Publications of the

MINNESOTA HISTORICAL SOCIETY

RUSSELL W. FRIDLEY
Editor and Director

JUNE DRENNING HOLMQUIST
Associate Editor

Selections from
"Minnesota History"

A FIFTIETH ANNIVERSARY ANTHOLOGY

Edited by RHODA R. GILMAN and

JUNE DRENNING HOLMQUIST

MINNESOTA HISTORICAL SOCIETY • ST. PAUL • 1965

Library of Congress Catalogue Card Number 65-25992
International Standard Book Number 0-87351-025-9

Introduction

THIS VOLUME of selections from *Minnesota History*, the quarterly of the Minnesota Historical Society, marks the fiftieth anniversary of continuous publication of the magazine. Its first issue, which appeared in February, 1915, as the *Minnesota History Bulletin*, stated that it was established "primarily for the purpose of keeping the members, and others who may be interested, in touch with the work of the Minnesota Historical Society" and to provide for "the timely publication of papers read at the meetings or contributed." In addition to such papers, the quarterly would "contain reviews of books pertinent to Minnesota history, notes on the activities of the society, perhaps occasional documents or reprints, and miscellaneous matter of various sorts." The statement added: "No attempt will be made to have a uniform number of pages in each issue; thus the temptation to publish articles of slight value in order to fill up space will be avoided."

During the years which have elapsed since its founding, the quarterly has continued to fulfill these stated purposes. It has informed the society's members of the growth and changes in the state's oldest institution and has provided an outlet for the publication of hundreds of documents and original papers dealing with the multifaceted history of Minnesota in its broadest sense. Its pages still carry reviews and notes calling attention to pertinent books and other publications, as well as reports on the society's activities. After a half century of publication, the back issues of the magazine constitute a virtual encyclopedia of Minnesota's past, and the sturdy volumes, uniformly bound in brown cloth, now fill a bulging five-foot shelf.

A careful look at the thirty-eight volumes of *Minnesota History* which have been published since 1915 reveals a surprising over-all consistency and continuity of purpose. This is doubtless due largely to the fact that the magazine has had only four editors. The initial issue of *Minnesota History* followed by three months the appointment of Solon J. Buck as superintendent of the society. He was the first professional historian to serve in that capacity, and he not only founded the magazine but he also led the institution into a new era. He was succeeded as editor in 1923 by another distinguished historian, Theodore C. Ble-gen, who held the post until 1939. After that a young lady, who began her long career with the society under Dr. Buck in 1919, became re-sponsible for the magazine's direction. She was Bertha L. Heilbron, whose association with the quarterly continued until her retirement in 1961. At that time the present editor, Rhoda R. Gilman, began her tenure.

Long before its golden anniversary occurred in February, 1965, the magazine had won a respected place among historical journals of the nation for the high quality of its content, its editorial standards, and its excellent printing and design. The word *Bulletin* disappeared from the title in 1925, and a new page size and format were adopted in 1952 to enable the quarterly to make greater use of illustrations as important historical source materials. Thus the magazine's content, appearance, and style have changed over the years to keep pace with developments in the historical profession and the technology of printing and publish-ing. The pages reflect a half century of growth and change in American culture, in the profession it serves, and in the society itself. They con-tain numerous articles that have broken ground in new fields of study and many others that have survived the years to become standard sources of information on particular topics. The roster of its authors and reviewers contains many names of distinction, and if the magazine itself can be said to constitute an encyclopedia in its field, its contribu-tors surely constitute a "Who's Who" in Minnesota history.

Because the quarterly has printed so many articles and documents of lasting interest, the society determined to mark the magazine's gold-en anniversary by calling attention to them in an anthology volume. It was felt that some of these outstanding pieces should be made avail-able to a new generation of readers. The frustrating task of selecting from the more than five hundred articles which have appeared over the years was undertaken by a committee of three: Dr. Blegen and Miss Heilbron, both former editors of the magazine, and Mrs. Gilman, its present editor. Together their terms of service cover forty-two of the journal's fifty years of publication. To provide a somewhat more detached view, June Drenning Holmquist, the society's associate editor, was asked to serve as a consultant.

The committee members quickly realized that their task was a for-midable one and that any group of selections decided upon would be unsatisfactory as well as arbitrary in some respects. Each member in-dependently reviewed all the published issues from 1915 to 1965. When they met to make their final selections, the three found a surprising unanimity among their choices. The twenty-six articles in this volume were included, first of all, because they have stood the test of time. Four additional criteria governed the committee's decisions: the importance of the subject, the breadth and depth with which it was treated, the continuing interest of the piece as a whole, and the readability of its presentation. Several representative articles were also selected, since the committee felt that the anthology should reflect the general contents and character of the magazine. Thus two lively documents were chosen from among the many which have been printed over the years, and one excellent example dealing with the backgrounds of a Minnesota community was included. No effort was made to represent the work of particular authors; nevertheless the committee felt that most of those whose contributions have significantly influenced the character of the journal were represented in the anthology.

It was decided, too, that certain topics which have received emphasis in the magazine should be included. Among them were the fur trade, pioneer social life, immigration, and third-party political movements in the state — all of which bulk large in the pages of *Minnesota History* during its first fifty years. The contents of the magazine reflect the changing interests of scholars. The early issues, for example, show a strong preoccupation with social and cultural history while those of the past two decades include an increasing number of studies on political and economic subjects. Therefore an effort was made to choose articles from the entire life of the magazine. In this the committee was not wholly successful, although the publication dates of the selections span the years from 1918 to 1962. The greatest concentration of articles dates from 1927 (volume 8). Four pieces from that year were included.

After the final agonizing selections had been made, the committee realized that a second anthology of equal length, quality, and variety could be compiled. Many articles and authors of distinction had been reluctantly omitted. Important aspects of the state's history were also slighted, among them the Sioux Uprising, the many Indian treaties, the story of education, and the development of railroads. Although music and literature are represented, art is missing, and its absence is especially notable because *Minnesota History* has published a large amount of work in the field of western and frontier art. This topic was not included because the illustrations important to such articles could not be handled satisfactorily in the format of the anthology volume. In addition, no truly biographical studies are present, and the part played by Minnesota's early business, political, and military leaders has been neglected.

In preparing these selections for publication, very few changes were made. Living authors were invited to review their articles, and several of them incorporated minor changes. When authors were no longer living or were unavailable, the editors made such minor alterations in dated material as seemed absolutely necessary. No attempt was made to revise the annotation, but significant new information on the topic is indicated by editorial notes appearing at the foot of the page. In one case an author revised his article for publication as a pamphlet a number of years after it appeared in *Minnesota History*, and the more recent version is included. Since editorial practices have varied somewhat over the years, an effort was made to achieve a uniform style in this volume — generally conforming with the current usage of the magazine. In all other respects, the material is presented as it originally appeared.

The twenty-six selections which follow are arranged chronologically more or less by the period covered in the article rather than by the year in which the piece appeared in the magazine. This arrangement is not meant to suggest that these articles constitute either a history of the state or a complete survey of the contents of the magazine. As the title states, they are selections. Taken as a whole, they present a fragmentary and disjointed picture of Minnesota, viewed by twenty-eight different authors. On the other hand, no integrated history from the pen of a single person could convey half so clearly a sense of the immense variety that characterizes Minnesota's past. As the state's early boosters never tired of pointing out, Minnesota lies at the heart of the continent. Waters from within its borders flow north, east, and south, and the state forms a part of the lake region and the plains, of the corn belt, and of the north woods. Its varied geography has provided equally varied resources, which in turn have made it a transition zone economically, politically, and ethnically.

It is hoped that the publication of this collection will stimulate interest in both the magazine and its subject. Much remains to be written in the field of Minnesota history, and the society's quarterly journal is a continuing enterprise. Building on the broad foundation already laid, it proposes to explore new aspects of the development of Minnesota, for history, like the magazine itself, is an unfinished record, not a completed book.

St. Paul, Minnesota   RHODA R. GILMAN
July 1, 1965   JUNE DRENNING HOLMQUIST

Contents

The Pipestone Quarry and the Indians

THEODORE L. NYDAHL

PIPESTONE QUARRY in southwestern Minnesota is associated with some of the earliest chapters in the region's history. When the first explorers and fur traders reached the area, they found it peopled largely by two diverse Indian tribes—the Sioux (or Dakota) and the Chippewa (or Ojibway) — and the quarry from which the Indians obtained the stone to make their calumets or peace pipes was already ancient. It became Minnesota's first national monument in 1937, and today it is undoubtedly the state's most popular Indian site. The following article by Theodore L. Nydahl, published in December, 1950 (volume 31), stands as one of the best available discussions of this legend-shrouded spot. Its author is dean of the school of arts and sciences in Mankato State College and coauthor of Minnesota History: A Guide to Reading and Study, *published in 1960.*

IN MINNESOTA'S deep southwest there is a section of land which may lay claim to being "classic ground." [1] George Catlin felt that way about it and used the phrase in referring to the area when he made his memorable trip of the 1830s. Minnesotans may have forgotten that Henry W. Longfellow pointed specifically to this spot in his *Song of Hiawatha*. Here are a few of his lines:

> On the Mountains of the Prairie,
> On the great Red Pipestone Quarry,
> Gitche Manito, the mighty,
> He the Master of Life, descending,
> On the red crags of the quarry
> Stood erect and called the nations,
> Called the tribes of men together.

Longfellow never actually saw this country. His mountains are the Coteau des Prairies. While we wouldn't think of calling them moun-

1

tains, several of the early explorers used that term in their reports. The name Coteau des Prairies, given to the area by the earliest French explorers, means Highland of the Prairies. This land feature of southwestern Minnesota was formed by the ice sheet of the last glacial epoch. It is the terminal moraine left by one of the massive lobes of this great ice sheet. The *coteau,* or highland, begins in the eastern Dakotas and runs southeasterly on into Iowa. Both the eastern and western slopes of the highland are in the main so gentle as to be almost imperceptible. In Pipestone County, stone outcroppings break that gentle declivity and give rise to the quarry.[2] And it is this quarry country that became classic ground, a view which grew with the years until the national government established there an Indian reservation, then an Indian school, and finally a national monument. But the thing that brought recognition as classic ground was the high regard which the Indians themselves had for the locality — a regard which, for some of them at least, was linked with spiritual considerations. Legends, often having a religious tone, had their setting in this locale. To the Indians who gave credence to these legends, this ground was *wakan,* or sacred.

The pre-Columbian Indian had a Stone Age culture. He lived close to nature, but in no sense was he master of mother nature. Rather he lived in awe of her and worshipped her various manifestations — sun, moon, waterfalls, fire, rocks. His spiritual feeling ran deep, touched albeit with a vein of superstitious awe. His worship tended to take on a negative characteristic in that he sought to appease the spirits so as to ward off evil which otherwise might be inflicted upon him.

The practice of smoking was widespread among the tribes of the red man. In consideration of his reaction to the practice, the white man from Europe could not have thought too poorly of the custom. One aspect of smoking, however, the white man did not adopt — the Indian's veneration of the pipe and tobacco, his use of them in a ceremonial manner. The Indian could and did enjoy smoking for the pleasure it afforded, and the Sioux has been labeled "an inveterate smoker." Now the Indian's nature was such as to be impressed with the mysterious character of rising smoke, its spirit-like quality, and he could be made to feel that tobacco and the pipe were gifts from the Great Spirit. A type of pipe, to which the French gave the name calumet, came into common use for ceremonial purposes. The bowl of the calumet, in which the tobacco was placed, was shaped from a hard substance, generally stone. Attached to the bowl was a stem two to three feet long, hollow centered to allow passage of the smoke to the mouth. The calumet seems to have been in veneration for centuries. It was used to make treaties or agreements more binding, to place strangers on a basis of friendliness, to insure safe passage through country held by other tribes, to promote peace. The peace pipe then was an Indian contribution.[3]

A firsthand portrayal of the role of the calumet appears in the narrative of Peter Pond, a Yankee fur trader from Connecticut who was on the Minnesota frontier from 1773 to 1775, even before American independence had been won. In quaint style, with abominable spelling, he tells of approaching a camp of the red men "with Our Loded Horses and Cuming Near the Camp Made a Stop and Seat Down on the Ground. I Perseaved five Parsons from the Camp Approaching — four was Imployed in Caring a Beaver Blanket finely Panted — the Other Held in his Hand a Callemeat or Pipe of Pece — Verey finely Drest with Differant feathers with Panted Haire. They all Seat By me Except the one who Held the Pipe. Thay Ordered the Pipe Lit With a Grate dele of Sarremoney. After Smokeing a fue Whifs the Stem was Pinted East and West — then North and South — then upward toward the Skies — then to ye Earth after which we all Smoked in turn and Apeard Verey Frendlye." [4]

Ceremonial pipes used by the plains Indians came in considerable proportion from Minnesota. In the red stone from the quarries of Pipestone County the Indians found a substance admirably suited to the shaping of their calumet bowls. One student suggests that the Indians "must have considered it a God-send when they first discovered a soft stone that could easily be carved with the primitive tools which they possessed." And if one may use the words of a twentieth-century Supreme Court ruling, the southwest corner of Minnesota became a place where tribes were "wont to gather under solemn truce to quarry," a spot regarded "by the tribesmen with sentiments bordering upon religious reverence." [5]

Knowledge of the Pipestone area reached only a comparatively few white men at first. And those few who did know of it learned largely through word-of-mouth presentations by the Indians themselves and by trappers and traders. Occasionally, however, an explorer might make a written statement of some report gained from the red men, although until the 1830s probably none saw the quarry firsthand.

There was the French explorer, Pierre François Xavier Charlevoix, who traveled in the Mississippi country in 1721. He wrote of the pipe of peace which, he said, "is ordinarily made of a species of red marble, very easily worked, and found beyond the Mississippi among the Aiouez (Ioways)." A few years after Great Britain took the interior of the continent away from the French, a British trader and explorer named Jonathan Carver spent parts of the years 1766 and 1767 in the Minnesota country and wrote an elaborate account of his travels. In this account he recorded that near "the Marble River, is a mountain, from which the Indians get a sort of red stone, out of which they hew the bowls of their pipes." Peter Pond, whose Minnesota journeyings followed Carver's by eight years, referred to a calumet "Made of the Read Stone of St. Peters River so Much asteamd among the Eastern and Southern Nations." [6]

In all these cases there is one brief reference to the Pipestone locale — no more. Not until the third decade of the nineteenth century does one meet with accounts which seek to elaborate upon the quarry country. Four persons visited the Pipestone Quarry during the 1830s and took pains to write about their findings — Philander Prescott, George Catlin, Joseph N. Nicollet, and John C. Frémont. The first two were independent adventurers; the last two were government explorers and were on the same expedition. [7]

At the time of his visit to the quarry, Philander Prescott was a fur trader working out of Mendota. In 1831 he traveled to his trading post on the Big Sioux, a branch of the Missouri River, where he wintered and traded, and then returned to Mendota. Both on the way out and on the way back he stopped at the quarry not only to observe, but also to work it. Other traders probably had done the same, but Prescott was different — he wrote about his experiences. Prescott's style of writing, like Peter Pond's, was crude but descriptive. The following excerpt from Prescott's "Reminiscences" reveals that Indians were in his company and that he worked with them in quarrying. He records that on his journey westward, probably in September, 1831, "we camped and dug pipe stone one whole day   we got out a considerable quantity but a goodeal of it was shaley and full of seams   So we got onley about 20 good p[i]pes after working the rock all day." Prescott goes on to describe the methods used by the natives in working the quarry: "the Indians have labored here verry hard with hoes and axes thy only tools th[e]y have except large stones which they use forr breaking the rock . . . the Sioux cl[e]are of[f] the dirt then get stones as large as two Indians can lift and throw it down as hard as th[e]y can and in this way break or crack the rock so they can get their hoes and axes in the cracks and pry out piec[e] after piec[e]   it is verry laborious and tedious." The old trader recalls that "after we had worked the pipe stone quarry until we were tired we made preparati[o]ns to be off as our Indians were getting alarmed for fear of enemies although I never heard of any of them being killed at the pipe stone quarry." [8]

Prescott waited two decades before writing his "Reminiscences" and they have remained unpublished for about a century. This was no way to gain nationwide attention for the land of the red pipestone. There must be more aggressive writing. That was furnished by George Catlin following his trip to the quarry in 1836. Fairly well-known even then, Catlin was to gain attention on a national scale as a painter and writer. His one passion was the American Indian, whose life he sought to portray. In his first years of travel among the aborigines of the United States, he tells that he heard frequent mention of the spot near the Coteau des Prairies where various tribes of Indians said they obtained the red stone for their pipes. In Catlin's own words, this was the case for "almost every tribe of Indians on the Continent." And so, he said, he "had contracted the most impatient desire to visit it." [9]

New York was the starting point of his trip. His quickest way to the country of the Sioux was by water — the Great Lakes, Green Bay, then the Fox, Wisconsin, and Mississippi rivers. From Fort Snelling he went up the Minnesota River to a point near New Ulm, then across country to the Coteau des Prairies, and over these highlands to the "classic ground."

Two trading posts of the American Fur Company provided stopping points — that of Le Blanc, or Louis Provençalle, at Traverse des Sioux and Joseph Laframboise's station at the Great Oasis. At Traverse des Sioux, Catlin tells that he ran into a gathering of Sioux who showed a sullen hostility to his mission. He and his traveling companion, Robert S. Wood, were called to a kind of council meeting, where they were told to turn back. A dozen or more Sioux braves spoke, and Catlin reported their words. A brief portion of one speech will give the tenor of their plea:

"*Brothers* — I speak strong, my heart is strong, and I speak fast; this red pipe was given to the red men by the Great Spirit —it is a part of our flesh, and therefore is great *medicine*. ('How! how!')

"*Brothers* — We know that the whites are like a great cloud that rises in the East, and will cover the whole country. We know that they will have all our lands; but, if ever they get our Red Pipe-Quarry they will have to pay very dear for it. ('How! how! how!')

"*Brothers* — We know that no white man has ever been to the Pipe Stone-Quarry, and our chiefs have often decided in council that no white man shall ever go to it. ('How! how!')"

Catlin endeavored to assure the Sioux that he was not a government official on a mission intended to wrest the quarry from them, but that he and his companion had heard that the "Red Pipe-Quarry was a great curiosity" and that they were merely interested in viewing it. "We have started to go to it," said he, "and we will not be stopped." And they proceeded on their way unmolested.

The country in and around the quarry impressed Catlin as having a "sublime grandeur." Topography then came in for some treatment, but by far the major portion of his portrayal of this "classic ground" was made up of a recital of the many legends which were linked to the locale. How many of these legends he obtained from the local Sioux and how many he had gathered on his travels over the country Catlin did not make clear. But he did emphasize that they were legends. "This place is great," he said, "(not in history, for there is none of it, but) in traditions, and stories, of which this Western world is full and rich."

All were legends, that is, except one. And that one? The quarry in Catlin's day was held by the Sioux, but at one time, he insisted, it had been "held and owned in common, as neutral ground, amongst the different tribes who met here to renew their pipes." He goes on to relate that "for centuries" pilgrimages had been made to the quarry "by all the neighboring tribes" to obtain the precious material for shaping their calumets. In the quarry precincts the war club and the scalping knife were put aside "under the fear of the vengeance of the Great Spirit." As support for this view, Catlin points to statements made to him by Indians of other tribes, to the pictographs carved in the quartzite and which, in his judgment, were *"totems and arms"* of visiting tribes, and finally to the many legends which sprang into existence only because of this earlier condition. The implication was that where there was so much legend there must be some basis in fact.

There are those who feel that Catlin here allowed his enthusiasm to lead him to overstatement. Questions are raised about the likelihood of an Indian tribe surrendering so valuable a property to the common use of all tribes and also of the difficulty that would be encountered in making regular pilgrimages by a tribe at some distance from the quarries. Henry H. Sibley, who had been in the Minnesota country two years when Catlin came along, was one who felt that misrepresentations had been made. Sibley had been irked by the man, and by his readiness to allow the report to grow that he was the first white man to visit the quarry when "it is notorious that many whites had been there and examined the quarry long before he came to the country." [10]

Calumets made of red pipestone have been found in many parts of the United States — in Indian mounds as far away as Ohio, Florida, and Louisiana. Deposits of red pipestone, or catlinite, as it has come to be called, have been reported in other places besides Minnesota: in

Wisconsin, South Dakota, Iowa, Missouri, Ohio, and Arizona. The Wisconsin deposits, however, are the only ones which seem to give evidence of having been worked before the white man arrived. It seems reasonable to hold, therefore, that most of the catlinite calumets found over the United States came from the quarry of the Coteau des Prairies. Indians the country over, of course, used several other materials for making their calumets. Then, too, several fur-trading companies manufactured red calumets for sale among the various tribes, a practice that began about the middle of the nineteenth century.[11] It is, therefore, possible that some of the red stone calumets found are not genuine, if to be genuine they must have been made by the Indians. In the writings of those who had early contact with the aborigines there is a body of testimony to be found which should make one thing clear — the red calumet was in common use among the plains Indians, especially those of the northern plains. In lesser amounts pipestone was used by Indians of the southern plains and also of the Mississippi Valley. The source of the stone for sacred red pipes of these Indians must have been in large part the Pipestone Quarry. While some of the red men went directly to the quarry, many of them could have obtained their calumets by trade or by other contact with the Indians of the northern plains.

Catlin's works were widely read, and people came to know of the Pipestone Quarry before there was a Minnesota. Another boost to interest in the region came when the justly famed Joseph N. Nicollet made his expedition of 1838, just two years after Catlin's visit. Nicollet had four companions on this government-sponsored venture, one of whom — John C. Frémont, the pathfinder — was to bask in the national spotlight for over two decades after his visit to the quarry. Nicollet had just completed a map of the upper Mississippi Valley, which was not only the first reliable map of the region, but was recognized widely as a singular contribution to American geography. His 1838 assignment was to study the country between the Mississippi and the Missouri rivers. Exacting — that was the way officials came to look upon his exploring and reporting. It helps to explain, too, why the people of Minnesota saw fit to give his name to a county, a town, and to a principal avenue in Minneapolis.

Three days the Nicollet party of five remained at the quarry. They, too, found Indians at work, and helped them. Nicollet noticed that the Sioux were encountering difficulty in removing the tough top layer of red quartzite, a necessary first step before they could get at the thin layer of catlinite below. They pleased the Indians by using gunpowder to blast away the top layer of the hard stone over a fairly large area.

They also found time to carve Nicollet's name, the initials of his companions, and the date in the hard quartzite. It is significant that this careful observer paid his respects to the ceremonial attitude which the Indians held toward the quarry. And there was recording of legend in his official report. He referred to the Indian belief in the opening of the quarry by the Great Spirit and to the salute of lightning with which the Great Spirit greeted any visitor to the grounds — views held at least by the "young Indians, who are very fond of the marvellous." Nicollet noticed that the grass before the "Three Maidens" had been killed for some great space by the profuse offerings of tobacco and food which the Indians had placed before these boulders as ceremonial offerings to bless their quarrying.[12]

The Three Maidens are large boulders of a substance wholly different from any rock formation in the vicinity. Newton H. Winchell speaks of them in his monumental survey of the *Geology of Minnesota,* noting three other smaller boulders, making a cluster of six and all resting on the surface of the red quartzite a short distance from the quarry. The six boulders were at one time a single boulder, which was split later through the action of frost. The original boulder must have been carried by a glacier and dumped near the quarry. And since the Three Maidens are each about twelve by twenty feet, the boulder must have been from fifty to sixty feet in diameter, making it more than likely the "largest ice-transported block known in Minnesota." The Three Maidens are composed of a red, coarse-grained granite, whereas the quarry is made up almost in its entirety of red quartzite, which Winchell claims is "the hardest stone in the state, or in the United States, probably, that can be stated to have been used for purposes of building." Catlinite is a softer stone made of fine clay which has been subjected to heat and pressure — indurated clay to use the geologist's term. The catlinite appears in a thin layer, generally from two to four inches thick. When the Indians first began quarrying, they dug out the part of the catlinite layer that was close to the surface. The layer, however, dips downward; thus, the more pipestone taken the deeper the Indians had to quarry for it. The task of removing the superincumbent layer of quartzite became increasingly difficult. In quarry pits now being worked, the catlinite layer is found at an average depth of ten feet.[13]

It was in the quartzite close to the Three Maidens that the numerous pictographs were found. Because of the hardness of the stone, the crude drawings of the Indians could not go deep, but for the same reason they have endured. Among them are representations of the turtle, bear, elk, wolf, buffalo, bird tracks, and the human form, all of which give emphasis to the concentration of Indian lore in the Pipestone quarry area.[14]

The name "Three Maidens" suggests legend, and of legend there seems to be no end in and around the land of the red pipestone. Prescott, Catlin, Nicollet — all gave reports of them. And the store of legend grew in the years following these earliest writers. At times the fables were new, but in the main they were variations of those reported in the 1830s. Handed down orally from generation to generation, it is not strange that they should have varied from tribe to tribe. Most of them are in some way related to the workings of Gitchi Manito or Wakantonka. These are Indian expressions which when translated become Great Spirit. Prominent among them is the peace injunction which Longfellow emphasized in the *Song of Hiawatha* — the plea of Gitchi Manito that the Indians wash off their war paint, bury their war clubs, and, as a symbol of their peaceful intent:

> Break the red stone from this quarry,
> Mould and make it into peace pipes.

The first calumet, or peace pipe, was, of course, shaped at the quarry by the Great Spirit. In legends explaining the origin of pipestone, it is always blood which gave the stone its color — buffalo blood from animals slain by the Great Spirit for food, human blood from those who died in an ancient, great catastrophe. The Pipestone Quarry, too, in Indian lore was the site of the creation of man. Wakantonka took the red stone, and from it shaped first man, then woman, and the two walked off together. There are several versions of the story of the origin of the human race, and they vary greatly. There is also a tradition of a flood ("freshet," Catlin calls it) in which men and women try to save themselves by seeking the top of the Coteau des Prairies. The "Leaping Rock" was a testing point where a young brave might demonstrate the sincerity of his love for a maiden by risking death in a leap from a high ledge to a solitary pillar of stone where, as Prescott put it, "there was nothing to hold onto and all he could do was to jump and stand right where he struck." As for the Three Maidens, in one of the manifestations of the Great Spirit two maidens disappeared for shelter under these boulders. Their spirits remained there, and offerings must be placed before them if one is to hope for good quarrying.[15]

A people who looked upon a place with the reverential awe with which the Indians seemed to regard the quarry of the red pipestone could hardly be expected to relinquish their control of the area without a protest. By the middle of the nineteenth century that "great cloud that rises in the East" had rolled to the borders of the Suland — and it was the Sioux who claimed the quarry in this century, no matter what the situation may have been in an earlier day. Then came the treaties of 1851 and the sale to the federal government of southern Minnesota. There was no mention of the quarry in the treaty of Traverse des Sioux. The Yankton Sioux were not party to that treaty, and they disputed the right of the Sisseton and Wahpeton bands to cede land held jointly with the Yankton. They claimed that their right to the quarry was as strong, if not stronger, than that of the other two bands, since their villages were actually closer to it. Grumblings continued through the 1850s, and whites who knew about this discontent were concerned. Congress appropriated twenty-one thousand dollars for payment to the Yankton Sioux, thinking that it might appease them. But Congress was due for a surprise; the Yankton tribe refused to accept the money. They wanted another kind of settlement. They finally obtained what they were after in the important treaty of 1858. That treaty was important for the whites as well as the Indians. It was for South Dakotans what the treaty of Traverse des Sioux was for Minnesotans. In it the Yankton band sold all their South Dakota lands to the United States except for a reservation of four hundred thousand acres. Five months of negotiation were required before the Yankton delegation of sixteen chiefs agreed to the terms of the treaty. They held out stubbornly for one point in particular. It was contained in Article 8, the first statement of which reads: "The said Yankton Indians shall be secured in the free and unrestricted use of the Red Pipestone Quarry." In fulfillment of the provisions of this article, the federal government set aside a reservation of 648 acres, the survey of which was completed in 1859, well in advance of the regular survey. And so was created a special reserve, comprising a little more than a section of land located immediately north of the present city of Pipestone. Except for a small grant of land for a railroad right of way, the reservation area today is the same as it was in 1859.[16]

In the opinion of Arthur P. Rose, who wrote a history of Pipestone County, the existence of the reservation delayed white settlement. He points to census figures for 1860 and 1870 to show that Rock, Lincoln, Murray, and Nobles counties, all bordering on Pipestone, had settlers in those years, while Pipestone had none. Not until 1874 could Pipestone County claim a resident. As reasons for this delay, Rose gives the presence of an Indian reservation in the Pipestone area, the many legends that were associated with the locale and with the name "Pipestone," and memories of the Sioux Outbreak of 1862. Careful examination of the record of early settlement of neighboring counties would suggest that while each of them could report residents at an earlier date, they were very few in number, and that for all of them the period of heavy influx was the decade of the 1870s, when the first pronounced rush to Pipestone lands occurred as well.[17]

Interestingly enough, the man who spearheaded the settlement of the county and the establishment of the town of Pipestone was attracted to the place, in part at least, because of its Indian lore. C. H. Bennett was the man, and to the day of his death he sought to safeguard that lore. On an exploratory trip in 1873 Bennett selected the land immediately south of the quarry as the site for the city he intended to found. In the next year he led a group from Le Mars, Iowa, into the county and he induced D. E. Sweet to guide another from Rock Rapids, Iowa. With their arrival, Pipestone, both town and county, were on the way. The next four years were discouraging to the town's founders; settlers came only in dribbles. Some moved away. The word "grasshoppers" tells the story. The boom year was 1878, with almost eight hundred land filings reported. A newspaper in Rock County, to the south of Pipestone, reported on March 17, 1878, that "Parties from Pipestone City who came down yesterday report meeting no less than twenty-two covered wagons enroute to that place." [18]

Bennett's interest in Indian lore took root and grew until it became a community tradition. In a meeting of town residents, few as they were in April, 1876, a motion was adopted "that we respect and enforce to the best of our ability the rights of the Indians to the Indian reservation." Unfortunately there were exceptions; a few squatters liked the lands of the reservation and hoped that a *fait accompli* would lead to legalization. It required troops to change their minds. Eviction of the squatters in 1887 ended an attempt to deflower the prairies of the reservation. In 1875 one of the pioneer settlers, D. C. Whitehead, had suggested that an Indian school on the reservation would be a boost to settlement as well as a benefit to the Indians. This idea was nurtured through the years by the community and, with the able support of John Lind in Congress, an act was passed in 1891 which called for the establishment of seven Indian schools over the country, with one to be located on the Pipestone Indian Reservation. The school's first building was erected in 1892. The choice of building material was fitting — the red quartzite of the quarry.[19]

The decision to establish an Indian school at Pipestone gave rise to an issue — an issue which moved in and out of Congress, the Court of Claims, and the United States Supreme Court for almost four decades.

It was not settled until 1928. The question was raised by the Yankton Sioux, 167 of whom signed a petition complaining that the decision to build a school on their reservation was made by Congress alone, without consulting the Indians. In their petition they expressed the fear that this represented an attempt by Congress to "invalidate, if not extinguish, their right to this property peremptorily and without compensation." In the courts the issue boiled down to this question: When the Pipestone Reservation was created by the treaty of 1858, did the federal government grant to the Yankton Sioux an absolute title to the land, or merely a right in the nature of an easement? If the Sioux had been given an absolute title, then at the time the Indian school was built the federal government should have compensated them for its exercise of eminent domain. After prolonged and complicated litigation, a decision was reached in favor of the Indians, and the Court of Claims held that the amount due them was $100,000.00 plus interest since 1891 — an amount which was fixed at $228,558.90, or a total of $328,558.90. Congress made the necessary appropriation, and the sum was distributed among the 1,953 members of the Yankton band. The Indians won the financial award, but by the same token "fee title to the reservation . . . passed to the United States." [20]

The march of years seemed to give increasing prominence to the sentiment that the Pipestone Quarry was meaningful enough in the traditions of the Indians to warrant some very special recognition. The sentiment grew slowly, but come it did: reservation — 1858, Indian school — 1891, financial award — 1928. This growing recognition did not just happen. It came only after untiring work by sympathetic and enthusiastic pioneers, by the persistence of the Indians themselves, and by the continuing effort of interested leaders of a later day. An agency which in a more recent period has been responsible for much effective work is the Pipestone Indian Shrine Association, composed of representatives of more than fifty local and state organizations. Miss Winifred Bartlett, president of the organization, was one of its most active spirits. Among aims announced by this association were three of significance: "to preserve the natural features of the typical prairie" of the Pipestone Reservation, "to honor the race that established its Shrine at this place," and to again make the quarry "a common meeting place for all the tribes." The culmination of this interest and of the trend which had been in evidence so long was the establishment by Congress of the Pipestone National Monument. It came in August, 1937, a century, more or less, after the visits to the quarry of Prescott, Catlin, Nicollet, and Frémont. Promotional work for the passage of the act creating the monument was done primarily by the Indian Shrine Association. The task of guiding the measure through Congress was undertaken by Senator Henrik Shipstead and Congressman Frank Clague.[21]

Now it will be remembered that the reservation as created in 1858 embraced slightly more than a section of land. The 1937 act designated as a national monument a little less than a fifth of the reservation, or 115.6 acres. This portion is in the southern part of the reservation, and it contains, as it logically should, all the features which the Indians cherished. The law establishing the monument declared that the quarry found therein should be accessible to members of any tribe who might choose to work it, and that quarrying was to be reserved exclusively to Indians. And so another goal was achieved by those who sought to build respect for the traditions of the red man. And Minnesota gained its first national monument.[22]

The monument grounds are a part of the national park system, and therefore are open to the public. The visitor, if he has imagination, may catch a glimpse of the emotional life of the first Americans. The press of white settlement, increasing difficulty in getting down to the catlinite layer, and the changed attitudes of the modern Indian have led to a complete disappearance of the quarry pilgrimages, but a few local Indian families still do occasional quarrying. The Pipestone community has continued to nurture interest in this classic ground. Annually, in midsummer, a pageant entitled the "Song of Hiawatha" is presented there. About a hundred and sixty people, some of them Indians, make up the cast. Interestingly enough, the person who in the early 1950s played the role of Gitchi Manito was an Indian who was descended not from the Sioux, but from the Chippewa, a tribe which in times past was the bitterest enemy of the Sioux.[23]

The Pipestone National Monument was established to honor America's first inhabitants. It is a symbol, too — a symbol of peace. Today's Minnesotan who gives thought to the Indian's record may at times give overmuch attention to the play of force in that record. He might well remember that even the Sioux, fiercely warlike as they were, had a hand in carrying forward the movement which would preserve as a monument at Pipestone a small corner of their ancient lands; and they did so, at least in part, because that corner represented in a very special way the strivings of their race for peace.

Fort Beauharnois

LOUISE PHELPS KELLOGG

FEW TRACES, either physical or cultural, remain from the period of almost a century (1671–1763) during which the flag of France waved over Minnesota. The area was on the western periphery of French influence, and only two points within the borders of the state were occupied for a significant length of time. They were Fort St. Charles on Lake of the Woods and Fort Beauharnois on Lake Pepin. The story of the latter post, which was located on the Mississippi River near present-day Frontenac, is here told by Louise Phelps Kellogg, who was a distinguished member of the staff of the State Historical Society of Wisconsin from 1901 until her death in 1942. Miss Kellogg's work has lived after her in numerous publications; among them are two substantial volumes on the French and British régimes in Wisconsin and the Northwest, published in 1925 and 1935. Scholarship in the intervening years has added few new details to this story of Fort Beauharnois, which was published in September, 1927 (volume 8) in honor of the two-hundredth anniversary of the founding of the post.

THE ERECTION of a permanent post among the Sioux Indians had been a favorite project of the French in North America from the days of the first discoveries in the West. Such a post was designed not only to secure an alliance with one of the most powerful western tribes, dwelling in one of the richest fur countries on the continent, but also to serve as a link in the chain of discovery by which the French hoped to cross the continent and open a land route to the western ocean. It must be remembered that no one at that time realized the great width of the continent, and there was always the hope that a route would be found, largely by waterways, which would lead as easily to the western ocean as the route by the Great Lakes furnished access to the interior.

When Du Luth in 1679 made his epoch-making journey to the home of the Sioux on Mille Lacs, he expected to push thence westward across the continent to the salt water described to him by his envoys

14

among the western branches of the Siouan people. He was making preparation the next year to pursue his discoveries in that direction, when the misfortunes that befell La Salle's party caused a complete reversal of his plan and turned his face eastward instead of westward. Had La Salle honestly kept to the terms of his concession and had he not surreptitiously attempted to tap the great beaver-bearing lands of the Sioux, expressly against the prohibition of the court, who knows what Du Luth might have accomplished in the latter years of the seventeenth century?

Then came Nicolas Perrot, the practical, the diplomat in Indian dealings, who in 1686 — after a winter at Trempealeau — built Fort St. Antoine on the northeast bank of Lake Pepin, and there carried on an advantageous trade with the Sioux. It was Perrot who formed the alliance between the Sioux and the French and who took possession on May 8, 1689, for France of all the Sioux territory about the head-waters of the Mississippi. Pierre Charles le Sueur, who was present at the last-named ceremony, and who was very popular among the tribes-men, cemented the alliance by escorting in 1695 the first Sioux chief and chieftess to the colony, introducing them to the great Onontio, Count de Frontenac, governor of all New France. Le Sueur also se-cured a concession to search for mines, and in 1700 mounted the Mis-sissippi in a sailboat and built the first French post in the interior of Minnesota.

The founding of Louisiana and the occupation of the lower Missis-sippi Valley in the early years of the eighteenth century gave an ad-ditional impetus to western discovery. Posts were built about Lake Superior, the northwesternmost of these being intended as a base for a far western push. To obtain accurate and definite information of possibilities for westward discovery and to ascertain the best routes thither, the regent, the Duc d'Orleans, sent in 1720 a special envoy to North America; and that his mission might not be made the subject of heedless gossip, it was disguised as a visitation of the French mis-sions of the interior. The ecclesiastic chosen for this examination was a discreet and able Jesuit, Pierre François Xavier Charlevoix.

Father Charlevoix left Montreal early in May, 1721, and with a retinue of voyageurs in two canoes made the journey around the lower lakes and reached Mackinac on June 28. Here he met Sieur de Mon-tigny, who was about setting out for his new post at the far end of the Bay of the Winnebago (Green Bay). There the regent's envoy might hope to learn much of the great Sioux country to which Montigny's new post was the entrance. At La Baye, Charlevoix was fortunate enough to meet a delegation of the Sioux, whom he questioned concerning their habitat and the possibility of traversing that country toward the west. The Sioux told him that some branches of their tribe traded with western tribesmen who lived on salt water, and Charlevoix took much encouragement from this report.

Upon his return he made a detailed report to the regent, recommending two routes for western exploration — one through the northwestern end of Lake Superior, one through the Sioux country, and as a preliminary for the latter he urged that a strong fort should be erected on the upper Mississippi and that the powerful tribe of the Sioux should be bound in firm alliance with the French. Matters of this kind moved deliberately in eighteenth-century New France. Recommendations approved in 1723 were not finally acted upon until 1727, but in that year elaborate preparations were made at Quebec and Montreal to occupy the region at the head of the Mississippi.

The chief reason for the delay in carrying out the recommendations of Charlevoix lay in the unsettled conditions of the region now known as Wisconsin, caused by the hostilities of the tribe called the Renards or Foxes. Since 1712 this fierce band of savages had been on the warpath against the French, had infested all the waterways and ambushed all the trading paths, had murdered many of France's red allies, and had even struck down many Frenchmen. In 1716 Captain Louis de Louvigny had led a war expedition along Green Bay and the Fox River, and had forced upon the Foxes a somewhat unstable peace, which remedied the situation but very little. In fact, Charlevoix on his voyage of 1721 had been obliged to take a longer route to the Mississippi than that by the Fox-Wisconsin waterway, because of the ravages of this tribe; and upon the Illinois River he saw ghastly evidences of their hostility to the Illinois Indians, France's faithful allies. In the course of this conflict the Foxes had succeeded in allying themselves with the Sioux at the headwaters of the Mississippi, and in procuring from them the promise of an asylum in the event of being driven from their homes in eastern Wisconsin. Thus an additional incentive to the erection of the post was the importance of detaching the Sioux from this alliance with the Foxes.

In order to reach the Sioux country, however, an expedition must pass through the territory of the rebel Foxes; therefore, Sieur de Lignery was sent to treat with this tribe and to make at least a temporary truce with them. Lignery, who was an old hand at Indian diplomacy, was successful in his efforts, and he arranged on June 7, 1726, that in the near future a further conference should be held either at Chicago or Le Rocher on the Illinois River, in which the Illinois Indians and the commandant of French Illinois would participate. Trusting in the results of this truce the new governor of New France, Charles de la Boische, marquis de Beauharnois, gave orders to prepare the expedition for the Sioux country, in accordance with the instructions he had received on leaving France.

Beauharnois was by far the ablest governor France had sent to the New World since the time of Frontenac. He was reputed to be a natural son of Louis XIV, and he had all the dignity and love of ceremony that characterized that monarch. Moreover, he had remarkably good judgment and a grasp of administrative duties rare in the officials of New France. Under the Marquis de Beauharnois Canada had for a score of years a governorship unsurpassed in its colonial history. The time seemed ripe, therefore, for an expansion of colonial influence and for recommencing westward exploration.

The first step toward founding the proposed post among the Sioux was the formation of a commercial company to finance the undertaking. The colonial treasury was always impoverished; but the merchants of New France were eager to participate in opening the vast territory of the Siouan peoples, which had so great a reputation for rich furs. The contract made by the governor with this company is an interesting document from the administrative and economic points of view. The promoters were to have a complete monopoly of the trade of the Sioux country for three years, with a preference for future years. In return they agreed to build a "fort of stakes, a chapel, a house for the commanding officer, and one for the missionaries." They were also to convey during the ensuing three years, free of cost, provisions and supplies for the commandant and his second in command as well as for the missionaries, the amount and weight of which were specifically stipulated; and they were to buy at Mackinac three or four extra canoes in order to transport these goods over the rapids and shallows of the Fox-Wisconsin waterway. This contract, signed at Montreal on June 6, 1727, is preserved in the archives of the Chicago Historical Society.

With regard to the members of this trading company we have some interesting information. Jean Baptiste Boucher de Montbrun and his brother François were grandsons of Pierre Boucher, first historian of the colony of New France, ennobled by the king for his services. He had an immense estate at Boucherville, where he lived in patriarchal fashion, his nine sons and their children around him. The elder Boucher died ten years before the date of this contract, at the ripe age of ninety-seven. His seventh son, Jean, sieur de Montbrun, was the father of the two young adventurers who planned to undertake the fur trade on this farthest frontier. Of the other partners, the Garreaus and Campeaus seem to have come from Detroit; the rest are unknown, save Paul Marin, who became one of the most distinguished officers of the Northwest, but whose personality is somewhat shrouded in mystery. He had been for some years at Chequamegon Bay, where doubtless he had had some knowledge of the Sioux. He was later to end the Fox wars and to make a fortune from his contact with the western tribesmen. Now, in mid-career, he visited the upper Mississippi probably for the first time.

The Sioux chiefs whom Charlevoix met at La Baye had intimated that they would welcome "black robe" missionaries in their villages; therefore it was determined to send two Jesuits to the new post as messengers of the gospel. Fathers Nicolas de Gonnor and Michel Guignas were chosen, the latter of whom became the historian of the expedition, giving the details with a lively pen.* Guignas joined the party at Mackinac, while the other missionary came out from Montreal. The governor asked from the king, in their behalf, a case of mathematical instruments including a six- or seven-foot telescope, thus indicating that they were to take scientific observations, and determine the latitude, longitude, and perhaps the altitude of the new post.

For commandant the governor chose Réné Boucher, sieur de la Perrière, an uncle of the Montbruns, who not only belonged to this well-known family but was a distinguished officer in the colonial troops. La Perrière had seen service during the intercolonial wars and had the unenviable distinction of having led the French and Indian raid of 1708 which resulted in the sacking of Haverhill, Massachusetts. He had visited the Sioux country in 1715 as a preliminary to Louvigny's expedition against the Foxes; and he had been destined for the command at La Baye, but another officer had been preferred in his stead. Having been promoted to a captaincy the previous year, La Perrière was eager to serve once more in the far West; although the command was desired by him, he nonetheless found the hardships of the journey and of the winter so great that, now nearly sixty years of age and worn by previous services, he was unable to remain at his new post throughout the first year.

The expedition left Montreal on the sixteenth of June, when shy, early summer was abroad in this northern land. We do not certainly know its route, but in all probability the way was up the Ottawa River,

*Father Guignas' record is in the form of a letter to Marquis de Beauharnois, May 29, 1728. It is published in translation in *Minnesota History*, 6:362–369 (December, 1925). *Ed.*

with its numerous portages, across the Mattawan Portage to Georgian Bay, and thence to the fort at Mackinac, the emporium of the western country. Not quite five weeks were employed in this toilsome journey, which was a customary one for the voyageurs and all the personnel of the fur trade. Nine days were passed at Michilimackinac, buying new canoes, repacking goods, joining in the social gaieties of the season, meeting old friends, and making new ones. The officers hoped an express would arrive from Montreal before their departure, but none came, and the first day of August they set forth from this northern post for their far journey to the Mississippi, strengthening themselves, writes Guignas, "against the pretended extreme difficulties of securing passage through the country of the Renards."

For a week the little flotilla crept along the north shore of Lake Michigan and the rock-bound coast of Green Bay, arriving on August 8 at the log fort known as La Baye, on the present site of the city of Green Bay. The commandant, François Amariton, received the travelers graciously and assured them that the way was open through the country of the Foxes. With but a brief delay, therefore, the expedition advanced along the lower Fox River, accompanied by Pierre Reaume, official interpreter at the Green Bay post, and Father Jean Chardon, its missionary, who took this opportunity to refresh himself by intercourse with his fellow Jesuits. On August 13, late in the evening, a group of Winnebago chiefs came into La Perrière's camp, bringing presents and offering peace calumets. The next day the French arrived at the Winnebago village on what is now known as Doty Island, a site occupied by this tribe for two centuries or more. Here they were welcomed with volleys of musketry and great demonstrations of joy.

Thence the French canoes crossed the northern end of Lake Winnebago, entered the upper Fox, and advanced to the first Renard village, where the Oshkosh suburb named Oakwood now stands. When their visitors arrived, the Fox chiefs ran down to the banks with their peace calumets and quickly arranged for an informal council. At this council, Reaume and Father Chardon were of great use in placating "these cutthroats and assassins," and this interview with a tribe "so dreaded and really very little to be dreaded" was amicably accomplished.

The next morning the interpreter and missionary returned to Green Bay, and the officers, rejoicing greatly at having passed the village of the Fox rebels, set themselves to overcome the winding mazes of the stream, at this time in summer filled with tall reeds and wild rice stalks. "Never was there a more tiresome voyage made than this. . . . We continued to grope our way, as it were, for a week; for we did not arrive until the [twenty] ninth, towards three o'clock in the afternoon, by pure chance (believing ourselves still far away) at the portage of the Ouisconsin." The portage quickly and safely crossed, they embarked upon the Wisconsin, "a shallow river upon a bed of shifting sand. . . . The shores are either bare and rugged mountains or low points with a foundation of sand."

Early in September the little flotilla of canoes reached the Father of Waters, and began its ascent. The chronicler accurately describes the appearance of the Mississippi: "This beautiful river is spread out between two chains of high mountains, barren and very sterile, regularly distant from each other one league [*three miles*], three quarters of a league, or half a league, where it is narrowest. Its centre is occupied by a chain of islands well wooded, so that in looking at it from the top of the heights, one would imagine that one was looking at an endless valley watered on right and left by two immense rivers."

On September 17, just as the sun touched the zenith, Lake Pepin was reached, and the middle of the southwestern shore where a low point juts into the water was chosen for building. The woods were dense but offered excellent chance for firewood, by the use of which they were partly cleared by spring. "The day after landing," says our chronicler, "axes were applied to the trees and four days later the fort was entirely finished." What he means by the fort is apparent in the next sentence: "It is a plat of ground a hundred feet square surrounded by stakes twelve feet high with two good bastions." Within this staked enclosure were the commandant's and missionaries' houses and the chapel, respectively thirty by sixteen feet, thirty-eight by sixteen, and twenty-five by sixteen. Outside the fort each man built for himself a house, and these with the blacksmith's shop and a warehouse for goods formed a considerable village. By the close of October all was snugly finished, and one might have seen from any neighboring height the little cluster of huts sending up through wattled chimneys tall columns of smoke into the surrounding forest.

It is not hard to picture this group of thirty to forty persons, most of them accustomed to the life of the woods, making all secure and snug for the long hard winter, which they knew would soon be upon them. Before shutting themselves in their inclosures, however, they had a great hunting excursion in the neighboring woods, but were disappointed in not finding such vast herds of deer as they had heard described. The lack of meat was supplied by the friendly Sioux, a band of whom, consisting of four or five hundred, had hastened to the place and pitched their tepees within sight of the fort, watching with wondering eyes all that these strange white men were doing. Their wonder and astonishment grew into awe and terror on November 14, when a celebration in honor of Marquis de Beauharnois was held. The little wilderness post had been christened in his honor, and on November 4, the day of his patron St. Charles, the missionaries said high mass for him in the morning. In the evening the jollification was to occur; the weather not being propitious, the celebration was postponed until the fourteenth, when "some very fine rockets" were sent aloft amidst the *vivas* for the king and the governor. When the simple tribesmen saw the stars falling from the rockets, the women and children fled in alarm to the surrounding forests, while the men besought the French to stop this dreadful "medicine," which made the very stars fall from the skies.

By this and other means, the visitors acquired a great reputation in this primitive world. The tepees of the red men soon disappeared, however, as it was time for the winter hunts, and save for a few stragglers and one band, which came in February, no customers appeared for the traders' goods until rather late in the spring.

Meanwhile, the inhabitants of this log village in the primeval wilderness settled down to a long test of endurance during the cold season; but accustomed as most of them were to the rigors of a Canadian winter, they were pleased to find the one on the upper Mississippi less severe; there was less snow than they expected and it had all disappeared by the end of March. Just as they were preparing to enjoy their liberation from the winter's confinement, however, a new misfortune occurred, for the river rose and inundated the point on which the buildings stood. The houses and the fort inclosure were filled to the depth of nearly three feet, and it was not until the end of April that the adventurers could reoccupy their "rather dilapidated" houses.

La Perrière found the flood, added to the cold of the winter season, seriously affecting his health, and so he was obliged to leave his command to his nephew, Pierre Boucherville, and with Father de Gonnor to take the long voyage to Canada. There he arrived so ill that he was not able to report to the governor, who drew from the missionary the facts about conditions in the Northwest. These facts were of vital concern to Beauharnois, for the Foxes had broken their truce, had massacred both French soldiers and Indian allies in the Illinois country, and he was determined utterly to destroy this rebellious tribe.

Lignery was ordered to proceed against them, and elaborate plans were made for the second invasion of the Fox River Valley. Large numbers of soldiers and their officers came up from Montreal, among whom were some of the best-known youth of the colony, such as Pierre Vaudreuil, who was later to be its last French governor. From Mackinac the force advanced, sixteen hundred strong, a fourth of which were Frenchmen. But alas for their hopes; Lignery's approach could not be kept secret, the Foxes were warned, and after a toilsome march along the lower Fox River the expedition reached the Fox villages only to find all the tribe had fled to the interior. "Lignery allows the Foxes to escape," was written by the minister upon the leader's report of the expedition. On his retreat Lignery burned the fort at Green Bay, and took off all the garrison.

Anxiety was great concerning the fate of the French traders and officers at Fort Beauharnois. With the woods swarming with angry fugitive Foxes, intent on wreaking vengeance on every white man, and with the Sioux former allies and friends of the Foxes, the situation on the upper Mississippi was critical. Lignery sent seven of his men overland to warn Boucherville that his post might soon be besieged. He paid two Menominee to guide his messengers, and they won safely through to the fort, where the garrison immediately recognized its danger. The Menominee sounded the Sioux at the Falls of St. Anthony and returned saying they had "Renard hearts." It only remained to escape as expeditiously as possible. On September 18, 1728, Boucherville laid the situation before his men, and all agreed that it would be impossible to hold the post. Lignery had suggested retreat by way of Lake Superior, but, taking into account the lateness of the season, Boucherville thought his best chance lay in running down the Mississippi to the Illinois.

The next day some of his men waited on him to state that they preferred to risk their lives to abandoning their goods. Despite the commandant's urging they insisted on remaining, and he reluctantly left them to their fate. Among these was Sieur de la Jémerais, who by his address was able to preserve himself and his companions and to "hold the fort" for another year.

Meanwhile Boucherville and his cousins the Montbruns, Father Guignas, and eight others took canoes on October 3, in the hazardous attempt to pass the hostiles unobserved. This they were not able to accomplish; just below the mouth of Rock River they were intercepted and taken captive by a band of Fox allies — Kickapoo and Mascoutens. The savages deliberated whether to turn the white men over to the Foxes to be burned or to keep them for a profitable ransom. The Montbruns, however, succeeded in escaping, and, alarmed by this circumstance, the captors consented to listen to the Frenchmen and finally agreed to abandon the Foxes and make peace with the white men. Boucherville and his men were escorted to Peoria, permitted to communicate with the officers in Illinois, and ultimately returned to Montreal, whither one of the Montbruns had hastened to notify the governor of their peril.

Meanwhile the little group at Fort Beauharnois had fared much better than they had dared to hope. Sometime that autumn they were dismayed by the approach of a large body of Foxes and Winnebago, who claimed that they were friendly and wanted to lodge around the fort. La Jémerais forbade them, and sternly threatened to fire if they came too close, whereupon they withdrew beyond gunshot and set up their wigwams. One of the traders imprudently ventured into one of their lodges to sell a trap. He was seized, and nearly lost his life. The Foxes, however, hearing from Fort St. Joseph, near the lower end of Lake Michigan, that the commandant there was mercifully inclined, begged for a Frenchman to accompany their chiefs thither to testify to their repentance and desire for pardon. La Jémerais volunteered to go, but found to his cost that the Foxes were not sincere. The truth was there were two parties among them; one wishing to approach the French, the other implacable in its hatred. After detaining the young officer twenty-one days, the Indians at last allowed him to proceed to St. Joseph, and he arrived finally at Montreal unharmed.

The prospects, however, for a profitable trade were very small, the Sioux company surrendered its contract, and sometime in 1729 Fort Beauharnois was entirely abandoned and probably looted and burned by hostile Indians.

The Sioux company was re-formed in 1731, with different backers and undertakers. The convoy, which was commanded by Godefroy de Linctot, stopped at Perrot's old wintering place near Trempealeau Mountain and remained there for five years, conducting a profitable trade with the Sioux and Iowa tribesmen. Father Guignas was missionary for this post also, but we have no such description as he wrote concerning Fort Beauharnois, and our knowledge of the post life is derived from inference. The garrison and traders were in constant danger, as the Fox wars continued, and in 1733 the commandant at the restored Fort La Baye was slain with several of his officers. Linctot was successful in maintaining a hold upon the Sioux; and in the spring of 1736 he removed his post to Lake Pepin — this time on the northeastern side — and resigned the command to St. Pierre. The latter was forced in 1737 to abandon this post and retreated with Father Guignas and the traders by the Lake Superior route.

It was fourteen years before conditions became sufficiently peaceful to admit of another post among the Sioux. In 1750 Paul Marin, who had ended the Fox wars, secured a concession and sent his son Joseph to reoccupy the Sioux country. Here again we are balked by lack of evidence, but there seems reason to believe that Joseph Marin built his post on or near the site of the destroyed Fort Beauharnois. There he remained for six years, conducting a trade of great proportions, which enriched the Marins and all their confederates and unmercifully exploited the fur-bearing animals of the Northwest. Paul Marin was in 1752 sent to the upper Ohio frontier, where he died the next year somewhere above Pittsburgh. His son Joseph seems to have remained at the Sioux post until 1756, when all the outlying garrisons were called in to aid in defending New France against the English.*

This last commandant of the Sioux post was in service on Lake Ontario and at Lake George; he was captured at the battle of the Plains of Abraham and after the conquest was one of the French officers who elected to live in France. So far as is known he never returned to the upper Mississippi or to America.

Neither Linctot nor Marin seems to have had the explorer's spirit, although the ministry continued to urge that the Sioux post should be made the basis of westward discovery. Paul le Gardeur, sieur de St. Pierre, however, who was a grandson of Jean Nicolet, carried the French flag far out upon the Saskatchewan and might have crossed to the Pacific had he not been summoned to a nearer frontier. Upon Paul Marin's death St. Pierre replaced him on the upper Ohio, and he was the officer to whom Major George Washington carried the summons of the governor of Virginia to retire from that region. St. Pierre was killed two years later in the naval battle on Lake George.

Thus the heroic daring and enterprise of the great line of French explorers was quenched by the bloody deluge of war, and the vast empire acquired by Louis XIV and Louis XV in North America became the spoil of France's bitterest enemy and rival. Even before the ink was dry on the capitulation of Montreal, British traders had pushed their way into the West and reaped where the French had sown. The very site of Fort Beauharnois was forgotten until Americans took possession, and in the nineteenth century American historians resurrected the sources for the French régime on the upper Mississippi.

Fort Beauharnois was well planned and well placed. It was one of the chain of posts which, sweeping around the great arch of French occupation from Quebec on the east to New Orleans on the south, safeguarded the French empire in interior North America. Had France

* For additional information, see Grace Lee Nute, "Marin versus La Vérendrye," in *Minnesota History,* 32:226–238 (December, 1951). *Ed.*

been able to people her colony, the political fortune of the Mississippi Valley might have been different.

We should not forget, however, that the French in the West, as well as in the East, aided the Americans in wresting what is now the United States from Great Britain. Even some of the descendants of the commandants at Fort Beauharnois were on our side during the Revolution. Timothée de Montbrun not only supported George Rogers Clark in the Illinois country, but was the commandant of that region under the American flag. Maurice Godefroy de Linctot was Clark's most trusted and able emissary among the northwestern Indians, making it possible for the Americans to maintain a foothold on the upper Mississippi until the signing of the treaty of peace in 1783 gave our new nation all the lands east of the Mississippi River.

So we do well to signalize the bicentenary of the founding of Fort Beauharnois in this year of 1927, while we recall the names and deeds of its officers and the strong push made by France to explore and occupy the headwaters of our greatest river and the land of the great tribe of the Sioux.

The Story of Grand Portage

SOLON J. BUCK

BRITISH FUR TRADERS, who succeeded the French in the Minnesota country after 1763, made Grand Portage on the north shore of Lake Superior one of the most important fur posts on the North American continent. In 1960 the site became Minnesota's second national monument. Although such later historians as Harold A. Innis, W. Stewart Wallace, and Milo M. Quaife have added significantly to our knowledge of the North West Company and its far-flung activities, this pioneering article published in February, 1923 (volume 5) remains the most comprehensive general treatment of Grand Portage, which was the company's headquarters in its heyday. The article was later revised by the author for publication as a pamphlet issued by the Cook County Historical Society in 1931, and the text as he amended it is reprinted here. Solon J. Buck, who served from 1914 to 1931 as superintendent of the Minnesota Historical Society, was also the founder and first editor of Minnesota History. *From 1941 to 1948 he was archivist of the United States, and for the next six years he occupied the post of assistant librarian of Congress. As a writer, Mr. Buck is best known for his book on* The Granger Movement, *published in 1913. He died in 1962 at the age of seventy-eight.*

MODERN MAP MAKERS have the disagreeable habit, in the interest of economy, of dismembering the state of Minnesota and depicting the northeastern corner separately on a little inset map.[1] Few people today realize that this triangle of land, so cavalierly treated by our draftsmen, was during many years the scene of more human activities than took place in all the rest of the state; that more than thirty years before the founding of Fort Snelling, which we are wont to look upon as the real beginning of Minnesota history, upward of a thousand white men were assembled year after year at a post within this area; and that here occurred the only military operations of the American Revolution within the borders of the state.

The explanation of the importance of this region is to be found in

26

its geography. The Pigeon River, which now forms the international boundary at Lake Superior, was, in the days when waterways were the only means of transportation, the best natural highway between the Great Lakes or the St. Lawrence system and the northwestern section of the continent, with its thousands of lakes and streams draining into Hudson Bay or the Arctic Ocean. But the Pigeon River, through the last twenty miles of its course before it flows into Lake Superior, is so obstructed by falls and by cascades in rocky canyons as to be impossible of navigation. On the Canadian side the land is too mountainous and the distance too great for portaging to be practicable; but on the American side the line of the lake shore is roughly parallel to the river, and about seven or eight miles from the mouth of the river a little bay forms a natural harbor from which a portage of about nine miles over not too difficult country can be made to the Pigeon River above the cascades.

That this Grand Portage or great carrying place, as it was early designated by the French, was used by the Indians for generations before the advent of white men in the region is almost a certainty, although apparently not susceptible of proof. When and under what circumstances the first white man crossed the portage and who he was are questions which cannot now be answered. Nor do we know who was the first white man to visit the little bay at the eastern end of the trail, which takes its name from the portage. Radisson and Groseilliers, the first white men thought to have visited Minnesota, are believed to have reached the north shore of Lake Superior in 1660, but it is not likely that they went as far east as Grand Portage.[2] Du Luth coasted along the north shore in 1679 and established there a fort or trading post, the location of which was near what is now Fort William, about thirty miles northeast of Grand Portage. It is highly probable, however, that Du Luth or some of his men entered the bay at Grand Portage, and they may have traversed the portage itself. Fort Kaministiquia, as Du Luth's post was called, was maintained for several years, then was abandoned, and was re-established in 1717. That the traders who made this their headquarters failed to discover and make use of the Grand Portage is unbelievable.[3]

The first white man to leave a record of the use of the portage, however, is the Sieur de la Vérendrye, who crossed it on his famous expedition along the boundary waters in 1731. In his account he calls it the Grand Portage and refers to it in such a way as to lead to the inference that it was already well known by that name.[4] From this time until the French and Indian War, French traders were pushing constantly farther and farther into the Canadian Northwest, and practically all the traffic passed over the Grand Portage route. A post was undoubtedly established at the eastern end of the trail, where goods destined for the trade were landed from the large canoes used on the lake and prepared for the nine-mile carry to the Pigeon River.[5] At the western end of the trail, where the goods were loaded into smaller canoes suitable for river transportation, some sort of shelter probably was erected during the French period, but of this no information has been found. During the last conflict between the French and the English in America, which terminated with the surrender of New France in 1760, the trade on Lake Superior and westward was abandoned, and the Indians had to go to the posts of the Hudson's Bay Company far to the north or to get along without white man's goods.[6]

In November, 1761, a British garrison took possession of the post at Michilimackinac or Mackinac between Lakes Michigan and Huron. Shortly before this, however, one Alexander Henry, who had outfitted at Albany, New York, arrived at the post prepared to engage in the Indian trade on the upper lakes, and soon after him, other English traders made their appearance in the vicinity. If a narrative written nearly sixty years afterward is reliable, a party of these traders, accompanied by a military escort, made its way through Lake Superior to Grand Portage in May, 1762, this being the first voyage through Lake Superior under the British flag. This, if true, would indicate that Grand Portage was recognized at this time as the most important place in the western part of Lake Superior. The Indians of the Northwest, however, did not welcome the substitution of the English for the French; in 1763 the post at Mackinac was surprised, the garrison was massacred, one of the traders was killed, and the others, including Henry, were taken captive. This outbreak, which was a part of the conspiracy of Pontiac, put an end to British attempts at trade in the Northwest until the close of the Indian war in 1765.[7]

In that year some traders made their way from Michilimackinac to Rainy Lake, doubtless over the Grand Portage, and every year thereafter apparently the portage was used by traders, who soon reoccupied the old French posts in the interior and established new ones. On July 19, 1767, a party of explorers led by Captain James Tute arrived at Grand Portage Bay, having made their way from the upper Mississippi to Lake Superior and then along the north shore. Jonathan Carver, who was a member of the party, in his manuscript journal in the British Museum, describes the bay as "about a mile and a half deep and about so Broad almost to the Bottom, being nearly square, in the Chops of

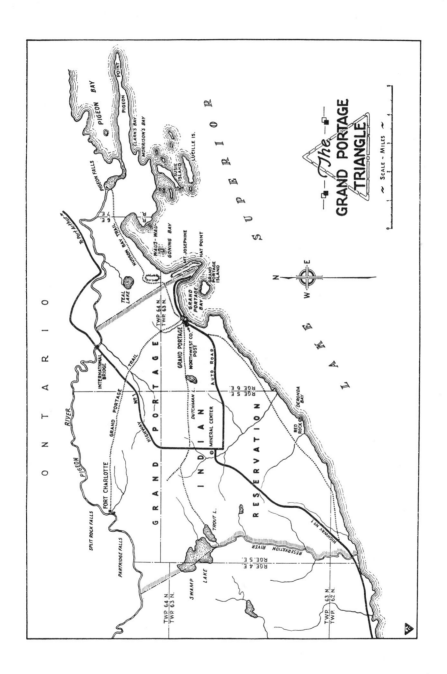

this bay or where it Communicates with the Lake is a very pleasant Island Lying in the Middle having a Little opening to the Lake on Each end, on This Island and Landing at the Bottom of the Bay is some of the best Land on all the north of Lake Superiour." Carver's "Survey Journal" indicates that at that time "the Landing Place and Indian Castle" were about halfway between the two hills that are known locally as Mount Rose and Mount Josephine. Carver reported that the country was "ownd by a Chief of the Chipeways who has a Large house and a few warriours here." Some Cree and Assiniboine Indians were camped there at the time on the lookout for traders who would relieve them of their dependence on the Hudson's Bay Company.[8]

The explorers, who were short of provisions, remained at the bay three weeks, hoping to receive supplies from Major Robert Rogers, the commandant at Michilimackinac, that would enable them to push on to the west, and in the meantime subsisting mainly on wild rice and fish obtained from the Crees. On July 23 six canoes of Rainy Lake Indians arrived from Michilimackinac, where they had been to visit the commandant, and on August 2 traders bound for the Northwest arrived in six canoes. Finally on August 7 a trader arrived with letters from Rogers indicating that no supplies would be sent, and on the following day the explorers started eastward along the north shore of the lake.[9]

It is evident from Carver's journal that none of the traders had a permanent establishment at Grand Portage in 1767. The number of traders operating through there increased rapidly, however, and considerable rivalry developed among them. In 1775 at least nine applications were made for licenses for the Grand Portage trade; and in one of them James McGill, Benjamin Frobisher, and Maurice Blondeau proposed to transport twelve canoes to the bay, with 102 canoemen and merchandise consisting of 1,000 gallons of rum and brandy, 24 kegs of wine, 90 bags of ball and shot, 150 guns, 150 bales of dry goods, 15 trunks of dry goods, 12 boxes of iron ware, 12 nests of brass kettles, 4 nests of copper kettles, 100 packages of carrot and twist tobacco, 50 kegs of lard and tallow, and 60 kegs of pork. When Alexander Henry arrived at the bay on June 28, 1775, he "found the traders in a state of extreme reciprocal hostility, each pursuing his interests in such a manner as might most injure his neighbour. The consequences were very hurtful to the morals of the Indians." The transportation of Henry's goods across the portage was "a work of seven days of severe and dangerous exertion."[10] A memorandum drawn up by General Frederick Haldimand in January, 1778, states that at that time the trade by way of Grand Portage amounted annually to forty thousand pounds and employed five hundred persons, who, "for about a month in the summer season, have a general rendezvous at the Portage, and for the refreshing and comforting those who are employed in the more distant voyages the Traders from hence have built tolerable Houses; and in order to cover them from any insult from the numerous savage Tribes, who resort there during that time, have made stockades around them." The memorandum adds that there was some "jarring" of interests at Grand Portage and that, because of the lack of officers representing the government in the region, the traders had found it necessary to provide some show and parade such as firing cannon to signalize the arrival of the brigades and distributing medals — the purpose of this being to impress the Indians.[11]

The antagonisms among traders representing separate interests, possible dangers from the Indians, and above all the fear that disaffected persons at the portage might send supplies to the American troops then operating in the Illinois country under George Rogers Clark, were the reasons for sending a military expedition from Mackinac to Grand Portage about June 1, 1778. On May 18 John Askin, the commissary at Mackinac, wrote to M. Beausoleille, the clerk of the Northwest traders at Grand Portage, that he would have "an officer and several soldiers to pass the summer" there, and directed him to have a house, equipped with a chimney, ready to receive them. The letter concludes with the following remarkable sentences, of which no explanation will be attempted: "I need two pretty Slave girls from 9 to 16 years old. Have the goodness to ask the Gentlemen to procure two for me." The officer detailed for duty at this northwesternmost point of British military operations during the Revolution was Lieutenant Thomas Bennett of the Eighth Regiment of Foot, and his detachment consisted of about twelve soldiers. While stationed at Grand Portage they constructed a small fort at the expense of the traders and laid out a road across the portage. Apparently they left in the fall, for the next year the traders petitioned for another detachment. Major A. S. De Peyster, in command at Mackinac, protested that, in view of the imminent danger of his being attacked by the rebels, he could not spare the troops; and no evidence has been found as to whether or not they were sent.[12]

By this time the Northwest trade had grown to such proportions and the competition between different interests was resulting in so many abuses that movements were under way for consolidation; and, after several preliminary "joint stocks," the famous North West Company was organized in 1783.[13] The next twenty years comprise the greatest period in the history of the Grand Portage. The North West Company about 1785 built a fort or stockade on the bay, which consisted of an enclosure of palisades twenty-four by thirty rods in size. The buildings within the fort, according to a contemporary description, were "sixteen in number made with cedar and white spruce fir split with whip saws after being suquared [sic], the Roofs are couvered with shingles of Cedar and Pine, most of their posts, Doors, and windows, are painted with spanish brown. Six of these buildings are Store Houses for the company's Merchandize and Furs, &c. The rest are dwelling houses shops compting house and Mess House — they have also a warf or kay for their vessel to unload and Load at." [14] The company had a vessel of ninety-five tons burden which made four or five trips to Grand Portage each summer. In the bay was a large canoe yard where seventy canoes were constructed annually for use in the trade.[15]

During July and August, Grand Portage was a very busy place. Here the brigades from Montreal, with goods for the trade of the ensuing winter, accompanied by two of the Montreal partners, met the wintering partners and other traders coming in from their posts scattered throughout the Northwest from the upper Red River to Lake Athabasca. Here was held the annual meeting of the company, at which arrangements were made and agreements entered into for the ensuing year. Here the employees received, and largely spent, their annual wages. The partners, traders, clerks, and guides, to the number of two or three hundred, lived in the fort and ate in the great dining hall, and outside were the camps of the pork-eaters and the winterers, as the canoemen from Montreal and the interior respectively were called. These engagés subsisted principally upon pork and hominy, with plentiful supplies of liquor and tobacco; but the food served in the dining hall included bread, salt pork, beef, ham, fish, venison, butter, peas, corn, potatoes, tea, and wine. There was even plenty of milk, for a herd of cows was kept at Grand Portage. In the evenings the great hall was often the scene of much merriment, and interesting accounts may be read of festive balls at which the dusky maidens of the forests are reported to have danced very well and to have conducted themselves with much propriety. Besides the resident Indians, many others congregated about the fort during the summer.[16]

The task of transporting the packs of supplies and furs across the portage was a long and arduous one and required the services of a hundred men for several weeks. Parts of the trail were often in very bad condition being "knee-deep in mud and clay, and so slippery as to make walking tedious." The packs weighed ninety pounds each and two or more were carried by each man on his back, the round trip of eighteen miles requiring about six hours. How many thousands of trips back and forth across this trail were made during the entire period it is impossible to estimate, but it is small wonder that the soil still shows evidences of the trampling of many feet. In 1788 the company requested a grant of land along the route to enable it to construct a wagon road over the trail. The request was denied by the council at Quebec, probably because it would have given the company a monopoly of the route, but later the trail was improved so that ox carts could be used on it.[17]

At the western end of the portage, where it met the Pigeon River, was another stockade enclosing several buildings, which was known as Fort Charlotte. Here the goods were stored until the traders were ready to load them into their canoes and start for the wintering grounds.[18] Of the history of this fort little has been ascertained as yet, but it evidently was a place of considerable importance for many years. On August 5, 1793, John Macdonell, a trader, noted in his diary* that "Mr. Donald Ross has been so long in charge of Fort Charlotte that he has acquired the respectable name of Governor."

The North West Company was not able to maintain a complete monopoly over the trade which passed across the Grand Portage. Rival companies were established from time to time, usually to flourish a few years and then amalgamate with "the Great Company." One of these rivals, the X. Y. Company, which operated from 1797 to 1804, had a separate establishment at Grand Portage and also probably at Fort Charlotte, for the map drawn by the surveyors for the boundary commission in 1824 indicates the outlines of two stockades at the western end of the portage, and in 1922 these outlines were located on the ground.[19]

At the very beginning of this period of the greatest activity on the Grand Portage, the land over which it ran became, by virtue of the Treaty of 1783, a part of the United States. The boundary, as laid down in the treaty, was somewhat indefinite, but it was generally understood by the traders that it had been fixed at the Pigeon River. So long as the military posts on the American side of the line in the Great Lakes region remained in the hands of the British, there was little likelihood that the traders would be disturbed; and those posts, for reasons which need not be considered here, were not surrendered until 1796. Soon after the occupation of Mackinac by an American garrison, how-

*Macdonell's diary mentioned here and in note 14 has since been published. See Charles M. Gates, ed., *Five Fur Traders of the Northwest,* 97 (Revised edition — St. Paul, 1965). *Ed.*

ever, intimations were given to the traders that a revenue officer might be sent to Grand Portage to collect duty on the great quantity of goods being imported there into the United States. As a result of this threat, and also, perhaps, of a desire to avoid the difficulties of the long carrying place, the North West Company began casting about for another route to the interior. In 1798 the Kaministiquia route, by way of Dog Lake to the boundary waters, was discovered, or rediscovered, for it had been known to the French; and in 1801 the company commenced the erection of a new headquarters at the mouth of the Kaministiquia River. To this, subsequently, was given the name of Fort William.[20]

Apparently the X. Y. Company retained its headquarters at Grand Portage until the union of the two companies in 1804,[21] but thereafter the greatness of the place was a thing of the past. A local trading post was maintained by the North West Company at Grand Portage until after the War of 1812, but the portage itself was little used, and apparently Fort Charlotte was allowed to fall into decay.[22] During this war a British trader is said to have visited Grand Portage for the purpose of endeavoring to enlist the Chippewa Indians there resident against the Americans.[23] At the close of the War of 1812, Congress passed an act excluding foreigners from the fur trade in American territory, and John Jacob Astor's American Fur Company purchased the posts of the North West Company south of the line. Lewis Cass, governor of Michigan Territory, in 1815 recommended the establishment of a United States military post at Grand Portage for the collection of duties and the enforcement of trade regulations. The recommendation was not followed, however; and, as the American Fur Company confined its operations on Lake Superior to the southern shore for several years, the Grand Portage band of Indians continued to be supplied from Fort William. "In the winter of 1824," according to Henry R. Schoolcraft, "persons in the service of the Hudson Bay Company [*which had absorbed the North West Company in 1821*] carried off in trains the band of Chippeways, living near old Grand Portage . . . after the arrival of an American trader."[24]

In 1831 a single trader was licensed for Grand Portage, but the principal activities at the place during the 1830s centered around the fishing industry conducted by the American Fur Company.* Grand Portage was a central station for these operations, and large quantities of Lake Superior fish were there assembled from various stations along

---

*For additional information on this point, see Grace Lee Nute, "The American Fur Company's Fishing Enterprise on Lake Superior," in *Mississippi Valley Historical Review,* 12:488–490 (March, 1926). *Ed.*

the north shore and packed in barrels for the export trade. In 1839 the establishment there consisted of two family dwelling houses, a "new store," two "mens houses, 1 Coopers Shop, 1 Fish Store, Stable Barn, Root house, &c below or near the beach, placed here and there without order or symetry." About three acres were under cultivation and produced over two hundred bushels of potatoes. The fishing business was unprofitable, however, and seems to have been abandoned when the American Fur Company sold out in the 1840s.[25]

The village of Ojibway Indians, which had been located near Grand Portage Bay apparently before the coming of the first traders, remained after the glories of the place had departed. In October, 1837, Father, later Bishop, Frédéric Baraga visited the village and baptized seven persons, and in the following July a Catholic mission and school for the Indians was opened there by Father Francis X. Pierz. This was abandoned in 1839, but in the spring of 1842 Pierz started another mission and school for the same Indians on the Pigeon River about a mile from its mouth. He was recalled in the fall, and the Indians were without a resident missionary until 1848, when three Jesuits reopened the mission on Pigeon River, only to remove it after a year to Fort William. Despite the intermittent character of these missions many of the Indians had been converted to Christianity, and missionaries continued to visit them once a year or oftener. Grand Portage is still an Indian village although most of its inhabitants wear white man's clothing and live in houses. The main automobile road along the north shore leaves it to one side, but it can be reached over a good side road, and it is visited every summer by many people attracted by the natural beauty of the place and by its historic associations.[26]

Perhaps the most interesting feature of the history of the Grand Portage in the nineteenth century is its connection with the boundary controversy. The region was carefully explored and mapped in 1822 by the surveyors of a joint American and British commission provided for in the Treaty of Ghent. When the commissioners held their final meeting in 1827, the representative of Great Britain offered to accept the Pigeon River route as the boundary, provided the line should be drawn through the portages, including the Grand Portage. When this was rejected, he offered to accept the river as the boundary, providing the portages should be free and open to the use of both parties. This offer also was rejected; but when the boundary controversy was finally settled by the Webster-Ashburton Treaty in 1842, it was on exactly these terms. This treaty is still in force, and British citizens would be entitled

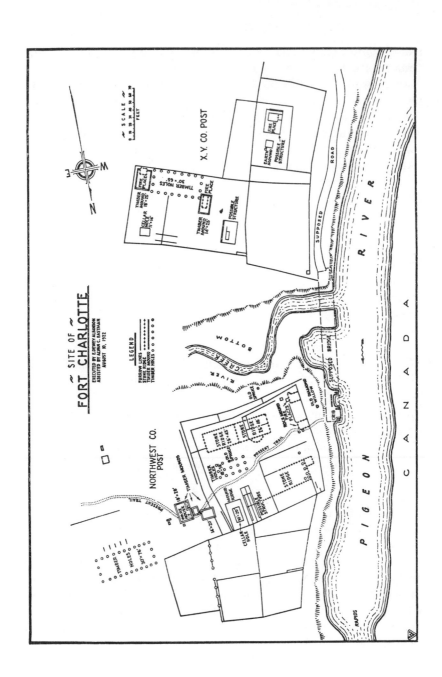

SITE OF

FORT CHARLOTTE

EXECUTED BY E. DEWEY ALBINSON
ASSISTED BY ALMA C. EASTMAN
AUGUST 10, 1922

LEGEND

FURROW LINES
STONE RIDGE
TIMBER MOUND
TIMBER HOLES

SCALE
0 10 20 30 40 50 60 70
FEET

NORTHWEST CO.
POST

X. Y. CO. POST

PIGEON RIVER

CANADA

today to demand the unobstructed use of the ancient trail over the Grand Portage.[27]

In 1854 the United States purchased the triangle north of Lake Superior from the Chippewa, but a tract extending from the lake to the Pigeon River and including the entire line of the portage was set aside as a reservation for the Indians. In the later years of the nineteenth century, this reservation was broken up, allotments were given to the Indians, and the remainder of the land, with the exception of reservations for possible hydroelectric development, was sold for lumbering purposes or opened up to homesteading. A number of settlers took up claims which lay across the portage, and it appeared for a time that the trail might be obliterated.[28]*

In the summer of 1922 a member of the staff of the Minnesota Historical Society and a representative of a Minneapolis newspaper explored the region and found it possible to trace the route of the portage throughout its length.[29] At the western end they discovered the cellars and other remains of old Fort Charlotte and remnants of an ancient dock on the banks of the Pigeon River. Later in the year the site was more thoroughly explored for the society by Mr. E. Dewey Albinson and Mr. A. C. Eastman, who had been spending the summer near Grand Portage. A map was made showing the locations of the various buildings, which were traced by the remains of the log piers driven in for foundations and by piles of stones, the remains of fireplaces and ovens. Several articles, such as knives, tools, and bits of broken china, were discovered — interesting evidences of the white man's sojourn in the wilderness. The outlines of what was probably the North West Company post on the bay can also be traced in part at the base of Mount Rose, and in the water near by were seen the remains of an old dock.

In a printed *Statement* concerning state parks submitted by the Honorable Ray P. Chase, state auditor, to the 1923 Minnesota legislature, he included a "Fort Charlotte State Park" among the proposed new parks and presented a map of it embracing the region from the western boundary of the Indian reservation to Pigeon Point. After discussing the historic associations of the region, Mr. Chase described its scenic attractions: "About two miles up the river from the site of old Fort Charlotte are the Partridge Falls, 45 feet high; just below the fort site the river runs through Split Rock Canyon, where it doubles on itself

* The trail and the site of Fort Charlotte are now within Grand Portage National Monument. The dock discussed below as well as portions of the stockade and dining hall of the old post have been reconstructed since this article was written. *Ed.*

in a hairpin turn and falls 144 feet in a series of cascades; and then, after several smaller falls, the water drops 70 feet in the Pigeon Falls, the highest and most beautiful waterfall in Minnesota, and flows out through an estuary and Pigeon Bay into Lake Superior. The rocky but forested shore of Lake Superior from Grand Portage to Pigeon Point, including Grand Portage and Wauswaugoning Bays, with Hat Point between them, Mount Josephine and other hills in the background, and a group of interesting islands, is the most picturesque part of the North Shore in Minnesota." [30]

Mr. Chase recommended that land embracing as many as feasible of the scenic and historic features of the region "be acquired promptly before the advent of homesteaders and speculators increases the cost." He suggested also "the erection of a building on the site of old Fort Charlotte, to serve as a starting point or terminus for canoe trips on the boundary waters, and the establishment of camp sites." He expressed the belief "that the Province of Ontario will co-operate by acquiring or reserving land on the Canadian side of the Pigeon River so that ultimately a great international park may be developed in this region."

No action has been taken by the state as yet (1931) on Mr. Chase's recommendations, but public interest in the region and its possibilities for park purposes has been increasing. The Quetico-Superior Council, formed in 1927 to promote the establishment by means of a treaty between Canada and the United States of an "international forest and wilderness sanctuary" of "some ten million acres of forested lakeland" along the Minnesota-Ontario border, proposes the inclusion of the Grand Portage and Pigeon River region within the reservation. Unfortunately this region is not included within the boundaries of the Superior National Forest. Most of it is already privately owned, and prompt action is necessary if private exploitation is to be avoided. Recent action of Congress makes it probable that Isle Royale will soon be a national park, and its development will increase the importance of Grand Portage as the nearest harbor.* If the state or interested private agencies would acquire the land in the region and present it to the national government, it is probable that Congress would gladly establish it as a national monument. This would ensure the protection and appropriate development of the area and would fit in with the larger plans for the great reservation along the border.

*Isle Royale became a national park in 1947. *Ed.*

The Settler and the Army in Frontier Minnesota

FRANCIS PAUL PRUCHA

WHEN THE TREATY of 1783 was signed following the Revolutionary War, the Minnesota lands east of the Mississippi River became part of the United States. With the Louisiana Purchase of 1803 much of what is now western and southern Minnesota passed into American hands, and the remaining portion in the northwestern corner fell to the United States when the forty-ninth parallel was fixed as the boundary by the Convention of 1818. With the transfer of the region to the United States, the soldier joined the fur trader as a major factor in the area's history. The United States Army represented the authority of the Great White Father in Washington and by its very presence opened the way for settlement. Francis Paul Prucha, who is a member of the history faculty in Marquette University at Milwaukee, has examined the role of the military on the northwestern frontier in numerous articles and in two books: Broadax and Bayonet *(1953) and* A Guide to the Military Posts of the United States, 1789–1895 *(1964). The following article appeared in September, 1948 (volume 29).*

THE FIRST DETACHMENTS of the United States Army to be garrisoned in what is now Minnesota slowly poled their keelboats up the Mississippi in the summer of 1819 to the point where Fort Snelling was to be built. They entered a wilderness almost devoid of white men, for they had not been sent to protect westward-moving frontiersmen They had not journeyed more than a thousand miles from their headquarters at Detroit to answer the call of white settlers who feared the tomahawks or scalping knives of the Sioux. Rather, they came to substantiate the claim of the United States to overlordship of the vast reaches of the upper Mississippi country, which long had felt the dominance of the British government. The English had indeed been defeated and had given up all rights to the area in 1783, and the young American government's claims had been upheld in the War of 1812,

39

but only the presence of army men would convince the Indians that the Great White Father at Washington at last meant to exert his authority.

In 1819 Minnesota belonged to the Indians — the Chippewa and the Sioux — except for small patches of land where the Minnesota and the St. Croix met the Mississippi. These Lieutenant Zebulon M. Pike had arranged to purchase from the natives for army posts in 1805. Since there were no white settlers in the region stretching out from Fort Snelling, there was no one to criticize the actions of the army garrison, to demand protection, or to squat upon lands reserved for military use.

Such a situation could not continue long. The garrison at Fort Snelling was a magnet drawing hardy pioneers into a region which soldiers had tamed. The post was a substantial guarantee against the Indian menace; its men made a success of cultivating the soil; and they set up mills to utilize the water power of the Falls of St. Anthony and to saw into lumber the rich timber along the rivers. Provisions were at hand to succor families hard pressed by a wilderness that exhausted their supplies as well as their bodies. In fact, it was as a haven that Fort Snelling was first sought out by Swiss and other refugees from Lord Selkirk's settlement on the Red River. These miserable and deluded people left the hardships caused by Canada's grasshoppers and floods, and beginning in 1821 several hundred drifted to Fort Snelling. For many of them this was but a stopping point on a journey to settlements in Illinois or Indiana, but some stayed in the vicinity of the fort, setting up homes on the military reservation by the sufferance of the kindhearted army officers. Soon they were joined by lumbermen and farmers traveling up the Mississippi. Finally, in 1837, by treaties with the Indians, the delta of land between the Mississippi and the St. Croix was opened to settlement, and the white men living there were enabled to obtain legal title to the lands on which they had been squatting.

By the same token, the army's isolation was gone. There appeared increasing numbers of white settlers, who looked upon the army garrison as subordinate to their wishes and needs. The army faced complaints and criticisms from disgruntled citizens who coveted military lands or called for new western posts and more aggressive protection as settlements surged up the rivers. The complaints often were expressed in the columns of frontier newspapers, and more than once they echoed in the halls of Congress as irate Minnesotans took their troubles to the source of army authority.

There were various reasons for dissatisfaction with the army in

Minnesota. Most of them can be traced to the location of the posts, the type and number of troops, the way in which they were used, and the annoying hindrances to settlement caused by the reservation for military use of land around the posts. Fundamentally, of course, the United States troops accomplished their mission, for they prevented Indian uprisings and furnished an umbrella of protection under which settlement advanced. Only in a situation of comparative security did people speak out about the irksome details of the army's presence which seemed to impede the fulfillment of manifest destiny.

As Minnesota developed before the Civil War and the frontier advanced beyond Fort Snelling, the army moved westward and northward. Large blocks of fertile prairie and rich forest land were purchased from the Indians by the terms of treaties negotiated in 1851, 1854, 1855, and 1858; new, permanent army posts were built on the Mississippi and Minnesota rivers to provide the protection that once Fort Snelling alone had furnished. In 1849 Fort Ripley was established on the Mississippi below the mouth of the Crow Wing River; and in 1853 Fort Ridgely was founded on the Minnesota, in the northwest corner of present-day Nicollet County, to guard against the Sioux who had been restricted to narrow strips of land along the upper river.

The war department considered these concentrations of troops the best means for overawing the red men and preventing attacks on isolated families in the river valleys. The number of men available to the secretary of war seems pitifully small to those accustomed to thinking of armies in terms of hundreds of thousands, but penny-pinching Congresses in the decades before the Civil War made a total of even ten to fifteen thousand men difficult to maintain. It took no small skill to distribute these meager forces along two extensive coasts and from Lake Superior to the Gulf of Mexico. By keeping men in sizable groups, the government hoped to use them most efficiently. "The multiplication of small posts," the secretary of war asserted in 1853, "however much it may appear to have been called for by the necessities of the service, is of more than doubtful policy. The system is expensive far beyond any good results that are attained by it. It is injurious to the decipline [sic], instruction, and efficiency of the troops, and it is believed that it often invites aggression by that exhibition of weakness which must inevitably attend the great dispersion of any force."[1]

Yet the "multiplication of small posts" and the dispersion of forces was what many Minnesotans demanded. The fingers of settlement into the western area of the state and the islands of settlers that sprang into being around such points as Pembina called for a military post near by as effective protection; and, as a corollary, the maintenance of garrisons in sections well populated and in little danger were severely denounced. The war department just did not move fast enough — or in enough directions — to keep pace with advancing settlement.

In 1858 the editor of the *Pioneer and Democrat* of St. Paul urged a new policy for the disposition of troops in an article entitled "Military Defence of Our Western Frontier." To him the "defenceless state of our frontier settlements, everywhere exposed to the incursions of tribes which recent events have shown to be capable of any atrocities" and the "proved inadequacy of the few companies which are cooped up at Forts Ridgely and Ripley to defend the immense extent of country which the emigration of the past few years has carried far beyond the line of protection afforded by those posts" required a reallocation of troops along the frontier and a "new system of military defences corresponding to the new disposition of the Indian tribes, and the new exigencies to which the recent extraordinary extension of our settlements have given rise." [2]

The *Sauk Rapids Frontierman* was even more explicit in its criticism, and its program for improvement is in sharp disagreement with the war department's policy of concentration. The editor of this small weekly journal gave voice to a proposal which would meet the demands of Minnesota citizens — a clear statement of dissatisfaction with things as they were. He asserted that "the mistake in our military system for the past thirty years, so far as it has referred to the defence of the Indian frontier, has been that too much money has been expended in the *building of Forts* and Barracks for troops, and that they have been *occupied too long* after the frontier has gone beyond them." Seldom during the past twenty years, he pointed out, had the frontier long remained stationary, nor had troops been needed at the same point for more than three or four years. Restraint imposed by the actual presence of troops in the neighborhood was needed, rather than a display of expensive military fortifications. "For all purposes of defence against Indians, or protection of the white settlements," the editor continued, "if, instead of vast outlays of money in erecting expensive barracks, cheap but comfortable quarters were provided and occupied only so long as the settlements were in their infancy, our little army would have been much more efficient, and at a comparatively trifling cost: it would have been able to prevent the waste of blood and treasure which our Indian difficulties have involved. . . . A large and inviting region of country is now open to settlement lying northwest of this place, and the advance settlements have already penetrated far beyond the reach of assistance from either the military posts or the volunteer troops of the more populous counties. . . . Troops have not been needed at Fort Snelling since the removal of the Sioux to their present position near Fort Ridgely, and even Fort Ripley has been useless as a military post since the removal of the Winnebagoes." The Sauk Rapids editor asserted that if the troops from these forts had been used on the remote frontier, somewhere on the Red River, the country in between would be filled with settlers, Dakota Territory would have twenty thousand settlers, and the soldiers would be free to move farther westward.[3]

The most insistent demands for a new disposition of soldiers came from settlers in the Red River Valley. There substantial numbers of French-Canadian half-breeds had congregated near Pembina, just south of the Canadian border.[4] Under constant threat of attack from Indians of Canada and Dakota, these men sent up cry after cry for military protection, and the government could not be deaf to their pleas forever. "For five years," complained the *Minnesotian* in 1854, "the Legislative and Executive authorities of Minnesota have been asking for a small appropriation to sustain a military force at Pembina. No appropriation having a greater degree of right and justice on its side has ever been asked by a frontier people; and yet the measure has been continually delayed from some cause or other, which we could never learn." Finally in February, 1855, Congress appropriated the small sum of five thousand dollars for the erection of a military post on or near the Pembina River, and in June of the next year two companies of infantry were sent out to explore the Red River country and determine the "most eligible site for a military post in that quarter." [5]

The outcome of the expedition was a recommendation that the fort should be located at Graham's Point on the Red River near the present city of Breckenridge. In the years that followed its establishment, criticism of the new post, named Fort Abercrombie, continued to pour from the settlement at Pembina, which was still without the protection it had demanded. It was alleged that the location had been decided upon with more regard to speculators than to the military needs of the region. One newspaper correspondent, who signed himself "Veritas," pointed out that the settlers were dissatisfied with Graham's Point as a fort site because it was in a region still unsettled and not well suited to agriculture. The editor of the paper likewise condemned the site and called for a military establishment farther north on the Red River. "The Government is so familiar with the language of appeals for military protection from the settlements of our extensive frontier," he noted ironically, "and has so often been seduced by false or exaggerated pretexts into useless and extravagant expenditures, that it has learned to see even in the most clamorous calls for assistance, and in the most alarming menaces of danger, only a conspiracy of contractors and town-site speculators to induce appropriations of the public funds for some one's private benefit. Fortunately the amount of money necessary for the construction and maintenance of a military establishment on the Pembina river, is not large enough to tempt the cupidity of the mercenary bands of contractors and lobby agents, while the situation is too remote from the sphere of real estate operations to afford any suspicion that the demand for Government appropriations is simply to lend importance to some town-site. In conceding Fort Abercrombie to the clamors of these men, the Government may now feel itself at liberty to provide for the real necessities of defence on the Red River." Nevertheless, the site of Fort Abercrombie was maintained. Not until 1870 was a post established at Pembina, after internal revolutionary disturbances in Canada and incursions of hostile Sioux across the boundary.[6]

Isolated white settlers were not the only ones interested in changing the locations of the army garrisons. Sometimes the Indians themselves were the center of the argument, for the army was as much their protector as that of the whites. Intertribal warfare had to be stopped if peace were to be maintained in any region, and the troops were influential in keeping Indian affairs in order. The army post was considered essential, too, for groups of Indians who had forsaken the ways of the tribe for those of the white man and who needed protection from their more warlike brethren. This was especially the case among the Indians of Joseph R. Brown's Upper Sioux Agency on the Minnesota near the mouth of the Yellow Medicine River. Brown had persuaded many of his charges to adopt the white man's clothes, houses, and agricultural pursuits, and he attempted to find for them the security they needed in their new way of life. The location of Fort Ridgely, to his mind, was not suited for the protection of his "farmer Indians." "However proper the location of Fort Ridgely may have been in 1852," Brown asserted in his report for 1860, "it is now within the settlements, and for all practicable purposes connected with the control of the wild Indians, troops would be as effective at Fort Snelling as at Fort Ridgely. Before assistance could be obtained from either post to quell disturbance or prevent hostilities, the evil would have been consummated, and the aggressors be far beyond the reach of foot soldiers." Brown cited as confirmation of his views the report of Captain A. A. Gibson, who had been on duty at the two Sioux agencies to attend to annuity payments. Gibson declared that Fort Ridgely should be situated at the Upper Agency, which had to bear the brunt of every contact with the wild bands to the north and west.[7]

The citizens of Minnesota were critical enough of the location of the posts that the army had set up in their midst, but when troops were for some reason withdrawn, the chorus of complaints invariably reached a new high pitch. The necessity for economy in the war department during the 1850s and the belief in official circles that large concentrations of troops would be more effective on the frontier than small separated detachments brought about the evacuation of Fort Ripley on July 8, 1857. The Chippewa of the northern area were considered peaceful, and the usefulness of the post was believed to have been diminished by the founding of Fort Ridgely. But no sooner had the troops disappeared than the Chippewa caused trouble. The action of the war department in withdrawing the soldiers was severely condemned. The *Pioneer and Democrat* called it "one of the most ill-advised measures ever perpetrated by the Federal authorities, in this Territory." [8]

When Fort Abercrombie was abandoned for a brief period in 1859–60, there were more complaints. They reached a bitter peak in the vitriolic columns of Jane Grey Swisshelm's *St. Cloud Democrat*. After denouncing the government for neglecting the people of Minnesota in various respects, the editor added: "And now they have directed the Troops to abandon the only stations between you and the savages, and intend that you shall protect yourselves and families from the Indians, or take the consequences." After Fort Abercrombie was reoccupied, however, Mrs. Swisshelm still found cause for complaint. "Now that the winter is over and the Indians have ceased to rob and maltreat the frontier settlements," she wrote, "the Administration has, as we are informed, ordered three or four companies to Fort Abercrombie. A most delightful way to spend the summer and a few hundred thousand of Uncle Sam's revenue. — But just as soon as Autumn and the starving, thieving savages approach the settlement, these same troops will be sent to New York or some other safe and agreeable winter retreat. No matter; our hardy pioneers are getting used to it, and can protect the army in addition to their other duties, without serious inconvenience." [9] An ardent abolitionist, Mrs. Swisshelm could not forget her prejudice against anything the Democratic administration did, and her attacks on war department activities were colored by her views. Nevertheless, she expressed in an exaggerated degree the feelings of frontier Minnesotans who feared for their security when the strong arm of the military disappeared.

The troops located in Minnesota were the subject of caustic comment by newspaper editors whenever some action displeased the settlers or the soldiers failed in their assignments. When six Indians who were being taken from Fort Snelling to Benton County in irons escaped from their military escort, the editor of the *Minnesota Pioneer* exclaimed: "Suffering this escape, is wholly inexcusable — shameful. Has it come to this, that 25 regulars are insufficient to guard half-a-dozen Sioux Indians? What is the service coming to? What are officers and men kept dressed up in regimentals for, at our garrison at an immense expense?" While the Sioux and Chippewa were engaged in one of their numerous conflicts in the summer of 1858, troops were withdrawn from the state, leading another editor to remark sarcastically, "The Indians being so quiet, peaceable and orderly in Minnesota, is thought to be the occasion for this retrograde march!" The writer continues by asking, "What! are the soldiers frightened at the Indian warfare so near them?" [10]

Inactivity of troops in the garrisons was a further point of contention. "The feverish excitement which certain interested persons have managed to keep up in regard to the dangers of a general Indian war upon our frontier," peevishly observed a writer for the *Minnesotian* of August 22, 1857, "is now aggravated by the inactivity of the troops recently sent here to protect the settlers. Some three or four companies, it will be recollected, were announced as having arrived several days ago; but we believe they are as yet all quietly resting at Fort Snelling, and recruiting themselves after their fatiguing march by railroad and steamboat from the Atlantic coast. Why they have not been despatched to the frontier quarters, which the people were led to believe was their original destination, is a question which perhaps cannot be answered except through Secretary Floyd's circumlocution office at Washington." The writer asserted that there were plenty of troops in Minnesota if only they were sent where they were needed. He believed that the settlers would continue to feel alarmed until the troops manifested "more activity and a more thorough disposition to do something to intimidate the refractory Indians." He suggested that "these soldiers be put upon active service, instead of idling away their time in comfortable quarters," adding that "They will then enjoy better health, and produce a more healthy state of affairs on the frontier of Minnesota." Mrs. Swisshelm had her bit to say, too, in 1860, after hearing a rumor that there was an Indian uprising along the Minnesota River.

"We insisted on sending to Fort Ripley for troops," she recorded, "for a probability that a single family had been murdered, appeared cause sufficient; but the rule as understood, appeared to be that the soldiers will not come until all the fighting is over." [11]

The *Henderson Democrat* did not want its censure of the army to fall on the men and officers stationed in Minnesota, for, wrote the editor, "It is the war department we blame for the inadequacy of the force in the Territory." He pointed out that "Infantry is very useful in its place, but I question if there is any officer in the army who will hold that it is the proper arm of the service for operations outside a garrison, in the Indian country. Mounted men are necessary to the successful pursuit of Indians, and a sufficient force of either mounted infantry or dragoons should be stationed in the Territory, and be held in readiness to march at any time it may be necessary, either for the protection of our settlements or the punishment of offences." Any increase in numbers, however, served to mollify the demands of the citizens. Commenting on a detachment of a hundred and fifty men who arrived in St. Paul in 1858, one observer noted, "An additional force has been long needed . . . for the more complete protection of the settlers on the Western frontier of the State, the number already stationed there being too limited for the purpose, and this new addition will, no doubt, have a beneficial effect on the Indians." [12]

While Minnesotans were quick to call for new cantonments of troops to protect western settlements, they were equally ready to condemn the continuation of posts in areas where the density of the population was itself adequate protection against the Indians. This hostility toward old posts in settled areas arose partly out of the wish that troops should be used in new regions where the Indian danger was still acute. But it was caused also by the settlers' eagerness to acquire the military reservations around the posts. When each post was established, an extended area around the actual fort was withdrawn from sale and reserved for use as garden plots, hay meadows, and wood land for members of the military garrison. Others were prevented from settling on these lands, although many people did locate on reserves through oversight or by permission of the army officers. In any case, settlers found the reserved lands attractive, and they made repeated attempts to persuade the federal government to curtail or abolish the military reservations, which, the pioneers argued, had served their military purpose and were a serious hindrance to settlement. Long after the Indian danger had been obviated by the removal of Indians from the state or by confining them to reservations, the question of reducing the military reserves continued to plague the relations between Minnesotans and the army.

Fort Snelling was located at the mouth of the Minnesota River, near the Falls of St. Anthony, and at the head of navigation on the Mississippi. Its reservation, embracing territory of obvious economic importance, was much coveted by the citizens of the territory. In 1838–39 the actual limits of the Fort Snelling reserve were well defined for the first time. At the same time the commanding officer advocated extending the reservation in order to control the liquor traffic near the post. His suggestion met with violent opposition from settlers in the area, who steadfastly refused to move and who attributed the proposal to various base motives. Irate citizens, meeting on November 16, 1839, adopted a series of resolutions condemning the officers, assailing the attempt to extend the reservation as "alike derogatory to the principles of common honesty and justice," and complaining because they were forced to abandon improvements on the military land and to face the hardships involved in moving. As a result of the settlers' complaints, a resolution protesting the extension of the reserve was sent to Congress by the legislative assembly of Wisconsin Territory. It stressed the importance of steamboat landings to the agricultural district, protested the loss of good agricultural land, much of which was improved and under cultivation, and charged speculation by the post officers.[13]

But resolutions and complaints had no effect, and the secretary of war, relying on the reports of government officials, ordered the squatters removed. This was done with considerable harshness by the soldiers of the fort, and the settlers, many of whom had been refugees from the Selkirk settlement, were forced to take up new residences farther down the Mississippi, where St. Paul later developed. More than a decade passed before any reduction was made in the size of the Fort Snelling Reservation.[14]

A beginning was made in 1849 on plans to move the Indians to the western part of the state in order to free the land around Fort Snelling for settlement. At the same time ambitious settlers began to work for a definite reduction in the size of the military reserve, realizing that Fort Snelling must soon pass from the picture as an important post. Their efforts were rewarded in 1852, when Congress finally passed a law redefining the boundaries of the reserve and directing that the area excluded be surveyed and sold at public auction. The people of Minnesota had been most anxious that the bill become law, and even before the final action the squatters had continued their improvements on the land. "Good houses are in course of erection, and farms are being systematically improved," reported the *Minnesotian*. "Particularly is this the case in the neighborhood of the Falls of Saint Anthony, and out at Lakes Calhoun and Harriet. Fort Snelling no more needs the use of these lands than she needs a battering train, were she called upon to lay siege to Crow Village. They are among the most fertile, well watered and timbered, and eligibly situated lands in the Territory. Now that the Indian title is extinguished upon the country all around them, the people have a right to demand that they be given up for their use." The *St. Anthony Express* hailed the act as a "measure imperiously called for by the state of affairs in this vicinity" and declared that the retention of the whole reserve by the government "would have operated as an embargo upon our town and the country adjacent." [15]

Two years passed, nevertheless, before any lands were sold under the provisions of the law of 1852, for the necessary surveys were not speedily made. But the limits then defined continued as the boundaries of the Fort Snelling reserve until after the Civil War. During part of that period, however, the reserve was owned by Franklin Steele, to whom it was sold in 1857. In 1871 the government and Steele came to an agreement by which the military holdings were reduced to about fifteen hundred acres. [16]

The question of opening to settlement the Fort Ripley Reservation on both banks of the Mississippi near the mouth of the Crow Wing was the cause of a long and bitter controversy in that area and in Congress. The story has been told elsewhere in great detail. [17] It is perhaps sufficient to note here that the reserve was not opened to homesteaders until 1880.

With variations, the same theme was repeated at Fort Ridgely. In 1854 the area around the new fort was surveyed, and the post commander issued a proclamation defining the limits of the reserve and prohibiting settlement on the military lands. But it was ten years before the interior department was asked to have the sections withdrawn from sale by the land office. In the interval between 1854 and 1864 many settlers took out patents on reservation lands at the St. Peter land office, and when the war department in 1869 began to threaten forcible ejection of squatters from military reservations, Minnesotans involved cried in anguish. [18] "We learn from the St. Peter *Advertiser*," reported the *St. Paul Pioneer*, of September 5, 1869, "that considerable alarm exists among the settlers on the military reservation at Fort Ridgely, caused by the recent order of the war department that settlers upon the military reserves shall be ejected by the commanding officers having jurisdiction. The settlers upon that reserve number 300 to 400

families, and they are expecting a detachment of soldiers, with bay-
onets fixed, to hasten their departure by a few gentle pricks of their
warlike implements."

Two hundred settlers signed petitions to the secretary of war, asking that the recent order to force settlers off the military reservation be
revoked. "We the undersigned residents of the Military Reservation at
Fort Ridgely, Minn would respectfully represent," the petitions ran,
"that many of us made entries of Lands, at the U S Land Office and
our homes, within the present limits of the reserve, while it was
public land and under the laws of Congress allowing homesteads to
actual Settlers on the public domain . . . and believing the reservation made in 1864 was made during an emergency and was intended
only to be temporary, others have settled here and are now occupying
and cultivating the soil. That an Enforcement of the recent order of
the War Dept for the removal of *all* Settlers from the Military reservation . . . would deprive hundreds of families of all their means of
subsistence the approaching winter, and would occasion suffering second only to the Indian Massacre of 1862." [19]

Governor William R. Marshall added his official voice in a telegram
to the president and was assured in a reply from the secretary of war
that the commanding officer would be instructed to respect the rights
of bona fide settlers on the Fort Ridgely Reservation. An order issued
by the commanding general of the Department of Dakota on October
21, 1869, protected the rights of holders of patents and land office certificates, but as the editor of the *Pioneer* warned his readers, "the order
relating to the Fort Ridgely settlers has been modified only — not revoked. . . . In cases where *settlers on the reservation held patents or
Land Office certificates,* they will not be removed. The order, however,
relating to squatters, or settlers without title, remains in force. . . .
The holders of patents and land office certificates are but a small number of the settlers." [20]

The war department soon indicated its willingness to relinquish the
reserve, but action was delayed because of complications in one of the
claims. Meanwhile, in 1868 and 1870, the Minnesota legislature
memorialized Congress to open the Fort Ridgely Reservation and to
perfect the claims of settlers living there. Eventually, as in the case of
Fort Snelling and Fort Ripley, the reserve at Fort Ridgely was abandoned and opened to public settlement under the land laws of the federal government.[21] The lands reserved on the Minnesota side of the
Red River for Fort Abercrombie, too, were returned to the body of
public lands at the request of Minnesota citizens.[22] Their pleas an-

swered, Minnesotans had little left about which to complain in their relations with the army and the war department.

It must not be concluded that Minnesotans allowed their criticism
of the army to affect their booster spirit. The newspapers might condemn military protection as inefficient and call loudly for new posts
or augmented garrisons, but their words were for the administration in
Washington and not for prospective settlers. Promoters realized that a
Minnesota pictured as a place in constant danger from Indian uprisings
would not attract newcomers — settlers who would help to develop the
resources of the territory and the state. When it came to fundamentals,
the army was doing its job. If any hint of criticism came from the East,
Minnesotans were quick to insist that everything was safe in Minnesota. Even the *St. Cloud Democrat,* in its issue of May 16, 1861, had
a good word for the army: "We beg to assure our Eastern friends once
again that there is not the slightest danger to the people of Minnesota
from Indians. The three forts — Abercrombie, Ripley and Ridgely —
in the Indian districts are well garrisoned and perfectly sufficient to
prevent all disturbances of this kind, were any imminent."

As settlers pressed forward on the advancing Minnesota frontier,
they called back over their shoulders to the federal government, asking it to send on soldiers. Fort Snelling anticipated settlement by two
decades; Fort Abercrombie was established in response to demands
from people already in the Red River Valley. The two posts symbolize
the lag in military protection against which voices of protest were
raised in Minnesota. When the Indian danger had been removed —
first in eastern Minnesota, then throughout the state — demands for
more posts and more troops gave way before complaints that military
reservations were impeding settlement. This phase, too, passed, and
eventually Minnesota's interest in the army paled into insignificance.

Wilderness Marthas

GRACE LEE NUTE

ON THE HEELS of the soldier and the fur trader followed the missionary, who became a third factor in the civilization of the frontier. He brought to the Minnesota wilderness — peopled in the 1830s and 1840s by Indians, traders, and a few settlers — not only the religious teachings of his faith, but also the customs, habits, and arts of homemaking which he and his wife had known in the older sections of the United States. This article, published in September, 1927 (volume 8), is one of many contributions to the pages of Minnesota History *made by Grace Lee Nute, who served on the staff of the Minnesota Historical Society from 1921 to 1957 and on the history faculty of Hamline University in St. Paul from 1927 to 1960. Miss Nute is at present in charge of organizing the papers of James J. Hill in the Hill Reference Library in St. Paul. She is perhaps best known for her many books and articles dealing with various aspects of the fur trade and northern Minnesota. Among them are:* The Voyageur *(1931),* The Voyageur's Highway *(1941),* Caesars of the Wildernesss *(1943), and* Lake Superior *(1944). Her interest in the missionary is indicated by this article and by a volume of* Documents Relating to Northwest Missions, 1815–1827 *(1942).*

THE HOUSEWIFE'S LOT has never been a heroic one.[1] Who has written epics on making beds or sweeping floors? Even historians, though often charged with too great attention to economic factors, have had little to say regarding the methods of operating that interesting economic unit, the family. If implements such as spinning wheels, cradles, and candle molds had not become popular as objects of art, how should we of today know anything of the way in which colonial housewives managed their homes?

Yet there have been periods in the development of the American frontier when the housewife's lot was neither humdrum nor unromantic. One of these was during the 1830s and 1840s when the edge of the fur-trader's frontier was to be found in northern Michigan, in Wisconsin, and in Minnesota. There the white woman had not ventured unless she were the wife of a missionary; there half-breed wives and mothers graced the traders' and missionaries' log houses on countless streams and lakes. Of these women reliable and detailed records have been preserved. The reason for this abundance of data lies in the fact that the missionaries and their wives were intrigued by the novel sights in their chosen fields and were accustomed to write of them in their letters and diaries. From these documents the following sketch of pioneer women has been constructed. Though it tells of but three women, it is representative of activities and customs of many others.[2]

The period was one of color and picturesqueness in this region about the upper Great Lakes. The fur trade was still practically the only material lure to white men; and the Indians still hunted in the winter, migrated to their sugar bushes in the spring, gathered wild rice in the late summer, and fished in the autumn. From her cabin door the housewife looked out over the water to watch her neighbors pass: blanketed Chippewa in birch canoes passing silently in pursuit of their traditional enemies, the Sioux; voyageurs in blue capotes and red, feather-decked caps speeding past with voices ringing out over the waters in the strains of *A la claire fontaine* or other folksongs from the valley of the Loire in the valorous days of Henri Quatre; and zealous youths from New England, Austria, and Switzerland following in their wake with faces aglow at the prospects of thousands of souls to be saved for the kingdom of God.

Into such scenes as these Hester Crooks Boutwell was brought as a bride in the fall of 1834. She was the daughter of a Chippewa half-breed woman and Ramsay Crooks, a prominent fur trader and businessman of Mackinac and the city of New York. Little is known of her early years except that she was born on Drummond Island in Lake Huron on May 30, 1817, and was well educated at her father's expense at the mission school at Mackinac. She has been described as a "woman of tall and commanding figure, her black hair and eyes indicating her Indian origin. She was a fluent conversationalist, and careful and tidy in her personal appearance." [3]

After the completion of her studies in the mission school, she acted as assistant to Miss Chapelle, one of the teachers, and in 1833 she went to Yellow Lake, in western Wisconsin, with the family of the missionary, Frederic Ayer. Here her work was to teach the "infant school," and a contemporary letter from Ayer states that she was "well fitted to teach on this plan." She was not to remain long, however, in this mission teaching little Chippewa. A young Easterner by the name of

William Thurston Boutwell had been sent in 1833 by the American Board of Commissioners for Foreign Missions as a missionary to the notorious Pillager band of Chippewa Indians at Leech Lake in what is now northern Minnesota. Earlier he had lived for a time at Mackinac, where he had been much interested in the mission, and here he must have become fairly well acquainted with Hester. At any rate, off on the shores of Leech Lake his thoughts soon turned toward her. His own words taken from a letter of January 23, 1835, tell the story of his unusual courtship better than any paraphrase could:

"To the eye of an Ind. nothing looks permanent until he sees the man come who is married & he sees him build his house. . . .

"I was willing to return alone. But experience had taught me, that to reside in a traders family, however I might be called a missionary, yet it was impossible to remove the impression from the Inds. mind, that I was interested in the trade.

"To build me a cottage & live alone, I could not live above suspicion, from the fact that single men, clerks in the Company's employ, who do so at their wintering posts, are in the habit of keeping a mistress. . . .

"In view of all those circumstances, what was my duty? In brief I must tell you, after a prayerful consideration of the subject, what I did. I cast my [eye] over this barren desolate land, & asked, is there a helper? Instead of going into the first lodge I should chance to fall upon & throwing down my blanket, Prov[idence] directed me to send a dispatch 3 days march across the wilderness to Yellow Lake with proposals to Miss Hester Crooks. The seventh day the messenger brought me an affirmative & the next day I packed up my effects, swung my pack & marched. The fourth day, Sept. 1st at 4 A.M. I arrived at Y. Lake. I had no time to loiter. Embarked the same day & started for Fond du Lac, wher[e] we arrived on the 11th. Here Br[other Sherman] Hall met us & on the same eve. united us in the indissoluble & holy bonds. Left F. D. Lac the next day, & arrived at this place [*Leech Lake*] Oct. 9th, 39 days from Y. Lake." One longs to have been at Yellow Lake to witness the surprise and flurry of the half-breed girl when Boutwell's wholly unexpected letter was received.

Boutwell kept a diary in which he describes this wedding trip to Leech Lake by way of the St. Louis River, Sandy Lake, and the Mississippi. It was an arduous journey by birch canoe, with execrable portages where "My dear Hester, like a true heart, followed me through mud and water half-leg deep" encumbered "with a few small cooking utensils." And what fine abode for a bride did she find at the end of the journey? A bark lodge for seven weeks! Then the new house was ready for occupancy. Boutwell, in his diary of December 2, 1834, describes it: "Quit my bark lodge, today, for a log mud-walled cottage. This is a palace to me, though I have neither chair, stove, table, or bed-stead. . . . Our windows, which are deerskins, admit a very imperfect light, scarcely sufficient to enable one to read. One bed and table, and a mat, spread on the floor."

But though the youthful bride may have found imperfect accommodations, she discovered that her neighbors were deeply interested in her. On October 9, 1834, Boutwell confided to his diary: "My wife, I find, is no small curiosity to this people, though one of their kindred, according to the flesh. Her manners and dress being that of an American woman, which most of the number never saw, excites the stare and gaze of all, young and old, male and female."

Here for almost a year Hester lived, cooking for herself and her husband, performing other household duties, visiting the Indians, and endeavoring to teach the children the rudiments of reading and writing and the basic principles of Christianity. Fish, wild rice, and Indian corn were the Boutwells' chief foods, and probably they had only two meals a day, as was the custom throughout the Indian country. The most competent person to judge of Hester's qualifications for the role of wife and housekeeper wrote thus of her at this time: "She has exceeded my highest expectations in culinary affairs, & given me more than one specimen of real N[ew] E[ngland] bread. She is not ashamed to work, & is always at something — when nothing calls for the employment of her hands, she is reading writing or translating, & thus improving herself or endeavoring to benefit others.

"To speak plain, she is deserving a better husband than I was ever made to become. She is all & more than I expected in her or any wife."

Then in June the young couple turned their faces eastward again, and the labors and hardships of the same arduous canoe trip were repeated despite the fact that Hester expected to become a mother in less than two months. On August 4 little Elizabeth Antoinette Boutwell opened her eyes in the mission home at La Pointe on Madeline Island in Lake Superior and just a month later she was baptized. On the fourteenth of September the family started on the long trip to Leech Lake, but a young woman accompanied them this time to assist Hester with her babe. One of the incidents of the trip was the baby's falling from her mother's back into the waters of the Mississippi. The fact that the mother was carrying the child on her back speaks for itself: only a woman of Indian blood would have adopted this expedient in order to have her hands free for carrying other things or for aiding her in traveling.

Life in the little mission at Leech Lake was not wholly without its dramatic quality during the next years. A scene that took place on June 24, 1836, before Hester's very eyes is described thus in her husband's diary: "This morning exhibited such a scene as I never before witnessed — a fight between two women, the Big Cloud's wife, and one of the Soldier's daughters. It commenced with billingsgate . . . each in turn reviling the other on her person. The Big Cloud's wife . . . at length . . . became so angry, that she got up and took a stick of wood upon which she was sitting, and laid it onto the other's head with all her might. Now commenced the battle. Each took her fellow by the hair, and pulled until both fell. Then they began tearing each others clothes. . . . Next she [*the soldier's daughter*] attempted to stab her with a knife. . . . My wife now went out and begged them to desist fighting before her door, and thus ended the affray."

The winter of 1836–37 was hard, both for Indians and whites, since only half as much rice and half as much fish as usual were secured in the fall. In April Hester and her husband were pestered from morning to night with appeals for food, and many a touching scene must have been enacted in the little log cabin.

In May, 1837, a baby boy joined the mission family and when he was fourteen days old, he, like his sister before him, took a long journey of several weeks' duration. On August 13 at La Pointe he was baptized Ramsay Crooks Boutwell after his rich, influential grandfather in New York. The latter was not unmindful of this little family in the faraway West, for in September, 1836, with his second wife and Hester's seven half brothers and sisters he arrived from New York at Mackinac, where one of his activities was to write to his son-in-law and to send a big bundle of newspapers and two boxes of good things. Sent by special conveyance, too, was "a 'Doll' for dear little Antoinette." The closing paragraph of his letter bespeaks his interest in his daughter and granddaughter: "Do I pray you write me often. All that concerns you interests me deeply. Kiss your dear Hester for me, and tell her to hug her Baby frequently for my sake. Give her an extra buss with the 'Doll.' "

No doubt to Hester's relief, Boutwell did not return to Leech Lake but went with his family to Fond du Lac, where, for a brief period, they lived with the family of another missionary, Edmund F. Ely, who also had married a woman with Indian connections, Catharine Bissell. She was born on November 25, 1817, and like Hester Crooks was educated at the Mackinac mission. On June 30, 1835, she went to La Pointe to assist in the mission school. Ely was there at the time and mentions her arrival in his diary. On July 12 she was admitted to membership in the La Pointe church. On August 30 in the same church she became the wife of Ely. Until October they remained at La Pointe and then Ely returned to his mission school at Fond du Lac taking his bride with him. Evidently the house to which they repaired on their arrival was hardly even the "palace" that Boutwell describes, for Ely's diary entry for November 7 reads: "We begin to feel comfortable in my house. Have mudded & whitewashed (or wht clayed) it — & put up our beds (bunks)." And the next entry reveals the trials of the pioneer housewife: "A Rainy Night last night, but our house was tight compared with what it was when the last rain fell. . . . Only the Eaves had any bark on — & our floor was completely drenched. We laid some boards on the floor — put our blankets on them. Piled up our trunks & boxes — on wh[ic]h we laid a pole & over this drew my Bed oilcloth — crawled under & slept out the Storm."

Ely's diary also tells of one of the little customs that soon developed in this new home: "Some days since, Catharine copied a Scripture promise on a Slip of paper, applicable to the state of mind she supposed me to be in. It was very seasonable. I answered in the same manner. It has become a daily exercise."

Early in the new year Ely was obliged to go to La Pointe and during his absence Catharine and a native convert carried on the school. Later, after his return, he and his wife visited one of the native sugar camps, the grove where maple sugar was being made. They "Had a pleasant walk . . . by moonlight & — arrived at the Camp just before break of day." These spring sojourns of the Chippewa at their sugar camps were an interesting phase of savage life, and Ely and his wife could hardly have become conversant with Indian customs without witnessing some of them.

One day in the spring Ely fulfilled a longfelt desire by going to view the beautiful rapids in the St. Louis River above the mission. He took Catharine with him, as he did on most of his trips afield. Once, in April, when he went alone, he returned to find his house closed and no wife to greet him. He learned to his dismay that she had started for the rapids early in the day. As he was starting out with others to search for her, he saw her coming across the Grand Portage road. "She had walked out for exercise in the morning . . . & having proceeded far on the way to Kokabika [the rapids], she concluded to go on, expecting to find me there — was much fatigued before arriving there. . . .

She rested a few moments & pursued our path over the high lands —
from lodge to lodge. Our tracks were fresh before her She pressed
on — Slipping & Stumbling. Having passed all the lodges, she must
reach home, or suffer. Had nothing on her feet but one pr Hose & a pr
of Seal Slippers. Her clothes were wet & heavy — excitement alone sustained her. With Bruised knees & wrenched Joints, she arrived — &
in a short time was scarce able to support herself on her feet."

Perhaps this was the cause of her severe preparturition illness; for
weeks she was very ill, and Ely was all attention to her, taking her out
on the bay for canoe rides whenever she felt able to leave her bed.
Finally, on May 29, he records in his diary, "This has been a day of
deep interest & anxiety in the Family. About 11 o'clock Catharine was
delivered of a *Daughter* both mother & daughter are doing well."

In this new object of attention and care Catharine's interests were
completely absorbed. A little diary in her handwriting has been preserved, wherein she records very naïvely her amazement at all the sweet-
ness and precocity of her little daughter. "We think her on the
whole a pretty good baby. She does not seem to complain without some
reason. She begins to notice those around her & appears pleased when
noticed. She is now seven weeks old." On July 22 the mother recorded:
"Sometimes it seems as if she was pleading to be taken up when she
catches an eye fixed upon her, her whole body eyes, arm, are all in
motion pleading." On one occasion the father made the entry: "Thurs-
day [July] 28. Baby's fond of listening to music, sometimes she shows
pleasure at the sound of the flute, rather fretful this afternoon." Another
entry characterizes her as lying in her cradle "hardly to be resisted."
Quite modern parents these were — see how they frowned on that
dreadful habit of rocking children to sleep: "Oct. 24. Her Father
knocked of[f] the rockers from the cradle. She had got in a habit of
being rocked to sleep & she could not sleep without We thought it
best to have her go to sleep without rocking. The First day she cried
very much. She wanted to be rocked. When she saw that it could not
be so she finally drop[p]ed asleep. The next day she did not cry. She
now goes to sleep without being rocked, which is altogether better."

The diary goes on through the excitement of the day when she held
out her hands to be taken, to the memorable occasion when she could
sit alone, and on to the red letter day in November when a tooth was
discovered. She had one habit that children in civilized communities
do not indulge: "Mary is very fond of sucking rabbit bones." Finally
she began to creep, and the day came when she imitated the class of
little Indians who were being taught the letter *k*. When she was eleven

months old her mother was delighted to find her standing alone, and at thirteen months she began to walk. Thus did this half-breed mother pass her days far from civilization but interested in the things in which all mothers are interested.

Other half-breed women who are mentioned casually in the diaries and letters already quoted, nearly all of whom were wives of fur traders, are Mrs. Vincent Roy, Mrs. Ambrose Davenport, Mrs. Pierre Cotté, Mrs. Henry Cotté, and Mrs. Lapointe. The diaries depict them journeying from place to place, as they did so frequently, attending mission classes, learning from the young Ely how to make bread, interpreting for the missionaries, making maple sugar, taking sleigh rides on the harbor ice, and in general living a half-savage, half-civilized life. One of them, Mrs. Charles Chaboillez at Red Lake, stands out as a more distinct personality than most of the others because of a description of her in a letter of Frederic Ayer dated February 24, 1843: "His [*Chaboillez'*] wife with much cordiality administered to our comfort during a week's tarry in their hospitable dwelling. . . . Mrs. C. is a half breed Ojibwa, and feels much interest in the spiritual welfare of the Indians. Her public station is favorable for her to exert much influence over the females." And again in July Ayer writes that she "was educated at Mackinaw school and is a member of the church."

In 1843 the record of certain white women in wilderness homes in the Minnesota interior begins. Again it is missionaries and their wives that have left the most detailed accounts of pioneer women. To Leech Lake and its neighboring lakes, Red, Cass, and Winnibigoshish, was sent a band of missionaries from Oberlin, Ohio. One of these, the wife of Dr. William Lewis, wrote many letters describing conditions as she found them. Several of these letters and a few of her coworker's, Mrs. Frederic Ayer, have been preserved.

In the spring of 1844 Mrs. Lewis took the long canoe journey from La Pointe to Leech Lake, where her husband had spent the winter. Her description of the journey is a succession of interesting pictures like the following: "We left La Pointe Tuesday May 7th in a bark canoe about 20 feet long. . . . Encamping is one of the beauties of *voyageing* as traveling is termed here. When a spot is selected with reference to smoothness and dryness the tent is presently set up and a blazing fire kindled before it. No scruples are had in cutting down the goodly cedars & firs & stripping off the boughs to form a bed or carpet over which an oil cloth is spread. This is our table also on which we spread a cloth & set our plates & cups, around which we sit in turkish fashion. I sometimes used my carpet bag for a seat. When our beds were unrolled & I had suspended my curtain I slept soundly as a queen in her palace."

When she reached the site of modern Duluth a novel and disagreeable experience was in store for her. A modern woman would hardly be shocked at the substitute for a gangplank that was universally employed when passengers (practically always fur merchants or male sight-seers) were carried. To early Victorian women, however, travel *à la* pickaback savored of frivolity, if not of immorality. Mrs. Lewis thus describes her feelings: "When we came to a good place [to disembark] the waves were so high that it was unsaf[e] to run the canoe ashore but one or two men held it with their oars while two others jumped into the water & began to unload as fast as possible. One offered me his back to take me ashore. Though my feelings revolted there was no alternative & I was soon safely landed."

Portaging was new to Mrs. Lewis, and she describes in detail the customs of the voyageurs, who acted as beasts of burden and adhered to almost inflexible rules made by earlier voyageurs in conveying canoes and baggage over such carrying places. Of one of these places she writes: "My feet too for the first time were wet. I had jumped over many a mud hole & walked many a tamarack pole but not till I came near to the end of the last portage did I get over the tops of my india rubbers   I found them excellent with moccasins over them to protect them from being torn by rocks & stones. A deceitful bog gave way & I sank down." It was with some difficulty that one of Mrs. Lewis' traveling companions helped her free herself. She also relates that her "bed was sometimes quite wet by water getting into the canoe."

Mrs. Lewis' most enlightening letter, written on December 17, 1844, contains two pencil sketches of her log house on Leech Lake, a plan of the interior, and a description of her ménage. Probably these pencil sketches are the first contemporary pictures of a home on Minnesota soil. They show a one-story log house with two chimneys and two "shed" additions with sloping roofs. An upturned canoe on the beach adds a vivid touch.

The plan shows a ground floor of two rooms, the kitchen and the combined bedroom and "sitting room." Apparently most of the beds were stationary but "Br. J[ohnson]'s on account of its great length & Br Spencer's because in the kitchen are made to turn up in the day time. The lines extending from the beds are curtains which constitute the only partition we have as yet between the bedrooms. It is designed to have one between the two doors . . . extending as near to . . . the fireplace as consistent with safety & convenience." Corners for

books are shown on the diagram and "Br J. has shelves suspended by
cords. In our corner is a small medicine cupboard with three shelves
extending from it over the window for books. The floor is carpeted
walls lined with rush mats and with our trunks, two chairs & some
stools, presents quite a comfortable aspect when we are all seated round
a fire of pine notts, by the light of which Sister J[ohnson] & myself sew,
while someone usually reads aloud. Br Spencer usually performs this
office. Is reading Bancroft's history of the United States which is very
interesting."

In the kitchen were "the stove, the most important article . . . the
cupboard for dishes & cooked food, of which we do not however keep
much on hand . . . a couple of shelves for water pails kettles &c,"
a wood box in one corner, "a ladder which swings up & is fastened to
the chamber floor by a hook," and "a trap door to the cellar. Our table
stands when not in use, during the day, before the window at the end
of the cupboard, and at night when it would interfere with the bed before it."

Later in the letter she describes how the women of the mission shared
in the household duties: "I thought you might like to hear a little of our
domestic arrangements & how our time is occupied. Well to be brief
as possible Sister J. & myself divide the work into forenoon & afternoon
& alternate a week at each. We are obliged to be in the kitchen one of
us nearly if not quite all of the day time. We get some time to sew in it,
sometimes besides teaching the children & reading to them & others
who come in. We rise early & usually have our breakfast out of the way
before any company comes in. This consists almost always of boiled
fish, & rice boiled the day before warmed in the stove oven. Our stove is
a great convenience. We have fish boiled baked or S[teame]d & wheat
or corn bread or boiled pudding for dinner, with occasionally the variety of a mess of beans or rabbits. We think we cannot afford to eat wheat
& corn on the same day as neither are plenty here   Our suppers are
rice with milk & sugar, with fruit two or three times a week. We have
some milk for breakfast. We use butter very seldom. . . . As we
have good appetites we can eat bread without butter & fish without
bread." She goes on to mention that she liked "to be tidy occasionally &
the winds here make rude work with hair   I am wearing my black cap
this winter. We find attention to appearance as important here as anywhere."

One of Mrs. Lewis' charges also believed in paying attention to her
personal appearance, though not in a way sanctioned by the pious
woman: "I have been tried with my [half-breed] girl Lucy somewhat.

She had improved . . . much during my absence, particularly in reading & speaking english but I found that vanity had taken possession of her mind. She is rather pretty looking & desire to increase her beauty had led her to use various substances as paint, not the vermillion with which the Indian girls thickly smear their faces but a delicate tinge that would do credit to the art of a city belle."

In this rude house several children were born to the mission families. Association with the Indian and half-breed children caused moments of anxiety for the parents, but the little folk seem to have had a happy childhood despite their frequent quarrels. They learned to speak both English and Ojibway and probably a smattering of the patois used by the French-Canadian voyageurs. Most of them had left the wilderness before the missions were abandoned in 1859.

These descriptions by a few of the women that Minnesota and Wisconsin claim as pioneers may serve to show that the homes of the wilderness in the thirties and forties were not devoid of charm and interest. The experiences of a few women like those mentioned illustrate very well the customary life in the rude structures that stood on the shores of many a river and lake. The names of most are unknown, but they ate the same food, saw the same pageant of savage life, and traveled the same waterways in the same manner as Hester Boutwell, Catharine Ely, and Lucy Lewis.

Two Letters from
Minnesota Territory

WILLIAM W. FOLWELL and
WILLIAM K. McFARLANE

IN 1849 Minnesota was admitted to territorial status by the United States Congress. It became a full-fledged state in 1858. The following pair of selections purport to be letters written during the territorial years, when immigrants poured in and land speculation was rampant. Such documents abound, and many of them have been printed in Minnesota History *over the years. One of these, however, is unique. It was written by William W. Folwell, president of the University of Minnesota from 1869 to 1884 and author of a highly respected four-volume history of the state. Folwell died just as the fourth and last volume went to press in 1929. Four years earlier the genial historian, who was then in his ninety-second year, read this letter complete with footnotes at the Minnesota Historical Society's annual meeting, preserving a perfectly straight face and giving no hint that the document was imaginary. The incident was typical of the Folwellian sense of humor — a humor which constantly brightens the pages of his monumental* History of Minnesota. *The scholarly hoax was published in March, 1925 (volume 6) under the title "Minnesota in 1849: An Imaginary Letter."*

No less interesting is the second (and genuine) letter by William K. McFarlane, which was published in December, 1926 (volume 7) under the title "A Pennsylvanian Visits the West in 1855." It is drawn from the longest series of documents to appear in Minnesota History *during its first fifty years, a series which ran from 1925 through 1931 under the general heading "Minnesota As Seen By Travelers."*

MINNESOTA IN 1849: AN IMAGINARY LETTER

St. Paul's Landing, M. T., July 10, 1849

Dear Mary:

It's a lively week I have had of it — no time to write.[1] If I could have written the letter would be still here waiting for the next down

63

boat. The trip from Galena up on the Doctor Franklin was truly delightful. I do not know how splendid the scenery along the Hudson and
the Rhine may be, but it must be something exceedingly beautiful to
surpass what I saw from Prairie du Chien (Dog's Prairie in English) to
the Falls. At one place near here the Mississippi widens out into a
broad lake, bordered by lofty cliffs or forested slopes. At the upper
(northern) end of the lake is a lofty detached peak which looks so much
like a barn that the early Frenchmen, who were here fifty years before
the Declaration of Independence, called it La Grange. Close to these
was a group of huts and tents in which I was told old Redwing's band
of Sioux — they pronounce it Sue — Indians are living. If I may judge
from the appearance of the individuals I saw as we passed the Indian
is not an object of beauty in every day clothes.

The boat stopped but a few minutes at this place to discharge a few
boxes and barrels of merchandize and went on a few miles to New Hope
on the St. Peter river just above its issue into the Mississippi. They are
now trying to call the place Mendota. The big man of this little hamlet
and indeed of the whole territory is Henry Sibley, who came there in
the year 1834 as manager of the American Fur Company. He lives
in a big stone house, near which is a huge warehouse. I found him busy
taking in furs collected in the foregoing season by Indians, trappers and
licensed traders. One of the traders, Renville by name, had come from
a post two hundred miles away on the edge of the buffalo range. The
furs when assorted and baled are shipped to St. Louis, the great fur
market of the upper Mississippi. Mr. Sibley asked me to dinner, which
was abundant with plenty of silver and linen and a bottle of good claret.
As he was occupied with his traders he left me to be entertained by
Mrs. Sibley; and I was entertained. Mrs. Sibley would be at home in
any circle no matter how select. From Mendota it is only two miles or
a little more to Fort Snelling, and the small village of St. Peter consisting of the dwellings and other buildings of the Indian agent, the post
sutler and civilian employes around it. We had to be ferried over the
St. Peter river in a flat boat. The post sutler is Mr. Franklin Steele who
has been out here almost as long as Mr. Sibley. For years his general
store served the whole neighborhood as well as the garrison of the fort.
I found Mr. Steele a little less affable than Mr. Sibley but courteous and
hospitable enough. I soon learned that Mrs. Sibley was Mr. Steele's
sister and that he had two other very handsome sisters, one the wife
of a doctor here in St. Paul's, the other engaged to a lieutenant of the
U. S. Army named R. W. Johnson lately out of West Point and ordered

to Fort Snelling. The situation of the Fort on a high and precipitous bluff was admirably chosen way back toward the beginning of the century by an army lieutenant sent up here with a small party to find the source of the Mississippi and if possible catch some Hudson's Bay traders carrying on an unlawful trade with Indians. The lieutenant — Pike was his name — without a scrap of authority bought of a small local band of Indians who had no right to sell a hundred thousand acres of land to include the site of the fort and the Falls for half a barrel of whiskey and a promise that some day the Great Father would pay them some money. I understand that a little before the fort was built an agent came up here and paid the Indians 2 cents an acre and some more whiskey. Mr. Steele intends to lay out a city as soon as the Indians are sent off towards the Missouri, which all agree will soon take place. There is no real fortification — only rows of barracks inclosing a parade ground, and a rather formidable round tower at the gateway, loop-holed for musketry.

Of course my next place to see was the Falls of St. Anthony, only seven miles away to the north. Mr. Steele was good enough to send me on in a two horse spring wagon with a young man named Stevens, now in his employ.[2] He came up here after the close of the Mexican war in which he had been a quartermaster. I have not yet met with such a genial joyous fellow as this Stevens, who believes that the greatest city in the Union will grow up around the Falls. Of the Falls one may quote Dr. Johnson's remark on the Giant's causeway "Worth seeing, but not worth going to see." I was disappointed in the scant height of the Falls, and the small volume of water, it may be unusual in this dry season, but the wooded banks of the narrow gorge below and the prairie above sloping back in terraces made a charming composition.

The village of St. Anthony is on the east side of the river. It is divided by two islands which are so near together they come near being one. There was little to attract settlers there till about a year ago when Mr. Steele got a sawmill he had built into operation. It is a small affair with a flutter wheel on a horse dam in the smaller, east, channel. The local humorist says of it "the saw goes up in the morning and comes down at noon." Still in the course of the season it turns out all the lumber just now needed. A number of frame houses have been built out of it, the first one by Ard Godfrey who came all the way from the state of Maine to build the sawmill. I forgot to tell you that on the west side of the river there is what may be called an already old saw mill built by soldiers from the fort years ago. There is also a very small flour mill later built to grind feed for the animals of the garrison at the Fort.[3] The only persons I fell in with at the Falls whom I would care to meet again were a storekeeper named William Marshall and his unmarried sister Rebecca. He is not especially handsome but she is. They live in rooms over the store on Main Street. Mr. Marshall is or has been a surveyor and some time last year he laid out for Mr. Steele a village called St. Anthony Falls. Miss Rebecca helped him make the map.[4] Mr. Marshall tells me he thinks of moving his store to St. Paul, because it is the larger place. I did not venture to advise him, but if he had asked me to, I would certainly have told him to stick by the Falls. The enormous power running to waste in these falls will be captured and set to work some day and it will work day and night, year in and year out, and the great big, rich city of this region will be at the Falls of St. Anthony. A man who was far up the river last winter tells me that there is pine timber enough close to water to last this whole northwestern country for three hundred years, if not longer.

The stage from the Falls to St. Paul is a two seated open wagon, drawn by two horses, but it landed me safely, after the eight mile drive partly along the wooded bank of the river and partly over a stretch of prairie fairly ablaze with wild flowers. I found a room at the Central House, partly log and partly frame on the edge of the high bluff near the steamboat landing, and set out to view the town. The site is about as unpromising as you could well imagine. After you climb a steep bluff from the riverside you have before you a series of humps running up to high hills a mile back. Between two of the humps there is a large duck pond. At several places the rock comes up three feet above ground. They tell me that the first settlement was made almost by luck. I will inquire about that and tell you more. A townsite has been laid out but the houses, some with bark or slab roofs, look as though they had been built wherever a level spot of land could be found. However there is plenty of fine scenery, free to all who have eyes to see with. Please don't imagine that the people living in these humble shacks are all of them cave men. There are some men and women here you could hardly match in Fort Wayne or any other city. One of them is a Vermont Yankee named Rice. I don't know that I have yet met just such a personality. Courteous, suave, even gracious, he makes friends with everybody; but he's no sycophant. For some years past he has been associated with Mr. Sibley at Mendota. But they did not get along well together and Mr. Rice has just moved here. The expectation is that he will make things hum. He has bought a big piece of land and will put up a big hotel — big for the place. So far Mr. Sibley has had things his own way in politics, but I should not be surprised if Henry M. Rice should some day relieve Sibley with all his stately dignity, of his labors in public station. In one of his journeys to Washington Mr. Rice made the acquaintance of a young Southern lady. In another journey this very year there was a wedding and the happily wedded pair are now living in one of the better shacks of St. Paul's — I say happily wedded, because she seems to have the same social gifts as distinguish her husband. With her beauty and graces she will soon be the social leader of this capital city.

Yes this is the capital city of the Territory of Minnesota, made so by an act of Congress passed on the 30 day of March of this year. It seems like a joke that President Taylor has appointed as governor a Pennsylvania lawyer, an ex-member of Congress, named Alexander Ramsey when there were many men out here who would not have declined the honor. I doubt if there is much truth in the yarn I heard at the hotel table that Mr. Ramsey would not accept the appointment till he made sure that he would not have to go round the Horn to get here. The new Governor came up near the end of May. Mr. Sibley had written him to come on to Mendota and be his guest. He stayed with the Sibleys nearly a month before he could find a house to live in. But he was over here attending to business meantime. On the first day of June he proclaimed the Territory to be organized, and a few days later he issued a proclamation dividing the territory into three judicial districts. Three whig judges had come up with him. Now you will have to take my word that the Territory of Minnesota is bigger than all New England, New York and Pennsylvania put together. In another proclamation issued three days ago Governor Ramsey divided up his immense empire into seven counties with Indian names. He also ordered an election of delegates to convene as a legislature early in September. From what I have seen of Governor Ramsey I like him. He has not the stateliness of Sibley or Steele, nor the genial voice and smile of Rice, but he is sturdily built, dignified enough, even-tempered and perfectly frank in expression. If he decides to burn his ships and stay here for good he may play a large part in the history of the territory he has come to rule over. But he will have to wait for he is the only Whig in the whole territory except the few federal officers who came up with him. In one respect Mr. Ramsey is very fortunate. Five years ago when he was 29 he married a Pennsylvania girl of 18. Although still young, she is really queenly in appearance, very well informed and altho' domestic is interested in her husband's public duties. Mrs. Rice may have to tolerate a rival as social leader in the Capital city. I have had a most interesting trip so far and shall have plenty of things to tell you about when I get back to old Fort Wayne.

Ever your faithful DICK.

P.S. The boat was late coming from Mendota and is delayed here. I will tell you about two or three notable characters I have met with or heard about. One of them is a young Presbyterian minister from Philadelphia who came this last spring. He is a man of talent, but somewhat erratic. He preached a sermon on the text "And he slew a lion in a pit on a snowy day." He has got a school started in what was a blacksmith shop. For seats they have ranged some planks on pegs driven into auger holes in the logs. He will build a small wooden church on a lot given by Mr. Rice.[5] Another very notable personage is James M. Goodhue who came up here in the spring and started a weekly Democratic paper, called the Minnesota Pioneer. He is well educated a very facile writer, with a vein of sarcasm which shades off into gall. Of one visiter to the territory he writes, "He stole *into* the Territory, he stole *in* the Territory, and he stole *out* of the Territory." My guess is that Mr. Goodhue is likely to lead a stormy life here.

There is another man, whom I have not seen, but his name is more heard on the street and in the hotel than that of any other. His name is Brown.[6] He came out to Fort Snelling with the first troops to garrison Fort Snelling. He was a minister's son somewhere in Pennsylvania, ran away from home when 14 years old and enlisted as a drummer boy in the Army. Some say he was rather a fifer, for he soon became principal musician and leader of the garrison band. After seven or eight years he quit the army and began a series of enterprises much too many to tell you about if the steamboat would wait till sundown. For a while he kept a grocery — that means grogshop in this region — on the east bank of the Mississippi. He did not "introduce liquor into the Indian Country," that would have been felony, but an Indian could slip over to his grocery in a canoe and get a well-watered drink of whisky. Brown — Joe Brown everybody calls him — has started a farm on Grey Cloud island in the river a little below this place, has been lumbering over on the St. Croix river, served a term in the Wisconsin legislature when this part of Minnesota was St. Croix County, Wisconsin. Last year there was a convention held over at Stillwater on the St. Croix river — folks there believe their town is to be the great city — as a starter towards getting the new territory set up. Brown was a delegate, and his experience in the legislature came in handy. He made most of the motions, and headed the important committees. It was on his motion that in the petition to be sent to the president the special request was made that the new territory be named Minnesota.[7] Brown had been out here fifteen years before Mr. Sibley came and knows more of men and things here than . . .[8]

A PENNSYLVANIAN VISITS THE WEST IN 1855

IN THE 1850s a general interest in impressions of the West was prevalent in the eastern part of the United States and letters from venturesome friends or relatives who traveled westward claimed much attention.[9] One can sense without difficulty the eagerness with which the following letter was read by the Pennsylvania friends of the writer; and a vivid picture of a frontier town it must have left on the minds of all who heard it. Nothing further is known of the writer. The letter was found with some others addressed to Samuel W. Sharp in the papers of Curtis H. Pettit, a pioneer resident of Minneapolis. Presumably this Sharp was the man of that name mentioned in the letter.

FALLS OF ST. ANTHONY MAY 25th 1855
MESSS IRVINE, STOUGH, BRICKER, SHARP, MCKENNEY, DILLER, DUNLAP, WOODBURY, &C
ESTEEMED FRIENDS
(Sketches of Minnasota by an Emigrant)
On a beautiful Sabbath morning we rounded the bend immediately below St Paul and the city burst upon our view   the white steeples of the churches towering aloft far above the surrounding Houses adds greatly to the appearance of the place   after firing our swivel as steamboats Generaly do we rounded to and went ashore   I have been in some *few towns* in my journey through life but a more motley Crowd than stood on the landing at St Paul I have never saw in any town of its size Irishmen, Dutch, Californians, nigers omnibus drivers, Boatmen, speculators Dandys, Gamblers Winnabages & Soux Indians half Breed, Frenchmen, & Hosts of others too numerous to minten   as we passed up to the American house (by the way kept about the same as the Franklin in Phi[ladelphi]a) the Bells were ringing for divine servic and the streets were thronged with as well dressed people as You would see in any of our large towns   the fact is there are numbers here from New York   when we landed at the American I saw one specimen of this Class Genus homo who was looking at the scenery through a large opera Glass and remarked to a bystander that it was *demed Foine* but wild.

Took a wash and went with some acquaint[a]nc[e]s to Epispocal Church   on our way passed the first Church (A Catholic one) erected in St Paul. 7 years ago St Paul was a little Hamlet without any present prospect of being any more in future than an ordinary Country town her buisness was then considered large at $131,000   now the buisness for last year may be summed up at $6,000,000   Four Daily & Weekly papers are published here and have a large Circulation   when standing on the Bluffs back of Town I could not help contrasting the present condition with what it was 10 years ago then the camping ground of Indians now covered with Handsome residences that would do credit to Phia   Gov Ramsey has a handsome one and can live retired as he has made his pile   front lots are held at $100 pr foot in the principal street prices that I think cannot be sustained at least I have found places of more Healthy grothe where a person can invest money to a better advantage.

After looking around and becomeing somewhat acquanted in St Paul I left for St Anthony one of the most romantick places on the Missippi   nature has done for this place what she has not done for many others viz the river here falls over the rocks some 20 ft and on both sides for 1½ miles leaves a butiful plain for building a city   the Lumber trade of St Anthony alone was $1,000,000 last year, and it is yet in its infancy but suffice it to say that after traveling over a considerable portion of Minnasota I came back & purchased a Property within ⅓ of Mile of Coperate limits of the City and if any of you ever visit the Falls of St Anthony your Friend Mc will be on hands to Welcome you   I was offered in the evening $500 for my bargain but dec[l]ined to take it   I would just mention to my Friends Irvine & Stough that the[y] brew splendid Ale one mile from my place and I occasi[o]naly indulge   I shall give you a description of the town at some future time

A word to persons intending to settle here   now I do not pretend to advise any one about Coming west but would say to those intending to settle in Minnasota that from actual observation I would Cons[i]der that the best portion of the Teritory lay south of the Missippi along the St Peters and bordering on sothron Iowa   there is as handsome land as ever the sun shone upon south of the St Peters and I intend to enter some before going home   a great part of that County is settled by Pennsylvanians   the Northeren part of the Country is more sandy and abounds in small Lakes   I have some property on a lake that is filled with splendid fish   the Country through the Lakes generaly is what is called oak openings and soil a dark sandy Loam   I love Minnasota for its clear springs of water   better is not to be had on the banks of **Big** spring. 4 Miles from St Anthony Lays 3 Lakes Called Crystal Lake, Lake Harriet & Lake of the Woods   if there is any thing more butiful than to stand on the shores of any of these Lakes and watch the setting sun the waves running on the pebly shore with a faint murm[ur] which almost lulls a person to sleep —

The glorious heaven the Lake so blue, the forests dark and still, your friend has not seen it.   by next year their banks will be studded with Farms   already unimproved Land near there is held at $10 pr A[cre] which in 6 mo. will prob. bring $15   Gentlemen you can form no Conception of the way property advances   This country as minnasota is but 5 years old   in Two more she will be knocking at the door for admission into the union   I have become acquainted with the Most prominent men about St Anthony and feel almost as much at home as if setting in Fri[e]nd Danls   all that is wanting is to hear the Hearty laugh of Bricker and the pleasant smile of my Friend the Dr & Stough   I have an excelent Boarding place and while I am writing this to you the Lady of the House (she is a splendid looking woman) is teasing me for writing to my *sweet Heart* in Penna   I of course take it all in good earnest for the sake of Conversation as I calculate to be pretty tolerably well acquainted about these diggings before I go east. She says one day Mr Mc you ought to have brought a wife with You   you *surely must* feel the want of one   Says I indeed Mrs Nourse I do feel the *want* and feel it *sensibly*.

To give You an entire account of My trip would fill some 5 sheets of Fools cap, and perhaps would create a smile on the most stoical Countanance   Suffice it to say that I have travelld into the indian County within 200 miles of Lake Itasca the head of the Missippi have slept in the midst of an encampment of 1200 Winnabagoes have crossed the Missippi on a Dug out and floted on it[s] Clar water at Sauk Rapids 100 miles above St Anthony   I have seen life in ways that I never did before   Came across one man in the indian County who keeps a Tavern and is married to an Indian squaw   he had two bouncing half Breed daughters good looking but dirty as the ——l they received us kindly but as I saw them cooking the meal I had no appetite for it though Hungry   in my next I shall give something more about the diferent soils &c   my thanks to Friend Stough & Bricker for favors received

Truly Yours
WM K. McFARLANE

The "Fashionable Tour" on the Upper Mississippi

THEODORE C. BLEGEN

THE MISSISSIPPI RIVER was pioneer Minnesota's principal con-necting link with the outside world. After 1823 steamboats plied its waters in increasing numbers, bringing mail, supplies, and settlers to the region. As early as the 1830s the boats also carried up the river a surprisingly modern-sounding cargo — tourists. The role of the Mis-sissippi in making the remote northwestern frontier familiar to the intellectual and literary travelers of the mid-nineteenth century is dis-cussed by Theodore C. Blegen in this article published in December, 1939 (volume 20). Mr. Blegen was the second editor of Minnesota His-tory *(1923–39), and his contributions span the entire fifty years of the magazine's existence, beginning with its fourth issue in November, 1915. The list includes articles, edited documents, bibliographical notes, book reviews, and annual reports dating from his years as super-intendent of the Minnesota Historical Society (1931–39). Since his retirement in 1960 as dean of the graduate school in the University of Minnesota, Mr. Blegen has returned to the society where he is now a research fellow. Among his recent books are:* Minnesota: A History of the State *(1963), and* Abraham Lincoln and His Mailbag *(1964).*

FROM THE DAYS of trail blazer and trader to those of lumberman, farmer, and town builder, rivers have been of great importance to the Northwest; and one in particular captured the imagination of the pioneers — the Mississippi.[1] It was the path of explorer and voyageur, the line of steamboat pageantry, the route of incoming settlers, the link of frontier with civilization. To all it was dignified by the term "the river"; and it is still "the river" — great in its sweep from Itasca to the sea, great in its span of the nation's history, great, too, in its role in American life. The very magnitude of "the river," geographically, his-torically, and in many-sided interest, perhaps explains why no historian has yet succeeded in writing the book of the Mississippi — a magnum opus that tells the story in its full range and interprets it in all its varied aspects. One must turn to Mark Twain, to the poets and singers, to the narratives of old steamboat men, and a hundred other sources to understand the meaning of the Mississippi and to know the glamour of the "War Eagle," the "Northern Belle," "Time and Tide," and other steamboats that churned its waters. The historians are doing their part, however, for they are piecing together this chapter and that in the story, hunting out and preserving the old records, and gradually building up materials for a broad history of the Mississippi.[2]

That history should include some account of the beginnings of the Northwest tourist trade, which has become, we are told, a major industry. It was the Mississippi and its steamboats that inaugurated the trade and spread the fame of Minnesota as a vacation land, promising to the enterprising tourist the adventure of a journey to a remote frontier coupled with the enjoyment of picturesque scenery and of good fishing and hunting.

Giacomo Beltrami, a passenger on the "Virginia" when that first steamboat on the upper river made its maiden journey in 1823, may perhaps be called the first modern tourist of Minnesota. The mercurial Italian was bent on a voyage of exploration, but he traveled up the Mississippi as a tourist who compared the wonders of its towering bluffs and wooded hillsides with the scenery of the Rhine. Beltrami recorded the astonishment of the Indians when they viewed the boat on which he was traveling. "I know not what impression the first sight of the Phœnician vessels might make on the inhabitants of the coast of Greece; or the Triremi of the Romans on the wild natives of Iberia, Gaul, or Britain," he wrote, "but I am sure it could not be stronger than that which I saw on the countenances of these savages at the arrival of our steam-boat." Some "thought it a monster vomiting fire, others the dwelling of the Manitous, but all approached it with reverence or fear."[3]

To another traveler goes the distinction of calling attention to the vacation possibilities of an upper Mississippi journey and also of giving it a slogan-like name. George Catlin, the well-known artist of American Indian life, made a trip by steamboat up the Mississippi from St. Louis to Fort Snelling and the Falls of St. Anthony in 1835. "The majestic river from the Balize to the Fall of St. Anthony, I have just passed over; with a high-wrought mind filled with amazement and wonder," he wrote. "All that can be seen on the Mississippi below St. Louis, or for several hundred miles above it, gives no hint or clue to the magnificence of the scenes which are continually opening to the eye of the traveller, and riveting him to the deck of the steamer, through sunshine, lightning or rain, from the mouth of the Ouisconsin to the Fall of St. Anthony."

After describing the scenery above Prairie du Chien, he said, "I leave it for the world to come and gaze upon for themselves." He proposed a "Fashionable Tour" — a trip "by steamer to Rock Island, Galena, Dubuque, Prairie du Chien, Lake Pepin, St. Peters, Fall of St. Anthony," and he expressed the opinion that "This Tour would comprehend but a small part of the great 'Far West,' but it will furnish to the traveller a fair sample, and being a part of it which is now made so easily accessible to the world, and the only part of it to which *ladies* can have access, I would recommend to all who have time and inclination to devote to the enjoyment of so splendid a Tour, to wait not, but make it while the subject is new, and capable of producing the greatest degree of pleasure."[4] One wonders why the modern boosters of Minnesota and the Northwest have not built a monument to George Catlin.

The idea of a "Fashionable Tour" up the Mississippi quickly spread. Each year saw increasing numbers of sight-seers who took Catlin's advice. Most of them in the earlier years were men, but there were a few women who were willing to hazard the dangers of a journey to the outposts of America. One of these, a vivacious lady of eighty years, was none other than Elizabeth Schuyler Hamilton, the widow of Alexander Hamilton. She had gone west to visit her son William in Wisconsin in the summer of 1837 and decided "to ascend the Mississippi to the St. Peter's." She journeyed to Fort Snelling on the new steamboat "Burlington," saw the Falls of St. Anthony and Minnehaha, and, as befitted a queen of fashion, was accorded a royal reception by the officers of the fort. "A carpet had been spread," wrote a friend of Mrs. Hamilton, "an armchair [was] ready to receive her, the troops were under arms, we passed between two double rows of soldiers, and a very fine band was playing."[5]

The "Fashionable Tour" was stamped with the approval of this distinguished lady, who was delighted with the Minnesota country and her experiences. The next year, in 1838, Captain Frederick Marryat, the author of *Mr. Midshipman Easy,* traveled up the river, saw the sights, witnessed a game of lacrosse, which curiously he said was "somewhat similar to the game of golf in Scotland," and studied "the Indians in their primitive state."[6] His *Diary in America,* published in England in 1839, recorded the entire experience — and his was but one of many narratives putting before the world the story of travel on the upper Mississippi. Something more was needed, however, to establish the popularity of the "Fashionable Tour." The impetus came from the motion pictures of our grandfathers, the panoramas, great unwinding rolls of painted canvas which artists exhibited in America and Europe to the accompaniment of lectures. As early as 1839 John Rowson Smith and John Risley presented a panorama of the upper valley. About a decade later John Banvard showed to the world a vast panorama of the Mississippi. His canvas, with its many scenes, purported to be three miles long, but unhappily it portrayed only the river below St. Louis. By 1849, however, three more Mississippi panoramas were giving the public a demonstration of the potential delights of the "Fashionable Tour." Henry Lewis had spent the summer of 1848 making a leisurely tour of the river between Fort Snelling and St. Louis and the next year began to exhibit his famous panorama, a canvas twelve hundred yards long and twelve feet high. Leon Pomarede and S. B. Stockwell, both associates of Lewis, soon had competing panoramas on display, and by the end of the 1850s there were a half dozen panoramas of the upper Mississippi touring the show halls of the nation and Europe.[7]

The panoramists tried to picture in faithful detail not only the river but also the life alongside it — the native Indians and their villages and the American towns and cities. In their attempts at realistic effects they used ingenious devices. Pomarede, for example, somehow managed to make real smoke and steam roll from the steamboats in his pictures.[8] And yet the artists felt the inadequacy of their efforts. Lewis wrote in his diary one day, "As I looked I felt how hopeless art was to convay the *soul* of such a scene as this and as the poet wishes for the pencil of the artist so did I for the power of descript[i]on to tell of the thousand thoughts fast crowding each other from my mind." [9]

Crowds of people went to see these travel "movies" of the 1840s and 1850s and thus toured the great river vicariously. The throngs that wished to view Banvard's panorama were so great when it was displayed in Boston and New York that railroads ran special excursions to accommodate them. In these two cities alone more than four hundred thousand people saw the exhibition. "The river comes to me instead of my going to the river," wrote Longfellow. Whittier, after seeing a panorama, sang of the "new Canaan of our Israel," and Thoreau, who not only viewed a panorama but also made the tour itself, envisaged a coming heroic age in which simple and obscure men, the real heroes of history, would build the foundations of new castles in the West and throw bridges across a "Rhine stream of a different kind." Risley's canvas, unwound before audiences in Oslo in 1852, touched the imagination of the Norwegian poet Vinje, who came away from the exhibition convinced that America was destined to conquer the world. Banvard's work had a run of twenty months in London, with admissions exceeding six hundred thousand.[10]

Meanwhile, people were coming singly, in honeymoon couples, in small groups, and sometimes in parties of hundreds to make the tour portrayed in the panoramas. Sometimes they chartered boats to carry them up the river and back, and often the steamboat companies, with an eye to increasing business, organized excursions of their own, advertising their plans far in advance through newspaper announcements and offering low rates. Such excursions were conducted from places as far away as New Orleans and Pittsburgh. Ordinarily the fare from St. Louis to St. Paul was $12.00. From Galena it was $6.00, though rate wars brought it at times as low as $1.00. The tours were made expeditiously. In 1850, for example, the "Dr. Franklin" left Galena on Thursday, spent one day in St. Paul, and was back to Galena on Tuesday. The round trip from St. Louis normally took eight or nine days, but might be made in six or seven on speedy boats. The idea of excursion boats reserved for patrons of the "Fashionable Tour" captured the fancy of travelers, and by the late 1830s such outings were not uncommon on the upper Mississippi.[11] The tourists could view the scenery, see Indians at firsthand, and enjoy their vacations without the hubbub and the annoyances encountered on vessels heavily loaded with freight for the frontier forts or fur-trading stations.

As the fame of the upper Mississippi Valley spread, travelers from the far South and the East increased in number. By the middle 1840s tourists from New York, Washington, Pittsburgh, and Cincinnati, as well as from New Orleans, St. Louis, and Galena were making the trip. Each traveler helped to spread the story of what was to be seen from the decks of a steamboat pushing upstream to old Fort Snelling.

The time came when one could go all the way from the East to the Mississippi by rail. The "Fashionable Tour" was thus brought more easily within the range of possibility for thousands of people. When the Rock Island Railroad was completed from Chicago to the Mississippi River in 1854, a special celebration was arranged which included a voyage in chartered steamboats up the river from Rock Island to St. Paul.[12] Twelve hundred persons in a flotilla of seven steamboats made the tour commemorating this union of steel and water. The party included ex-President Millard Fillmore, the historian George Bancroft, Professor Benjamin Silliman of Yale, and a regiment of journalists. Charles A. Dana of the *New-York Tribune,* Samuel Bowles of the

Springfield Republican, Thurlow Weed of the *Albany Evening Journal,* and Epes Sargent of the *Boston Transcript* were among the writers whose detailed reports advertised Minnesota not only to prospective settlers but also to those interested in an unusual kind of pleasure jaunt.[13] The journey upstream was enlivened by music, dancing, popular lectures, mock trials, and promenades from boat to boat. Four of the steamboats, for example, were lashed together as they plowed their way up through Lake Pepin. At the river towns there were gala receptions, with addresses of welcome by local citizens and responses by the visiting dignitaries. Everyone talked about the marvels of the Mississippi scenery and the coming greatness of the West, and everyone accepted the view of Catherine Sedgwick that the "fashionable tour will be in the track" of this excursion.[14]

St. Paul was out in force to welcome the visitors, to listen to the praises of Fillmore and Bancroft, and to provide vehicles for a trip to the Falls of St. Anthony and Minnehaha. Dana, writing to the *New-York Tribune,* described the infant town of St. Paul. There were, he wrote, "Brick dwellings and stone warehouses, a brick capitol with stout, white pillars, a county court-house, a jail, several churches, a market, schoolhouses, a billiard-room, a ten-pin alley, dry goods' stores, groceries, confectioners and ice-creamers, a numerous array of those establishments to which the Maine law is especially hostile, and a glorious, boundless country behind." [15]

There were a few discordant notes in the general hymn of praise, however. One journalist wrote: "As the Upper Mississippi must now become a route for fashionable Summer travel, it is only proper to say that those who resort here must not yet expect to find all the conveniences and comforts which abound on our North River steamers. Everything is very plain; the staterooms are imperfectly furnished, but the berths are roomy; the table is abundant, but butter-knives and sugar-tongs are not among its luxuries." [16]

In due time these and many other luxuries appeared. Companies, competing sharply for traffic, vied with one another in bettering accommodations, providing well-furnished staterooms, improving steamboat architecture, serving good food, rigging up bars where, as Mark Twain says, "everybody drank, and everybody treated everybody else," employing bands and orchestras, and in other ways adding to the attractions of the "Fashionable Tour." And when large and luxurious river boats docked at the St. Paul levee, their captains liked to invite local citizens on board to see the wonders of the ships and to join in "grand balls," as was done, for example, when in 1857 the "Henry

Clay" brought up an excursion party from St. Louis. The captains and pilots, the envied monarchs of the river, took unbounded pride in their boats. One pilot in after years recalled the "Grey Eagle" as "long, lean, and as graceful as a grey-hound" — the "sweetest thing in the way of a steamboat that a man ever looked at." Steamboats, he believed, had souls; and his idea of heaven was the "Grey Eagle" plying "celestial waters, carrying angels on their daily visits, with their harps," Daniel Harris, captain, and himself the pilot.[17]

Immigrants

The general picture of beautiful boats, luxury, and gala entertainment must not close one's eyes to another side of river traffic — the vast throngs, on most of the boats, of immigrants who crowded the lower decks while the tourists occupied cabins and balconies on top of the decks. Coming in ever-increasing swarms, the immigrants accounted for great profits to the steamboat companies, and, with the expansion of freighting, they help to explain why, in the 1850s, the number of steamboat arrivals at St. Paul sometimes ran to more than a thousand in a single season. Bound for the Promised Land, the immigrants faced, as Dr. William J. Petersen says, the hazards of "runners, blacklegs, and gamblers, explosions, tornadoes, and devastating fires, snags and sand-bars, poor food and wretched accommodations, sickness, suffering, and death." When cholera and other diseases broke out on board ship, they were likely to spread with appalling rapidity. On one occasion a traveler complained because the towel in the washroom was filthy. "Wal now," said the purser, "I reckon there's fifty passengers on board this boat, and they've all used that towel, and you're the first on 'em that's complained of it." [18]

What did the people who made the "Fashionable Tour" in early days see? For most, the magnificence of the scenery made up for torment by mosquitoes and the inconvenience of crowded quarters. Indeed, many were so delighted that they accepted philosophically the hazards of explosions and collisions. The scenery held them spellbound upon the decks of the steamboats through the days, and often far into the nights. Said one traveler: "I had taken my impressions of the Mississippi scenery from the descriptions of the river below St. Louis, where the banks are generally depressed and monotonous. But nothing can surpass the grandeur of the Upper Mississippi. Is it then strange that I was fascinated while floating through these Western paradises, over which the moon shed her soft, shadowy light, and where the notes of the whippo[or]will rose and died far away, as I had heard them in my boyhood's home?" [19]

Another tourist wrote: "We came . . . on the Steamer Yankee, and a delightful trip we had. The scenery of the Upper Mississippi, for wildness, beauty and grandeur, is unequaled and perfectly indescribable.

"We had grand moonlight scenes on this glorious river, that were perfectly enchanting. It seemed as though I could gaze all night; that my eyes would never tire or be satisfied, in beholding the beauty and grandeur of its ever-varying banks and lofty hills." [20]

And Frødrika Bremer, the kindly and observant visitor to America from Sweden, wrote: "I have . . . seen the scenery on the upper Mississippi, its high bluffs crowned with autumn-golden oaks, and rocks like ruined walls and towers, ruins from the times when the Megatherium and mastodons walked the earth, — and how I did enjoy it!" [21]

Sometimes a traveler, vexed by the slow progress of his boat, annoyed by its unscheduled stops on sand bars, or wearied alike by travel and by travelers, failed to join the usual chorus. Ida Pfeiffer, an Austrian lady of wealth, had sober second thoughts. "This is a grand thing to think of at first," she wrote, "but after a few days one gets tired of the perpetual monotony of the scenery." Even she relented, however, when her boat entered Lake Pepin, for the sight of it, she said, "almost made me amends for my long and tedious voyage up the river." George T. Borrett, an English visitor, made the journey during a period of extremely low water. He chronicles his impressions with solemn detail: "A broad expanse of extremely shallow water; a number of oddly-shaped marshy-looking islands, a tortuous channel in and out amongst them, very difficult of navigation, and intersected by frequent sandbanks, on the top of which the keel of our boat grated at every other bend in the stream, with a dull sound that brought home to the passengers the uncomfortable apprehension of the possibility of sticking fast on one of these banks and seeing much more of the Mississippi than we had bargained for; a low vegetation on most of these islands, very much like that which may be seen on any of the alluvial deposits on the Thames; a range of steep bluffs on either bank rising abruptly from the water's edge, sparsely wooded and bare alternately, but bold in outline and precipitous. Such was my first impression of the Mississippi scenery, and such it is now, for there was little or no variety." The "Father of Waters" appeared to him "very much in the light of an imposter." "I think it extremely doubtful," he said, "whether, in his then state of aqueous insolvency, proud little Father Thames himself would have owned him even for a poor relation." [22]

Borrett's boat was crowded, the accommodations were inadequate, and he found the company intolerable. Ida Pfeiffer shared his scornful attitude toward the fellow passengers and was especially indignant at the impudence of two young ladies who patted her on the shoulder and genially called her "grandma." She also thought that the manners displayed at the dinner table were somewhat less than perfect, particularly the strange custom of certain people of pelting "each other with the gnawed cobs of Indian corn." In the evening, she says, the ladies took possession of the ten available rocking chairs, "placed them in a circle, threw themselves back in them, many even held their hands over their heads, stuck their feet far out, and then away they went full swing."

Let us draw the distressed Ida away from this shocking spectacle and introduce her to a fellow sufferer, Anthony Trollope, the English novelist, who made the "Fashionable Tour" in Civil War days. The author of *Barchester Towers* also had many melancholy reflections to record. "Nine-tenths of the travellers," he exclaimed, "carry children with them. . . . I must protest that American babies are an unhappy race." The parents seemed to Trollope as untalkative as their babies were discontented and dyspeptic. "I found no aptitude, no wish for conversation," he said; "nay, even a disinclination to converse." And poor Trollope's cabin was too hot. This circumstance led him to generalize about the effects upon Americans of their taste for living in the "atmosphere of a hot oven." To that taste he attributed their thin faces, pale skins, unenergetic temperament, and early old age.[23]

When Catlin made his tour in 1835, there was only a lonely frontier outpost at the junction of the Minnesota and Mississippi rivers and a rough trading post close by to signalize white civilization at the northern terminus of the "Fashionable Tour." The characteristic note of the region was Indian life. Catlin, like Marryat a few years later, was entertained by a Sioux game of lacrosse and by a variety of Indian dances. From Fort Snelling south into Iowa, the wilderness was broken only by an occasional Indian village or trader's post. Charles Lanman in 1846 felt that at St. Peter's, at the mouth of the Minnesota River, he was "on the extreme verge of the civilized world, and that all beyond, to the ordinary traveller," was "mysterious wilderness." In 1852 Mrs. Elizabeth Ellet thought it "curious to see the primitive undergrowth of the woods, and even trees, left" in portions of St. Paul "not yet improved by buildings." In walking from her hotel to the home of Governor Ramsey, she "passed through quite a little forest . . . and saw a bear's cub at play — an incident in keeping with the scene." She was attracted by the "curious blending of savage and civilized life. . . . The lodges of the Dakotas had vanished from the opposite shore . . .

but their canoes yet glided over the waters of the Mississippi, and we met them whenever we stepped outside the door." [24]

Mrs. Ellet found "excellent quarters" in the Rice Hotel in St. Paul. St. Anthony, she reported, "has but recently emerged from a wilderness into the dignity of a village." "In the summer months the town is much resorted to by visitors, especially from the southwestern States. These have come in such numbers that no accommodations could be found for them, and they were obliged to return with but a glance at the curiosities they had come to view. Now the state of things is more favorable to the lovers of fine scenery; an excellent hotel — the St. Charles — having recently passed into the proprietorship of Mr. J. C. Clark, and under his excellent management, already obtained a reputation as one of the best in the northwestern country." [25]

Mrs. Ellet boarded one of Willoughby and Powers' stagecoaches for what was called the "grand tour." It consisted of a drive from St. Paul to St. Anthony, then out to Lakes Harriet and Calhoun, "thence to the Minnehaha Falls and Fort Snelling, and by the Spring Cave to St. Paul, arriving in time for the visitors, if in haste, to return with the boat down the river." Shortly before Mrs. Ellet's arrival, the beauties of the Lake Minnetonka region began to be appreciated, and during her stay in St. Paul she took advantage of an opportunity to visit what in due time was to become one of the most popular summer resorts in the Northwest.[26] Frontenac, White Bear Lake, the St. Croix country, and many other places became widely known as ideal for vacation seekers.

When Charles Francis Adams, Jr., went up the Mississippi in 1860, he did so not for the sake of the "Fashionable Tour" but as a minor figure in a political junket. This excursion was headed by William H. Seward and the elder Charles Francis Adams, whose purpose was to win the Northwest for Lincoln and the Republican party. To the observant and sensitive Charles Francis, Jr., however, it was a sight-seeing tour of the wild and woolly West, and in his diary he gives us vivid pictures of the changing scenes, describes steamboat races, and reveals an eye for the picturesque. After the speeches and cheers at Prairie du Chien, he found himself on the deck of a Mississippi steamboat proceeding upstream at night. Of this experience, he wrote: "To me it all seemed strange and unreal, almost weird, — the broad river bottom, deep in shadow, with the high bluffs rising dim in the starlight. Presently I saw them wood-up while in motion, and the bright lights and deep shadows were wonderfully picturesque. A large flat-boat, piled up with wood, was lashed alongside, and, as the steamer pushed steadily up stream, the logs were thrown on board. As the hands, dressed in their red flannel shirts, hurried backward and forward, shipping the wood, the lurid flickerings from the steamer's 'beacon lights' cast a strong glare over their forms and faces, lighting up steamer, flat-boat and river, and bringing every feature and garment out in strong relief." [27]

The early pioneers were not so absorbed with the task of building cities, towns, and farms that they closed their eyes to the recreational attractions of Minnesota. They were, in fact, belligerent boosters. Every newspaper was a tourist bureau; but James M. Goodhue, the editor of the *Minnesota Pioneer,* was perhaps the leading promoter of them all. He intoxicated himself with his own superlatives. In 1852 he invited the world, and more especially the people of the South, to make the "Fashionable Tour," to breathe the marvelous air of Minnesota and be healed of earthly ailments. In true Goodhuean style, he asked: "Who that is idle would be caged up between walls of burning brick and mortar, in dog-days, down the river, if at less daily expense, he could be hurried along through the valley of the Mississippi, its shores studded with towns, and farms, flying by islands, prairies, woodlands, bluffs — an ever varied scene of beauty, away up into the land of the wild Dakota, and of cascades and pine forests, and cooling breezes? — Why it is an exhilarating luxury, compared with which, all the fashion and tinsel and parade of your Newports and Saratogas, are utterly insiped." He pictured the miserable life of a southern planter and of his "debilitated wife and pale children, almost gasping for breath." "What is such a life to him and those he loves, but death prolonged?" he asked. "A month in Minnesota, in dog-days, is worth a whole year anywhere else; and, we confidently look to see the time, when all families of leisure down South, from the Gulf of Mexico along up, will make their regular summer hegira to our Territory; and when hundreds of the opulent from those regions, will build delightful cottages on the borders of our ten thousand lakes and ornament their grounds with all that is tasteful in shrubbery and horticulture, for a summer retreat." [28]

In this, as in many other fields, Goodhue the booster was Goodhue the prophet. Even before the Civil War large numbers of people from the South flocked to Minnesota as a summer resort; and the habit was resumed not long after Appomattox. Folk from east and west joined in exploiting the vacation attractions of Minnesota. The day of the "Fashionable Tour" on the upper Mississippi passed when steamboating declined in the face of railroad competition. The fame of Minnesota as a summer resort had been established, however, and the railroads made the lakes and rivers even more accessible than they had been when sleek vessels graced the river in its golden age.

Keeping House
on the Minnesota Frontier

EVADENE A. BURRIS SWANSON

THE FRONTIER HOME and its management are topics which have attracted only a limited amount of detailed, first-rate research. The study here reprinted was published in September, 1933 (volume 14) as one of a series of four articles by the same author dealing with frontier domestic architecture, food, and furniture. Drawn from a master's thesis by Evadene A. Burris, who is now Mrs. Gustav A. Swanson of Ithaca, New York, this article and its companions have become standard reference sources for later historians seeking information on the home life of the Minnesota settler in the 1850s and 1860s. Mrs. Swanson is at present curator of the College of Architecture in Cornell University at Ithaca.

NEW SETTLERS in Minnesota Territory worked hard to re-establish the kinds of homes familiar to them in the life they had forsaken when they followed the lure of the frontier.[1] Traditional practices were modified to meet local conditions. One of the first problems that faced the settler and his wife was that of making a home comfortable and pleasant for habitation. How this problem was met in the 1850s in the Minnesota region — the frontier of the upper Mississippi Valley — is disclosed in a variety of contemporary and other records that illuminate the common life of the people.

Methods of lighting cabins and houses varied throughout the villages and rural districts. The flickering light from the hearth was the only illumination provided in the cabin of Edward Drew in the first year that he lived in Minnesota Territory. The next year he lived in a cabin containing a cookstove. There, because no tallow was available, he used rough lard placed in a dish with a strip of rag for a wick. The dish was put on the stove to keep the grease melted. Sometimes two or three wicks were put in a dish of melted grease to increase the lighting surface. Turnips and beets were occasionally hollowed out and used as receptacles for lard, tallow, goose grease, or vension fat. Three sticks were thrust into the beet for legs. Tallow dips were made by dipping the wick into tallow, cooling and redipping it until the desired size was obtained. These candles were made symmetrical by slight rolling while the tallow was still soft.[2]

Candles that were made in molds were superior to other varieties. The candlewick was twisted and doubled, the cut ends slipped through the tiny hole at the bottom of the mold, and a knot tied. A piece of wire strung through the doubled ends held the wicks in line on the top, and the tallow was poured into the molds. When the knots were cut, the candles could be lifted out of the mold by the wire at the top. Candlewick was carried by the leading stores throughout the territory. An early settler in Faribault recalled the "meanest man in town," a miser who bought up all the candlewick in stock and then tried to exact exorbitant prices from the housekeepers, thereby gaining for himself the nickname of "Candlewick Brown." [3]

Sperm and star candles were advertised in the stock of many St. Paul stores, and by November 11, 1857, a candle manufactory was in operation in that city. Elizabeth Fuller, a St. Paul woman, lists frequently in her account book for 1857 boxes of star candles which were purchased.[4] The headline, "In Darkness," in the *Minnesota Pioneer* of March 19, 1853, carried a startling message, for the supply of candles in St. Paul stores had been exhausted. The dependence upon candles for illumination was soon removed, however, by the introduction of kerosene lamps and gas. Camphene and burning fluids were sold by the Minnesota Drug Store in St. Anthony in 1856, but these burning fluids were not as safe to use as candles. A solution was advanced in 1860: "To those who have become disgusted with star and tallow candles, (and who has not?), and are no longer willing to risk the lives of their children by using burning fluids, we would say . . . that the best article for illuminating that has ever been brought to the city . . . is kerosene." [5]

A druggist in Rochester bought five gallons of kerosene and six lamps from a Chicago agent traveling by stage to St. Paul. He sold one gallon of kerosene for $1.40, and a marble lamp for $1.40.[6] The announcement of a new commodity in St. Paul was made by the *Pioneer and Democrat* on December 15, 1859, when Messrs. Wheeler and Son of St. Anthony advertised a stock of lamps that were designed to burn an article known as coal oil or kerosene, which gave a better light than the best quality of candles or ordinary burning fluid. So many purchasers were found in private families that there was danger that a stock consisting of twenty barrels of kerosene would be exhausted before the opening of navigation.

An analysis of the comparative burning value of different kinds of lighting fluids indicated that one gallon each of sperm oil, lard oil, and whale oil burned sixty, sixty-three, and sixty-five hours respectively, while one gallon of Breckenridge coal oil burned a hundred and seventy hours. Coal oil would not explode or congeal, and a lamp with a small wick gave light equal to six sperm candles. A bill which provided for the inspection of petroleum oils for illuminating purposes was considered, but not passed, by the Minnesota legislature in 1865.[7]

While kerosene lamps brightened up the interiors, lanterns were devised to carry outside. Whale oil was often used in a lantern made with a glass door in one side and tin perforated with holes in the shapes of stars and diamonds on the other. A possible source of supply for oil when all the whales had been killed caused speculation among the early settlers.[8]

Gas made its first appearance in St. Paul in the business section. Greenleaf and Chappell, jewelers, installed a plant that was said to equal the expensive works of large cities. St. Paul's "Great White Way" made its official opening with a grand illumination on September 19, 1857, when street lights were put in operation. A few days later the amount of gas consumed nightly was estimated at approximately ten thousand cubic feet, and the following suggestion was offered: "Bills for gas, we suppose, will be made out monthly." John P. Kennedy received employment in the following months installing equipment in houses for the use of gas. A. E. Ames's home in St. Anthony was furnished throughout with gas pipes in October of 1857. The gas company suffered serious losses during the next year, and St. Paul officials, after bickering with the city council, were forced to turn off many of the street lights to cut down expenses. Citizens were urged to dispense with candles and lighting fluids, and support the public utility.[9]

The problem of keeping the house warm in winter was no slight worry to the immigrant who arrived in the territory in the late summer months. According to the reports given to a visitor in St. Anthony in 1850, there was cold weather from the middle of November until May. Frost remained on the trees for six weeks at a time, although the sun might shine every day. The ordinary snowfall was from one to two and one-half feet, and it remained on the ground from the time it first fell until spring, for winter thaws were rare.[10] A good supply of fuel was necessary, and the ordinary kind for a frontier community was wood. "What We Burn in St. Paul," ran a caption in the *Pioneer and Demo-*

crat of August 29, 1857. "This may seem to our readers a singular inquiry in a city so far to the Northwest that coal has not yet been discovered, and where the only other natural lignite is wood . . . but our object was to direct attention to the source of supply . . . Mr. S. J. Albright's wood yard, getting his supply from a portion of the 'Big Woods' bordering on the Minnesota River." In winter, when the country roads were blocked, steamboats landed wood at the wharves.[11]

In the home of Charles Kimball in Superior, a frame house of four rooms, two stoves — one in the kitchen and the other in the parlor — consumed about twelve cords of wood a year, according to the memory of one of the occupants. The itemized bill for wood in 1857 for the Fuller home in St. Paul amounted to $239.75 for 43¾ cords of wood.[12] There was some question of honesty in the measurement of a cord, and for several years it was considered advisable to have a city wood measurer in St. Paul. This office was abolished before 1859 because of the additional charge on each cord. In 1866 a law provided for an official wood inspector for the town of Faribault. His fee for certifying a load of wood was ten cents per cord.[13] With the introduction of gas in St. Paul, the resulting by-products made possible another kind of fuel in the form of coke, which could be purchased at twenty-five cents a bushel from the St. Paul Gas Company. Peat was another natural resource which, it was hoped, would do away with wood for fuel.[14]

The property of Joseph S. Johnson in the middle 1850s included part of what is now Loring Park and the high bluff to the south of it, taking in land on Oak Grove Street, Clifton, Groveland, and Ridgewood avenues. Here he constructed his home so that the kitchen door faced the lake. This arrangement was convenient for trips to the springhouse to fetch milk and butter. The water supply in winter was obtained by melting ice on the back of the kitchen stove. An elaborate three-story house with a spacious observatory depended even in 1860 upon a spring for its water. A springhouse built on a farm near St. Paul in 1859 was of "octagon form, fifteen feet in the clear, half of which is under ground." It was surmounted by a handsome cornice. The building was considered an ornamental and useful addition to the property.[15] For those who had no spring or running water near their homes, the "wheelbarrow man" made deliveries. In August of 1856, his business warranted the purchase of a two-wheeled cart by means of which he distributed spring water to the "thirsty denizens" of St. Paul.[16]

Well water could be obtained in the Minnesota River Valley by digging from ten to twenty-five feet. The water was either pumped or brought up with a large bucket. Lewis Harrington, in his diary for

July, 1856, mentioned working on a well. He spent about a week in putting on the curbing and making the windlass. Pumps could be purchased in 1851 from F. S. Newell of St. Paul, who carried well, cistern, and house pumps of all sizes.[17] A town pump erected by the citizens of St. Paul for a common supply of water became a subject of some difficulty. On March 27, 1850, the announcement appeared in the *Pioneer* that "several citizens who defrayed the expense of digging a public well and placing a pump in it, at the corner of Jackson and Third Street wish us to give notice that horses must not be watered there." The issue finally led to an ordinance of the town council imposing a penalty of five dollars for the offense of watering horses or cattle at the town pump. In the advertisement of a house that was for sale in 1852, mention was made of the fact that it was watered with a well and with a running stream. The *Pioneer* commented on October 30, 1854, that "notwithstanding the innumerable springs surrounding our city, S. McConnell in the past season has dug upwards of forty wells." A reactionary spirit in Wasioja looked upon the mechanical contrivance with suspicion: "a pump is an outrage upon the 'sparkling beverage of nature,'" he writes. "They do well enough for city people who never know what they eat or drink, but go it blind on their faith." [18]

Plans for a city water system in St. Paul did not materialize in the fifties, although various schemes were considered as early as 1852 for "St. Paul Hydraulics." An aqueduct covered with a stone arch and a road running over it was planned. By 1857 comes the query, "Can we have pure water in St. Paul?" Lakes Como and Phalen were reported as possible sources, both clear and pure, that any city might be proud of having in use for its citizens.[19]

The problem of drainage for cellars flooded with rain water was discussed in 1857 in connection with a city water plant. The water, it was argued, was insufficient for putting out fires — indirectly causing high insurance rates — and overabundant in filling up cellars. The city engineer was instructed to draw up plans for a general sewerage system. The unfortunate financial reverses of the gas company and adverse financial conditions made the actual enterprise impossible, but public-spirited individuals were busy analyzing the situation and stirring up favorable public opinion for such projects.[20]

In getting soft water for laundry purposes, one of the first mechanical inventions used in the house became popular. This was the pump. When it was connected with the cistern, a water barrel under the eaves was no longer needed. Although troughs to guide the rain water along the roof into a receptacle continued to be used, cisterns were considered a convenience in well-equipped houses. Dr. Ames had a cistern with a capacity of thirty barrels in each wing of his conservatory.[21]

Devices for refrigeration in rural districts were somewhat primitive, and various formulas were exchanged to preserve foods. One method of hardening butter without ice was to set the dish in a water-filled saucer, cover the saucer with an inverted flower pot, drench the pot with water, and set it in a cool place. Submerging dishes in springs was a possible measure, and the springhouse or cellar for milk, butter, and water was an indispensable part of the well-equipped farm. One woman complained of having no closet or spot in the house where she could keep anything frozen, and when she received a gift of some oysters, she buried them in the snow.[22]

The rivers and streams offered such a generous supply of ice that it was not difficult to store it in winter. One enterprising citizen of St. Paul made the situation easy for residents of that city by building in the winter of 1851 an icehouse with a capacity of nine hundred tons. On May 27, 1852, the *Minnesota Pioneer* reported that "Charles Symons brings us thick, blue ice to our very doors, every morning, cheaper than we can afford to go into our own houses after it." Businessmen found it practical to continue to put up their own supply. In February of 1860, William Coulter, a St. Paul butcher, laid in a store for his use the following summer, when he planned to have two carts running with the provision baskets of his customers, in each of which would be placed a quantity of ice to preserve the meats. John S. Prince was putting in a supply which it was hoped would prove equal to the task of cooling all the claret punches that the public would consume in the next season.[23]

An unusual harvest was reported in the year 1860, when a news item headed "Sky-Tinted Ice for the South" announced that "this is the first year that our generous ice crop has been gathered to any great extent for the southern market, notwithstanding the unequalled facilities for transportation by river clear down to the tropics. . . . Several barges are loaded . . . for St. Louis, with this blessed summer luxury, and hereafter its export will take rank among our productions." The legislature found it expedient in 1866 to pass a law prohibiting persons or companies from taking ice from the Mississippi, St. Croix, or Minnesota rivers without erecting suitable safeguards around the place from which the ice was taken.[24]

Improvements in the mechanics of the refrigerator were described in the *Saint Paul Daily Pioneer* on July 21, 1866, when J. B. Holmes offered for sale a refrigerator which had a "passage of current of fresh air through all its compartments by a simple but ingenious invention." It required only a small quantity of ice, and answered all the purposes of a cellar with none of its inconveniences.

Special techniques of housekeeping were involved in cleaning and laundry work. One of these was soapmaking, an important skill of the economical housewife. Jane Grey Swisshelm objected vigorously to the boxes labeled "soap" coming from St. Louis, Cincinnati, and other places. "Where oak wood is used for fuel, and mess pork in cooking, as they are here, every family should make its own soap, until factories are started in the vicinity at least. At our house we make even our own toilet soap," she wrote.[25] A writer for the *Minnesota Pioneer* of June 28, 1849, assumed that every housewife knew how to make soap, but as all might not know the best way, the process was carefully described. It was recommended that the grease be cleansed by boiling in deep lye so that the refuse of bacon rinds, scraps of pork, and old bones, would sink to the bottom. Lye which was strong enough to bear an egg was to be boiled and poured into the soap barrel until all the grease was taken up. If luck was with the housewife, the soap would "come" at the end of this process, as the lye and grease would unite. Sometimes the action failed, although the lye seemed strong enough when tested. In this case, advised the writer, "put in fresh lime. The acids immediately leave the lye to unite with the lime, and the lye becomes caustic. . . . Some sorts of wood contain much acid, others little. Beech belongs to the first, and hickory to the last. Soap boilers who use ashes made of all sorts of wood indiscriminately put in a peck of quick lime to a bushel of ashes, and they never fail to get soap."

City dwellers were not without commercial aids in laundry work, however, for in 1855 washing powders were advertised which miraculously made such labor easy and pleasant. "Oh dear, 'tis such hard work to wash." "Not if using Bond & Kellogg's Washing Powder" ran one advertisement. A complaint was registered in one case by "Soap and Water," who protested that they were beaten out of the tub by a compound of iniquity that imparted whiteness with a fatal facility, but in equal ratio effected destruction.[26]

In some families brooms were made of splints and manufactured at home. The raising of broom corn was encouraged, and the manufacture of brooms was considered hopefully as the beginning of industrial development in the Northwest. Samuel Clotworthy brought to St. Paul in 1855 some brooms that he had made of corn grown in Minnesota. In the early sixties a Faribault man manufactured about three thousand brooms, all of which were sold in Minnesota.[27]

Goose plucking was an activity that afforded lively exercise. A settler in Newcastle, Iowa, described this procedure. A goose hatched early in the spring was relieved of its feathers four times during the season, she declared, and if half a pound of feathers from each goose was gathered in the four scrimmages, the process was deemed a success. The fine soft feathers were used for pillow and mattress ticks, while the long ones were twisted into feather dusters.[28]

The construction of fences around the dwelling place was a task common to both city and rural dwellers. Alice Mendenhall George said that her father was busy after he built their cabin putting up a fence which was seven rails high. A picture of a log cabin that was built in Douglas County in 1867 shows a little fence around the lonely structure, and views of St. Paul in 1857 and 1867 reveal inclosures around the property of city dwellings. Lack of fences was a sign of indolence to Mrs. Swisshelm, and after a sojourn in Wasioja, she reported it "like Owatonna, only more so — not a fence worth the name, no trees, no shrubbery, no garden — I did not see one man, woman, or child doing anything to make their home look like places to live in." In Mantorville, on the other hand, she was favorably impressed by the home of Zeno B. Page, a roomy, airy house built on the best Pennsylvania plan, surrounded by substantial fences. St. Cloud itself was a model in this respect, for "spring fences were going up around every St. Cloud house, and smiling gardens peeped out at one." Governor Ramsey had a rail fence in which nails were used built around his property in 1851.[29]

Rail fences were sometimes laid to a height of six, eight, or ten rails. The first layer was laid zigzag on the ground, and the ends of each succeeding layer interlocked, so that alternate rails were parallel in each section of a fence. A "worm" fence had no corner stays, but a "stake" and "rider" fence had a reinforcement for the junction of each section. Two stakes were braced in a slanting position to form an "X," and the top or "rider" rail rested in the crotch and locked the structure. A man could split about a hundred rails in a day.[30]

J. A. Willard, in explaining the advantages of Blue Earth County to settlers, described several methods of fencing that were being tried on the prairie, such as hedge and ditch and turf fences. The ditch and turf fence was made of earth dug from a ditch and formed into a wall. When the grass grew over it, it made a perfect barrier for hogs as well as cattle, he declared. Wire fencing with one board at the top was also being tried in 1868. An act of the state legislature in 1867 placed the sum of three hundred dollars at the disposal of the Minnesota State Agricultural Society to pay premiums for continuous half miles of live hedge fences. Paling fences around cabin yards were built of logs placed upright and fastened by a top and bottom rail frame. Such fences were intended to protect the occupants of a home not from the attacks of enemies but from the shots of hunters. The neat inclosures of city dwellings were a real defense in many cases, for they shielded vegetable gardens from the invasions of stray hogs and cattle.[31]

In the original clearing of the ground, settlers cut down so many trees that replanting became necessary. The *Pioneer and Democrat* in 1856 urged the citizens of St. Paul to plant shade trees. The elm was recommended. The *New Era* of Sauk Rapids announced that many citizens were beautifying their residences by setting out forest trees for shade and ornament. The editor of that paper reported on the success of an experiment in growing Kentucky blue grass in the yard around his home. The seeds had been brought from Daviess County, Kentucky. The grass in the spring of 1860 was six to eight inches high.[32]

In the gardens of a St. Paul nursery were dahlias, lilies, peonies, gladioli, lilacs, snowballs, and choice roses, as well as a variety of ornamental shrubs and trees, including mountain ash, balsam fir, red cedar, arbor vitæ, and Norway spruce. A complete catalogue was prepared in 1855 by L. M. Ford and Company, proprietors of the Groveland Nursery. Although their first tree had been planted only four years earlier, the stock included deciduous ornamental trees, evergreen trees, ornamental shrubs, and climbing and trailing shrubs. The proprietors claimed that they possessed over a hundred varieties of roses. All the beauties of the old-fashioned flower gardens were open to the housewife, for this nursery could supply plants of clematis, spirea, geranium, delphinium, phlox, narcissus, tulip, iris, and lily. The nursery was conveniently located "near the Halfway House between St. Paul and St. Anthony, Minnesota Territory," so the public of both cities could be served. Verbena, camelia, heliotrope, pink, nasturtium, gilly-flower, jessamine, fuchsia, winter chrysanthemum, veronica, and oleander were some of the flowers cultivated by a St. Paul greenhouse in 1860.[33] Bushes and plants evidently shared a corner with more practical provisions in the cargo of steamboats on the river, so the exchange of "slips" and potted plants became widespread through the territory. Mrs. Swisshelm acknowledged a gift of lilac and damask and blush rose bushes sent to her by friends in St. Anthony on the steamer "Enterprise." [34]

"Dr. A. E. Ames, of Minneapolis, enjoys the reputation of possessing one of the finest and most expensive flower gardens in the Northwest," declared the *Pioneer and Democrat* of July 17, 1859. His conservatory was composed of a central building measuring ten by twenty-four feet, and thirteen feet high, with two wings, each eighteen by twenty-two feet and six feet high. In each corner of the edifice were turrets three feet square and twelve feet high surmounted by spires. These gave the structure the effect of an Oriental mosque, and the unusual design was proclaimed very pleasing to the eye. A furnace in the central building with pipes running to the wings heated the conservatory, and water for the flowers was pumped from a cistern. The cost of construction was sixteen hundred dollars. A. M. Radcliffe was the architect and Charles Clark the builder.

The lightning rod was a form of protection considered necessary by the houseowner of the fifties. "Almost everyone has erected a lightning rod on his domicil," declared the *St. Anthony Express* on August 25, 1855. A primitive way of reckoning expenses is recounted in the story of a man who put up seven lightning rods on a livery stable in exchange for a horse. Terms as quoted in 1855 for supplying and putting up lightning rods and conductors were eight dollars per forty feet. This included a superior article, according to the advertisement, for the points were made of a silvered composition and were warranted to stand for years without tarnishing, the insulators were of glass, and the rods were square and twisted.[35]

Some civic responsibilities of the houseowner contributed to the safety and beauty of town life. An ordinance of 1857 required the resident of each dwelling house in St. Paul to place a fire bucket outside his door ready for action in case of emergency. Frequent notices were printed to remind citizens that sidewalks must be swept clear of snow by ten o'clock on a morning following a snowstorm. Individual enterprise aided in clearing the streets of rubbish when St. Paul prepared a reception for ex-President Fillmore, Thurlow Weed, George Bancroft, and other distinguished guests in 1854. The ladies of St. Paul found it necessary at one time to repair the sidewalks so that their full skirts would not be caught or torn. Numbering the houses was proposed in 1857.[36]

An early settler in Mankato declared that the mosquitoes were more aggressive in their hostility than wolves or Indians. Smudge pots were burned all day. Windows and doors were covered with netting and beds were draped with it at night.[37] Mice were a great bother in cabins and shanties, and their number did not seem to decrease with an increase in the number captured. One pioneer mother claims that if women had mounted chairs to escape, they would have occupied permanent places on top of the furniture. Edward Drew described an ingenious mousetrap which he devised in his cabin at Wabasha Prairie. He placed bait under a butter dish or bowl and by means of some strips of wood arranged a spring to release the bowl on top of the mouse. The success of this device is indicated by his report of eighty-nine victims. A cat was a priceless acquisition, according to Marshall Comstock, who felt that he had made a good bargain when he purchased one for five dollars in 1854.[38]

Dogs, however, were not in such demand. That they were an unnecessary extravagance was the verdict of the *Pioneer and Democrat* on July 2, 1859. "It costs as much to keep a dog as it does to feed an individual. . . . In these weak and piping times of little work and less pay, it behooves us all to economize — to cut off every source of waste and extravagant consumption." A little boy moving into Minnesota in 1865 had been making great plans for the dog which he would have in his new home. His disappointment in the shortage of pets in the community colored the first few months of his life there until he was given a dog of his own. A pioneer woman wrote in 1853 "have puppy too called Dash after the one at home . . . pointer brown and handsome." [39]

Servant problems did not perplex many of the pioneer mothers in rural communities. The tasks of housekeeping were distributed among members of the family, and no extra expense was incurred for service. One family in Minneapolis did engage an Indian boy to assist with the housework. Hewing wood and drawing water were chores which did not appeal to his fancy, and he disappeared after a short trial. A St. Paul woman in 1853 had a nursemaid for her little boy, a German girl, "the most comical piece you ever saw . . . keeps us laughing constantly." In 1859 people who needed extra girls for housework, cooking, and needlework, or men or boys for any kind of work, could apply at an intelligence office on Third Street in St. Paul. No fees were charged for the service unless it was necessary to advertise for desirable people to fulfill requests.[40] Most pioneer housekeepers, however, relied upon their own abilities to keep their homes clean and attractive.

The transition from the self-sufficiency of cabin life to the co-operative spirit of the town is well illustrated in simple domestic practices. The amazing progress of the decade of the fifties in techniques of housekeeping is apparent in all the activities described. The substitution of gas for candles and of refrigerators for springhouses illustrates the progressive character of the frontier.

Christmas and New Year's on the Frontier

BERTHA L. HEILBRON

MANY STUDENTS of frontier life have pointed to the isolation and the meager opportunities for social life on the frontier. This article demonstrates that the early Minnesotan's existence was not totally bleak and grim. It also constitutes a provocative comment on the social customs of the day. By her own admission, Bertha L. Heilbron "had a hand" in thirty-five of the thirty-seven volumes of Minnesota History *published before her retirement as editor of the magazine in 1961. She is now a research fellow of the Minnesota Historical Society. As editorial assistant, assistant editor, and editor (1948–61), she not only guided the destinies of the magazine, but in her own right made a sizable contribution to its contents. Many of her articles deal with aspects of western art — an interest which is also reflected in two books:* Making a Motion Picture in 1848: Henry Lewis' Journal of a Canoe Voyage *(1936), and* The Thirty-Second State: A Pictorial History of Minnesota *(1958). The contribution here presented made its appearance in December, 1935 (volume 16). As a source of information on holiday cheer in pioneer Minnesota it remains unsurpassed.*

"CHRISTMAS DAY: Serenade this morning at 3 oclk by the musicians from Fort Snelling." Thus reads part of an entry for December 25, 1827, in a diary, now faded and yellow with age, kept at old Fort Snelling by Major Lawrence Taliaferro, Indian agent at the post for two decades after 1819. The early morning serenade was merely a prelude to the events of that Christmas Day of 1827. At daylight there were "3 Rounds by the French Inhabitants of the Post with the usual complements [*sic*] of the Season." And then the "Indians both men & women called at 11 oclk . . . in considerable numbers to see & shake hands & express the feelings of the day — which they appear to have taken up within the last Eight years from the Whites. The feelings of their hearts were expressed before I was aware," writes Taliaferro, "by a few *Yel-*

94

low Kisses — & amusing Scene." Year after year, as the agent continued in office at Fort Snelling, the Indians appeared at his door on Christmas morning. By 1836 he must have been heartily tired of the yuletide attentions of the Indian women, for on December 25 of that year he complained: "had of course to undergo various salutations on the *cheek* from many & old as well as young women — a custom derived from our Canadian population — not a very agreeable one." [1]

Taliaferro might have observed that the Indians took over from the Catholic French-Canadians the idea and the method of celebrating both Christmas and New Year's. From the land to the north, the fur trade attracted to the Minnesota country hundreds of these people, most of whom served as voyageurs, or boatmen. Their daily work brought them into close contact with the natives. To the voyageur the midwinter holidays were gala occasions, days for merrymaking, for "drinking and fighting," for feasting and dancing. One trader described a Christmas ball where the "main point to which the dancers' efforts seemed to tend, was to get the largest amount of exercise out of every muscle in the frame." The dancing was done to the music of "one vile, unvarying tune, upon a worse old fiddle," with a "brilliant accompaniment upon a large tin pan." John McKay, a trader who had charge of a post for the Hudson's Bay Company on Rainy Lake, entertained a rival trader of the North West Company and his family at breakfast and dinner on Christmas Day in 1794. In the evening his guest invited him with his men to a dance, but, recorded McKay, "the Negroe who played on the fiddle got beastly drunk and spoiled our diversion." The daily diet of the voyageur was corn and suet, which was furnished by his employer; on Christmas, New Year's, and other holidays he was given sugar, flour with which to make cakes or puddings, a measure of rum, and other luxuries reserved for special occasions. McKay gave his men seven quarts of brandy on Christmas, 1793, and again on New Year's, 1794. The men who braved a Minnesota winter to explore the snow-covered plains and forests and frozen rivers of the north observed Christmas in much the same way as did the voyageurs. Lieutenant Zebulon M. Pike, who set out in December, 1805, from his fort near Little Falls in an effort to find the source of the Mississippi, on the twenty-fifth "Gave out two pounds of extra meat, two pounds of extra flour, one gill of whisky, and some tobacco" to each member of his expedition, "in order to distinguish Christmas." [2]

When missionaries began to work among the Minnesota Indians, particularly among the Chippewa, they found that the natives made much of New Year's Day. They celebrated the holiday, which they called "Kissing day," after the manner of the French-Canadian traders and voyageurs. The puritanical religious leaders often were obliged, much against their wishes, to observe the day in the native manner. William T. Boutwell, who went to Leech Lake in 1833, found that the Indians there were in the habit of visiting the resident trader on January 1 to receive presents, "when all, male and female, old and young, must give and receive a kiss, a cake, or something else." They seemed to expect similar treatment from Boutwell, for on the first day of 1834 they caused the pious missionary considerable annoyance by appearing at his cabin at breakfast time. He relates the incident as follows: "Open came our door, and in came 5 or 6 women and as many children. An old squaw, with clean face, for once, came up and saluted me with, "bon jour," giving her hand at the same time, which I received, returning her compliment, "bon jour." But this was not all. She had been too long among Canadians not to learn some of their New Year Customs. She approached — approached so near, to give and receive a kiss, that I was obliged to give her a slip, and dodge! This vexed the old lady and provoked her to say, that I thought her too dirty. But pleased, or displeased, I was determined to give no countenance to a custom which I hated more than dirt." [3]

At Red Lake twelve years later a band of missionaries planned a New Year's celebration which seemed to please the natives, who "honored" them "with a salute of two guns." The missionaries at this place recognized the Indian custom and took part in the celebration. According to Lucy M. Lewis, the wife of one of the missionaries, all the mission workers gathered at early dawn at the house of their leader, "the most convenient place to meet the Indians who assemble to give the greeting and receive a cake or two & a draught of sweetened water. It is the custom through the country to make calls & receive cakes." But instead of offering kisses, these Indians sang a "New Year's hymn learned in school for the occasion." The Red Lake missionaries marked New Year's Eve by assembling the pupils of the mission school and giving them presents. In 1845 the gifts consisted of flannel shirts for the boys and "short gowns" for the girls. The Indian children "came with cleaner faces & hands than usual," wrote Mrs. Lewis, "as a little soap had previously been distributed." The custom of giving the Indians presents during the holiday season was continued by later missionaries, and it doubtless had an influence in creating good will. In 1881 Bishop Henry B. Whipple, "with his usual kindness, sent an abundant supply of Christmas candy to all the Indian churches and stations" of the Episcopal church in northern Minnesota. A hundred pounds was sent to White Earth and fifty pounds each to several other stations, including those at Red and Leech lakes. This, according to one writer, "was enough to sweeten the whole Ojibway nation and gave many an Indian boy and girl and man and woman the only taste of candy they have during the year. It made a great many people happy." [4]

While missionaries were introducing the white man's customs in northern Minnesota, settlement was progressing in the southern part of the territory, and a few well-defined communities that were to become cities were established. They were peopled by newcomers, many of whom came from New England or other parts of the East, bringing with them the social customs of their old homes. By 1850 the gay and often crude Christmas celebration of the voyageur and the Indian had been replaced in Minnesota by a more conventional and refined holiday. The observance was, however, far from puritanical. People went to church on Christmas, but they also attended balls or other parties "gotten up with as much elegance and taste as can be displayed in any of the great cities," they arranged for amateur theatricals and community Christmas trees, and they enjoyed elaborate dinners. In St. Paul, according to a statement in a local newspaper, the Christmas season of 1850 was "rich in social entertainments and interesting religious exercises."

A "Grand Christmas Ball" at the Minnesota House in Stillwater was the "great centre of attraction" for "those who love worldly pleasure" during the holiday season of 1849. W. E. Hartshorn, the proprietor of the hotel, announced that he planned to "surpass anything of the kind yet got up in the Territory," which was then only eight months old. A week later St. Paulites saw the New Year in at a ball held at the Central House, where a local editor witnessed the "largest collection of beauty and of fashion we have ever seen in the West." A ball at Moffet's hotel in St. Paul ushered in the Christmas festivities of 1850. On the following night there was a ball of "unusual splendor" at Brewster's hotel in Stillwater, which was "attended by more than one hundred gentlemen and ladies, eight cotillions occupying the floor at once." A year later the holiday season was inaugurated a few days before Christmas in St. Paul by a "Ladies' Fair" held in Charles H. Oakes's "large, new elegant mansion house, well warmed and illuminated from the basement up to the observatory." An idea of pioneer St. Paul society may be gained from a contemporary report of this affair. The gathering was one of "intelligence and real respectability," made up of "beautiful, well dressed women and girls" and "genteel and accomplished men." They displayed "an easy elegance of manners

and a pleasant tone of refined conversation, that was truly delightful."
A frontier editor left the fair "with a better opinion of the elements of
society in St. Paul and higher hopes of the early predominance here, of
a christian spirit of enlightened morality and high-toned civilization." [5]

One of the forms of entertainment provided for guests at this Christmas fair was a post office, "where pertinent, ludicrous and appropriate
letters could be obtained." The celebration reached its climax, however, in a supper, at which tables were arranged for "one hundred
persons, in a style of sumptuous elegance." Turkeys, chickens, frosted
hams, "the more staple meats, including buffalo tongue," oyster soup,
lobster soup, sardines, pastries, sauces, ice cream, jellies, and "pi-
quants of every description" were among the dishes served. It is evident that delicacies were not lacking on the frontier Christmas table.
Another St. Paul menu of 1851 included chicken, ham, turkey, lobster, oysters, sardines, buffalo tongues, pastries, jellies, pecans, and
ice cream. In that year turkeys, brought by sleigh from Iowa and Illinois, sold in St. Paul for $1.50 and $2.00 each. Many a pioneer family, however, sat down to a holiday table that was not graced by the
king of birds. On Thanksgiving Day, 1850, which was celebrated in
that year on December 26, a Minneapolis family had a dinner of
stewed oysters, boiled vegetables, baked pork and beans, cranberries,
mince and cranberry pies, cheese, and nuts. The cranberries gave to
the meal a distinctly local flavor, for they grew wild in many parts of
Minnesota. One Minneapolis pioneer recalls that he picked the cranberries for his Christmas dinner of 1848 "in what is now Columbia
Heights," where the "bushes were loaded with them." Other frontier
products found a place on many a menu. A Christmas dinner served
in Fillmore County in 1854 included bear meat, prairie chicken, and
venison. The bear meat was furnished by an Indian chief who, with his
squaw and six warriors, joined the white settlers of the vicinity for a
yule celebration. After dinner the Indians entertained their hosts with
races, a ball game, and dances. Among the dishes served at a Christmas
gathering in 1852 at Winona, which was then known as Wabasha
Prairie, were wild goose, venison, and coon. The menu included also
five kinds of cake, three kinds of pie, and doughnuts fried in coon
grease. Guests at the table of Governor Alexander Ramsey during the
holiday season of 1850 dined "on a saddle of venison." Turkeys were
served regularly on Christmas in the home of Ignatius Donnelly at Nin-
inger in the 1870s. On his holiday table there appeared also such
delicacies as wine, homemade cider, and mince pie. [6]

Luxuries seem to have found their way even to the remote Minnesota frontier. At Crow Wing, near Fort Ripley on the upper Mississippi, in 1860 a Christmas dinner of oyster soup, roast turkey, plum pudding, coffee, and "fixins" was enjoyed by Mr. and Mrs. Samuel B. Abbe and their guests. The oysters had been sent to Mrs. Abbe by a friend at St. Cloud. With her husband she had only recently removed from St. Paul to Crow Wing, where he was a trader and a townsite promoter. Their first Christmas at this remote post was far from lonely. A few days before the holiday they attended a party at the home of Clement H. Beaulieu, a French and Indian mixed-blood who traded in the area. He "sent to St. Cloud (eighty miles) for music." In a letter written on December 30, 1860, Mrs. Abbe reports that her host served "an elegant supper," and though she did not consider the party "quite as elegant as some of our St P[aul] affairs of the kind [it] was n[o]t to be despised. The garrison were all present & all down from the Agency . . . and the *arrow*stocracy of Crow Wing." [7] After church services on Christmas morning the Reverend and Mrs. E. S. Peake, local missionaries of the Episcopal church, went home to dinner with the Abbes. In the evening they all attended a party at Fort Ripley, where there was a Christmas tree, and where Mrs. Abbe received a "very pretty embroidered cushion" and her husband "came into possession of a watch case with a mouse in it." Among the guests were the wives and daughters of the commandant and the post surgeon, and six or seven bachelors. "The young ladies are having a good time generally," commented Mrs. Abbe. She herself approved of only one or two of the young men; the others she found "like the rest of the brass buttons."

On Christmas morning "the grave and devout will be at church," wrote an editor of 1849. Churchgoing was a natural part of the frontier holiday observance; in fact, it was taken for granted and was seldom a subject of comment. A Swedish Lutheran pastor who arrived in Minnesota late in 1857 preached in St. Paul on the Sunday before Christmas, at Scandia two days before the holiday, and at both East and West Union on Christmas Day. He complained that he found it necessary to prepare his sermon in a saloon near Shakopee, "where several drunkards made a lot of disturbance until late at night." At Faribault the yule celebration began in the Episcopal Cathedral at six in the morning with a carol service, which by the late 1870s was looked upon as "one of the time-honored customs of the parish." The cathedral was always decorated for the holiday; on one occasion it was banked with evergreens and the "chancel was literally ablaze with the light of gas burners and tapers." A parishioner recorded that the carols heard at this service "were old and familiar Christmas songs, many of which were learned by most of us as Sunday school children in the far off parishes of Eastern cities and villages." At Morris in 1882 an Episcopal congregation that had been organized only a year earlier had a Christmas festival that "drew forth a glad observance of its sacred memorials. The church and chancel were made both beautiful and fragrant by wreaths and festoons of evergreen; and the service enlivened by rich anthems of praise." [8]

In many frontier homes children received Christmas gifts, but some pioneers found it impossible to provide even such simple objects as homemade toys, popcorn balls, and candy. They told the disappointed youngsters that "it had been a bad year for Santa Claus' business" or that "Santa Claus has not learned the way up to Minnesota yet." A pioneer woman who passed her childhood near Le Sueur recalls that the Christmas of 1861 was an especially thrilling one, for she received a "pink calico apron, a stick of striped candy, an apple, and a doll about seven inches long, with china head, hands, and feet." She records that the doll was "the first and only one" she ever had. A decade later, a community Christmas celebrated in a schoolhouse near Silver Lake in Martin County was marked by a "graceful red cedar well lighted with candles and well loaded with presents, as was also a table nearby, and the floor." Bushels of popcorn balls were piled beneath the tree, which was loaded with stockings made of mosquito netting by the women of the neighborhood and filled with candy, nuts, and popcorn. Among the gifts were mittens, suspenders, leggings, neckties, slippers, dolls, drums, dolls' clothing, books, pictures, boots, and other articles of clothing. In order to provide decorations for a Christmas tree at old Fort Garry, near the present site of Winnipeg, "tin foil and gilt paper were stripped off packages in the shop and twisted into fantastic shapes, bright beads and berries were strung upon cords, slices of yellow soap were cut into hearts, stars, etc., carefully covered with coloured paper, candles cut down and fitted into holders made by the tinsmith." [9]

Gifts received by adults were worthy of note. Governor Ramsey recorded in his diary for December 25, 1850 — the first Christmas that he spent in Minnesota — that he received "as a Christmas present a fine long sleeved pair of fur gloves and a pretty segar case." He noted also that a prominent St. Paul man presented Mrs. Ramsey with a "very handsome painting in a gilt frame, lady shading her face with a fan." A variety of gifts could be purchased in the local shops. In 1849 St. Paul merchants, confectioners, and bakers were prepared for the holiday trade. They advertised among other things stocks of cigars, tobacco, pipes, toys, "fancy dry goods," and Christmas cakes. "But if all our St. Paul merchants fail to supply you with what you want," a local paper suggested, "just step up to the Sutler's store, at Fort Snelling." A stock of goods received by one St. Paul shop just before Christmas, 1850, was brought up the river as far as Red Wing by steamboat and transported from there on the ice. As time went on the custom of giving presents to both young and old became an established one, and merchants continued to cater to the holiday trade. A Swedish traveler who was in St. Paul a few days before a Christmas of the early 1870s remarked upon the "newly arrived articles . . . intended as gifts for the coming holidays" to be found in the local stores. The "number and costliness" of the gifts exchanged by Americans amazed him. "The presents are sent with a message if the giver is someone outside the family," he explained, "or they are distributed by a dressed-up Christmas mummer, who here goes under the name of 'Santa Claus.'" An unusual gift received by a minister at Sauk Centre from his congregation in 1882 was a "Christmas card, the design upon which consisted of a unique arrangement of seventy-five dollars and fifty cents in gold and silver coin." [10]

Amateur theatrical performances sometimes marked the holiday season. The people of Hastings assembled at Burges' Hall on Christmas Eve of 1857 to witness a "grand musical festival" entitled "The Flower Queen." The rose, the lily, the crocus, the violet, and the like were impersonated by members of a "juvenile singing class connected with the Dakota Institute." On what was, in all likelihood, a frigid winter night, these youthful Minnesota pioneers sang:

> We are the flowers, the fair young flowers,
> That come at the voice of Spring.

Only seven years after the railway village of Glyndon in Clay County was platted, on December 24, 1879, a playlet known as the "House of Santa Claus" was produced there for the local Sunday school children. Despite a temperature of thirty-five degrees below zero, the youngsters turned out to see this play, sing Christmas anthems, and receive gifts and sweetmeats. At a masquerade given at Dodge Center on Christmas night, 1882, one of the guests was dressed as Oscar Wilde, "knee breeches, big buckled shoes, low collar, sunflower and all," and two women appeared in costumes "composed entirely of newspapers, the fit and style being very elegant." [11]

Sleigh rides often were planned for the Minnesota holiday season. A pioneer St. Anthony woman recalled that on Christmas Day, 1849, the young people of St. Anthony and St. Paul joined forces for a ride to a point nine miles above the falls. She related that "The sleighing was fine, and being well protected with fur robes the drive was delightful." Rides from St. Paul upstream to Fort Snelling on the ice, or down the river to Red Rock or Point Douglas, or across country to Stillwater or St. Anthony, sometimes were arranged. "Away we go," wrote one pioneer, "with bells jingling, horses blowing icicles from their nostrils — ladies alternately laughing and screaming . . . young men driving like Jehu." A sleighing party given in 1852 at Wabasha Prairie "had for its object the taking to ride in one sleigh of every lady then resident" in the settlement. "Stops were made at all the 'shanties' then on the prairie, and where occupants were found at home calls were made, while at the vacant ones the names of the callers were written in lead pencil upon the door." [12]

A sleigh ride was an enjoyable feature of a Christmas party given in 1866 in Minneapolis by Mr. and Mrs. John T. Blaisdell, and it was recalled many years later by one of the guests, Walter Stone Pardee, who in 1866 was a homesick boy recently arrived from New England. He related: "Likely there were 20 children on hand. Long before dark Mr. Blaisdell got all who cared to go, into his big farm sleigh, that was bedded in straw, and he took us for a ride to the back of his farm, half a mile west, and this was at Lyndale Avenue of today. The air was crisp, clear and cold, and the boys and girls especially were wonderfully stimulated to enjoy the substantial food soon to be offered. The road was out of the common way. . . . Not a house was to be seen along the route . . . in the region where there are hundreds of costly homes. . . . But that 1866 afternoon our brisk team pulled us merrily along thru snow drifts on just plain farm upon much of which Mr. Blaisdell raised wheat. As to houses in sight even on Nicollet Avenue, there were only two or three such as would be on 160 acre farms. A little white school house some way out was the biggest building to be seen until far away at Lake Street were two or three farmhouses." [13]

The farm in time became Blaisdell's Addition to the city of Minneapolis. After the invigorating ride, Blaisdell drove back to his "hospitable home," where the "New England supper came on." "The table was piled with the substantial and the fine," recorded Pardee. "As at Dave Harum's Christmas dinner, 'Sairy was for bringing in and taking out, but folks at table did their own passing.' " The feast was followed by a "jolly evening," with the "usual kissing games . . . sedate marchings about the big room and near-attempts at dancing." Pardee remarked that the Christmas affair pleased him, "for it was New England again."

In frontier Minnesota calls were the order of the day on New Year's. "The custom of observing this day, after the old Dutch fashion, is becoming firmly established," read a St. Paul newspaper of the early 1850s. On the first day of the year "ladies remain at home and see company. Gentlemen make short calls, and take a slight refreshment everywhere." From ten in the morning to four in the afternoon were considered the proper hours for making calls. Propriety seems, however, to have been disregarded by some elements of the frontier population. Shortly after midnight of New Year's Eve in 1852, for example, Governor Ramsey was surprised by a "visit, salute, and musick from some 30 Germans." Since he "was up reading the mail," he "called them in and treated them." This was only the beginning of a strenuous New Year's observance for Minnesota's first governor, for at daybreak the Indians began to call on him, and they kept coming "until noon, in which time some 300 called." In addition, the governor recorded in his diary, "very many citizens called upon Mrs. R." A year earlier, on January 1, 1851, he noted that the "practice of calling upon the lady of the house obtained very generally in town. Upwards of one hundred persons called on us." Among those who visited the Ramsey home on the first day of 1854 was Charles E. Flandrau, later a well-known Minnesota judge. This was his first New Year's in St. Paul, and he found to his delight that "everybody kept open house and expected everybody else to call and see them. . . . There was great strife among the entertainers as to who should have the most elaborate spread, and the most brilliant and attractive array of young ladies to greet the guests," according to Flandrau. "A register of the callers was always kept, and great was the victory of the hostess who recorded the greatest number." Flandrau added his name to many a register that winter day of 1854, for he reported that he was one of four "young frisky fellows" who "started out together with a good team and made one hundred and fifty calls by midnight." When he had made the rounds of the "principal houses" in the territorial capital, he went on to "Fort Snelling, with its Old School Army officers, famous for their courtesy and hospitality," and while in the neighborhood he called also upon "Henry H. Sibley, at Mendota, to whom the finest amenities of life were a creed." [14]

New Year's was marked in many other ways. The beginning of the year 1850 was observed by the Minnesota Historical Society, then only a few months old, with special exercises held in the Methodist Church of St. Paul. The Reverend Edward D. Neill, an active member of the new society, delivered an address "which was not merely instructive, but thrillingly eloquent," on the "French Voyageurs to Minnesota during the Seventeenth Century," and a band from Fort Snelling provided music. "Write your history as you go along, and you will confer a favor upon the future inhabitants of Minnesota," advised Neill. A gay New Year's ball at Shakopee in 1856 was given for the benefit of a missionary, Samuel W. Pond, and his home mission work. "I had nothing to do with it but to share in the spoils with the Fidler," was Pond's somewhat apologetic comment on the affair. On New Year's Day, 1878, a steamboat left the landing at St. Paul for a river excursion to Fort Snelling, its decks crowded with passengers clad in linen dusters and carrying palm-leaf fans. It may be imagined, however, that underneath the dusters were heavy, warm coats. The excursion was planned by a St. Paul real-estate dealer, who took advantage of unseasonable weather to advertise the Minnesota climate and "to deceive the eastern public into the belief that orange trees and magnolias are in full bloom in a Minnesota January as a regular thing." [15]

The traditional American custom of issuing a carriers' greeting at New Year's, long established by newspapers of the Atlantic coast, was adopted in pioneer Minnesota at an early date. On January 7, 1853, the *St. Anthony Express* circulated an "Address of the Carrier of the St. Anthony Express to His Patrons." In doggerel verse, the newsboys of the little community that is now a part of the city of Minneapolis voiced their hopes for the future:

> When five thousand souls our streets shall throng;
> And no one doubts but what they will ere long;
> We hope to leave you still the weekly news,
> To write your verses and collect our dues.

A *Carriers' Address to the Patrons of the St. Paul Daily Press* issued in 1866 expressed the gratitude "Of countless thousands that the war was done," and told of

> . . . that horrible and dark eclipse
> When, by a dastard's hand, our martyred chief
> Was foully murdered!

An *Annual Address* distributed by carriers of the *St. Paul Pioneer* in 1867 spoke of a beautiful dream, in which a "guardian spirit" announced to the carrier:

The happy scenes thus pictured on New Year,
Reflect the homes which take THE PIONEER.

The optimism of postwar Minnesota is reflected in the following lines:

Our busy merchants scarce find leisure
To send to bank their surplus treasure.
Mechanics, laborers, lawyers too,
Find work enough for all to do,
(Doctors sedate must find it funny,
That they alone can't make much money.) [16]

By the middle 1860s holiday celebrations in Minnesota were being influenced by people other than those from New England and the East. Europeans from England, Germany, and the Scandinavian countries were settling in the North Star State by the thousands, and each group brought from the homeland its own method of celebrating the winter holidays. Hugo Nisbeth, a Swedish traveler who visited Minnesota in 1872, commented: "It is not only the Scandinavians who celebrate Christmas here in America in a true ancient northern fashion, but even the Americans themselves have in late years begun to give more and more attention to this festival of the children and have as nearly as possible taken our method of celebration as a pattern." He drove out onto the prairie near Litchfield, where he spent the Christmas holiday with one of his countrymen who was living in a sod house, built half above and half under ground.

Upon his return to Sweden, Nisbeth published a book about his travels in which he told about the frontier festivities. The day before Christmas was spent in preparing for the celebration; among other things a "small sheaf of unthreshed wheat was set out for the few birds that at times circled around the house, in accordance with the lovely old Swedish custom." As in the fatherland, the principal celebration took place on Christmas Eve. "There was no Christmas tree, for fir trees are not yet planted in this part of Minnesota," he recorded, "but two candles stood on the white covered table and round these were placed a multitude of Christmas cakes in various shapes made by the housewife and such small presents as these pioneers were able to afford, to which I added those I had brought." Nisbeth was disappointed because the traditional Swedish Christmas dishes, *lutfisk* and rice porridge, were not served, but he observed that the "ham which took the place of honor in their stead banished all doubt that the settler's labor and sacrifice had not received its reward." After the meal the children were given their presents. "The gifts were neither costly nor tasteful, but they were *gifts* and that was all that was necessary," remarked Nisbeth. He related that "on the wooden horse I had brought, the little three-year-old galloped over the hard-packed dirt floor of the sod house with as much joy and happiness undoubtedly as the pampered child upon one polished and upholstered." [17]

The Christmas customs of the French-Canadian, of the New Englander and the Easterner, of the Scandinavian and the German, and of various other Europeans are among the contributions these groups have made to Minnesota life. They transplanted, too, scores of other national practices and characteristics, which, modified by the new environment, make up the social fabric of the North Star State.

The Hutchinson Family in the Story of American Music

PHILIP D. JORDAN

MANY THREADS have gone to make up the fabric of Minnesota, and the pattern has not always been woven within the limits of the state or the region. This article, published in June, 1941 (volume 22) deals with a colorful family singing group of the nineteenth century which carried its own brand of entertainment across America and helped shape the nation's cultural growth. The family's link with Minnesota was unique: it left an imprint upon the state's map as well as upon its music. Philip D. Jordan pursued his interest in the Hutchinsons beyond this paper, which he presented as an address before the ninety-second annual meeting of the Minnesota Historical Society in 1941. His book entitled Singin' Yankees *(1946) told their story in full. Among the many other works authored by Mr. Jordan, who is professor of history in the University of Minnesota, are* The National Road *(1948),* Uncle Sam of America *(1953), and* The People's Health: A History of Public Health in Minnesota to 1948 *(1953).*

TO ST. PAUL, a city bearing the proud name of a little wilderness mission church, have come through the years many men. Here black-robed Jesuits intoned the Mass; dragoons of the army of the West grounded their muskets; Indians, daubed with black and vermilion, sullenly trod frontier streets; fur trappers, with short pipes in clenched teeth, swung bales of green hides; and Mississippi River gamblers, thin-lipped, with derringers up their handsome broadcloth sleeves, shuffled cards to the musical clink of bottles. Men of America were all these. But perhaps the strangest were the Hutchinsons, the men with the high-standing collars.

John, Judson, and Asa Hutchinson, of a famous troupe of family singers from New Hampshire, first arrived in St. Paul early in November, 1855. On Friday, the sixteenth, they left Minneapolis with two wagons and four horses to explore McLeod County in the vicinity of

107

the Hassan River, now known as the South Fork of the Crow River. There they selected a site for the future town of Hutchinson. On December 2, 1857, Judge Charles E. Flandrau gave public notice of the entry of the town. Previously, however, the Hutchinsons with eleven others had organized the Hutchinson Company, an association of joint stockholders with elected officials whose duties were clearly and legally defined.

Briefly, the company was to promote settlement, apportion land among emigrants, reserve certain lots for schools and churches, and maintain order. Liquor was forbidden, as were bowling alleys, billiard tables, and gambling devices of all types. On November 21, 1855, it was voted at Glencoe that women residents of Hutchinson "shall enjoy equal rights with men and shall have the privilege of voting in all matters not restricted by law." Perhaps this was the first application of the women's rights principle in the Territory of Minnesota. The *St. Anthony Express* commented as follows upon the Hutchinson colonization project: "With a clear sky above, the rich land below, we may expect to see in a short time a large town built up in Hutchinson." The community did thrive, despite the Indian uprising of 1862, and today it stands as a fitting tribute to New Englanders who recessed from singing long enough to father a community in Minnesota.

The three Hutchinson brothers responsible for this project were little known in the Minnesota region. There they were only another factor exerting itself in the great migration of the 1850s. But in the world at large — in New England, New York, Pennsylvania, Ohio, Illinois, and even in Ireland, Scotland, and England — the Hutchinsons had won acclaim before the middle of the century as the most prominent troupe of family singers on tour. It was not until the era of President Jackson that folklore, narrative, and legend indigenous to American experience became popular. Then, of course, there tumbled from pens of particularistic authors a host of plots, characters, and scenes that truly reflected the democratic pith of the times.

At least thirty itinerant bands, including the Baker, Hughes, Thayer, Cheney, Peak, Orphean, and Hutchinson families, were delighting American audiences a century ago in one- and two-night stands. In Minnesota, they gave concerts in St. Paul, Hutchinson, Little Falls, and Rochester, to mention but a few places. They sang in theaters, churches, schools, and even on the streets. The Druid Horn Players, "dressed in the costume of the ancient priests of Old Britain," attracted huge crowds; and members of the Old Folks Concert Troupe of thirty mixed voices clad themselves in the styles of 1760. The concerts usually were advertised by local newspapers, by handbills, and not infrequently by one or more members of the troupe parading through a town. A Kilmiste family performance was announced by an older player who walked the streets with a chicken feather in his hat and made a "donkey of himself."

Such American troubadours, colorful in long-tailed blues, became ideal interpreters of American life. They sang about America for Americans. They answered the criticism of the supercilious *New York Mirror,* which, in 1839, asked, "When shall we have in America a characteristic national music?" They justified the faith of the *Springfield* [Ohio] *Republic,* which declaimed that true American music will "partake of our free air, and of the free thought of our glorious land — and it will not swell in sounds alone as does that imported from France and Italy; but in words as well as tones, it will have thought in it." Family concerts contained little of the operatic, less of the classical, and none of the mystical. Rather, they emphasized the melodramatic, the comic, and the sentimental. Programs included songs that were robust, told a story, or pointed a moral. The chorals, hymns, anthems, and glees were sung in a simple, unaffected way with emphasis upon clearly enunciated words. Frequently the performers sang *a cappella.*

Among the more prominent itinerant family singers interpreting the spirit of the times in music were the renowned Hutchinsons from New Hampshire, the "Old Granite State." "The magic of their inspiring melody once felt, can never be forgotten," wrote a Minnesota editor. From the time of their first concert in 1839, the Hutchinsons were constantly in the news and were considered the type example for similar bands. They wrote more original words and composed more music than did any other troupe. It was not until 1843, however, that Judson, John, Asa, and sister Abby felt sufficiently assured to leave their native state. Finally, friends persuaded them to attempt a program in New York City. With timid faith they arranged for their debut in the Broadway Tabernacle, where many concerts were given. Success was immediate. "The immense audience," noted the *New-York Tribune,* "were perfectly delighted and could scarcely be prevailed upon to release them from constant duty. We have seldom listened to sweeter melody than theirs."

Nearly all the Hutchinsons' programs began or ended, as did concerts of most other group singers, with a family song which commonly sketched their origin, early life, and principles. In St. Paul, late in 1855, the Hutchinsons began their program with such a song, "The Old Granite State."

Ho! we've come from the mountains,
We've come down from the mountains,
    Of the old Granite State.
We're a band of brothers.
We're a band of brothers.
We're a band of brothers.
    And we live among the hills;
        With a band of music,
        With a band of music,
        With a band of music,
    We are passing round the world.

Our dear father's gone before us,
And hath joined the heavenly chorus,
Yet his spirit hovers o'er us,
    As we sing the family song.
        Oft he comes to hear us,
    And his love doth cheer us,
        Yes, 'tis ever near us,
    When we battle against the wrong.

We have four other brothers,
And two sisters, and aged mother;
Some at home near each other,
Some are wandering far away,
    With our present number.
There are thirteen in the tribe;
    'Tis the tribe of Jesse,
And our several names we sing.

David, Noah, Andrew, Zepha,
Caleb, Joshua, and Jesse,
Judson, Rhoda, John and Asa,
And Abby are our names.
    We're the sons of Mary,
        Of the tribe of Jesse,
        And we now address ye,
    With our native mountain song.

Liberty is our motto,
And we'll sing as freemen ought to,
Till it rings o'er glen and grotto,
    From the old Granite State.

"Men should love each other,
Nor let hatred smother,
EVERY MAN'S A BROTHER,
AND OUR COUNTRY IS THE WORLD!"

And we love the cause of Temperance
As we did in days of yore;
We are all Tee-totlers,
And determined to keep the pledge.
Let us then be up and doing,
And our duties brave pursuing,
Ever friendship kind renewing
As we travel on our way.
Truth is plain before us,
Then let's sing in chorus,
While the heavens o'er us
Rebound the loud huzza.
Huzza! huzza! huzza!

The second number on a typical family program usually was a dramatic and colorful narrative, having as its theme some horrible human tragedy. Americans enjoyed this type of song, and two groups, the Bakers and the Hutchinsons, specialized in it. Frequently, these troupes selected the "Vulture of the Alps," described in contemporary handbills as a "thrilling song portraying the agonized feelings of a parent at the loss of an infant child, snatched suddenly from its companions by the ravenous vulture." Even today a slight tremor rides through the body at the first two lines.

One cloudless Sabbath summer morn, the sun was rising high,
When from my children, in the lawn, I heard a fearful cry.

"The Maniac," describing the "progress of insanity," offered opportunity to yowl and figuratively to tear at asylum chains. The refrain, "No, by heaven, I am not mad," rolled forth in bloodcurdling screams. It was a breath-taking performance, leaving singers, as well as audience, exhausted. Two other clamorous numbers were "The Great Railroad Wreck" and "The Ship on Fire." The latter began with a tremendous thunderstorm, with passengers and crew on bended knee, and ended with the vessel bursting into flame. It was strong stuff, so realistic, indeed, that in Canton, Pennsylvania, one Dutchman, overcome by the song, forgot himself, rushed from the theater, yanked an alarm, and had fire engines in the streets before the singers could stop him.

In 1861, during a private White House concert, Lincoln, holding Tad by the hand, requested that "The Ship on Fire" be sung.

For a concert in New York on May 17, 1843, the Hutchinsons chose another lamentable tale — "The Snow Storm" by Seba Smith — now quite forgotten, but then a favorite narrative. It told of the sufferings of a mother who, in 1821, wandered with her child over the Green Mountains in search of a husband whom she later found frozen to death.

> The cold wind swept the mountain's height,
> And pathless was the dreary wild,
> And mid the cheerless hours of night,
> A mother wandered with her child.
> As through the drifted snows she pressed,
> The babe was sleeping on her breast,
> The babe was sleeping on her breast.
>
> And colder still the winds did blow,
> And darker hours of night came on,
> And deeper grew the drifts of snow,
> Her limbs were chilled, her strength was gone.
> "O God!" she cried, in accents wild,
> "If I must perish, save my child,
> If I must perish, save my child."

Then, the audience having wetted the programs with sentimental tears, tragedy turned to fun. Horror was usually followed by a type of backwoods humor, not too rough, but with a pronounced element of the exaggerated ridiculous. Many songs of this kind were performed in hundreds of concerts, in the effete East, on the western plains, and even on the mining and cattle frontiers. "One always feels better for having laughed," noted a Minnesota editor, "almost to the destruction of waist-bands, vest buttons, and lacings."

"Ten years ago you knew me well," sang the Bakers, "but now true love is past, and I must answer no." There was a nice young man who courted a daughter fair and stole the family silver. Another affable rogue taught a Sabbath school class and ogled every lass. And the tragic tale of Johnny Sands who neatly disposed of Betty Hague is well known to many music lovers. "Not Married, Yet," first published in 1841, began plaintively, "I'm single yet — I'm single yet — Ye gods, what are the men about."

Another example of the humorous song is "Squire Jones'es Daughter," which was sung by Whitehouse's New England Bards and is, in parts, suspiciously reminiscent of "Oh! Susannah." "Bobbin' Around," a celebrated Yankee song of 1855, brings into music the literary characters of Josh and Sal, a "gal" whose beauty could not be judged by externals. "For I Should Like to Marry," the duet which follows, exemplifies a whole group of songs.

GENT

Yes! I should like to marry,
If that I could find
Any pretty Lady,
Suited to my mind:
Oh! I should like her witty,
Oh! I should like her good,
With a little money,
Yes, indeed I should.
Oh! I should like to marry,
If that I could find,
Any pretty Lady,
Suited by my mind.

Oh! I should like her hair
To cluster like the vine;
I should like her eyes
To look like sparkling wine:
And let her brows resemble
Sweet Diana's crescent;
Let her voice to me
Be always soft and pleasant.
Yes I should, etc.

LADY

Oh! I should like to marry,
If that I could find
Any handsome fellow,
Suited to my mind:
Oh! I should like him dashing,
Oh! I should like him gay,
The leader of the fashion,
And dandy of the day.
Oh! I should like to marry,
If that I could find,
Any handsome fellow,
Suited to my mind.

> Oh! I should like his hair
> As "Taylor's" wigs divine
> The sort of thing each fair
> Would envy being mine.
> He mustn't be too short;
> He mustn't be too burly;
> But slim, and tall, and straight,
> With moustache and whiskers curly.

None knew the value of satire better than did the Baker, Peak, and Hutchinson families, and scarcely a program lacked their cutting tributes to contemporary follies. The pomposity of waxworks proprietors, traveling showmen, militiamen, and the modern belle all were castigated. But bitter scorn, it seems, was reserved for Congressmen and physicians. "The Congressional Song of Eight Dollars a Day" was a favorite.

> At Washington full once a year do politicians throng,
> Contriving there by various arts to make their sessions long;
> And many a reason do they give why they're obliged to stay,
> But the clearest reason yet adduced is *eight dollars a day.*

The attack upon the medical profession is aptly illustrated by two old favorites, one ridiculing the prevalent custom of prescribing mighty doses of calomel and the other describing medical students whose Latinish prescriptions seem to have had only one translation — "gin." "Calomel" begins and ends with the following verses:

> Physicians of the highest rank
> To pay their fees we need a bank,
> Combine all wisdom, art and skill,
> Science and sense in Calomel.

> And when I must resign my breath,
> Pray let me die a natural death,
> And bid the world a long farewell,
> Without one dose of Calomel.

"O, Stay," the maiden said, "and rest thy weary head upon this breast." Longfellow's "Excelsior" perhaps sets the pattern for the hundreds of love scenes and sentimental ditties of the middle years. Shy maidens, "simpering, sniggling, and smiling," are really too abundant, and brave swains lurk almost everywhere. Bachelors lamented:

Who sets for me the easy chair,
Sets out the room with neatest care,
And lays my slippers ready there?

And 'Zekiel was, well —

'Zekiel crept up quite unbeknown
    And peeked in through the winder,
And there sat Hulda, all alone,
    With no one nigh to hinder.

Sometimes, as in the "Humbugged Husband," sung in the 1840s by Jesse Hutchinson, true love cries piteously:

'Tis true that she has lovely locks,
    That on her shoulders fall —
What would they say to see the box
    In which she keeps them all.
Her taper fingers it is true
    Are difficult to match:
What would they say, if they but knew
    How terribly they — s-c-r-c-h?

But perhaps a gardener, who has a sense of humor, tells his sad story best of all in the "Horticultural Wife."

She's my myrtle, my geranium,
My sunflower, my sweet marjorum;
My honeysuckle, my tulip, my violet;
My hollyhock, my dahlia, my mignonette.
    Ho, ho! she's a fickle wild rose,
    A damask, a cabbage, a China rose.

She's my snowdrop, my ranunculus,
My hyacinth, my gilliflower, my polyanthus;
My hearts-ease, my pink, my water-lily;
My buttercup, my daisie, my daffydowndilly
    Ho, ho! etc.

We have grown up together, like young apple trees
And clung to each other like double sweet peas;
Now they're going to trim her, and plant her in a pot
And I am left to wither, neglected and forgot.
    Ho, ho! etc.

> I am like a bumble-bee, that don't know where to settle,
> And she is a dandelion, and a stinging nettle:
> My heart's like a beet root, choked with chickweed;
> My head is like a pumpkin running off to seed.

Long before "Father, Dear Father, Come Home with Me Now" was composed by Henry Clay Work and published by Root and Cady in 1864, temperance songs were upon nearly every musical program presented by bands of family singers. The Cheney and Hughes families were particularly arid, and the Bakers specialized in the "Inebriate's Lament." Antialcoholism was part of the singers' stock in trade, and they belabored the cup that cheers with vigor. Indeed, one of the first public appearances of the Hutchinsons was before the American Temperance Union in New York. Back and forth across the nation from Boston to Leavenworth, sometimes traveling with John Henry W. Hawkins, father of the Washingtonians, a temperance society organized in Baltimore in 1840, and sometimes with John B. Gough, famous temperance orator, they described luridly the sot who dissipated his wages, kicked his children, and beat his wife. Tavern keepers dreaded the sight of handbills announcing concerts by these unbridled prohibitionists. They detested such titles as "Don't Marry a Man if He Drinks," "Father's a Drunkard and Mother Is Dead," and "The Temperance Deacon." Local temperance societies, on the other hand, welcomed them and churches opened wide their doors, secure in the knowledge that "King Alcohol" would be dethroned. Sons of Temperance, ladies' temperance unions, and cold-water principles were the rule of the day.

> Oh! cold water, pure cold water,
> Raise the shout, send it out,
> Shout for pure cold water.

"Which Way Is Your Musket A-pinting To-day?" stimulated perhaps by a tour through Iowa in 1880, rapidly caught temperance acclaim and was included in many prohibition songbooks.

> The issue before us is plain and unclouded —
>   Shall our nation be ruled by King Alcohol's sway?
> I candidly ask every qualified voter
>   "Which way is your musket a-p'intin' today?"

But of all the antisaloon songs which flooded the nation between

1830 and 1850, none stands out clearer and is more typical than "King Alcohol," written to commemorate the conversion into a temperance hall of old Deacon Giles's distillery in Salem, Massachusetts. It was sung in Rochester and elsewhere when the Hutchinsons were on tour in Minnesota.

> King Alcohol is very sly
>   A liar from the first
> He'll make you drink until you're dry,
>   Then drink, because you thirst.
>
> King Alcohol has had his day
>   His kingdom's crumbling fast
> His votaries are heard to say
>   Our tumbling days are past.
>
> The shout of Washingtonians
>   Is heard on every gale
> They're chanting now in victory
>   O'er cider, beer, and ale.
>
> For there's no rum, nor gin, nor beer, nor wine,
>   Nor brandy of any hue,
> Nor hock, nor port, nor flip combined
>   To make a man get blue.
>
> And now they're merry, without their sherry
>   Or Tom and Jerry, champagne and perry
>   Or spirits of every hue.
> And now they are a temperate crew
>   As ever a mortal knew.
> And now they are a temperate crew
>   And have given the devil his due.

No narrative of the spirit of mid-century America in music would be complete without mention of the vast song literature which pictured the great trek westward. Audiences listened breathlessly to fascinating tales of the weary emigrant, to fabulous accounts of the California discoveries, and to stirring recitals of the overland trail. Later, Kansas emigrant aid societies and "Pike's Peak, or Bust" were to find expression in song. Sang the members of one traveling troupe:

> Cheer up, brothers, as we go
> O'er the mountains westward ho!

> When we've wood and prairie land
> Won by our toil
> We'll reign like kings in fairy land
> Lords of the soil.

The Hutchinsons, composing a song to honor a Massachusetts band of forty-niners, expressed the great American belief in Sacramento gold riches.

> As the gold is *thar,* most any *whar,*
> And they dig it out with an iron bar,
> And where 'tis thick with a spade or pick,
> They can take out lumps as *heavy as brick.*

Some traveling troupes and lone artists reached San Francisco to perform in rude amusement centers. Their songs, commented an English journal of 1850, "are universally popular, and the crowd of listeners is often so great as to embarrass the players at the monte tables and to injure the business of the gamblers."

But it remained for Captain George W. Patten of the Second United States Infantry, author of *Voices of the Border,* to pen a typical tragedy of manifest destiny and of the "shining land where the gold-mines lay." Patten was stationed at Forts Ripley and Ridgely in Minnesota and at Fort Abercrombie in Dakota before the Civil War. In the early 1850s Patten's command was stationed at Fort Miller, near the San Joaquin River, to protect emigrants who were crowding the California trails on their trek to the diggings. One evening, so Patten tells, a family of gold seekers, exhausted and starved, arrived at the banks of the swollen San Joaquin. The mother had been buried on the plains. Within a short time an infant and its sister also died, "leaving the disconsolate father to prosecute his further journey to the gold mines alone." Patten added that the last words of the dying emigrant child were to be conveyed to the "ear of the world through the medium of song." When George P. Reed of Boston published Patten's delineation of the episode in 1853, with music and piano accompaniment by "an Amateur," its success was immediate. Abby Hutchinson frequently included it on her programs. "The Emigrant's Dying Child" is a sentimental interpretation of the hardships endured on the overland trail.

> Father, those California skies
> You said were bright and bland,
> But where tonight my pillow lies,
> Is this the land of Gold?

'Tis well my little sister sleeps
Or else she too would grieve,
But only see how still she sleeps
She has not moved since eve.

And when you pass this torrent cold,
We've come so far to see,
And when you go on beyond for Gold,
O think of Jane and me.

The Hutchinsons, after an extended tour of England and Ireland in 1845, gave much of their time to the abolition movement, a cause in which they had been interested for many years. They popularized the "Emancipation Song," "The Slaves' Appeal," and "Little Topsy's Song."

They were intimate friends, as well as co-workers, of William Lloyd Garrison, Gerrit Smith, Wendell Phillips, and other leaders of the antislavery group. "We were inspired with the greatness of the issue," wrote John Hutchinson, "finding our hearts in sympathy with those struggling and earnest people . . . and we sang for the emancipation of the millions of slaves in bondage." The "Negro's Lament" was one of the most popular of their selections.

Forced from home and all its pleasures,
    Africa's coast I left forlorn,
To increase a stranger's treasures,
    O'er the raging billows borne.
Men from England bought and sold me,
    Paid my price in paltry gold;
But though slave they have enrolled me,
    Minds are never to be sold.

This was first sung at a meeting of the Boston Antislavery Society in Faneuil Hall in January, 1843. "The powerful description of the singing of the wonderfully gifted Hutchinsons," ran a comment in the *Liberator* of Boston on February 24, 1843, "does not surpass the reality of their charming melodies. The effect on the thousands who listened to them was, in fact, indescribable. They added immensely to the interest of the occasion; and the manner in which they adapted their spirited songs (nearly all of which were original and impromptu) to the subjects that were under discussion displayed equal talent and genius."

Perhaps the most famous of all the antislavery songs in the Hutchinson repertoire was the stirring and dramatic "Get Off the Track." The words were written by the Hutchinsons and adapted to an old slave melody. After its introduction in 1844, it became, with *Uncle Tom's Cabin*, among the more powerful instruments aimed at the Southern slave system.

> Ho! the car emancipation,
> Rides majestic through the nation,
>   Bearing on its train the story,
>   Liberty! a nation's glory.
>   Roll it along! Roll it along!
>   Roll it along! through the nation,
> Freedom's car, Emancipation.
>
> Let the ministers and churches
> Leave behind sectarian lurches,
>   Jump on board the car of freedom,
>   Ere it be too late to need them.
>   Sound the alarm! Pulpits thunder,
>   Ere too late to see your blunder.
>
> Hear the mighty car-wheels humming:
> Now, look out! the engine's coming!
>   Church-and-statesmen, hear the thunder
>   Clear the track, or you'll fall under.
>   Get off the track! all are singing
>   While the "Liberty Bell" is ringing.

N. P. Rogers first heard this song in 1844. "It represented the railroad," he wrote in the *Herald of Freedom* in June, 1844, "in characters of living light and song, with all its terrible enginery and speed and danger. And when they came to the chorus-cry that gives name to the song — when they cried to the heedless proslavery multitude that were stupidly lingering on the track, and the engine 'Liberator' coming hard upon them, under full steam and all speed, the Liberty Bell loud ringing, and they standing like deaf men right in its whirlwind path, the way they cried 'Get Off the Track,' in defiance of all time and rule, was magnificent and sublime."

When, however, slaveholders would not "get off the track," the Hutchinsons did their bit to further the conflict by popularizing "The Battle Cry of Freedom" until it was "soon shouted in camps, on the march, and on the battlefield." Nor was this enough. John Hutchinson determined to take his singers into the camps of the Army of the Potomac. Unfortunately, however, they included in their programs Whittier's stirring "Ein feste Burg ist unser Gott," an inflammatory abolition poem set to the music of Luther's great hymn. General McClellan thereupon expelled the singers from the Union lines on the ground that abolition was not the primary object of the war. Undaunted, the troupe appealed to Lincoln. Secretary Chase, it is said, read in a cabinet meeting the lines judged offensive by McClellan. Lincoln listened attentively and then is reputed to have said, "It is just the character of song that I desire the soldiers to hear." By presidential order, therefore, the Hutchinsons were readmitted to Union camps and barracks.

Musical America was not unmindful of America, the land of promise, and of America, the strong. Patriotism could not be denied the composer, and songs praising victory and liberty and country probably begin with John Dickinson's "The Liberty Song, or In Freedom We're Born," written in Massachusetts early in 1768. The Yankee war song of the Revolution entitled "The American Hero, or Bunker Hill," written by Nathaniel Niles, originally appeared as a broadside in 1775.

As colonial conflicts passed into the dimming long ago, jauntier melodies replaced the ponderous harmonizing of the academic era. One must not forget "Corn Cobs or Yankee Notions," a folk development derived from the earliest version of "Yankee Doodle." The words of "Corn Cobs or Yankee Notions" were first printed in the *American Comic Songster* for 1834. Ballads, such as "Old Colony Times," became popular. The first stanza was sung from Maine to Georgia, and at least as far west as Nebraska.

> In good old Colony Times,
> When we were under the King,
> Three roguish chaps fell into mishaps,
> Because they could not sing.

The nineteenth century saw a tremendous increase in sectional and patriotic songs. Every artist strove to place at least one song of "God and Country" upon his program. They were not difficult to find. The *United States Songster*, published in 1836, lists fourteen, among them "The Star Spangled Banner," "Hail Columbia," "The Hunters of Kentucky," "The Boys of Ohio," and "All Hail to the Brave and Free."

Not until the roaring 1840s did a pronounced element of humor creep into this type of song. During this decade almost countless compositions based upon differences in geographic areas were published and included on concert programs. Henry W. Dunbar's "We've Left Our Mountain Home" and "The New England Farmer" frequently were listed as favorites. Typical of the lighter songs springing from the rich sources of Yankee ingenuity is "Away Down East." It tells of a man from Indiana who "took his bundle in his hand to seek this fabled land." And what a land it was, "a place of applesauce and greens, a paradise of pumpkin pies, a land of pork and beans!" Little wonder that the weary Hoosier remained forever in regions "Away Down East," whetting his jackknife and consuming apple brandy.

"Uncle Sam's Farm" was dedicated to "all creation" by Jesse Hutchinson and was published by Reed at Boston in 1850. The verses which follow invite the people of the world to share the personal freedom and the rich treasures of the United States.

> Of all the mighty nations in the East or in the West,
> The glorious Yankee nation is the greatest and the best;
> We have room for all creation, and our banner is unfurled,
> With a general invitation to the people of the world.
>   Then come along, come along, make no delay,
>   Come from every nation, come from every way;
>   Our lands they are broad enough, don't feel alarm,
>   For Uncle Sam is rich enough to give us all a farm.
>
> St. Lawrence is our Northern line, far's her waters flow,
> And the Rio Grande our Southern bound, way down in Mexico.
> While from the Atlantic ocean, where the sun begins to dawn,
> We'll cross the Rocky Mountains far away to Oregon.
>
> While the South shall raise the cotton, and the West the corn and pork,
> New England manufacturers shall do up the finer work;
> For the deep and flowing water-falls that course along our hills,
> Are just the thing for washing sheep and driving cotton mills.
>
> Our fathers gave us liberty, but little did they dream
> The grand results to follow in the mighty age of steam;
> Our mountains, lakes, and rivers, are now in a blaze of fire,
> While we send the news by lightning on the Telegraphic wire.
>
> While Europe's in commotion, and her monarchs in a fret
> We're teaching them a lesson which they never can forget;
> And this they fast are learning, Uncle Sam is not a fool,
> For the people do their voting, and the children go to school.

Songs such as those mentioned reflect the spirit of American life. They sing of a brave people and of a great democracy. The faded sheet music of yesteryear is a key to the nation's past. Social historians now search for tunes sung by the Hutchinsons and other traveling family troupes, for they are eager to capture the spirit of the nineteenth century and to gain an insight into the life of the common man.

Health and Medicine in Rochester, 1855-1870

HELEN CLAPESATTLE SHUGG

READERS OF Minnesota History *during its first half century have been treated to numerous articles which demonstrate how much local history can contribute to an understanding of state and national trends. This article is an outstanding example of the worth of local material in the hands of a skilled and imaginative writer, for it deals with frontier medicine in a town which was to become a world-famous medical center. It appeared in September, 1939 (volume 20), two years before Helen Clapesattle's internationally known study of* The Doctors Mayo *was published. At that time, Miss Clapesattle was assistant editor of the University of Minnesota Press. In 1944 she became its editor in chief, and from 1953 to 1956 she was its director. Now Mrs. Roger W. Shugg, she resides in Chicago.*

SINCE THE TURN of the century, when the amazing achievements of the Mayo brothers began to attract observers and reporters, the "paradox of Rochester" has been a theme for many writers.[1] Here is a sophisticated, cosmopolitan city with some ten hospitals, thirty hotels, and other buildings near skyscraper size, a city on whose streets mingle great and small from all nations, a city that houses the world's largest medical clinic — and that city not Minneapolis, or Chicago, or some populous center on the eastern seaboard, but a little river valley town in midwestern America, away from the beaten trails of travel, among the cornfields, dairy farms, and market villages of southern Minnesota. That is the paradox. As one writer rhetorically phrased it, "Rochester . . . only a pin point on the maps of commerce, but a starred capital on the charts of medical science."

That is Rochester now, and it makes us wonder about Rochester then, in its early years, before the Mayo Clinic, or even the Mayo practice from which this institution has grown, dominated the city's activities and its fame. During the decade and a half from 1855 to 1870,

Rochester grew from a stagecoach station consisting of a few rough shacks in the underbrush on the banks of the Zumbro into a busy, booming town of about four thousand inhabitants. In the first years it was merely an ambitious village in the trade area tributary to the towns on the Mississippi where the steamboats stopped. Its location at the heart of the system of river valleys that veins the fertile acres of Olmsted County made it a natural center for the everyday trade of the vicinity, but the larger commerce flowed to and from Winona, Lake City, Wabasha, Minneiska, or Reads Landing.

Then settlement thickened and the railroad came. Rochester read its future in the caravans of prairie schooners that rolled slowly through the town, often to camp on the outskirts in a lively mixture of children, cows, and horses around the wagons and the cooking fires before moving on to homes in the hinterland. The weekly newspaper added a column or two of special news for Irish readers, and one of the storekeepers wrote a postscript to his advertisement: "German, Norwegian, Swedish, and Danish spoken at our store." When at last in the fall of 1864 the railroad, moving westward from Winona, reached Rochester and a grain elevator was built alongside the tracks, the farmers forsook the road to the river towns for the shorter one to Rochester. Pioneer businessmen, restless, always watching for new promising locations, got the "Rochester emigration fever." Coming from near and far, they helped to build warehouses, open banks, and establish wholesaling firms. Soon Rochester had become a grain market and distributing center of enough importance to command the attention of trade journals and manufacturers in Milwaukee and Chicago.

Those were the days when wheat ruled Rochester. Wheat yields and wheat prices determined its prosperity. During the middle 1860s harvests and the machines to handle them were increasing; productive soil, a demand for wheat, and competition among buyers made profits high. In the fall, or when sleighing was good in the winter, the roads into Rochester were lined with a procession of farmers on the way to dump their loads of grain into the wide-mouthed hoppers of the elevator. They and their wives and daughters, who had come along "to do a little trading," thronged the streets and the stores. Wheat buyers and speculators helped to fill the hotels and saloons, often to overflowing. Later in the decade, when glut and monopoly had rounded the corner, Rochester was an outstanding center in the "people's movement" that demanded legislation to relieve the pressure of hard times.

When the district court was in session or when it was time for taxpaying, the settlers roundabout drained into Rochester, the county seat, making their business the occasion for a holiday. State and county fairs brought crowds so in excess of the available accommodations that visitors slept on straw in the churches and paid fifty cents a night for the privilege. State conventions met there too — fraternal orders, schoolteachers, church leaders, temperance enthusiasts, spiritualists. Fourth of July celebrations, horse races, baseball games, Masonic festivals, and exhibitions by the Turnverein drew spectators from a wide area. Word went out that Rochester was a paradise for shows and showmen, and all sorts came — circuses, menageries, magicians, minstrel troupes, and musicians. Concerts by artists like the Black Swan, a popular Negro contralto, and Ole Bull, the Norwegian violinist, brought listeners from places as far away as Mantorville, Kasson, Owatonna, and even Winona — because, commented the Rochester reporter loftily, the residents there were "not content to endure the inconvenience incident to such small places in being deprived of first-class entertainments." [2]

In short, early Rochester was a flourishing district capital, both economic and social. It was therefore also a promising center for the practice of medicine, for the people were quite likely to seek their doctors where they found their supplies and their amusements.

What need had they for doctors? That is not such an idle question as it may seem, for early Rochester and its vicinity were a community of pioneers, and part of the halo of romance with which we have framed the pioneers is an impression of their vigor, endurance, and robust health. That idea is not justified by the facts available. If the early settlers were a youthful people and therefore strong, they were also prodigal of their health and strength in their struggle with frontier conditions. Overexertion and overexposure, poor sanitation and careless hygiene, ignorance and superstition worked their customary harm, and the pioneers recorded aches and pains, plagues and accidents they suffered.

Early Rochester seems to have known most of our common ills. Many diseases were not yet clearly differentiated and frontier physicians were not greatly concerned about medical nomenclature, so that it must be left to the medical men to guess what specific ailments were meant by such general diagnoses as congestion of the brain, inflammation of the bowels, heart disease, spine disease, lung complaint, and fever. But rheumatism, pleurisy, dropsy, neuralgia, pneumonia, apoplexy, dysentery, and cancer appear in the records by name. Coughs and colds and croup kept the children out of school. Measles, mumps, whooping cough, diphtheria, typhoid fever, and smallpox struck in recurrent epidemics. [3] What were called cholera morbus and cholera infantum appeared frequently. And on one occasion yellow jaundice was so prevalent that visitors remarked about the number of saffron faces they saw on the streets.

The more malignant of the epidemic diseases worked a frightful havoc when they appeared. Diphtheria and typhoid fever in particular sometimes wiped out entire families in a few weeks. Not infrequently the deaths of two, three, or even four members of one household were reported in the same obituary column. But it seems to have been the threat of smallpox that caused the greatest panic, perhaps because it was known to be contagious. How to prevent it by vaccination was also generally known, and one writer remarked that a smallpox scare now and then was a good thing, because it sent the whole community to the doctor to be vaccinated.

Since such scares, however, smallpox or any other kind, were not good for business or immigration, sickness in Minnesota was like the ague in Indiana, "always somewhere else." Its presence in a town was usually left unreported until it was gone or until some rival town got word of it and gleefully published the damning news. Then the local editor denied the report if possible or at least tried to minimize it. Sometimes the charges and countercharges were bitter. In January, 1864, a returning soldier traveling through Rochester was taken ill at one of the hotels. After waiting three days the proprietor called a doctor, who pronounced the case smallpox. Amid great excitement the man was quickly moved to an empty log cabin a mile away, where he later died. Then the *Rochester City Post* reported the incident briefly, congratulating the city that no further cases had appeared.

But sensational rumors spread, and the Owatonna and Chatfield papers published them. In righteous anger they told how the "heathen" of Rochester had allowed the man to freeze to death through neglect and exposure, how they had let his body lie for several days until it was stiff and then had buried it by sticking it feet foremost into a swamp and tapping it on the head with a fence post driver. "Satan would despise one of his associates who would treat one of his imps thus," they said. Indignantly the Rochester papers made what denial they could. The man had not been neglected. He had been moved because the hotel was crowded and prompt action was necessary to prevent the spread of the disease, but the city fathers had hired a nurse to take care of him. Perhaps the house they moved him to was not just the place for a sick man in cold weather, but they could hardly be blamed for not anticipating the unusual cold spell that followed. Perhaps the low temperatures had accelerated his death, but as for the story of his burial, that was too absurd to need refuting. It was just a malicious attempt to spread reports prejudicial to Rochester.[4] Whatever the truth in this incident, instances of panic-stricken cruel neglect of those ill with small-pox and cholera were not uncommon on the Minnesota frontier.

A real smallpox epidemic came in the winter of 1868–69. Early in 1868 a public-spirited citizen of Grand Meadow, near High Forest, sent a warning to the people of Rochester. There was smallpox in his neighborhood, he said. Some of the townsmen were trying to check the pestilence by making everyone who had it stay at home. But most of the residents were Scandinavians, and they had an idea that if God intended a man to die of smallpox there was no use in his trying to avoid it. So they were going about from house to house without con-cern, and some of them were even insisting upon making an overnight visit to Rochester. The disease did not appear there, however, until late in the year. This time the city council authorized the construction of a pesthouse, a "city hospital" they called it, at a cost of fifteen hundred dollars, but the worst of the epidemic was over before the building was ready for use. Again neighboring papers spread the story, to the serious detriment of business in Rochester. The local editors did their best to still the panic with soothing items for their country readers, who had been "unnecessarily alarmed" and whose "wrong impressions" they desired to correct. They accused their rivals of deliberately encouraging a scare in order to further their own interests at Rochester's expense.[5]

The excitement did not subside until April, 1869 — only to be fol-lowed by a siege of measles, whooping cough, cholera morbus, and typhoid fever. In fact, 1869 is one of the two years in the sixties that especially deserve the name of "sickly season." The other was earlier, in 1863. At the end of that year the editor pointed out that the unusual mortality of the past year, due doubtless to the unseasonable weather, had made the cemetery dear to many, and that therefore it ought to be fenced in and improved in appearance.[6]

Effective measures for the prevention and control of epidemics were lacking. Their coming waited upon the passing of individualism in matters of health and upon the advance of medical science to explain the methods and agents of infection. It is difficult to determine what the state of opinion about the cause of disease was in the Rochester community. Many laymen seem to have agreed, more or less definitely, with the Scandinavians of Grand Meadow that pestilence was an act of God which they could do little to prevent. Others made wild guesses at more material causes. They said, for instance, that typhoid fever came from old wallpaper left hanging one layer upon another, or that the prevalence of diphtheria was due in part to the fumes given off by kerosene lamps when their owners tried to save oil by turning them low. Since at that time few learned men of medicine accepted the theory of personal infection, it could hardly have been general in Rochester; yet the instances of panic and of attempts at isolation show that the view was present in practice.

Perhaps the most widespread explanation for the cause of epidemics, and one more fruitful in effects than scientifically accurate, was the theory of miasmata. These were thought to be poisonous substances, effluvia, rising from stagnant water or putrid matter like an imperceptible gas, floating in the air, especially in night mists, and generating disease. This theory, old in the literature of epidemiology, seems to have become current on the American frontier as an explanation for the incidence of malaria near the marshes and low-lying river bottoms of the states bordering the Ohio and the lower Mississippi, but it was also made to account for many other diseases, both communicable and not. Minnesotans used it to explain the healthfulness of their climate: moisture being the main vehicle for these atmospheric poisons, "perturbation of the air" dispelling them, and low temperatures destroying them, Minnesota's dry, windy, and cold climate was peculiarly inhospitable to miasmata.[7]

An editor of the *Rochester Post,* probably J. A. Leonard, who was once a doctor, confessed to skepticism about this miasma theory. He quoted approvingly from a correspondent who thought the pollution from filthy cellars and outhouses went down, not up; who described how it seeped down through a few feet of loose soil to the impervious limestone table and then flowed along to pour itself into nicely drilled wells, from which it was pumped up, "a clear solution of all this nastiness" to flavor the Mocha or the oyster stew.[8] It is too bad the name of that correspondent was not preserved, for he was a broad jump ahead of most of his neighbors.

Whatever Leonard's own ideas, he and his colleagues made good use of the miasma theory to persuade their fellow citizens to clean up Rochester. They warned unceasingly about the danger of disease arising from common "nuisances": the cows and pigs and sheep that ran loose, fouling the city thoroughfares; the pools that stood undrained in cellars or vacant lots; the piles of filth and offal that accumulated in the streets and alleys, in the pigpens and stables, around the slaughterhouses, and on the river banks.

The Rochester charter of 1858 had given the city council power to abate such nuisances and to create a board of health, but except for some little-heeded ordinances against cows and pigs running at large, nothing was done until June, 1864. Then the stench from twenty dead horses dumped on the river bank without burial brought so many complaints that the council was moved to action. It named three laymen to a board of health, with orders to remove all nuisances without delay, and at the same time declared all slaughterhouses within the city limits to be nuisances. The objectionable carcasses were quickly removed, but there activity apparently stopped. A year later, after the citizens had petitioned the council for the "abatement of nuisances in the city prejudicial to health," another board was appointed, three doctors this time, but results were as conspicuously absent as before. Finally, when rumors came that cholera was abroad in 1866, an ordinance was passed providing for a permanent board of health, its members, two doctors and one layman, to be appointed annually. A companion ordinance gave the board orders and authority to clean up the city's filth. Perhaps the activity of this board helped Rochester to escape the cholera that year. There was one death from the disease, but the victim was a passing immigrant and no further cases were reported.[9]

One other factor that cannot be ignored in considering the state of health in early Rochester is the fact that Minnesota was then one of America's sanatoria for tuberculars, or consumptives, as they were called. However preposterous the booster's claims for the curative powers of Minnesota's climate may seem to us now, there is no disputing the fact that many persons within the state and in the East believed those claims and acted on their belief. Invalids suffering from lung and bronchial complaints made up an appreciable element in Minnesota's population — and, it must be admitted, in her graveyards. There is ample testimony to this fact. A Boston journalist traveling through the state wrote that he was surprised at the agriculture and industry he found, because, he said, he had been "accustomed to think of Minnesota as a State peopled with men and women in the last stages of consumption." When Horace Greeley came to speak at the state fair in 1865, he wrote to the *Tribune:* "There are hundreds here — perhaps thousands — who came to save their lives, and all insist that the climate is an antidote to pulmonary affections. . . . Many are well here who believe they would have been dead years ago had they remained at the seaboard." One of those believers wrote with less restraint: "Minnesota all the year round is one vast hospital. All her cities and towns, and many of her farm houses, are crowded with those fleeing from the dread destroyer. . . . Ask any man you meet in Minnesota what induced him to come here. One-half, at least, will tell you it was for the health of himself or some member of his family."[10]

There is some reason to believe that Rochester even then was attempting to specialize as a resort for these health-seekers, but whether that or not, it got its share of those who came, for it was one of the more easily accessible spots in the state away from the crowded hotels and boardinghouses in St. Paul, which the invalids were advised to avoid. Some of the visiting consumptives stayed with resident friends or relatives, others took rooms at a hotel or boardinghouse, and a few lived in the home of the local doctor whose professional skill they trusted to aid the climate in making them whole again. An amusing bit of evidence of the presence of such persons in Rochester is the advertisements directed to them. One dry goods store, for example, called to the special attention of "Invalids" its sale of double-breasted red flannel underwear, and another promised "Consumption Cured — Saved from Death and the Doctors" to the women who wore its "Kid-Fitting Skeleton Corsets."

If the age of the pioneers was not unusually healthy, neither was it enviably safe. The pace of living may have been slower and the peril to life and limb less unnerving, but the age had its own dangers. There was, for instance, the new and imperfect kerosene lamp, which frequently exploded, throwing its blazing liquid over anyone within range. There was the hot coal stove or the open fireplace, which surprisingly often set fire to the mother's clothes as she got too close while cooking dinner or rocking the baby to sleep. On Rochester streets there was the hazard of uncovered cellar openings which strangers or unwary homefolk stumbled into at night. And there were countless horses that kicked, or threw their riders, or upset buggies and cutters and sent the occupants to the doctor. It was an accident of this kind that gave the newspapers their first bit of copy about William J. Mayo, when he was only eight years old. The *Rochester Post* told how "Willie" Mayo's pony had bolted, throwing its rider off and breaking his arm, how the boy had remounted and ridden home, alone, to get his father's ministrations. Surely the mishap was not the rider's fault, however, for only a year later he won second place at the county fair in a trial of horsemanship.

The greatest cause for concern was the many accidents with the new farm machines, for the farmers and their wives seem to have been slow to learn that moving mechanisms do not yield to human bodies. The most troublesome contrivance was the tumbling rod between the horsepower and the separator in the threshing machine. Its turning knuckles took relentless hold of any loose sleeve, billowing skirt, or flapping trouser leg that came near it. So numerous and sometimes horrible were the accidents from this source that in 1868 the state legislature passed a law requiring all owners or operators of threshing machines to enclose the tumbling rod in a wooden case. But the law was observed in the breach, even by those it was designed to protect, and threshing machine disasters multiplied.[11] The whirring knives of the reapers, too, were hard on feet or fingers that got in their way. In 1870 a writer from Rochester to the *Saint Paul Daily Press* reported: "We hear of an unusual number of accidents occurring from malmanagement of those in charge of reapers, etc. The maimed from carelessness would crowd the largest hospitals in New York or Chicago. Dr. Cross and other surgeons are engaged night and day." [12]

By no means all these ills and accidents meant cases for the practicing physicians. The many miles that so often separated patient from doctor and a suspicion that doctors did more harm than good, surviving from the then recent days of heroic dosage and copious bloodletting, had taught laymen to prescribe for themselves. Knowing what to do for the family fevers and bruises was a part of mother's job, and if the illness was too acute for her to handle she could call upon some community grandmother, wiser still in the ways of plasters and poultices. Together they sometimes performed great feats of healing. Only as a last resort, usually, did they send a messenger for the doctor.

For chronic ailments, when home remedies had failed to give relief, there was an endless supply of nostrums waiting on the druggists' shelves. Each of the innumerable balsams, compounds, pills, powders, liniments, and tonics whose advertisements filled the columns of the early papers was warranted to work miracles in an incredible assortment of ills. Hamlin's Wizard Oil, for example, would cure everything from bunions to diphtheria; Dr. Poland's White Pine Compound was a sure specific for all lung complaints and kidney diseases; Dr. Smith's Electric Oil would quickly soothe a teething baby, or in only a few more applications banish the worst case of rheumatism or erysipelas.

Sometimes the proprietors were lyrical in their claims. One of them wrote: "Millions of people whose lives appeared to be at the last ebb, worn out by fever's consuming fires, by consumption's insidious advances, by racking torments of inflammatory rheumatism, have been cured by the use of Brandreth's Pills." Another was moved to verse:

> Light shall again the faded eye relume,
> And rosy health the faded cheek resume.
> The deaf shall hear, the trembling limb be strong,
> And groans of anguish mellow into song.

The less scrupulous vendors were clever in devising tricks to part the fool and his money. One such trick, fairly common, may be illustrated by the scheme of the Reverend Edward A. Wilson. (In this type the advertiser was always a minister, a returned missionary, or a Bible salesman.) In a modest card he announced that having been restored to health by a simple remedy after several years' illness from consumption, he was anxious to share his good fortune with fellow sufferers. To all who wished it and would send him their address, he would return a copy of the prescription free of charge. His only object was to spread information that would be a blessing to the sick. After the card had been running for some weeks, the Rochester editor exposed the racket. A "verdant friend" of his had sent for the prescription, but when it came he found it contained several ingredients so rare that no Rochester druggist had ever heard of them. In case this should be so, the Reverend Mr. Wilson generously offered to send the dry ingredients for three dollars and thirty cents or a bottle of the liquid for four dollars, express unpaid.[13]

The battle of the 1860s was among the bitters. There was a host of them contending for the right to heal the dyspeptic's stomach and improve his disposition. There were Red Jacket Stomach Bitters and Wahoo Bitters, both resting their claims on Indian formulas; Swain's Bourbon Bitters, especially for the "delicate tastes" of the ladies; Hoofland's German Bitters, warranted to relieve depression of spirits for whichever side should suffer defeat in the coming election; and Dr. Walker's California Vinegar Bitters, a "true root and bark medicine," not a "vile, fancy drink" like other bitters, "sweetened and spiced to please the taste and lead the tippler on to drunkenness."

Rochester entered the lists with a contestant of its own, the Gopher State Bitters. The formula was Dr. A. T. Hyde's and it was manufactured and sold by Daniels and Company, grocers and druggists of Rochester. It had a notable success for a time, took a first prize at the Minnesota State Fair, and won enough reputation outside the state (if a Chicago newspaper is to be believed) to contest the market in Chicago with the celebrated and firmly established Hostetter's Bitters of Pittsburgh. Rochester was proud of its bitters, and for a long time their price of eight dollars per case was listed in the market quotations along with the prices of wheat, flour, hides, and wool.[14]

If the balsams and the bitters failed the sufferer, he could resort to one of the traveling physicians of sundry kinds who went from town to town, staying at each for a few days or weeks and then moving on before their powers were tried too far. They all went to Rochester, sometimes three or four of them at once. Some of them announced specialties — in diseases of the eye and ear, the heart, the lungs, or the feet — and these might be accepted as legitimate practitioners, journeyman predecessors of the modern specialist, had they not claimed so much and bragged so loudly.

More spectacular were the various healers who claimed supernatural powers. Some of these must have found the people of Rochester unresponsive, for they had been disillusioned by one of this kind. Dr. William P. Duvall, the "Natural Healer and Practical Physician of the Western Healing Institute," had come to Rochester fresh from triumphs in St. Paul and Winona. He had issued a two-page supplement to both local newspapers, telling the stories of his cures and describing his method of healing. He used neither medicines nor instruments, only the natural healing power he had been exercising for thirty years. The patient had merely to sit calmly for a few minutes and all pains and ailments would pass away. In certain specified diseases several treatments might be necessary, but for most of them one would suffice. Dr. Duvall had been at work in Rochester only a few days before he had added some of the city's well-known residents to the list of those bearing public witness to his powers.

But from Rochester Dr. Duvall moved on to Owatonna, where after a brief courtship he married a local belle. A few weeks later, in Janesville, Wisconsin, Mrs. Duvall died. A post-mortem examination revealed a lethal dose of strychnine, and investigation disclosed that all three of Dr. Duvall's former wives had died under similarly suspicious circumstances. He was tried for murder, convicted, and sentenced to life imprisonment. Then the Rochester papers, wise after the event, said he had only pretended to cure by his "senseless mummery" over the patient, that he had "fleeced a great many credulous people out of their hard-earned dollars." [15]

Such quacks were numerous and successful in the day of the open door in medicine. Anyone who wished could add "M.D." to his name and enter into practice; no one had legal authority to question his qualifications, for all but three of the states having restrictions on medical practice had repealed them during the first half of the nineteenth century. The reason for this was a complex of circumstances. The laity, in reaction against the puking, purging, and bleeding that had become the rule in medical practice, were ready to turn a willing ear to the doctrines of such medical sects as the homeopaths and the eclectics and such health cults as hydropathy and Grahamism, which had sprung up to contest the place of the regular profession in the popular favor. The latter was ill equipped for the struggle. Medical science had progressed far enough to discredit old systems and theories, but had not yet developed a body of tested knowledge and practice to take their place; and the ranks of the profession were filled with poorly trained practitioners, turned out by the proprietary medical colleges, many of them little more than "diploma mills," which had been established in the Middle West to meet the demand for doctors on a rapidly expanding frontier.

Moreover, that was the period marked by "the rise of the common man," and the democratic Americans who could see no need for the trained person in government were not likely to appreciate his worth in medicine. Add to these factors the jealous individualism that could find only selfish and mercenary motives in any demand for the regulation of medical practice, and the reason for the fate of regulatory legislation becomes clear. The upshot was a period of uncertainty and confusion, in which the only way of judging a physician was by his fruits in practice. There were about as many irregular practitioners as regular, and the boundary between the two was indefinite and shifting. Most laymen employed one as readily as the other — and the quack as readily as either.

After the Minnesota State Medical Society was reorganized in February, 1869, it gave considerable time to the question of quackery. At its first session the following resolution was adopted: *"Resolved, By the State Medical Society assembled, That in case the Legislature now assembled, desire to protect the citizens of this State from quackery, it is the duty of this Society to co-operate with the Legislature, and lend its assistance in framing all needful laws upon the subject; and that Drs. Willey, Sheardown and Stewart, be appointed a committee as the organ of the Society, for this purpose."* [16]

The sequel might be guessed. The legislature of 1869 passed "An act to protect the people of Minnesota from empiricism and imposition in the practice of medicine." This made it unlawful for anyone to practice medicine in Minnesota unless he had graduated from a two-year medical course or could show a certificate of qualification from some state, district, or county medical society. But the sponsors of the bill had failed to include adequate means for its enforcement, they had not guarded sufficiently against the fake sheepskins of the diploma mills, and they had not considered how easy it would be for the irregular sects to organize medical societies and issue certificates of qualification. (The eclectic physicians, for instance, immediately gathered at Owatonna to organize the Minnesota State Eclectic Medical Society, of which Dr. N. S. Culver of Rochester was made secretary.) Either because of these defects or because of public opinion that the bill was "class legislation" for the sole benefit of the profession — a charge vigorously denied at the state society's annual meeting in 1870 — the law was considered a failure, and at the next session of the legislature the doctors worked as hard to get it repealed as they had to get it passed. They succeeded, and nothing more was done to standardize medical practice by law in Minnesota until 1883.[17]

The various medical sects were all represented in early Rochester, the homeopaths in particular being very popular. Their status in the community and in the profession is illustrated by the story of the Drs. Cross. Dr. Edwin C. Cross came to Rochester in 1858. He had received his training at the best of the eastern medical schools, but he announced himself as a "homeopathic and hydropathic physician and surgeon." His practice grew, so that in 1860 his brother, Dr. Elisha W. Cross, came to work with him, and the Cross brothers established what might, by a sizable stretch of the imagination, be considered Rochester's first clinic. They called it the Rochester Infirmary. They had bought a store building on Broadway and furnished it with "all the appliances afforded by similar institutions in the largest cities."

Patients needing surgical treatment were invited to the infirmary where, they were assured, they would find a full supply of surgical instruments made to order for the Drs. Cross by the best of French instrument makers. The doctors would take care of surgical cases either at the infirmary or at the patient's home, and they promised special attention to persons coming from a distance. Dr. E. C. Cross offered his personal services in cases of "the sore eyes incidental to this climate" and guaranteed "Prairie Itch cured or your money refunded." The infirmary was also a dispensary for the little white homeopathic pills, the thirty-four kinds of which could be bought individually or in ready-made assortments for family use.

But the specialty at the infirmary was baths — "Shower Baths, Full Baths, Half Baths, Sitz Baths, Douches, Plunges, and all other Baths necessary for the treatment of diseases . . . fully supplied with an abundance of *Pure Soft Water*, at any required temperature. . . . Also Vapor Baths, pure or medicated, for the treatment of diseases of the skin." There were special bathing apartments for the ladies, and the proprietors generously announced that their soft water baths were "open to the healthy public for the purposes of cleanliness, whenever they may choose to use them." During the hot summer months the local editor recommended the shower baths at the infirmary, along with the soda fountain at the drug store, as an aid in keeping cool. By 1866 the brothers had parted company professionally and the Rochester Infirmary had disappeared from notice in the papers, but Dr. E. C. Cross was advertising a "medical institute" that sounds much like the old infirmary and was publicly defending homeopathy as a branch of medical science.[18]

Their advertising, if not their homeopathic and hydropathic practice, might stamp the Drs. Cross as irregular practitioners today, but not so then. They had the most extensive and profitable practice, probably, in all southern Minnesota; they were both appointed to medical positions with the Union forces in the Civil War; they were active members of the Olmsted County Medical Society; and they were admitted to membership in the state society in 1870.

The careful public impersonality of present-day doctors was not maintained in the 1860s. Most reputable physicians limited their paid advertising to a simple business card stating their system of practice and their office address, but they all told the editor about their accident cases or unusual operations. Few issues of the Rochester papers in the late 1860s were without one or more accident stories in which the name of the attending physician was given, along with a brief statement of the treatment or operation necessary and the patient's condition. Unfortunately for the historian, this custom of "reporting cases to secular journals" was frowned upon by the medical societies and so gradually died out.

These newspaper notices provide good evidence of Rochester's position as a center for the practice of medicine and surgery, for cases were reported from all over Olmsted County and from across the lines in Dodge, Fillmore, and Steele counties. Sometimes the Rochester doctor had been called in consultation, or to perform an operation the local doctor did not feel equal to. But often the patient himself had sent a messenger directly to Rochester to bring the doctor whose success he had read about in the paper, or had heard about, perhaps from some neighbor or some friend in town the last time he was there.

There is not time to discuss the methods of medicine and surgery then, and there probably is no need, for so much has been written lately about the horse-and-buggy doctor, his kitchen surgery, and preantisepsis methods. The Rochester doctors were of their time in that respect. They operated under whatever makeshift arrangements could be devised in the patient's home or in a room of some city boardinghouse. They usually used an anesthetic, but not always. Their surgery was still largely of the emergency sort, a weapon of necessity not of choice, a way of staving off death not of securing health. A few of them might on rare occasions perform a tonsillectomy, remove a cancerous sore, or tap a tumor; but most of them limited their operations to reducing dislocations, trephining for fractures, setting bones, and amputating mangled or gangrenous members. Especially the last. They resorted to amputation so often that persons with missing extremities must have been commonplace in the community.

A number of these Rochester men were professionally alert and exerted themselves to keep up with the new developments in medical and surgical science. At least three of them spent a winter in New York attending lectures and clinics; several were active in the state medical association; and they tried having a society of their own. The birth year of the Olmsted County Medical Society is usually given as 1882, but there was an earlier organization. It was formed in 1868 with half a dozen Rochester doctors as members. After its first session, at which the principal business was the adoption of a common bill of prices, activity lapsed until the spring of 1869. Then the society was very active for several months, holding sessions every two weeks at which papers were read and discussed. To one familiar with the programs of present-day medical meetings, the topics of those papers may seem queer. Dr. William W. Mayo read the first two, on the "Progressive Creation of Life." A few weeks later Dr. E. C. Cross contributed one on the "Origin and Distribution of the Human Race," and at the next session Dr. Mayo read Professor Thomas H. Huxley's lecture on the "Physical Basis of Life." One is tempted to guess that those medical brethren were debating evolution, then the newest thing in scientific theories. There was also a paper on "Electricity and Lightning Rods" and one on "Inventions," the latter by John H. Whitney, a Rochester inventor who had been made an honorary member of the society. He was reported to have described an "entirely feasible appliance for aerial navigation." There were papers on medical topics too, one by Dr. Hector Galloway on the "Philosophy of Disease," in which he made the interesting prediction that medical science would someday discover ways to cure all diseases but cancer.[19]

This story of health and medicine has an intrinsic appeal, both for those who are interested in the history of Rochester and for those who are curious about the ways of life in an earlier day. But it has significance too, for it suggests what the next decades were to make clear, that early Rochester was a potential medical center and that it may therefore have contributed in some measure to the seeming paradox of Rochester today.

When America
Was the Land of Canaan

GEORGE M. STEPHENSON

THE HISTORY OF IMMIGRATION and immigrant groups oc-
cupies many pages in the thirty-nine volumes of Minnesota History.
No statement concerning it is more poignant than this account by
George M. Stephenson, in which he lets the Swedish writers of
"America letters" describe in their own words the forces that drew
them across the sea and their reactions to the new land. Research for
this paper, which was published in September, 1929 (volume 10), was
done during the two preceding years, while Professor Stephenson was
studying in Sweden on a Guggenheim Foundation fellowship. A mem-
ber of the history faculty in the University of Minnesota from 1918 to
1952 and a Fullbright lecturer in various Swedish universities after his
retirement, he was the author of eleven books, including A History of
American Immigration, 1820–1924 *(1926) and* John Lind of Minnesota *(1935). Professor Stephenson died in 1958 at the age of seventy-*
four.

VOLUMES HAVE BEEN WRITTEN on the causes of emigration
from the various countries of Europe to the United States, and it may
appear superfluous to add to the numerous articles that have appeared in print.[1] A plethora of emigration statistics is available;
monographs have appeared by the score; and it would seem that the
subject has been attacked from every conceivable angle. But the historical profession still awaits the man with the magic touch, who by a
process known only to the master can convert this tremendous mass of
material into a masterpiece of historical synthesis. This master must
sound the depths of the human soul, and he must analyze the noblest
as well as the basest emotions that play on the human heart. He will
not concern himself with the people on whom fortune has smiled
graciously, nor will he relate the exploits of the battlefield and portray

the lives of kings and nobles; he will study the documents that betray
the spirit, hopes, and aspirations of the humble folk who tilled the soil,
felled the forest, and tended the loom — in short, who followed the occupations that fall to the lot of the less favored majority that exists in
every land.

Emigration from Sweden was a class movement that spread from
the rural districts to the cities and towns. The fever sought its victims
among those who were not inoculated with the virus of social distinction and economic prosperity; and when the epidemic was transported
three thousand miles across the water, it took a more virulent form.
In fact, it was transmitted most effectively by the thousands of letters
that found their way from America to the small red cottages hidden
among the pine-clad, rocky hills of Sweden.

It has become a commonplace that emigration from Sweden began
in earnest after the close of the American Civil War, when, according
to a newspaper account published in 1869, "the emigrants, as if by
agreement, gathered from the various communities on certain days,
like migratory swallows, to leave, without apparent regret, the homes
and associations of their native land, in order to begin a new life on
another continent." [2] Statistically this statement is accurate enough,
but historically it is entirely misleading. Emigration from Sweden began
in earnest in the decade of the 1840s, when the first "America letters"
found their way back to the old country. These letters made a tremendous impression on certain persons at a time when a new world —
a new and ideal world — was dawning in literature and in the press.[3]
Into this realm of the idealist the "America letters" fell like leaves from
the land of Canaan. They were not only read and pondered by the
simple and credulous individuals to whom they were addressed, and
discussed in larger groups in homes and at markets and fairs and in
crowds assembled at parish churches, but they were also broadcast
through the newspapers, which, unwittingly or not, infected parish
after parish with the "America fever." The contents of these documents from another world were so thrilling and fabulous that many
editors were as glad to publish them as were the recipients to have
them published. The result was that the most fanciful stories were circulated about the wonderful country across the Atlantic — a land of
milk and honey.

A correspondent from Linköping wrote to a Jönköping paper in
May, 1846, as follows: "The desire to emigrate to America in the
country around Kisa is increasing and is said to have spread to neighboring communities. A beggar girl from Kisa, who has gone up into

the more level country to ply her trade, is said to have painted America in far more attractive colors than Joshua's returned spies portrayed the promised land to the children of Israel. 'In America,' the girl is reported to have said, 'the hogs eat their fill of raisins and dates that everywhere grow wild, and when they are thirsty, they drink from ditches flowing with wine.' Naturally the gullible *bondfolk* draw the conclusion from such stories that it is far better to be a hog in America than to be a human being in Sweden. The emigration fever seizes upon them, and the officials are so busy making out emigration permits that they cannot even get a night's rest." [4]

One cannot escape the suspicion that this beggar girl from Kisa had read or had heard discussed a letter written at Jefferson County, Iowa, on February 9, 1846, by Peter Cassel, who the previous year had led a party of twenty-one emigrants — men, women, and children — from this parish. The departure of this man in his fifty-sixth year at the head of a large company of emigrants — large for that time — created a sensation in his parish and in neighboring parishes; and information about his adventure was eagerly awaited by his large circle of friends and relatives. And they were not disappointed. In describing the wonders of America, Cassel's pen vied with Marco Polo's. Iowa's corn, pumpkins, and hogs, seen through the medium of his letters, appeared as monstrous to the peasants of Sweden as Gulliver to the inhabitants of Lilliput; and in contrast with the earnings of the American farmer the income of the Swedish husbandman shrank to insignificance. Even the thunder in Sweden sounded like the report of a toy pistol, compared with the heavy artillery of the heavens in America.[5]

In his first letter Cassel wrote thus: "The ease of making a living here and the increasing prosperity of the farmers . . . exceeds anything we anticipated. If only half of the work expended on the soil in the fatherland were utilized here, the yield would reach the wildest imagination. . . . Barns and cattle sheds are seldom, if ever, seen in this vicinity; livestock is allowed to roam the year around, and since pasturage is common property, extending from one end of the land to the other, a person can own as much livestock as he desires or can take care of, without the least trouble or expense. . . . One of our neighbors . . . has one hundred head of hogs. . . . Their food consists largely of acorns, a product that is so abundant that as late as February the ground is covered in places. . . . Corn fields are more like woods than grain fields."

This *bonde* (landowning farmer) not only was impressed with America's rich soil, its forests, its abundance of coal and metals, its rivers and lakes swarming with fish, but also wanted his friends at home to know that in other respects he had found a better world: "Freedom and equality are the fundamental principles of the constitution of the United States. There is no such thing as class distinction here, no counts, barons, lords or lordly estates. . . .[6] Everyone lives in the unrestricted enjoyment of personal liberty. A Swedish *bonde,* raised under oppression and accustomed to poverty and want, here finds himself elevated to a new world, as it were, where all his former hazy ideas of a society conforming more closely to nature's laws are suddenly made real and he enjoys a satisfaction in life that he has never before experienced. There are no beggars here and there never can be so long as the people are ruled by the spirit that prevails now. I have yet to see a lock on a door in this neighborhood. . . . I have never heard of theft. . . . At this time of the year the sap of the sugar maple is running and we have made much sugar and syrup." [7]

If the beggar girl from Kisa had heard this letter read and discussed by simple-minded folk, little wonder that her imagination ran away with her. Surely Joshua's spies could not have found a more ideal land if they had gone to the ends of the earth. And this girl was not the only purveyor of "information" about America. In many parishes stories were current that in Gothenburg there was a bureau that provided emigrants with all the necessities for the journey — free of charge; that several vessels were waiting to transport emigrants to the promised land — also free of charge; that in two days enough money could be earned to buy a cow that gave fabulous quantities of milk; that all pastures were common property; that the grass grew so tall that only the horns of the grazing cattle were visible; that there were no taxes in that fortunate land; that rivers ran with syrup; that cows roamed at large and could be milked by anyone.[8]

There may have been occasional "America letters" published in the newspapers of Sweden prior to 1840, but they were rare, chiefly because the few Swedes in America were usually adventurers or deserters from vessels, who did not find it expedient to let their whereabouts be known. The interest of the press in these letters began with the publication in *Aftonbladet,* in January, 1842, of a long letter from Gustaf Unonius, a young man who had received some notice as the author of a volume of poems before emigrating with his bride and a few of the "better folk" in the early autumn of 1841. He used the columns of this widely read Stockholm daily to inform his friends and acquaintances, especially in and around Upsala where he had been a student, about his experiences in the new world.

Unonius was essentially a student and his letters were carefully phrased, with the advantages and disadvantages of America weighed in the balance; but he could write after a residence of one month in Wisconsin that it was unlikely that he would ever return to his native land, because he found his youthful dream of a republican form of government and a democratic society realized. He found no epithets of degradation applied to men of humble toil; only those whose conduct merited it were looked down upon. "Liberty still is stronger in my affections than the bright silver dollar that bears her image," he wrote. Three months later he could write: "I look to the future with assurance. The soil that gives me sustenance has become my home; and the land that has opened opportunities and has given me a home and feeling of security has become my new fatherland." The readers of his letters learned that the young idealist, seeking to escape from the trammels of an older society, had found something that approached a Utopia on the American frontier, although his writings about it resembled more the reflections of a man chastened by unaccustomed toil and hardships than the song of a pilgrim who had crossed the river Jordan.[9]

Within a few weeks an emigrant who preceded Unonius to Wisconsin by three years was heard from through the same journalistic medium, the man to whom the letters were addressed having been prompted to publish them by reading the Unonius document. The writer was John Friman, a member of a party consisting of a father and three sons, who settled at Salem, Wisconsin Territory, in 1838. The serious illness of the youngest son necessitated the return to Sweden of father and son, but the eldest son remained to carry on the correspondence with the "folks back home." [10]

In a later letter the young pioneer told about his first meeting with Unonius in the latter's home at New Upsala: "We are healthier and more vigorous than we ever were in Sweden. Many people from England and Ireland have already come here. Last fall, in October, a few Swedes from Upsala came here from Milwaukee, Mr. Gustaf Unonius and wife, married only six weeks when they left Sweden. A relative, Inspector Groth, and a Doctor Pålman have settled on a beautiful lake near a projected canal, twenty-eight miles west of Milwaukee, Milwaukee County. They have named the settlement New Upsala *and the capital of New Sweden in Wisconsin*. They are expecting several families and students from Upsala this summer. . . . I visited New Upsala last fall. They wanted me to sell out and move there. Father has probably heard of them. Last fall Unonius wrote to *Aftonbladet*. I

hope his letter will awaken the desire to emigrate among the Swedes.
. . . Altogether we own two hundred acres of land, and when we have
our farm fenced and eighty acres broken . . . I wouldn't trade it for
a whole estate in Sweden, with all its ceremonies. Out here in the woods
we know nothing of such. . . . Give our love to Herman and say to
him that we hope his health will be better than it was the first time he
was here." [11]

Herman's health was restored sufficiently to enable him, in company
with a young man from another city, to undertake the journey to the
"states" a few weeks later. Imagine the sorrow of the father when he
received a letter informing him that Herman had entirely disappeared,
his companion, who had arrived at the Friman farm in due time, being
unable to give a satisfactory explanation of the mystery.[12] The public in
Sweden was informed of the misfortune through the publication of the
letter in the papers, and interest was even more quickened by the letter from the father of the companion, answering *seriatim* the charges
of the elder Friman brother that Herman was the victim of mis-
placed confidence in his fellow traveler; [13] for weeks thousands eagerly
searched the columns of the papers for the latest word about "brother
Herman." The wonderful adventures the prodigal son related when he
finally accounted for himself at the Friman farm not only cleared the
name of his companion and relieved the anxiety of both fathers, but it
gave to the "America letters" a halo of romance that made them, in
a very real sense, news letters from the rich, mighty, and romantic land
out there in the West.[14] The muse of history suffers no violence by the
assertion that one of the most interesting and widely read features of
the Swedish papers were the "America letters."

In that unique and valuable work that emerged from the survey of a
commission appointed by the Swedish government to seek out the
causes of emigration, appeared a volume entitled "The Emigrants' Own
Reasons," comprising letters written at the request of the commission
by Swedish immigrants who had lived a longer or shorter period in the
United States and Canada.[15] These letters have their value, but it must
be recognized that the writers unconsciously injected into them the
retrospections of several months or years. There is, therefore, a vast
difference between these letters and the "America letters" — naïve
accounts of experiences written for relatives and friends, who were as
simple and naïve as the writers themselves, and before retrospection
had wrought its havoc. It is just this "unconscious" and naïve quality
of the "America letters" that opens for the historian windows through
which he can look into the cottages in Sweden and into the log cabins

in the adopted country. The student of emigration who is satisfied with poring over statistics, government reports, and "social surveys" will never sound the depths of one of the most human phenomena in history. The much-abused psychologist in this instance is an indispensable colaborer with the historian, for the theme of the historian of emigration is the human soul. The emigrant was a product of his environment, but he was not held in bondage by it; his soul could not be shackled, even though his body was the slave of harsh taskmasters.

In the large the contents of the "America letters" written in the years from 1840 to 1860 may be divided into two categories: (1) impressions of and experiences in America; and (2) comments on conditions in Sweden. With the exception of a few letters written by men of the type of Gustaf Unonius, the great mass of them were the products of men who had only a meager education and who grew to manhood before the generation that enjoyed the advantages provided under the act of 1842, by which every parish was required to provide a public school. The spelling is faulty, to say the least, and the punctuation is atrocious. New York becomes "Nefyork" and "Nevyork"; Chicago, "Sikago" and "Cicaga"; Illinois, "Elinojs"; Iowa, "Adiova" and "Jova"; Pennsylvania, "Pensarvenien"; Galesburg, "Gillsborg" and "Galesbury"; Albany, "Albano" and "Albanes"; Troy, "Troij"; Princeton, "Princeldin"; Rock Island, "Rockislan" and "Räckarlan"; Peru, "Pebra" and "Perru"; and Henry County, "Hendi counti." Not only were liberties taken with American place names but even many innocent Swedish words were mutilated beyond recognition.

But the person who has the patience to spell his way through a mass of these documents cannot fail to acquire a profound respect for the ability of the writers to express themselves and for their sound and wholesome instincts. They reveal that in their native land they had thought seriously, and even deeply, about their own problems and those of their communities — probably more than they or their neighbors at the time realized; but it was during the first weeks and months in America that they gave vent to their feelings and emotions and tried the powers of expression that had previously lain dormant. America gave them a basis for comparison and contrast: church, government, society, and officials at home appeared in an entirely different light; and the contrast was such that the emigrant had no desire to return in order to relate to his countrymen his strange experiences; on the contrary, he did all in his power to urge them to follow his example — to emigrate. The emigrant became an evangelist, preaching the gospel of America to the heavy-laden. For him the year of jubilee had come.

There are, of course, among the "America letters" that have been preserved a number that express regret that the transatlantic adventure was undertaken and reveal a feeling of bitterness towards those who had painted America in such attractive colors and in that way had lured the writers into poverty and misery; but the overwhelming number of them are almost ecstatic in praise of the adopted country and bitterly hostile to the land that gave them birth. Some writers even went to the length of ridiculing or deriding those to whom their letters were addressed for remaining in a land unworthy of the man and woman of honest toil and legitimate ambition.

Extracts from two letters written before 1850 are illuminating in this regard: "I doubt that any one will take the notion of returning to Sweden, because the journey is too long and expensive; and even if these considerations were minor with certain individuals, I doubt that they would go, for the reason that nothing would be gained. . . . Not until this year have I fully realized how grateful we ought to be to God, who by His grace has brought us away from both spiritual and material misery. How shall we show our appreciation for all the goodness the Lord has bestowed upon us! In like manner does He bid you, my relatives and friends, to receive the same grace and goodness, but you will not heed His voice. What will the Lord render unto you now? He will allow you to be deprived of all this during your entire lives and in the future to repent bitterly of your negligence. We have the word of prophecy . . . and you will do well to heed it. . . . Ought not a place of refuge and solace be acceptable to you? . . . Now I have said what my conscience prompts me to say and on you rests the responsibility for yourselves and your children." [16]

The other letter contains the following admonition: "Tell Johannes . . . and others not to condemn me for failing to return home at the appointed time, as I promised and intended when I left Sweden, because at that time I was as ignorant as the other stay-at-homes about what a voyage to a foreign land entails. When a person is abroad in the world, there may be many changes in health and disposition, but if God grants me health I will come when it pleases me. If it were not for the sake of my good mother and my relatives, I would never return to Sweden. No one need worry about my circumstances in America, because I am living on God's noble and free soil, neither am I a slave under others. On the contrary, I am my own master, like the other creatures of God. I have now been on American soil for two and a half years and I have not been compelled to pay a penny for the privilege of living. Neither is my cap worn out from lifting it in the presence of gentlemen. There is no class distinction here between high and low, rich and poor, no make-believe, no 'title sickness,' or artificial ceremonies, but everything is quiet and peaceful and everybody lives in peace and prosperity. Nobody goes from door to door begging crumbs. . . . The Americans do not have to scrape their effects together and sell them in order to pay heavy taxes to the crown and to pay the salaries of officials. There are no large estates, whose owners can take the last sheaf from their dependents and then turn them out to beg. Neither is a drink of *brännvin* forced on the workingman in return for a day's work. . . . I sincerely hope that nobody in Sweden will foolishly dissuade anyone from coming to this land of Canaan." [17]

This letter may be said to be a prototype of the "America letters." It contains a mass of details, and almost every sentence breathes a deep-seated dissatisfaction with government, institutions, and society in Sweden and at the same time a remarkable satisfaction with everything American. This tone is characteristic even of letters written by persons whose first experiences in the new country were anything but pleasant. A man from Småland, who emigrated with his wife and eight children in 1849 — one of the "cholera years" — buried one of his daughters on the banks of an inland canal, suffered several weeks with malaria, and just escaped being cheated out of his hard-earned savings, was happy over his decision to emigrate and looked to the future with high hopes for a better existence in spiritual as well as material matters.[18] Another enthusiast, who had been exposed to dangers of various kinds, wrote: "We see things here that we could never describe, and you would never believe them if we did. I would not go back to Sweden if the whole country were presented to me." [19]

It is obvious that statements like these were topics of lively discussion in the cottages of Sweden. The astonished people naturally hungered for more information and some of them inquired of their "American" friends how the morals of this marvelous country compared with those of their own communities. Where everything was so great and rich and free, and the population was recruited from all parts of the world, how could the Americans be so honest, sympathetic, and kind as the letters pictured them? A correspondent in 1852 gave his explanation of the miracle. The country was large, he said, and the rascals were not concentrated in any one place; and if such persons did come to a community, they found no evil companions to add fuel to their baser instincts. Moreover, if they did not mend their ways, a volunteer committee of citizens would wait upon them and serve notice that they had the choice of leaving the community or submitting to arrest. The Americans would not brook violations of law, and therefore drunkenness, profanity, theft, begging, and dissension were so rare as to be almost entirely absent. This letter of recommendation did not stop here. It praised the observance of the Sabbath and asserted that the young people did not dance, drink, or play cards, as was the case in Sweden.[20]

Unlike the earlier travelers in America, who usually belonged to the upper classes in Europe, the emigrants found the moral standards on a much higher plane than in Sweden. During a residence of nine months in the new Utopia one emigrant had not heard of a single illegitimate child — yes, one case had actually come to his knowledge, and then a Swede was the offender. He found whisky-drinking very unusual and the advancement of temperance almost unbelievable. In a midwestern town of about two thousand inhabitants (the seat of a college with seven professors and 339 students) one had to be well acquainted in order to purchase whisky or strong wine. "From this incident you may judge of the state of temperance in American cities," he confided. After a residence of four years in southeastern Iowa, Peter Cassel testified that he had "dined in hundreds of homes," and had "yet to see a whiskey bottle on the table. This country suits me as a friend of temperance, but it is not suitable for the whiskey drinker." [21]

It is hardly conceivable that the Swedish immigrants were unanimously enthusiastic about temperance, whether voluntary or imposed by law, and the student of American social history would dot the map of mid-nineteenth-century America with thousands of oases; but it is nevertheless a fact that the Middle West, to which most of the immigrants gravitated, was in striking contrast to Sweden, where every land-owning farmer operated a still and where the fiery *brännvin* at that time was as much a household necessity as coffee is today. Men, women, and children partook of its supposed health-giving properties in quantities appropriate to the occasion. To many immigrants who had heard the speeches or had read the tracts of the great apostles of temperance in Sweden, George Scott and Peter Wieselgren, and had patterned their lives after their precepts, the rural communities of Iowa, Illinois, Wisconsin, and Minnesota must have approached their ideal.

We must not be deluded into thinking that all the earlier Swedish immigrants were saints or models of virtue, but many of their letters bear testimony to the fact that there was profound dissatisfaction with the state of religion in Sweden. The writers had listened attentively to pietistic pastors and Baptist and lay preachers with sufficient courage to violate the conventicle act or to incur the displeasure of the church authorities, many of whom made merry over the flowing bowl and served Mammon rather than God. One cannot escape the conclusion that religion played a greater role in stimulating the desire to emigrate than writers have hitherto suspected; and if the student of immigration wishes to understand why the Swedes in America have turned away in such numbers from the church of their fathers in favor of other denominations or have held aloof from all church connections, he will find a study of religious conditions in the homeland a profitable one. It is by no means purely accidental that the beginnings of emigration coincide with the confluence of various forms of dissatisfaction with the state church.

The immigrants quickly sensed the difference between the pastors in America and Sweden. In 1849 a writer put it thus: "There are also Swedish preachers here who are so well versed in the Bible and in the correct interpretation that they seek the lost sheep and receive them again into their embrace and do not conduct themselves after the manner of Sweden, where the sheep must seek the shepherd and address him with high-sounding titles." Another requested his brother to send hymnbooks and catechisms, because the old copies were almost worn out with use. "We have a Swedish pastor. He . . . is a disciple of the esteemed Pastor Sellergren [*Peter Lorenz Sellergren, a prominent evangelistic pastor in Sweden*]. . . . During the past eleven months he has preached every Sunday and holiday; on week days he works the same as the rest of us, because his remarkable preaching ability makes it unnecessary for him to write his sermons. One Sunday I heard him preach for over two hours, and he was as fluent the second hour as the first." [22]

A faithful disciple of the prophet Eric Janson drew an even sharper contrast between the two countries: "I take pen in hand, moved by the Holy Ghost, to bear witness to the things I have seen, heard, and experienced. We had a pleasant voyage . . . and I was not affected in the least with seasickness. . . . My words are inadequate to describe with what joy we are permitted daily to draw water from the well of life and how we have come to the land of Canaan, flowing with milk and honey, . . . which the Scriptures tell us the Lord has prepared for his people. He has brought us out of the devilish bondage of the ecclesiastical authorities, which still holds you in captivity. . . . Here we are relieved of hearing and seeing Sweden's satellites of the devil, whose tongues are inspired by the minions of hell and who murdered the prophets and Jesus himself and snatched the Bible from Eric Janson's hands and came against us with staves, guns, and torches, together with ropes and chains, to take away the freedom we have in Christ. But praised be God through all eternity that we are freed from them and are now God's peculiar people. . . . This is the land of liberty, where everybody can worship God in his own way and can choose pastors who are full of the Spirit, light, and perfection. . . . Therefore, make ready and let nothing hinder you . . . and depart from Babel, that is, Sweden, fettered body and soul by the law." [23]

The legal prohibition of conventicles and its consequences were fresh not only in the memory of fanatical Eric Jansonists but also in the mind of a former master shoemaker from Stockholm, who wrote: "The American does not bother about the religious beliefs of his fellow men. It is the individual's own affair to worship God according to the dictates of his conscience, without interference from prelates clothed with power to prescribe what one must believe in order to obtain salvation. Here it is only a question of being a respectable and useful member of society." [24]

Another letter describes the situation in America as follows: "It is not unusual for men of meager education to witness for the truth with much greater blessing than the most learned preacher who has no religious experience. There are no statutes contrary to the plain teaching of the Word of God which prohibit believing souls from meeting for edification in the sacred truth of our Lord Jesus Christ." [25]

The sum and substance of the religious situation in America and Sweden is graphically stated in the words of an emigrant: "America is a great light in Christendom; there is a ceaseless striving to spread the healing salvation of the Gospel. The pastors are not lords in their profession, neither are they rich in the goods of this world. They strive to walk in the way God has commanded. They minister unceasingly to the spiritual and material welfare of men. There is as great difference between the pastors here and in Sweden as there is between night and day." [26]

One of the highly prized advantages America offered to the immigrant was the opportunity to rise from the lowest to the highest stratum of society. He found a land where the man whose hands were calloused by toil was looked upon as just as useful to society as the man in the white collar. The man who chafed under the cramped social conventions of Europe could not conceal his joy at finding a country where custom and tradition counted for little and where manual labor did not carry with it a social stigma. He had probably heard that the American people had elevated to the highest position of honor and trust such men of the people as Andrew Jackson and William Henry Harrison, but the actuality of the democracy in the "saga land" proved to be greater than the rumors that had kindled his imagination back home. And so he sat down to write about it to his countrymen, who read with astonishment that knew no bounds such statements as the following:

"The hired man, maid, and governess eat at the husbandman's table. 'Yes, sir,' says the master to the hand; 'yes, sir,' says the hand to the master. 'If you please, mam,' says the lady of the house to the maid; 'yes, madam,' replies the maid. On the street the maid is dressed exactly as the housewife. Today is Sunday, and at this very moment what do I see but a housemaid dressed in a black silk hat, green veil, green coat, and black dress, carrying a bucket of coal! This is not an unusual sight — and it is as it should be. All porters and coachmen are dressed like gentlemen. Pastor, judge, and banker carry market baskets." [27]

And read what a boon it was to live in a land where there were no laws minutely regulating trades and occupations and binding workers to terms of service: "This is a free country and nobody has a great deal of authority over another. There is no pride, and nobody needs to hold his hat in his hand for any one else. Servants are not bound for a fixed time. This is not Sweden, where the higher classes and employers have the law on their side so that they can treat their subordinates as though they were not human beings." [28]

The writer of this letter had probably felt the hard fist of his employer, because at that time physical chastisement was by no means unusual. If it was a great surprise to learn that a fine pedigree was not a requirement for admission to respectable society and to all classes of employment, no less sensational was the fact that the inhabitant of the western Canaan was not required to appear before an officer of the state to apply for a permit to visit another parish or to change his place of residence. In Sweden, of course, this official red tape was taken for granted, or its absence in America would not have called forth the following comment: "I am glad that I migrated to this land of liberty, in order to spare my children the slavish drudgery that was my lot; in this country if a laborer cannot get along with his employer, he can leave his job at any time, and the latter is obliged to pay him for the time he has put in at the same wage that was agreed upon for the month or year. We are free to move at any time and to any place without a certificate from the employer or from the pastor, because neither passports nor certificates are in use here." [29]

This newly won freedom was, in some cases, too rich for Swedish blood. One of the first pastors among the immigrants was rather disturbed about the conduct of some of his countrymen: "This political, religious, and economic freedom is novel and astonishing to the immigrant, who sees the spectacle of twenty-two millions of people ruling themselves in all orderliness. As a rule, the Swedes make use of this liberty in moderation, but a number act like calves that have been turned out to pasture. In most cases their cavorting is harmless, but sometimes they run amuck. They seem to think that a 'free country' gives them license to indulge in those things that are not in harmony with respect, uprightness, reliability, and veneration for the Word of God. . . . A rather characteristic incident illustrates this. A small boy, upon being reproved by his mother for appropriating a piece of cake, replied: 'Why, mother, aren't we in a free country now?' " [30] Making due allowance for the orthodox pessimism of a minister of the Gospel in every generation, historical research applied to certain Swedish settlements confirms the observations of this shepherd.

To a Swede, whose tongue was trained to flavor with cumbersome titles every sentence addressed to superiors and carefully to avoid any personal pronoun, the temptation to overwork the second person singular pronoun in America was irresistible. The Swedish passion for high-sounding names and titles gave to the humbler members of society designations that magnified by contrast the grandeur of those applied to the elect. In his own country the Swede was shaved by Barber Johansson, was driven to his office by Coachman Petersson, conversed with Building Contractor Lundström, ordered Jeweler Andersson to make a selection of rings for his wife, and *skåled* with Herr First Lieutenant Silfversparre. There were even fine gradations of "titles" for the members of the rural population. Every door to the use of *du* was closed except in the most familiar conversation. The youngest member of the so-called better classes, however, might *dua* the man of toil, upon whose head rested the snows of many long Swedish winters. Can the sons of those humble folk in America be blamed for abusing the American privilege of using *du?* What a privilege to go into a store, the owner of which might be a millionaire, and allow one's hat to rest undisturbed! How much easier it was to greet the village banker with the salutation "Hello, Pete!" than to say "Good morning, Mr. Banker Gyllensvans!" "When I meet any one on the street, be he rich or poor, pastor or official, I never tip my hat when I speak," wrote an emigrant from Skåne in 1854. "I merely say 'Good day, sir, how are you?' " [31] On the other hand, what a thrill it was for the immigrant to be addressed as "mister" — the same title that adorned the American banker and lawyer and the first title he had ever had! "Mister" was much more dignified than "Jöns," "Lars," or "Per."

The equality that the law gives is not the equality of custom. The lack of political rights is comparatively easy to remedy, but social customs are harder to deal with because they are not grounded in law. From his birth the Swede was hampered by restrictive conventions which, though not always seen by the eye, were always felt by the emotions. The walls between the classes of society and various occupations were practically insurmountable. A person could not pass from a higher social class to an inferior one, even though the latter better became his nature or economic status, because that would be an everlasting disgrace. If a *bonde* had come into financial straits, the step down to the condition of a *torpare* [32] would have wrecked his spirit.

Class distinctions in America did not assert themselves in the same way; very often the foreman and laborer were neighbors, sat in the same pew, and belonged to the same lodge. One immigrant wrote of this in 1854 as follows: "Titles and decorations are not valued and esteemed here. On the other hand, efficiency and industry are, and the American sets a higher value on an intelligent workingman than on all the titles, bands, and stars that fall from Stockholm during an entire year. It will not do to be haughty and idle, *for that is not the fashion in this country, for it is to use the axe, the spade, and the saw and some other things to get money and not to be a lazy body."* [33]

If the men appreciated the equality in dress and speech, the women were even more enthusiastic. In the old country married as well as unmarried women were labeled with titles of varying quality and their work was more masculine, judged by the American standard. In the "promised land" they were all classified simply as "Mrs." or "Miss," and the heavy, clumsy shoes and coarse clothing gave way to an attire more in keeping with the tastes and occupations of the "weaker sex." In Sweden the maid slept in the kitchen, shined shoes, and worked long hours; in America she had her own room, limited working hours, regular times for meals, and time to take a buggy ride with Ole Olson, who hailed from the same parish. If she had learned to speak English, she might even have a ride by the side of John Smith — and that was the height of ambition! And for all this she was paid five or six times as much as she had earned in Sweden. In letter after letter one finds expressions of astonishment and enthusiasm over this equality in conversation and dress. One writer relates that the similarity in dress between matron and maid was such that he could not distinguish between them until the latter's peasant speech betrayed her. It is easy to imagine the thorn of envy in the hearts of the women in Sweden when they learned how fortunate their American sisters were. Another letter contains the information that the duties of the maid were confined to indoor work in the country as well as in the city and that even milking was done by the men, an amusing sight to a Swede.

It is rather strange that there was not more serious complaint about the hard work that fell to the lot of the immigrants. It is true that more than one confessed that they did not know what hard work was until they came to America, but there was a certain pride in the admission. It was probably the American optimism that sustained their spirits. They saw everything in the light of a future, where the "own farm" plus a bank account was the ultimate goal. This feeling of independence and self-confidence was also heightened by the vast distances of the Middle West, its large farms, billowing prairies, and cities springing up like magic.[34] In contrast with the small-scale agriculture and the tiny hamlets of his native parish, the immigrant felt that he was a part of something great, rich, and mighty, the possibilities of which were just beginning to be exploited. Said a Swedish farmer in 1849: "Here in Illinois is room for the entire population of Sweden. During the present winter I am certain that more grass has been burned than there is hay in the entire kingdom of Sweden. . . . The grass now is just half grown, and the fields give the appearance of an ocean, with a house here and there, separated by great distance."[35]

The Swede who came to the Mississippi Valley found a frontier society, with many institutions in advance of those of an older society and without the multitude of officials that strutted and blustered in Sweden. In fact, as one immigrant wrote, he was hardly conscious of living under a government, and the system of taxation fooled him into thinking that there were no taxes at all. The salary of the president of the United States was a mere pittance compared with the income of the royal family — a fact not omitted in the letters.[36]

Not a few of the "America letters" go to extremes in setting forth contrasts between "poverty-ridden Sweden" and the rich and mighty republic. Here is an example: "We hope and pray that the Lord may open the eyes of Svea's people that they might see their misery: how the poor workingman is despised and compelled to slave, while the so-called better classes fritter away their time and live in luxury, all of which comes out of the pockets of the miserable workingmen. . . . We believe that all the workers had better depart and leave the lords and parasites to their fate. There is room here for all of Svea's inhabitants."[37]

Quotations from the "America letters" could be multiplied to show the reaction of the Swedish immigrants to the American environment, but a sufficient number have been presented to demonstrate that they were unusually responsive to the impressions that rushed upon them soon after they had cast their lot with their brothers and sisters from Great Britain, Ireland, Germany, Norway, and Holland. And not only that, but their letters remain to record the fact that in America they found a society that nearly approached their conception of an ideal state. This explains why students of immigration agree almost unanimously that the Swedes assimilated more rapidly and thoroughly than any other immigrant stock. After all, why should anyone be hesitant about taking out naturalization papers in the land of Canaan? Some letters written by men who had had scarcely time enough to unpack their trunks read like Fourth of July orations: "As a son of the great republic which extends from ocean to ocean, I will strive to honor my new fatherland. A limitless field is opened for the development of Swedish culture and activity. Destiny seems to have showered its blessings on the people of the United States beyond those of any other nation in the world." [38]

The Sweden of 1840–60 is no more and the America of Abraham Lincoln belongs to the ages; but for hundreds of thousands of people in the land of the midnight sun America, in spite of the geographical distance, lies closer to them than the neighboring province. In some parts of Sweden the "America letters" from near relatives brought Chicago closer to them than Stockholm. They knew more about the doings of their relatives in Center City, Minnesota, than about Uncle John in Jönköping.

In deciphering an "America letter" the historian is prone to forget the anxious mother who for months — perhaps years — had longed for it, and the letter that never came is entirely missing from the archives and newspaper columns. But if he turns the musty pages of the Swedish-American newspapers, his eyes will fall on many advertisements similar to the following: "Our dear son Johan Anton Petersson went to America last spring. We have not heard a line from him. If he sees this advertisement, will he please write to his people in Sweden? We implore him not to forget his aged parents and, above all, not to forget the Lord." [39]

If many letters were stained with tears in the little red cottages in Sweden, there were not a few written by trembling hands in the log cabins of Minnesota and later in the sod houses of Nebraska. And sometimes the heart was too full to allow the unsteady hand to be the only evidence of longing for parents and brothers and sisters, as the following quotation reveals: "I will not write at length this time. Nothing of importance has happened, and if you come, we can converse.

God alone knows whether that day will ever dawn — my eyes are dimmed with tears as I write about it. What a happy day it would be if, contrary to all expectations, we children could see our parents." [40] Miraculous things happened in the land of Canaan; it could transform a conservative Swedish *bonde* into a "hundred per cent American" in spirit, but it could not so easily sever the ties of blood. Neither could the storm-tossed Atlantic prevent sisters, cousins, uncles, and aunts from accepting invitations embalmed in "America letters" to attend family reunions in the land of Canaan.

The Literature of the
Pioneer West

HENRY STEELE COMMAGER

FOR SOME IMMIGRANTS America was the land of Canaan, but others found it to be "on the border of utter darkness." A Minnesota author, writing in the Norwegian language, laid bare the darker side of the immigrant experience in one of the great novels on the pioneer West — Ole E. Rölvaag's Giants in the Earth, *which was first published in 1924. Soon after an English edition of the work appeared in 1927, Henry Steele Commager contributed the following perceptive evaluation of* Giants in the Earth *to the December, 1927, number of* Minnesota History *(volume 8). Mr. Commager is professor of history and American studies in Amherst College, Amherst, Massachusetts. He is one of the country's foremost living historians and the author of such well-known books as* Majority Rule and Minority Rights *(1943),* The American Mind *(1950), and* Freedom, Loyalty, Dissent *(1954).*

THE SAME YEAR which has witnessed America's coming of age in the profound historical and critical studies of Mumford, Parrington, and Beard,[1] has witnessed, with singular appropriateness, the appearance of the most penetrating and mature depiction of the westward movement in our literature. It is O. E. Rölvaag's *Giants in the Earth,* and it inspires this encomium because it chronicles as no other volume has that combination of physical and spiritual experience which is the very warp and woof of American history. It indicates in the realm of fiction the same attitude which has already expressed itself in criticism and in history — that the story of America is not the story of physical and material development and expansion to the utter exclusion of the spiritual or psychological. The westward movement ceases to be the victim of romance and becomes a great physical and spiritual adventure. It ceases to be the proud epic of man's conquest of earth and becomes the tragedy of earth's humbling of man.

For a generation American history has been concerned with the

156

significance of the frontier, and American literature with the son of the middle border. These two avenues of approach have led us in history to a wholesome, if occasionally somewhat arid, economic realism, and in literature to romance, but we have not yet come out on the high-road of understanding. Historians, economists, and sociologists have given us their various evaluations of the physical processes and institutions of the frontier and of the westward movement, and novelists have sublimated the chronicle and symbolized it for all time in the covered wagon. But history is no more a physical than a psychological phenomenon, and the significance of the westward movement and of the frontier for the development of the American character and the American mind is to be discovered neither in statistics of population growth nor in the campfire songs of the western trails, but rather in the psychological experiences of the individuals and communities that participated in the great enterprise.

This more mature and reflecting attitude toward the westward movement made its appearance, as might well be suspected, somewhat earlier in criticism than in fiction. Indeed, the earliest travelers in America were frequently struck with the psychological aspects of the frontier experience and of the influence of pioneering on the American mind: thus Crèvecœur and the Duc de Liancourt at the time of the Revolution, thus Harriet Martineau and Mrs. T. A. Trollope and Fredrika Bremer in the first half of the nineteenth century, and thus those two major observers, Alexis de Tocqueville and James Bryce. Nor were American critics unaware of this aspect of the frontier. Henry Adams, with his customary penetration, suggested something of the influence of environment not only on the economic development of the frontier but on the cultural and spiritual as well, and touched on the disparity between the grandeur of the physical environment and the meanness of the cultural experience.

This conception of the westward movement as a cultural phenomenon, as a chapter in the history of the American mind and American psychology, did not gain general acceptance. Historians continued to write of the West as an economic concept. And where the psychological aspect was touched upon, it was commonly clothed in general terms, in pretty phraseology, usually in a romantic idealism somewhat more appropriate to fiction than to history. Historians described the buoyant pioneer and the zest and energy of pioneering, and even Adams grew lyric in the prospect of the plowboy some day going to the field whistling a sonata of Beethoven. The West was the vessel of idealism, the stronghold of democracy, the promise of progress, the vindication of the great American experiment. The scientific school of Frederick Jackson Turner and his followers directed attention more exclusively to the economic realities of the westward movement, but they did not fundamentally alter the idealistic conception.

This idealistic conception communicated itself to the literature of the West, though to be sure the process was one of interrelations and interactions. From the day of James Fenimore Cooper and Montgomery Bird and William G. Simms to Owen Wister and Emerson Hough and Zane Grey and Herbert Quick, the westward movement was portrayed as a crusade, symbolized in the covered wagon and celebrated in that magnificent chorus that Hamlin Garland has given us:

> Then over the hills in legions, boys,
> Fair freedom's star
> Points to the sunset regions, boys . . .

Ah, that was it. The sunset regions! Out where the West begins! And Whitman consecrated it with one of his most inspired lyrics:

> Have the elder races halted?
> Do they droop and end their lesson, wearied over there beyond the seas?
> We take up the task eternal, and the burden and the lesson,
>   Pioneers! O pioneers!
> All the past we leave behind,
> We debouch upon a new mightier world, varied world,
> Fresh and strong the world we seize, world of labor and the march,
>   Pioneers! O pioneers!

But there were skeptics who doubted the authenticity of the creation story. They had witnessed, perhaps, the labor, and they distinctly remembered that it had been painful and arduous. They repudiated the aureole of romance and glamour which a past generation had thrown over it and offered instead their own narrative, bearing the authentic stamp of personal experience. The new realism found its first expression in two volumes strangely neglected by the brilliant author of the *Mauve Decade*. Edward W. Howe, in *The Story of a Country Town*, offered a tragedy too stark, a masterpiece too honest, for the generation of the *fin de siècle* and allowed a later generation to hail *Main Street* as original; and Hamlin Garland, in *Main-Travelled Roads*, presented farm life in Wisconsin and Iowa in all its grim and unprepossessing actualities, "with a proper proportion of the sweat, flies, heat, dirt and drudgery of it all."

In the course of the next three decades the ranks of the heretics grew until realism became orthodoxy. The continuity from the *Story of a Country Town* to *Main Street,* from *Main-Travelled Roads* to *Iowa Interiors,* is an obvious and unbroken one. The realistic school of the middle border has attained respectability: it numbers among its disciples Willa Cather and Margaret Wilson, Frank Norris and Edgar Lee Masters, Ruth Suckow and Edith Kelly, and even William Dean Howells and Francis Grierson, with their neglected stories of early Ohio and Illinois; and it has achieved the comfortable recognition of learned dissertations, ponderous bibliographies, and rather uncertain interpretative essays.

Indeed, it has achieved more than this doubtful beatification. For by one of those curiously consistent developments from radicalism to conservatism, from realism to romanticism, the archleader of the rebels himself, Hamlin Garland, waved the magic wand of romance over the scenes of his boyhood and enveloped them in a nimbus of beauty, and we might paraphrase Ariel that

> Nothing of him that doth fade
> But doth suffer a land-change
> Into something rich and strange.

The result is the *Son of the Middle Border,* the classic narrative of pioneer life in the West, and it portrays in colors of incomparable loveliness the heroic saga of the westward movement. There is realism here, to be sure, but over it all Garland has thrown something of the lovely grace of a day that is dead and will never come back to him: "It all lies in the unchanging realm of the past — this land of my childhood. Its charm, its strange dominion cannot return save in the poet's reminiscent dream. No money, no railway train can take us back to it. It did not in truth exist — it was a magical world, born of the vibrant union of youth and firelight, of music and the voice of moaning winds." [2]

But this was not the West of *Main-Travelled Roads,* nor even of *Rose of Dutcher's Cooley.* The *Son of the Middle Border* is the most exquisite presentation of pioneer life in our literature, but the criticism of Mumford is pertinent: "The post-Civil War writers who deal with Roughing It, A Son of the Middle Border, or A Hoosier Schoolmaster, to mention only a few examples, had already abandoned the scene of the pioneer's efforts and had returned to the East: they made copy of their early life, but, though they might be inclined to sigh after it, because it was associated with their youth, they had only a sentimental notion of continuing it." [3]

With the exception, indeed, of Willa Cather, the writers of the middle border were overwhelmingly concerned with the physical and material aspects of life. It is the taking up of the land, the struggle with the soil, the physical environment that dominates the scene. Their interest is centered upon the economy of the westward movement. To a certain extent, therefore, their stories are propaganda; they form the literary chapter in the history of the agrarian revolt.

This chapter in American literature, then, furnishes a striking parallel to the synchronous chapter in American historiography. *Main-Travelled Roads* is the literary articulation of Solon J. Buck's *Granger Movement,* and the *Son of the Middle Border* of Turner's "Contributions of the West to American Democracy." With their attention fixed so largely upon the taking up of the land, the novelists of the middle border emulate the historians of the middle border, and the interpretation is an economic one.

The appearance of the volumes of Mumford, Parrington, and Beard seems to mark the beginning of a new era in American historiography — the "sober second thought" of the historian, the intellectual maturity of the critic. The emphasis in these studies is on the cultural and psychological aspects of American history rather than on the economic, though Beard's volumes may be something of an exception to this generalization. It appears, indeed, that in American as in European historical writing we are entering upon that era of psychological interpretation which Professor J. W. Thompson prophesied some time ago. Nowhere is this more evident than in the criticism of the westward movement. From the economic point of view that phenomenon was an epic. From the psychological point of view it was a tragedy. The intrinsic subjectivity of the facts of history which Carl Becker celebrates with such malign satisfaction never received apter illustration.

It is fitting and not altogether without significance that this new attitude in history should find concomitant literary expression. It is for this reason that we can hail *Giants in the Earth* as a milestone in American literature. It is not only that it portrays more completely than any other novel the synthesis of what Arthur M. Schlesinger, Sr., has happily termed the "two grand themes of American history" — the westward movement and immigration. It is rather because for the first time, adequately, in the literature of the middle border the primary concern is not economic but psychological; the main interest of the story centers not on the taking up of the land but on the effect of that experience upon the characters. For the first time a novelist has measured the westward movement with a psychological yardstick and found it wanting.

We do not necessarily imply that Rölvaag is either the first or the only author to call attention to the psychological aspects of the westward movement. Neither Garland nor Howe, nor their numerous successors, have ignored this element. Willa Cather, indeed, in her remarkable *O Pioneers!* and *My Ántonia,* has dwelt intelligently and sympathetically upon the problem. To a certain extent she may be said to anticipate Rölvaag and some passages from her volumes might serve as a text for *Giants in the Earth:* "But the great fact was the land itself, which seemed to overwhelm the little beginnings of human society that struggled in its sombre wastes. It was from facing this vast hardness that the boy's mouth had become so bitter; because he felt that men were too weak to make any mark here, and the land wanted to be let alone, to preserve its own fierce strength, its peculiar, savage kind of beauty, its uninterrupted mournfulness." [4] But, withal, Miss Cather records the triumph of Alexandra and of Ántonia over their grim environment, and her novels are panels rather than murals.

Hamlin Garland has furnished us, perhaps, with the explanation of the partial failure of the novelists of the middle border to penetrate the spiritual life of the frontier. He was looking back upon his first courageous efforts, when he said, "I intend to tell the whole truth." He confesses, however: "But I didn't! Even my youthful zeal faltered in the midst of a revelation of the lives led by the women on the farms of the middle border. Before the tragic futility of their suffering, my pen refused to shed its ink. Over the hidden chamber of their maternal agonies I drew the veil." [5] Rölvaag is not less tender, but he is inexorable. The even tenor of his tale nowhere falters, nor does he choose to draw the veil of silence over the "tragic futility" of the women's suffering, over the "hidden chamber of their maternal agonies." Indeed, it might be said that his volume is primarily concerned with the "futility of their suffering," and the emphasis is not so much on suffering as on futility. Of all tragedies the most poignant is that of futility. Not to have suffered, but to have suffered in vain, ah, there's the rub!

And futility is the moral of *Giants in the Earth.* Of what avail is the conquest of the soil by man; the scars which man inflicts upon the virgin earth are as nothing to the scars which nature inflicts upon the souls of men. Against physical environment men can indeed struggle, and they can emerge successful. The earth can be made to yield its bountiful crops, the forests timber, and the rivers fish. Men can build homes to shelter them from the fury of the elements, they can close out the bitter cold and the fierce storms. To the indomitable courage and energy of man nature must yield her grudging tribute. But what of the souls of men here on the distant plains? What of the infinite loneliness, of the secret fears, of the primeval silences that shake the faith of men? What of that concern with the salvation of the physical being that sacrifices the salvation of the soul? And what of the pleasures of social inter-course, the homely comforts of a homely culture, the social and reli-gious and family life of simple folks? Aye, man might wrest a living out of nature here on the dreary prairies, but nature would wrest civilization from man. And what indeed shall it profit a man that he gain the world if he lose his soul? The life is more than the living, and living could be achieved only at the cost of life itself.

This literary diagnosis of the spiritual realities of pioneer life har-monizes strikingly with the critical interpretation of Mumford; the narrative and the interpretation are complementary, and passages from the latter merely point the moral and adorn the tale: "The vast gap between the hope of the Romantic Movement and the reality of the pioneer period is one of the most sardonic jests of history. On one side, the bucolic innocence of the Eighteenth Century, its belief in a fresh start, and its attempt to achieve a new culture. And over against it, the epic march of the covered wagon, leaving behind it deserted vil-lages, bleak cities, depleted soils, and the sick and exhausted souls that engraved their epitaphs in Mr. Masters' Spoon River Anthology. . . .

"The truth is that the life of the pioneer was bare and insufficient: he did not really face Nature, he merely evaded society. Divorced from its social context, his experience became meaningless." [6]

Per Hansa, buoyant, vital, lovable, with his hand to the plow and his eyes fixed hopefully upon a golden future, and Beret, his wife, dis-consolate and sick at heart, physically, mentally, spiritually stricken by her cruel experience — these are Rölvaag's symbols for the hope of the romantic movement and the reality of the pioneer West. The symbolism is sustained and terribly convincing. It is Beret, at first a tragic figure in the background, who gradually dominates the scene, just as spiritual tragedy overwhelms physical phenomena. Her experi-ence, subtly and profoundly described by Rölvaag, loses its immediate application and becomes as universal as that of Goethe's Margarete. It is this ability to universalize, to translate the experience of his char-acters into spiritual values of catholic and transcendent significance that stamps Giants in the Earth as a work of genius.

The "two grand themes of American history" Rölvaag has infused with a profound psychological significance. Immigration ceases to become the story of Americanization and becomes the problem of spiritual adaptation and acclimatization. The westward movement is metamorphized from an economic enterprise or a romantic epic and becomes a struggle against the "power of evil in high places." The characters of this drama are not hailing "fair freedom's star," but "facing the great desolation." Not for them the triumphant song of "Pioneers! O pioneers," but the silence "on the border of utter darkness."

It is upon the eternal verities that Rölvaag concentrates — on birth and death and suffering — and he recites them with a profound understanding and a tender sympathy and yet without sentimentality. The birth of Peter Victorious is the focal fact of the book; he is for Per Hansa a symbol of victory, for Beret a symbol of sin. Over him this strangely and beautifully mated pair wage their silent battle for life and salvation, and when Per Hansa wins and the child is restored to grace and the mother to sanity, it is by a religion which is the harbinger of death. It is the "eternal yea" and the "eternal nay" echoed here on the western plains, but Per Hansa's magnificent "yea" was to be choked out by the icy hand of death. "The Great Plain drinks the blood of Christian men" — it is the handwriting on the wall of American history.

Wendelin Grimm and Alfalfa

EVERETT E. EDWARDS and
HORACE H. RUSSELL

A GERMAN IMMIGRANT, little honored in his own day, played an outstanding role in the development of modern agriculture. He was Wendelin Grimm, a Carver County farmer whose dogged persistence and devotion to the "everlasting clover" he brought with him from Germany gave the northern Midwest its most valuable forage crop. Although other more desirable types of alfalfa have now been developed, Grimm alfalfa reigned for some eighty years as the most important variety produced in the United States. Everett E. Edwards, a native Minnesotan, was associated with the Bureau of Agricultural Economics of the United States Department of Agriculture from 1927 until his death in 1952. He was the author of numerous bibliographical works published by the department, and he served for twenty-one years as the editor of Agricultural History *(1931–52). Horace H. Russell, his collaborator in the writing of this paper, was on the staff of the Social Security Board in Washington, D.C. The article, which is one of several contributed by Edwards to* Minnesota History, *was published in March, 1938 (volume 19).*

GRIMM ALFALFA is one of Minnesota's main contributions to American agriculture, and its history is an interesting and significant story of a hardy forage plant that was brought to America in the 1850s by a German immigrant named Wendelin Grimm.[1] Although millions of Europeans migrated to the United States in the course of the nineteenth century, Grimm stands out as an individual farmer who made an important specific contribution to American agriculture. He left his native Külsheim, a little agricultural village between Tauberbischofsheim and Wertheim in the Tauber Valley of the duchy of Baden, Germany, in 1857. Since he was nearly forty years of age when he emigrated, he retained many of his old farming methods and interests. Like many other immigrants he brought with him some of his

164

favorite possessions. Among them was a bag of alfalfa seed, weighing not more than twenty pounds, which was destined to become the basis of his important agricultural contribution. Grimm reached Chaska in Carver County about September 1, and there he bought 137 acres in the northwest quarter of section 4, range 24 west, Laketown Township.

In the spring of 1858, Grimm planted the seed he had brought with him in order that he might have a crop of alfalfa, as had been his custom in the old country. The soil was favorable, but the winters were more severe than those of his native village, and he did not have immediate success. Some of the alfalfa plants winterkilled, but he carefully saved the seed from those that survived and replanted the field. Thus he continued year after year, trying to grow what he considered an essential crop. Some years his field winterkilled very little, but in others it died out almost entirely. Yet he always saved seed from the plants that survived and replanted the following spring. After years of persistence, the alfalfa became acclimatized and no longer winterkilled. The scientific importance of his work Grimm probably never realized.

Detailed information about Grimm as a farmer is lacking, but reports gathered from the neighbors of his community have been repeatedly used. Charles Kenning of Bird Island, who was acquainted with Grimm, emphasized the fact that for many years he made little headway, and only by persistent care did he finally succeed in raising hardy alfalfa. A near neighbor, Henry Gerdsen, is authority for the story of an incident that must have made Grimm feel that his efforts in growing alfalfa in America were worth while. In the summer of 1863, Grimm drove a number of fat cattle past Gerdsen's home on the way to market. Gerdsen, surprised to see such fat animals when feed was scarce and his own cattle were lean, asked Grimm where he had obtained his corn. Grimm, long conscious of the feed value of alfalfa, proudly answered: "Kein Körnchen, nur ewiger Klee," — "not one kernel, only everlasting clover."

George Du Toit, the proprietor of a store at Chaska, knew Grimm for many years. It was through him that Grimm did much of his trading, including the buying of garden and field seeds. Du Toit remembered him as a man with the rudimentary education of the average German-born citizen, good common sense, and a determination in his undertakings. The storekeeper also said that, in his memory, the only time that Grimm's alfalfa nearly died out entirely was in the winter of 1874–75. It is interesting to note that this was the severest winter since the forties. Joseph, Grimm's older son, who lived with his father until 1876, when he went south, recalled that six years after the alfalfa was planted the family dug a driveway for a bank barn and found that the "roots of this clover had penetrated more than 10 feet deep through the clay soil." [2]

Wendelin Grimm's alfalfa or "everlasting clover," as it was commonly called, grew and thrived year after year, but it received little early notice commercially. Grimm himself did nothing to bring his contribution to the attention of the agricultural world. Only the farmers in his neighborhood planted it and relied on it as a permanent source of fodder and of fertility for the soil. They obtained seed from Grimm and sowed fields for themselves. In this way alfalfa spread in Carver County, but it was raised largely within a radius of perhaps ten miles of the Grimm farm. It may also have been used a little in other localities. Grimm is reported to have bought a threshing machine in 1865 from an implement dealer who advised him to produce alfalfa seed for commercial purposes. Whether this suggestion was given as an aid to Grimm, or merely as a talking point to dispose of the thresher, is not known. According to Joseph Grimm, who operated the machine, 480 pounds of seed were produced on three acres in 1867 and sold in Minneapolis for fifty cents a pound. The failure of hardy alfalfa to spread in Minnesota during the early years of its development was probably due, as Joseph Grimm said, principally to the fact that livestock was grazed on vacant lands and there was plenty of open range. After the passage of the Enclosure Act in 1871, fences were erected and more attention was given to feed crops, and especially to alfalfa, in Carver County. In 1889 this county produced nearly fifty per cent of the alfalfa grown in Minnesota.[3] Ten years later it was still the leading alfalfa center of the state, producing a third of the total crop. Prior to 1900, it was generally believed that the farmers of Minnesota could not grow permanent stands of alfalfa, and those few who knew that it was being grown in Carver County attributed its success to local soil conditions.

The first person to take an active interest in bringing Grimm's hardy alfalfa to the attention of the outside world was Arthur B. Lyman of Excelsior. About 1880, on a visit to Tobias Ottinger at Victoria in Carver County, he learned of the superiority of alfalfa over red clover and induced his father to plant a field, which winterkilled because ordinary seed was used. Ten years later, when teaching school in Dahlgren Township, Carver County, he again came in contact with this forage plant which withstood the wintery weather. This time he took a handful of Grimm alfalfa hay home and showed it to his father, who bought seed in Minneapolis and tried again. As before the crop winter-killed. Lyman, still believing in alfalfa, obtained seed from the Grimm neighborhood and persuaded his father to try again. The result following the first winter was not encouraging, but the second winter more plants survived and from then on the alfalfa continued to flourish.

Lyman was very enthusiastic over his father's success with Grimm alfalfa and was anxious to disclose the facts to someone who would bring it to the attention of Minnesota farmers. In 1900, at a picnic excursion on Lake Minnetonka, he met Professor Willet M. Hays, head of the Agricultural Experiment Station of the University of Minnesota in St. Paul, and to him he told the story of his discovery. Hays decided to make a personal investigation in Carver County. Accompanied by an assistant, Andrew Boss, he drove the thirty miles to Excelsior and made an extensive tour of inspection with Lyman as guide. After three days, he decided to start trials with the plant at the experiment station, and made arrangements with Lyman to procure all the Grimm seed possible. Lyman obtained as much as he could by increasing his own alfalfa fields to "over one hundred acres." Cold, rainy seasons prevented the harvesting of large supplies for two years, but at the end of that time he again agreed to furnish seed because there were constant demands for it from other experiment stations.[4]

From this time on more interest was taken in the possibilities of developing and introducing hardy alfalfa as a forage crop for the Northwest. Lyman was invited by Professor Hays to read a paper on the subject at a session of the annual meeting of the Minnesota State Agricultural Society, held at the Masonic Temple in Minneapolis on January 12, 1904. A general discussion of alfalfa, and especially of the hardy variety grown in Carver County, followed the reading. Most noteworthy of the remarks and questions was the comment by William J. Spillman, a member of the federal department of agriculture: "I cannot help but be impressed with this paper read by Mr. Lyman . . . as of vital importance to the future of agriculture in the State of Minnesota and in the Dakotas. We have been searching the world for a variety of alfalfa that would do just what this variety does. We sent a man to Turkestan this summer at great expense to get something of that kind, but here we know we have what we sought." [5] Professor Hays continued to give considerable attention to Grimm alfalfa, and in March, 1904, he issued a *Press Bulletin* in which, officially at least, this hardy alfalfa was referred to as Grimm alfalfa for the first time.

From 1901 to 1920 experiments to compare Grimm alfalfa with other alfalfas and other species of forage plants were conducted at various experiment stations in the Northwest. The first were started at the Agricultural Experiment Station of the University of Minnesota. Careful statistical records were kept, using genuine Grimm seed, commercial seed, Turkestan seed, Iowa seed, and some unidentified varieties. In 1902 similar experiments were begun at the North Dakota Agricultural Experiment Station at Fargo and also at the substation at Dickinson. Comparative studies in Montana and Kansas showed that Minnesota Grimm yielded three times as much hay as other alfalfas. Hardy strains were developed also in South Dakota; one of the best was known as Grimm S.D. 162.

After Dr. Spillman heard about Grimm alfalfa at the meeting of the Minnesota State Agricultural Society in 1904, the United States department of agriculture became actively interested, and Professor Hays continued to give encouragement from Washington after his appointment as assistant secretary of agriculture. Charles J. Brand and Lawrence R. Waldron made exhaustive comparative tests at Dickinson. Their study brought them to the conclusion that Grimm alfalfa was a natural cross between the common purple blossom alfalfa, *Medicago sativa,* long familiar to agriculturists, and a wild yellow flowering kindred species, *Medicago falcata,* which in some devious way had strayed from its original home in Asia to western Europe.[6]

Brand had obtained alfalfa seed from the region of Grimm's old home in Germany for comparison with that developed by Grimm in Minnesota. With reference to its ability to resist cold winter weather, the conclusion of Brand and Waldron was: "In comparative experiments with Grimm alfalfa and the old German Franconian alfalfa the latter has proved to be much less hardy under our northern conditions than the Grimm, which points to the probability that the German lucern that Mr. Grimm brought with him has been greatly modified during its fifty years' sojourn in Minnesota. . . . Under identical conditions and with identical treatment, adjoining rows of these strains killed out very differently. In the old German strain 64 out of 85 plants winterkilled, while in a sample of Grimm grown in North Dakota only 2 out of 70 plants were killed. . . . The Grimm killed out less than 3 per cent, while the old German lost more than 75 per cent." [7]

Other observations were made by Brand and John W. Westgate, who started in 1906 to make a critical, botanical, agronomic, and historical study of alfalfa, officially directed by the United States department of agriculture. After three years of study, Westgate concluded that a certain per cent of *Medicago falcata,* the hardy drought-resisting wild alfalfa of Eurasia, was indicated in the Grimm strain, and that it was this ancestry rather than acclimatization since its introduction in Minnesota that made it so hardy a plant. Brand, in his summary, called attention to the hardiness and consequent great potential value of Grimm alfalfa. This had been amply substantiated by the results of his investigations and also by the experiences of many northern farmers, who time and again had planted seed of ordinary strains of domestic and foreign origin only to have their fields gradually deteriorate to a point where they were no longer profitable. Such fields had to be plowed up and resowed with Grimm to obtain enduring stands.[8]

Ten years of tests comparing Grimm with other varieties of alfalfa confirmed all beliefs in its hardiness and superiority over other forage plants as a general feed crop for the Northwest. Grimm was recommended at all times, but little headway was made in establishing it as a leading forage crop because the farmers did not know how it should be raised and treated under differing soil conditions. Methods were found, however, that eventually aided certain localities in its cultivation. In Carver County the soil had always been favorable to a good stand, but where the land contained quantities of acid, alfalfa did not grow successfully. The farmers had to learn that, to counteract such conditions, they must apply lime to their fields. Inspection of the roots in alfalfa fields also revealed that poor stands were often caused by lack of alfalfa bacteria, whose presence is essential if the plants are to thrive and to fertilize the soil. The methods of inoculating new seedings had to be explained and demonstrated.[9]

Although the large-scale production of Grimm alfalfa was slow in developing, its seed was much in demand and at all times scarce. In 1914, forty thousand pounds of seed were distributed among farmers widely scattered throughout the northwestern counties of Minnesota. Many seed companies handled what Grimm alfalfa seed they could get, and probably much that was purported to be of this variety, but it was Lyman who concentrated his attention on producing and distributing the seed on a large commercial scale. His early experience in furnishing seed for the farm school and the encouragement and influence of Hays afforded him an unusual opportunity. He leased land in Montana, Idaho, and the Dakotas, where the dry climate seemed to be most favorable to seed production. Grimm alfalfa failed to seed well in wet years or in humid surroundings. Lyman directed the farmers whose fields he had leased in the production of pure Grimm alfalfa seed. The growers were required to deliver all seed to him for inspection, and a pedigree was kept for each field planted. Advertisements in farm journals and pamphlets telling of the value of Grimm alfalfa and including a short history of its discovery gave publicity to "Lyman's Grimm Alfalfa Seed." It is not known to what extent Lyman's business grew, but in 1915, twenty-five thousand dollars worth of seed was sold, and at no time was his production great enough to meet the demand. The seed was always high in price, selling for as much as a dollar a pound.[10]

By 1920 Grimm alfalfa was being grown in widening circles. It had spread to many states of the Northwest where the winters brought sub-zero weather and to the Canadian West, and it had been tried in the states to the southward. In the warm, humid regions, however, the results proved very unsatisfactory, so its growth in such places was not advised. The alfalfa acreage in Minnesota increased from 658 acres in 1900, to 2,288 in 1910, 45,419 in 1920, and 702,578 in 1930. The focal point up to 1924 was always Carver County, but so great was the expansion that by 1930 no less than eighteen counties had a larger acreage. During the ten years from 1910 to 1920, Grimm alfalfa was becoming a standard hay crop in Minnesota, endorsed by many growers. The best results appeared in the western part of the state and portions of the eastern half. The leading counties in seed production were Grant, Kittson, eastern Roseau, central Marshall, eastern Polk, Norman, Otter Tail, Wilkin, Becker, Crow Wing, Chippewa, Lac qui Parle, Todd, and Stevens. In southwestern Minnesota and the Red River Valley, excellent hay crops were obtained, but the fields produced seed only in dry seasons.[11]

Farmers in North Dakota became interested in Grimm alfalfa after seeing the results at the North Dakota demonstration farms. Some began extensive production of seed and, as a result, the North Dakota Grimm Alfalfa Seed Producers' Association was incorporated in 1916. Its objects were to register Grimm alfalfa fields to keep the variety pure, to assure purchasers that all the seed they bought was genuine North Dakota-grown Grimm, and to furnish this seed to buyers at prices consistent with the product. The bylaws provided for inspection and verification of fields to insure against fraud or possible error. The Grimm fields in North Dakota were registered by application, and growers stated under oath that genuine seed was the source from which their crops were grown. In 1917, its first year, the association handled seventeen thousand pounds of seed.[12]

A similar organization in Minnesota, the Minnesota Grimm Alfalfa Growers Association, was formed at Morris in August, 1924. The businessmen of the town agreed to donate and build a warehouse to be used for storing the pooled seed of all members of the organization. Articles and bylaws were drawn up providing for the use of genuine seed and fair terms of production. In order to equalize freight costs, it was agreed to average the cartage, thus giving a farmer who lived two hundred miles from Morris the same advantage as one who shipped only ten miles. The Minnesota Crop Improvement Association also became actively interested in Grimm alfalfa, and required that seed for certification be traced back, under affidavit, to Carver County.[13]

Although increasing attention was being given to the production of Grimm seed, the acreage was slow in reaching a commanding figure. The *Northwest Farmstead* took a leading interest in expanding the acreage of alfalfa, recommending Grimm as the variety to be grown in Minnesota. After emphasizing alfalfa for a number of years, it started a most arduous campaign on August 1, 1923, and during the following year published some two hundred articles endorsing Grimm and revealing the value of alfalfa as a protein feed and a soil builder. The campaign slogan was "An Acre of Alfalfa for Every Cow in Minnesota." To teach the farmers how to grow alfalfa successfully, Charles R. Hutcheson, a specialist on the subject, was engaged to go to all parts of Minnesota to test the soil and explain to the farmers and businessmen "what to do and how to do it" in order to succeed with alfalfa. He came to be known as "Alfalfa Hutch," and as a result of his work many alfalfa clubs were formed to further its growth. An example of the interest taken is shown in a letter from Lynn Sheldon, county agent of Redwood County, to the *Northwest Farmstead:* "Redwood County farmers have sown over 15,000 pounds of Grimm alfalfa this spring [*1924*] according to reports from various seed handling agencies. About one half of that amount was ordered through the county agent and orders were placed with the various seed distributing agencies handling good seed at right prices." [14]

The production of a forage plant so hardy as Grimm alfalfa, with its permanence, enormous yields, high protein content, economy as a crop, and value as a soil builder and weed throttler, is almost without parallel in plant history. It is impossible to compute in dollars and cents what it has meant to the nation. Minnesota, therefore, owes a great deal to the diligent German pioneer who knew that he must have good feed for his livestock and, through perseverance and hard work, developed what is the outstanding forage crop in the Northwest today. Who should be honored for bringing Grimm alfalfa to the attention of the agricultural world and fostering its development is a question that cannot be answered easily. Much credit, however, should be given to Lyman, Hays, Boss, Brand, Waldron, Westgate, Hutcheson, and others for their interest in alfalfa work. The various alfalfa associations and the campaign of the *Northwest Farmstead* should not be overlooked.[15]

To pay homage and tribute to the German pioneer who developed Grimm alfalfa, a monument was unveiled and dedicated on June 10, 1924, on his old farm. Over four hundred people gathered for the occasion, including many of Grimm's descendants. His granddaughter, Miss Clara Adelmann of Minneapolis, drew back the American flag that covered the monument — a bronze tablet attached to a native boulder. The inscription reads: "Commemorating Wendelin Grimm, resident of Minnesota 1857–1891, who originated Grimm Alfalfa on this farm. Erected June 1924 by Grimm Alfalfa Growers Associations."

Speakers at the dedication services included Dean W. C. Coffey, of the college of agriculture in the University of Minnesota, who declared that he felt that Grimm's contribution to the livestock industry was as great as that of the breeders. George W. Kelley, editor of the *Northwest Farmstead,* gave his reaction to the occasion in the following editorial, and its text may well serve as a conclusion for the present discussion: "The world knows not its greatest benefactors. Frequently it raises to eminence the demagogue and the time server. Fame it often gives to those responsible for its most disastrous calamities.

"Sometimes, though, it is given to a few to recognize and pay tribute to a patient man or woman who in obscurity and perhaps in poverty has worked out great benefits to humanity.

"Such an occasion was that . . . when eminent men from several states joined with hundreds of his former neighbors in dedicating a monument to the late Wendelin Grimm. . . .

"Civilization advances. Such monuments indicate it. Perhaps some day our historians will tell more of the work of such men and glorify less the authors of death and devastation." [16]

Monte Cassino, Metten, and Minnesota

AUGUST C. KREY

THE OLD-WORLD ROOTS of a pioneering Minnesota religious institution are traced in the following article by a scholar who was especially interested in the medieval foundations of Western civilization. In the thirty-eight years that have elapsed since September, 1927, when this paper was published in volume 8, St. John's Abbey at Collegeville has further demonstrated the vitality of the tradition here described. On the eve of its centennial in 1956, the abbey and its adjacent university embarked upon an ambitious construction program that promises to make it one of the state's architectural landmarks. August C. Krey served on the history faculty of the University of Minnesota from 1913 to 1955. He was the author of a volume of essays entitled History and the Social Web *(1955). He took an active interest in the work of the American Historical Association and the Minnesota Historical Society; at the time of his death in 1961 he was a member of the honorary council of the latter institution.*

IN FOLLOWING THE DEVELOPMENT of civilization through early European history it is necessary to dwell at some length upon the Rule of St. Benedict.[1] This rule, better described as a constitution for the government of men living under certain conditions, is known as one of the great governmental documents of history. It came into being during the critical years when the old Roman Empire of the West was breaking down and western Europe was coming under the rule of those vigorous but untaught tribesmen from the north known as the Teutons. Among the Romans at that time there was an intense interest in the Christian religion. For some time hundreds, and even thousands, of people, persons of wealth, of prominence, and of social position, as well as persons of the humbler walks of life, had renounced the affairs of the world and had turned their thoughts exclusively to the attain-

173

ment of eternal salvation, which they hoped more certainly to deserve through a life of self-denial.

This spirit of self-denial is one which all ages have lauded. Asceticism had begun in the East and was already a century old when the West took it up. Even in the East the thought had arisen that this practice required some organization and should be made of some service to society. It remained, however, for the West to realize this thought in its fullest form. This was the work of Benedict of Nursia, a Roman to whom succeeding centuries have reverently paid their respect under the title of St. Benedict. Benedict was of that race of Romans which had conquered and ruled nearly all the civilized world for upwards of five hundred years. Something of the genius of his race was apparently preserved in him. The problem of ruling others was not of his seeking. It was thrust upon him by the many persons who crowded around him to learn to live as he lived — a life of perfect self-denial. After several unhappy experiences with such groups, one of which nearly cost him his life, he finally devised a form of government which, while it satisfied the spirit of self-denial in quest of individual salvation, also struck most clearly the less selfish note of service to humanity.

According to tradition, this form of government, known as the Rule of St. Benedict, was finally formulated at Monte Cassino in the year 529.* In Benedict's community, among the mountainous hills to the south of Rome, with the blue waters of the Mediterranean off in the distance, this rule proved its excellence during the remaining years of his life. For the benefit of his sister, Scholastica, Benedict made some slight modifications in his rule to suit the needs of women following a religious life. Thus were founded the first two Benedictine communities for men and women. The Rule of St. Benedict is a masterpiece in the art of government. Others have drawn up on paper regulations which, if followed, would constitute a counsel of perfection. The world has seen many such — Benedict's rule was not that. It was, instead, a form of government under which men of religious zeal could live and work harmoniously together day in, day out, through the changing seasons of the year and the changing outlook of passing years without losing their zest either for religious salvation or for service to humanity. In its provision for work as well as prayer, in its recognition of the varying needs of illness and of health, in its adjustment to the changing seasons, and in its appreciation of human nature, the rule laid down a form of government which men could follow, whether among the

* The ancient abbey and the town of Cassino were destroyed during World War II. They have since been rebuilt. *Ed.*

heaping snows of the Arctic Circle or under the glaring sun of the equatorial zone, whether in southern Italy in 529 or in central Minnesota in 1927. And under all these conditions the ideals remained the same, personal salvation and humanitarian service.

Monte Cassino, however, is as far away as southern Italy and as long ago as fourteen hundred years. It was a religious community in which Romans were striving for salvation and incidentally helping people within a radius of not more than eighty miles and usually not more than ten. Perhaps another chapter of history may help to make clear what connection that community has with Minnesota.

Everybody knows of Gregory the Great. He too was a Roman. Three-quarters of a century had elapsed since the Rule of St. Benedict was formulated, and the times, in Italy at least, were even more out of joint than they had been in Benedict's day. Nevertheless the community at Monte Cassino still continued, though Benedict had been dead nearly half a century. Other communities had been formed under the government of this rule. Gregory himself had chosen early to follow a religious life. He used the vast estates to which he had fallen heir for the purpose of founding monasteries, and in all of them the Benedictine rule was observed. When Gregory became pope he decided to extend the sphere of usefulness for which Benedict had provided. He sent Benedictine monks as missionaries to regions not yet Christian. The St. Augustine and forty companions whose memory is so dear to English Christians in all lands today were Benedictine monks, and the community they founded at Canterbury was such a community. In fact the missionary movement that converted the Anglo-Saxons was a Benedictine service. From the monasteries that grew up in England other monks went out to carry on the work among their kinsmen on the continent. It was a Benedictine monk from England who succeeded in carrying Christianity to the heathen folk of Germany, and German Christians today are as grateful to the Anglo-Saxon Boniface as the English are to Augustine. The textbooks for the training and guidance of converts which Boniface carried with him to Germany were written by the Venerable Bede. The work which Boniface began so successfully was continued after his time, and for the next four centuries the advance of Christianity northward and eastward on the continent was marked by Benedictine monasteries.

In their work in England and even more in Germany the Benedictine monasteries realized the ideals of service which their founder had set before them. The people among whom they worked were not yet civilized and the life they led was still a semiroving one. The Benedictine monks had to teach these people not only the fundamentals of the Christian religion, but also the fundamentals of civilized life. The monastic clusters of buildings, which the monks themselves literally built, gradually became the nuclei of permanent villages and towns. In fact some of the cities of Germany today owe their origin to these early monasteries. From the monastic center the Benedictine monks went out to convert the heathen and to minister to those already converted. At the monastic center the monks taught the growing youth letters, and taught both them and adults agriculture, industry, and, in general, the arts of civilization. The importance of their work early won the recognition and support of the great Carolingian kings. Charlemagne's father and Charlemagne were especially interested in them. The cooperation of these two rulers with the Benedictine monks is best illustrated in the case of the Saxons and Bavarians, the most vigorous and turbulent of the German people. The taming of the Saxons, so far as they were tamed, was accomplished more by the planting of Benedictine monasteries than by the crashing of Charlemagne's sword.

One trait of the Benedictine rule for which Benedict himself had provided is fully revealed by the spread of Benedictine monasteries through the north of Europe. Though the monasteries sent out missionaries, and these founded new communities, the latter were cut off from organic connection with the parent community almost as soon as they were self-sustaining. Sentiment and tradition often preserved the memory of the earlier connection more or less fondly, but there remained no authoritative bond. This has sometimes been spoken of as a defect of the Benedictine rule, and later new orders arose in which an organic connection was maintained between scattered communities. Whether a defect or not, the fact remains that each Benedictine community became essentially a part of the region in which it was located. There were undoubtedly many advantages in this fact. The people of the region would not continue to look upon the Benedictine community as foreign. The original monks would quickly be replaced by others who had been born and reared in the region, and thus the feeling of community between the people and the monks would facilitate both the work of conversion and more material education. Whether for good or ill, this Benedictine characteristic of the separate entity of each monastery is an important fact in the history of the order.

One of the monasteries established during this great missionary period was the Monastery of Metten. This was built on the northern side of the Danube Valley some miles east of Ratisbon in the year 801. Charlemagne then ruled that territory, and the monastery was in a sense built under his auspices. The people among whom it was built were Bavarians, already Christian, but on the border of Bohemia and the land of the Avars. The work it did in the early years was exactly the kind of work that the greater monasteries established by St. Boniface were doing. It trained missionary priests, taught the arts of peace, and, in general, served as a force for improvement in the region round about. About a hundred years after its founding its buildings were destroyed by the great invasion of the Hungarians, then a wild people recently come from Asia. It was rebuilt, and, when Otto the Great finally defeated the Hungarians and established the Ostmark as a protection against them, Metten embarked upon a more peaceful career. Presumably, some of the monk-priests it trained took part in the missionary work among the Hungarians and Slavs, but that work was soon accomplished. Secular hierarchies were established there, and the missionary duties of Metten came to an end.

Metten was never one of the largest, nor was it the most important of the Benedictine monasteries. From the tenth century on it was a Bavarian institution essentially, contributing its services to the locality about it. The centuries came and went and Metten continued to render its services. Its fortunes fluctuated with those of the region in which it stood. There were times when its abbots were unusually able, when its community was unusually large, and its influence radiated out over all Bavaria. There were other times when its community was small and its abbots neither distinguished nor important. There were times when the chief interests of the monks were apparently concerned with the administration of their properties, which had grown considerably, and other times when Metten was a leader in learning and art and zeal.

A few specific incidents will illustrate the fluctuations in the career of Metten. Its destruction by the Hungarians in the tenth century has already been mentioned. Early in the thirteenth century its buildings were destroyed by fire and years were required to repair this damage. Two hundred years later, in the fifteenth century, Metten was famous for its beautiful manuscripts and ornamental books, some of which are still preserved as models of calligraphy. Two hundred years after that, in the seventeenth century, the abbot of Metten stands forth as a leading figure in the religious organization of Bavaria. The great church with its two spires, which so impresses visitors today, was built in the eighteenth century. In 1803, almost exactly a thousand years after it was founded, Metten and its properties were confiscated by the state and its twenty-three monks scattered. This was in the days of Napoleon and under his influence. Almost a generation passed before it was re-established around one of those twenty-three monks who still remained. Since then it has again grown, and upon the outbreak of the World War [I] it was famous for its school, and its community consisted of seventy members, mostly priests.

The establishment of Monte Cassino in Italy in 529 thus marks the foundation of an order whose influence was widened by the work of Pope Gregory the Great and later by that of St. Boniface and other English monks. We have seen this rule spread with the help of Frankish kings until it led to the foundation of Metten in eastern Bavaria in 801. That monastery was to continue under the Benedictine rule right down to the present day. Monte Cassino and Metten are linked, and 529 has been brought into touch with 1927, but we are still some distance away from Minnesota.

Visitors to St. Paul are usually shown what is called "the old German church," the Church of the Assumption, as one of the most picturesque of the older sights of that picturesque city. And tourists as they drive along the highway that leads westward out of St. Cloud marvel at the church at St. Joseph, which seems too large for the little village that clusters about it. They are yet more puzzled by the church steeples that peer out over the trees four miles belond, at Collegeville.* Yet all three and many more spots in Minnesota and the Northwest serve to establish the connection between Minnesota and Metten and Monte Cassino.

There are doubtless people still living in St. Cloud and its vicinity who remember a little group of three priests who arrived there in the spring of 1856 and built themselves a wooden structure on a farm some two miles south of that city. Less than a year later the territorial legislature of Minnesota passed a law recognizing as a "body politic and corporate" the members of the religious order of St. Benedict — Demetrius Marogna, Cornelius Wittmann, Bruno Riss, and Alexis Roetzer being mentioned by name — and their associates and successors in office. The bill recognized this order "as instituted for scientific, educational, and ecclesiastical purposes" and authorized them to establish an institution or seminary to be known as "St. John's Seminary." This seminary was actually opened on November 10, 1857, having one professor and five students.

Thus began in Minnesota a community living according to the Rule of St. Benedict and dedicated like Monte Cassino to the twofold ideals of religious salvation and humanitarian service. It is perhaps fitting in light of the title of this paper to note that the leader of this little band

* Portions of the steeples referred to by the author were removed in 1960. *Ed.*

was originally an Italian nobleman. The connection of Minnesota and Monte Cassino is thereby made a bit more intimate. The Very Reverend Demetrius Marogna, however, was not an abbot. His title was that of prior, and his community was a priory of the Monastery of St. Vincent in Pennsylvania. The latter had been founded only a few years before by Benedictine monks from Metten in Bavaria. It was there that Father Demetrius had entered the novitiate and from there he had been sent to Minnesota. The Minnesota priory was not long kept under tutelage. The parent monastery cut it adrift in 1858. Scarcely well enough established to be recognized as a monastery, it justified the confidence of its parent by toddling along as a canonical priory until 1865, when, through the efforts of the abbot of St. Vincent, it was raised to the status of an abbey or monastery by the Pope. It is interesting to note that the name of the monastery at this time was "St. Louis on the Lake."

The coming of this little band of monk-priests was due indirectly to the efforts of an interesting missionary priest, Father Francis Pierz, who had worked among the Indians and whites of this Northwest for many years. Father Pierz was one of those rare individuals who thrive on hardship that would kill most people. He lived to be ninety-five years old, though he had spent many of those years in tramping the forests and fields of the region in an age when there were no roads to ease the journey of the weary traveler and very little shelter to temper the rigors of sub-zero winters. Father Pierz came to love this region, to regard it as God's own country. In his enthusiasm he saw in the woods and lands, the lakes and streams of Minnesota an abundance of natural resources even beyond the vivid imagination of later realtors. When settlement began up here Father Pierz launched an eloquent epistolary campaign through German Catholic newspapers of the country urging Germans who were Catholics to settle here. It was his enthusiastic urging that attracted the early settlers of this race and religion. When they arrived he sought to minister to them, but found the work too great for his declining energy. He was then already past seventy years, and he sought for others to carry on his religious work. One of his assistants, a young priest returning from an emergency service in midwinter, was frozen to death. The authorities really did not require such an incident to convince them of the need of special help. There was need both of persons who were trained to endure hardships and of persons who understood the language and customs of these settlers. Bishop Joseph Cretin of St. Paul finally wrote to missionary societies in Bavaria for aid, and was directed by them to the Monastery of St. Vincent in Pennsylvania, which had been established under the leadership of Father Sebastian Wimmer, himself a monk-priest from Metten in Bavaria.

With the establishment of the Benedictine foundation in Minnesota, additional members continued to come for several years. Some of these had entered the order at Metten, others at St. Vincent. It was not long, however, before the community was recruiting its new members from Minnesota and surrounding regions. Indeed, the second abbot of the institution, Father Alexius Edelbrock, was a boy in St. Cloud when the first fathers came there. He had been one of the first students of old St. John's Seminary, but because his father opposed his desire to become a priest and monk he had gone to St. Vincent to enter the order. When his education was completed the abbot there sent him back to Minnesota, and he became one of the strong personalities in the history of the community as well as an interesting and important figure in the history of the state and the Northwest. Of pioneer stock, accustomed from earliest boyhood to pioneer life in Minnesota, he was eminently fitted to cope with the problems that arose. Under his leadership the monastery grew in membership, in material resources, and in influence. He was one of that iron age of strong men in Minnesota, the age of James J. Hill, Archbishop John Ireland, and Bishop Henry B. Whipple, with all of whom he was well acquainted and among whom he occupies an honorable place.

It is not the purpose of this paper to present a systematic history of the community in Minnesota.* That would be too long a story, and it is better left to others more familiar with the detailed development of the community and the Northwest. Only a few of the more salient features of its work and importance can be pointed out here.[2]

That first community had barely begun its work when it realized the need of added help from women in educational work. So a call was early sent to Bavaria for women who were willing to undertake educational work under the hardships of pioneer life. The first group of Benedictine sisters responded to this call in 1857, just a year after the arrival of the fathers, and thus was founded the Convent of St. Benedict, now flourishing at St. Joseph. Its work was to care for elementary education, minister to the sick, and serve as a refuge for those in need. As at Monte Cassino, so here in Minnesota, the Benedictine monastery and convent grew up within a few miles of each other, and both con-

* Two recent volumes on the history of the community are: Colman J. Barry, *Worship a.id Work: Saint John's Abbey and University 1856–1956* (Collegeville, 1956), and Sister M. Grace McDonald, *With Lamps Burning* (St. Joseph, 1957) dealing with the College of St. Benedict. *Ed.*

tributed to the development of a wide locality. The central establishment at Collegeville, with its large and growing community of priests
and brothers, was not only a shelter for the priests but also a school
center. It offered opportunities for higher education in communities
which in themselves could not have afforded even an elementary
school. The sisters looked after the primary instruction, going out to
settlements large enough to maintain school buildings of their own, or
receiving at their convent the children of people in smaller settlements
or on scattered farms. The fathers performed this service in higher
education. The chief function of the latter was religious. They journeyed out from the monastery to conduct services in small and scattered settlements. Where the community was large enough to support
a resident priest, fathers were sent to remain for extended periods,
sometimes years. While most of their work was among the white people, they did important work also among the Indians and still carry
on their work on the Indian reservations in the state.

The distance to which the work of these Benedictine communities
was extended seems almost incredible. The monastery has helped to
serve needy communities as far away as northwestern Canada and
even the Pacific Northwest of this country. The sisters have supplied
elementary teachers and nurses almost as widely. The Canadian work
of the men has now reached a stage where it supports an independent
monastery, whose abbot was in charge of college work at St.
John's in the early 1920s. The sisters, too, have seen their work increase to such proportions as to warrant the separate establishment in
1900 of a community at Duluth, the Convent of St. Scholastica. The
sisters there carry on both educational and nursing work, just as do
the sisters of St. Benedict at St. Joseph. Even so, there are more than
nine hundred professed members of the latter community, the largest
Benedictine community of women in the world.

To the historian of early European history it is peculiarly interesting
to watch the growth on Minnesota soil of an institution whose work
he has so often followed in those earlier years of European civilization.
It is amazing to find repeated here so much of what occurred around
Monte Cassino, or at the monastery of the Venerable Bede in Anglo-
Saxon England, or at Fulda in western Germany, or at Metten in eastern Bavaria. Only the names and dates are different. The successful
qualities of those earlier monasteries, particularly in England and
Germany, where the work was of a pioneer character, reappear in the
Minnesota community. Like them, the Minnesota monastery was pe-
culiarly fitted to cope with pioneer problems. It was practically as self-

sustaining in the material needs of life as were they. Its priest members could likewise serve the scattered small groups of their flock over a radius of many miles.

It is interesting also to note how truly the Minnesota communities have run the course of the older monasteries in identifying themselves with the localities in which they were established. Originally the monks came from Germany to serve the needs of the German Catholic settlers of this region. They spoke German as their native tongue, both monks and settlers, and they conducted their work among the adults in German. But from the very opening of their seminary in 1857 they carried on instruction for their younger pupils in English. Many of the fathers still speak German fluently, but it is already apparent that most of them speak English more readily. Where English was the acquired tongue in 1857, German has become the acquired tongue for those of the present generation. In this, both monastery and convent have served a very important function in easing the transition of these settlers from their German origin to American society. The composition of the communities reflects a similar development. Whereas the earlier membership was almost exclusively of German origin, the 1927 membership, while it still has many German names, probably a majority, embraces also Irish, Czech, Polish, French, English, and even Scandinavian names. This is still more true of the students enrolled in the schools. One infers from newspaper accounts of St. John's University that the students there engage in football, basketball, and baseball games, have trained coaches for the purpose, and have a very creditable record of competition with other colleges of the state. In other words, the institution has become within little more than half a century an integral part of the characteristic life of the state.

Their part in the cultural life of the state is no less impressive and no less typical of Benedictine traditions. They did not rear an imposing Gothic or Romanesque or Renaissance edifice on the prairies when they arrived in 1857. Their first community dwelling and seminary or college was a log house measuring some twelve by twenty feet. As their needs required, the building was enlarged and new buildings added. The location was changed several times, and on their present location the cluster of buildings reflects further stages in growth. Those buildings give some evidence too of the influence of an education that is in touch with ideas of Europe as well as of Minnesota, but mostly evidence of a close connection with Minnesota and the Northwest itself. Architecturally, the buildings are, and presumably have been since

1857, like and just a little in advance of the general taste of the surrounding society.

One cannot visit St. John's without becoming aware of the regard
for art and science prevailing there. It is present in the care with which
the grounds are kept, and trees, shrubs, and flowers planted; and in the
location and character of the buildings. Within the chapel the vest-
ments and other articles of religious service reveal this taste and interest
in art. The library is a truly impressive one, and, while dominated
by the interest in theology and church history, it has a considerable number of secular works. It is quite evident that the traditional
intellectual interests of the Benedictine Order are not forgotten. There
is, therefore, nothing surprising in the fact that the horticultural ex-
perimentation of some of the fathers there has resulted in the development of several fruits adapted to this climate. Nor is it surprising to
find, among the many protests against the so-called antievolution bill
which confronted the legislature in 1927, a series of vigorous resolutions from St. John's University. In both art and learning this monastery has held an active and important place in the history of Minnesota.

Or, putting it in another fashion, one may think of the Roman
Benedict and the equally Roman Gregory back there in Italy of the
sixth century, or the Anglo-Saxon Bede and the equally Anglo-Saxon
Boniface of the eighth century, or the Frankish Charlemagne at the
opening of the ninth, as well as of that long line of Bavarian Benedictines at Metten as contributing to the history of Minnesota or even
to that of Stearns County. Each of them took part in forging the chain
which links Monte Cassino and Metten and Minnesota. The Benedictines of Minnesota are neither Bavarian nor Anglo-Saxon nor Italian;
they are American and Minnesotan, but they carry on the traditions of
a glorious past which links them to the rest.

This survey is only a reminder of the fact that our civilization is
composed of the achievements of the past, particularly of the European
past. As our legal institutions hark back to English history, even farther
back than Magna Charta; our common language to the England of
Chaucer, Wycliffe, and Shakespeare; so many of our social and economic institutions and most of our religious institutions were fashioned
in the various countries of Europe anywhere from one hundred to
more than two thousand years ago. The Benedictine strand from
Monte Cassino to Metten to Minnesota is but one of the many strands
from which the multicolored warp of Minnesota and western civilization is woven. It is this multicolored and multiform character of our

civilization which distinguishes us from any of the countries of Europe today.

Although the Monastery of St. John and the Convents of St. Benedict and of St. Scholastica are very definitely linked with their European past, much more important to us is their part in the development of Minnesota and adjacent regions. Just as Monte Cassino contributed to the maintenance of Roman and Italian civilization, Canterbury and Wearmouth to the making of English civilization, Fulda and Metten to that of German civilization, so St. John's has definitely contributed to the making of Minnesota as we have it today. It served to stabilize that first scattering German Catholic element which came here in the 1850s. Its establishment encouraged other Germans to come here, and it is probably one of the most important, if not altogether the most important, factor in explaining the great influx of those settlers into this region. From its very beginnings in this state the Benedictine community set about the problem of teaching these German people the arts of American life. It had the twofold problem of learning those arts itself and then of imparting them. The great strides which have been made toward this goal in this section are in no small measure due to the work of the Benedictines. The thorough identification of the interests of these monks and nuns with those of Minnesota and the nation is further illustrated by their intelligent and effective co-operation in dealing with other problems of the region, such as the Indian problem and various phases of educational work. Their contributions to domestic science and art, and their work in hospitals and care for the sick are noteworthy. Their connection with a long, definite past renders them somewhat more picturesque, but their real importance to Minnesota lies in their work as a Minnesota institution. While perhaps they have not yet given us a Minnesota Bede or Roswitta, they have already made modest contributions in both fields of endeavor suggested by those illustrious names, and their past efforts are clearly an earnest of even greater efforts in the future.

Some Frontier
Words and Phrases

LEROY G. DAVIS

*SOME OF THE MOST memorable contributions to Minnesota His-
tory have come from authors who were not professional historians but
who were able to recount vividly their own recollections of the frontier
experience. One of these was LeRoy G. Davis, a Sleepy Eye lawyer,
who had arrived in southern Minnesota via covered wagon in 1866 as
a boy of seven. From his keen memory and lively pen came a series of
reminiscences, picturing life in the expanding state of the 1870s and
1880s. In the essay here reprinted from the September, 1938, issue
(volume 19), Davis lists some of the Yankee expressions brought to
Minnesota by settlers from New England — expressions which must
have mightily puzzled the European immigrants who were the Yankee's
neighbors in many parts of the state. Present-day readers may be surprised at the number of these phrases which are still in current use. The
article below is drawn from a manuscript volume of reminiscences
in which the author describes many aspects of pioneer life in southern
Minnesota. Mr. Davis, who died in 1957, also published a collection
of legends (1924) and a book of poetry (1937).*

WORDS, ACCENTS, and pronunciations used by pioneers whose
ancestors talked and wrote the old Yankee version of the English
language in the New England hills and along the narrow winding
streams of the East were undoubtedly modified in the West. There the
settlers met with and adjusted themselves to new living and working
conditions, material and otherwise, met and associated with settlers
from many sections of the Old and New Worlds, and often lived in
communities that lacked schools and churches. I say the old New
England English, for one may now travel for a week through Yankee-
land without hearing a half-dozen people speak the language as their
grandparents did back in the sixties of the last century. But I shall not
attempt here to explain the how or why of that. Many words and

185

phrases and practically all the accent or dialect pronunciations have passed into oblivion. But in the late sixties and the seventies they were still commonly used by New Englanders, New Yorkers, and other native Americans who settled in southern Minnesota. A few words still have a place in the vocabularies of the people, and some of these words are still pronounced in the old way, as "crick" for "creek," "ant" for "aunt," "laff" for "laugh," and the like.

Among the natives — the Yankees and near Yankees — many very expressive words and phrases were used in common conversation. These were well understood by the natives themselves, but their purport was often lost at first on the foreigners, many of whom never came to understand them all. If a speaker wished to convey the idea that another person was naturally dull, he called him a "numbskull"; if he was bright enough naturally, but had been easily fooled by someone, he was a "chump." If the speaker harbored more or less ill will against another, the latter "didn't know enough to carry guts to a bear," he "didn't know as much as a sore foot," he was a "saphead," he "didn't have the gumption of a louse," he "hadn't as much sense as a farrow cow," he was a "blockhead," a "stick-in-the-mud," a "reg'lar toby's [donkey's] hind leg," "no great scratch," or maybe a "mullet head." It might also have been said that he "hasn't got sense enough to last 'im over night," or that he "wasn't fit fer a taller drag."

A stingy person was "tight as the bark to a tree," an "old miser," or a "skinflint." A woman would refer to another whom she did not like or about whom she had heard derogatory stories as a "hussy" or a "hen hussy." If the reference was to a man, he might be called an "old blatherskite," a "scallawag," a "hen granny," or some other scorching epithet. Whichever expression was used would usually be preceded by "darn" or an equally descriptive adjective.

Some common expressions carried their meanings more or less clearly and openly, notwithstanding idiomatic obscurity in the form, as "scarce as hens' teeth." "The jumping off place" was used to describe a place about as far west as the women wanted to go. The "bat's end o' the world," "let the cat out o' the bag," "he'll stick like a dog to a root," "run Big Fraid, Little Fraid's after ye," "he's plannin' some scullduggery," "she's made 'er bed an' now she's got tuh lay in it," "out o' the fryin' pan intuh the fire," "full o' gimp an' gumption," "ye're as much mistaken as if ye'd burnt yer shirt," "as useless as a last year's bird's nest," "he got comeup-with," "I'll knock 'im intuh the middle o' next week," "don't open yer yawp," "hitting two birds with one stone," "jealous pated," "go tuh grass," "go tuh pot an' see the kittle bile," "birds of a feather flock together," "looks like he's been drawn through a knothole," "he makes a mountain out of a molehill," "stay on yer own side o' the dish," "give 'im an E an' he'll take an Ell," "root hog 'er die," "you've got tuh either fish 'er cut bait," "the more haste the less speed," "between the devil an' the deep sea," "give the devil his due," "ye might as well eat the devil as drink his broth," "smart as a whip," and "love'll go where it's sent" were sayings frequently used by the pioneers.

How wonderfully expressive were the following: "It smells strong enough to knock an ox down," "ye're a dreadful knowin' critter," "now I'm in a peck o'half bushels," "I'll bust yer biler," "going at a hen canter," "stands to reason," "the pesky thing is all out o' kilter," "like a thousan' o' brick," "tough as a biled owl," "more than ye c'n shake a stick at," "licketty split," "till ye're blue in the face," "crazy as a bedbug," "called him everything he could lay his tongue to," "right hand runnin'," "it ain't what it's cracked up tuh be," "can't git head nor tail to it," "as cunnin' as a red pig a runnin'," "it's as easy as fallin' off a log," "if ye don't like it ye c'n lump it," "blind as a bat," "full of the old Harry," "I'll make 'im scratch gravel," "I wish he was in hell with his back broke," "hell-bent fer 'lection," "let 'er rip," and "skee-daddle." If a neighbor needed help in case of sickness or trouble, the settlers said that "we'll all clap to and help 'im out." "I can't guttle it down" or "I can't muckle it" were expressions for "I can't eat it." "I want tuh know" expressed wonder or incredulity. If two men wanted to settle a mutual running account without bothering to look up books or figures they would "jump accounts" — that is, call it even.

And what modern expressions are capable of more carrying power than these: "as big as all out doors and part in the house," "like all possessed," "as near as ye c'n put yer eye out," "that can't hold a candle tuh mine," "quick as a cat ever licked 'er ear," "that's no all-killin' matter," "that's a whopper [*a big lie*]," "he'll turn up missin'," "don't buy a pig in a poke" and "mind yer p's an' q's"? Uncouth? Yes, perhaps. But what depths of possible meaning these expressions imply and what a wide range of application they have!

The following did very well for terse and meaningful character descriptions: "narrer contracted," "he ain't got no backbone," "he thinks he's the biggest toad in the puddle," "crooked as a ram's horn," "he c'n lie faster than a horse c'n trot," "he thinks he's a little god and a half," "he's got enough brass in his face tuh make a ten-pail kettle," "they're the offscourin's o' the earth," "as full of the devil as an egg is full o' meat," "he's a reg'lar bigbug," "thinks he's some punkins," "he's a wolf in sheep's clothing," "dumbhead," "old rip," "terror tuh snakes," "backbiter," "half baked," and "he don't know enough tuh ache."

And here are more idioms and often-used words and phrases that added rugged richness to the ordinary conversation of the pioneers: "Homely as a hedge fence," "like all git out," "one boy is half a man, two boys no man at all," "cutting up didoes," "bugbear," "boogaboo," "brat," "three jerks of a cat's tail," "I like the cut of his jib," "it ain't tuh be sneezed at," "strain at a gnat an' swaller a sawmill," "crack o' doom," "dark as a nigger's pocket," "busy as a bee in a tar bucket," "it rained pitchforks," "beller like a bay steer," "if wishers had horses beggars might ride," "sure as ye're a foot high," "hustle yer boots," "he'll go up like a rocket an' come down like a stick," "run like a heeter," "afoot an' alone," "ye can't make a whistle out of a pig's tail," "every which way," "unbeknown," "by good rights," "the hull kit an' caboodle of 'em," "all cluttered up," "don't git on yer ear," "don't git yer dander up," and "the hull shootin' match."

If one did a thing with more than ordinary energy, it was said that he went at it with "hammer an' tongs"; he would "spruce up" when getting ready to go to a party or to go courting; he was "off the first four miles" if he was liable to be absent when needed; he was said to "feel his oats" if he thought too much of himself; and when he began to feel at home in a place, he was said to be "wonted." One often spoke of a boy as a "little bugger," though the expression "stiff-necked old bugger" also was common. To "go snucks" was to go into partnership. To "hoof it" was to walk, but if one walked a considerable distance and someone asked how he came, he would say that he "rode shank's mare." To be "tight" was to be drunk. One spoke of a "hunk" of bread or cake. A "little cutup" was a lively child, and a "flutterbudget" was a lively or nervous person. "They're in cahoots" was said of people who were thought to be scheming to do something disliked by the speaker. "Got a hen on" was said of a person planning something he did not yet wish to discuss or reveal. If a person died it was reported that he had "kicked the bucket." If a person entered or left a house unceremoniously he "boused" in or out. "Scram" has replaced the old word "git" for "get out" or "go away." Here is a mother's advice to her grown boys — perhaps hard to take, but well meant: "Don't tie yer love tuh any girl's apern strings till ye know ye c'n get 'er." But if a woman wanted her daughter to "keep company" with John Doe, she said: "Why don't ye set yer cap fer Johnny, he'd make a good per-vider."

The following expressions were often used as expletives by those who for some reason did not want to swear: "the devil an' Tom Walker," "gosh all fishhooks," "so help me jumping John Rogers," "jumping Aunt Hannah," "Land o' Goshen," and "by cracky." "In all my born days" and "for land sakes alive" were used chiefly by women for emphasis, and "not by a jugful," "what in Sam Hill" or "what the Sam Hill," and "Zounds an' garters," by men.

If an undesirable person or family left the neighborhood, their departure was described as "good riddance tuh bad rubbish." It was often said that there was a "nigger in the wood pile" or "the devil's in 'im as big as a woodchuck," or "she'll do it if the devil stands tuh the door." "All around Robin Hood's barn" was expressive as covering a good deal more territory than was necessary or truthful.

What these words and idiomatic expressions lacked in grace and delicacy was made up for in stark expressiveness. The pioneers who used them in everyday conversation did so very often and on many diverse occasions, giving them the shades of meaning demanded by the circumstances.

On the Trail of the Woodsman in Minnesota

AGNES M. LARSON

MANY NEW ENGLANDERS were drawn to pioneer Minnesota by the magnificent stands of white pine and hardwoods which covered the northern half of the state. From the time the first commercial sawmill went into operation at Marine Mills on the St. Croix River in 1839 until the early years of the twentieth century, loggers from Maine and other states to the east harvested the vast forests to build farmhouses, cities, and fortunes. Between 1848 and 1903, for example, it is estimated that about eleven and a half billion board feet of lumber were cut in the St. Croix Valley alone. The colorful traditions of this major nineteenth-century industry and its lumberjacks are described by Agnes M. Larson in the following article, which was published in December, 1932 (volume 13). Its author later wrote a full-length History of the White Pine Industry in Minnesota *(1949) which remains a standard reference on the subject. She retired in 1960 after a distinguished teaching career in the history department of St. Olaf College at Northfield.*

WHEN THE PILGRIM FATHERS chopped the first white pine to provide them with shelter in the immense wilderness to which they had come, they little realized that they were launching one of America's greatest industries, the manufacture of lumber.[1] As people sought haven in America in ever greater numbers they began literally to absorb the pine around them, and they looked for new forests to supply the needs of the ever-growing population. Then began the trek of the woodsman into regions of untouched monarchs. The woodsman became an explorer. He moved ever westward. He marched in the vanguard of civilization. Surely he, no less than the fur trader and the cowboy, deserves a place in the history of the West — and his name, like theirs, is passing into history. The kingship in the north woods of the "jack," the "riverman," and the "cruiser" is sinking into oblivion.

On the shores of the Atlantic the woodsman found the first white pine. It fell before his ax in Maine, and New York, Michigan, and Wisconsin in turn gave up their supplies. Westward, ever westward, moved this woodsman. The white pine in the region of the upper Mississippi was the last to go. There it had stood serenely for centuries. It had known only the red man as he glided in and out, and saws and axes were not tools peculiar to him. But one day these same pines sensed tragedy. The "army of axes" was upon them, and the harvesting of the white pine was to continue until its disreputable relative, the jack pine, was all that remained.

It was in 1836 and 1837 that the woodsman began his work within Minnesota's boundaries. Pines, centuries old, faced the woodsman's ax, and the monarchial achievement of the ages came crashing down. As the gold diggers sought California and the Klondike, so the "pine hungry" lumbermen were attracted to the forests of Minnesota. Hither trekked men from Maine — men who had driven logs on the powerful Penobscot, like Daniel Stanchfield; or who had lived on the banks of the Androscoggin, like William D. Washburn; or who had labored on the banks of the turbulent St. Croix, which separates Maine from Canada. The names of many Maineites who came into the upper Mississippi territory are well known in Minnesota today — DeLaittre, Bovey, Eastman, Stanchfield, Morrison, and Washburn. On the banks of the Mississippi and of its tributaries, they found what they sought, and in the region of the virgin pine they settled down to make their homes. Tozer, Hersey, Staples, McKusick are names familiar in the St. Croix lumber region, and the men who bore them likewise came from Maine and New Brunswick in quest of forests. Stephen Hanks, who logged on the Snake River, a branch of the St. Croix, in 1841, found that most of his coworkers were old loggers from Maine and other eastern logging states.[2] Men old in the business of lumber today give to the men of Maine unstinted praise: "Maineites knew logging."

These newcomers did not come as single men in big gangs, here when the season was on and gone when it was over. They came to stay, they brought their families. They settled in the woods and carried on logging as their chosen lifework. If they had little farms, these were but incidental to their chief business. The first operators in the pine forests of Minnesota were pioneers who ventured into the new country to cut timber for a livelihood, and not for speculation.[3]

Though the early woodsmen were largely from New England there were some New Yorkers, some French and Scotch from Canada, some Irish, and occasionally a German, a Norwegian, or a Swede. The Scotch who came into Minnesota from Canada were from the Glengary district below Ottawa. MacDonald, MacIntosh, MacLain, and MacLaughlin are names still heard in Minnesota. The Scotch loggers were men of repute, and they often developed sufficient skill to be advanced to the position of cruiser; others became foremen of camps; and some went into the business of logging for themselves.[4]

Then came also the hardy, rawboned French-Canadian, who was proud of his hairy chest which showed through the unbuttoned collar of his black and red flannel shirt. This French-Canadian was full of imagination; he had a store of songs; and he was known for his speed and general efficiency. He was said to have been "born with an ax in his hand," and he moved with the "tall pine." He was at home in no other place, and when the pine was gone he, too, was gone.[5] He excelled as a sawyer, but was also known widely for his skill in handling the cant hook. He could serve both as a top loader and a landing man, and so he was much in demand. The Canadian played no humble part in the development of the lumber industry.

The meagerness and simplicity of the conditions under which the woodsman worked offer a strange contrast to the later methods used in lumbering by "big business." A shanty, low and dark, served as the woodsman's living quarters. It was built of logs; its sides were never more than four feet high, and the roof was steep and sometimes ran almost to the ground. "One had to learn to stoop in those days," according to a tall lanky Irishman of eighty-one summers, who has lived his life in the logging camp and knows its evolution. The gables were built of logs, for windows were very rare. The shanty varied in size, depending upon the number in the crew. One on the banks of the Snake River in 1841 was twenty-five by forty feet.[6] Moss and clay filled the openings between the logs to keep the warmth in. The shanty had but one big room, where at least twenty men lived during the coldest days of the year.

The life of the shanty centered about a big open fire, which baked the bread, dried the clothes, gave cheer and warmth, and illuminated many a squaw dance.[7] Sleeping quarters were at one end of the room. Beds of balsam boughs a foot deep gave rest at night. With their heads to the walls and their feet to the fire, the men slept side by side covered by large blankets — so large that each served for many men.[8] Strange it must have been at night to see by the glow of the fire the bewhiskered faces of the lumberjacks peering out above the blankets. There were whiskers like Paul Bunyan's and there were those like Abraham's of old. A grindstone, a wash sink, and a barrel of water were also parts of the equipment of the men's sleeping quarters.

At the farther end of the shanty was the kitchen. Cooking was not very complex. It was done over the open fire or in the bean hole. The cook had a wooden crane by which he moved the red-hot kettles over the burning logs. Bread was baked in a reflector standing beside the open fire. Beans were put into a Dutch oven and buried in the bean hole, which was alongside of the big fire. They cooked mysteriously at night while the men slept, and were ready to be served in the morning with boiled salt pork. Both dishes appeared again at noon and at night, and for a change on Sundays the salt pork was fried. Bread, sometimes in the form of hot biscuits, salt pork, blackstrap, and bean-hole beans, eulogized by the early woodsmen, formed the regular diet. Once in a while a mince or an apple pie appeared. Venison, fish, and fowl were sometimes a happy change, and one lumberjack speaks of being served with a "fine mess of red squirrels in a delicious stew." [9] The early woodsmen ate and slept in the one-room Maine shanty or hovel, where their cooking and baking were done. They lived together like one family. Such were the humble beginnings of a big industry in Minnesota.

John Boyce was the first to assemble a crew to cut pine in the region of what is now Minnesota. In a Mackinaw boat he traveled from St. Louis in the fall of 1837, setting camp where the Snake River rolls into the proud St. Croix. His outfit consisted of eleven men and six oxen.[10] More meager still was the crew of Franklin Steele, who became a prominent lumber promoter in Minnesota. When he first "fleshed his ax" in the wilderness of the St. Croix in 1837 his outfit consisted of an ox, a cart, and six half-breeds.[11]

Ten years later camps began to appear on the Rum River, a tributary of the Mississippi, where Anoka now stands. In 1847 Daniel Stanchfield placed the first logging camp there with twenty men to cut the pine. And in 1848 Sumner W. Farnham, a son of the surveyor of logs on the St. Croix River in Maine, established a second logging camp on the Rum River.[12] By 1852 twenty-two firms of loggers were operating on this river alone. In that year Minnesota's lumber brought a net revenue of $2,500,000 — a sum more equally divided among the "bone and sinew" of the territory than that from almost any other trade.[13]

Pine was plentiful and water on which to transport the logs was there, but food was scarce, and that which was to be had was very expensive. A logging team required much food. In the usual outfit in 1852 there were from six to eight oxen and from twelve to fourteen men. Two of the men were choppers, two or three were swampers, two sled tenders, two barkers, two sawyers, one a teamster, and one a cook.

Three hundred bushels of corn, two hundred bushels of oats, twenty barrels of flour, a hundred and fifty pounds of lard, ten bushels of beans, six hundred pounds of beef, and fifteen tons of hay were the foodstuffs necessary for such a crew during five long cold winter months.[14]

In 1836 Joseph N. Nicollet found that at Fort Snelling fifteen dollars were paid for a barrel of flour and twenty-five dollars for a barrel of pork. These articles had no doubt been purchased for five or eight dollars in St. Louis. In 1837 Franklin Steele paid four dollars a barrel for beans, eleven dollars for flour, and forty dollars for pork. Even in the late 1850s, wheat cost four dollars a bushel and flour ten dollars a barrel.[15] The woodsman used to fine advantage meadow hay, wild rice, and maple sugar, but there were not enough farmers in Minnesota to supply him with the necessary corn, oats, and wheat. Such provisions must all come from down river.[16] In 1846 Stephen Hanks bought at St. Louis for John McKusick, who was then the lumber magnate of Stillwater, several tons of food, including uncured bacon, eggs, beans, hominy, and dried apples. At Bellevue above St. Louis he bought fifty barrels of flour and several barrels of whisky. At Albany, Illinois, on the same trip, he purchased oxen and horses, paying fifty dollars in gold for a yoke of oxen. St. Louis was a market for lumber and from St. Louis in turn came the lumberman's provisions. But the exorbitant prices resulting from the distance from the source of supply and difficulties of transportation worked a real hardship on the loggers. In 1853 logging teams on the Rum River were reduced in number for this reason.[17]

The virtues of the Minnesota climate were extolled as a means of attracting settlers. "We wish all the world were here in Minnesota to enjoy the magnificent weather which now 'comes off' daily," reads an item in the *St. Anthony Express* of June 14, 1851. "Skies are blue and air as balmy as Italy can boast, and an atmosphere so pure as to defy the approach of disease — of such marvelous virtue indeed as might 'create a soul under the ribs of death.'" Territory and state attempted vigorously to attract settlers, and prominent Minnesotans carried the gospel of the North Star State to Europe — Franklin Steele, for example, to England, and Hans Mattson to Sweden. Minnesota did eventually become an agricultural state, but it was lumber providing a market for farm produce that first gave agriculture an impetus there. Pillsbury's Best and Gold Medal Flour owe something to Minnesota white pine and the early woodsman.

The early period of logging in Minnesota could well be called the hand-tool period. It was a period of heavy lifting, when plain brute strength figured. It was a period of slow motion, when the deliberate movement of the ox and the hand of man made power. The Maine men brought to the Minnesota forests the go-devil and the ax and that instrument so necessary in the drive, the peavey.[18] The chopper was an artist in the opinion of the woodsman. To swing the ax and strike right every time was the work of an expert, and therefore the chopper could command wages above those of other woodsmen.[19] These men did not know the crosscut saw. It had not seen the light of day. It had not yet come to replace the ax, and to take from the chopper the position which he later jealously had to guard.

There was no hewing out of log roads during the period of early logging in Minnesota. The pines stood thick on the banks of streams. A go-devil, a wishbone-shaped affair with a crossbar — only the crotch of a hardwood tree — was the chief means of transportation in the woods. This rough sled sufficed to take the trees from where they fell to the landing, whence they should go downstream when the spring freshet came. When the chopper had finished his work and the tree was prostrate on the ground, the swamper came to lop the branches. Then followed the barker, who ripped the bark from underneath so the tree would slide more easily.[20] The ox pulled it through the brush and snow to the landing, where it was made into logs ready for the spring drive.

The cant hook, used in rolling logs, was not so important among the tools of the early Maineites. It seems to belong rather to the Canadian, who cut the trees into logs where they fell. Thus the loggers could carry bigger loads to the landing. This brought about a change in the mode of transportation in the woods, which led to the use of bobsleds, bigger teams, bigger loads, and log roads. Early logging in Minnesota, it is evident, was a combination of the ways of the Maineites and those of the Canadians.[21]

But heavier market demands were forcing a speedier output, for settlements in Iowa, Kansas, Nebraska — the great treeless prairie states — were calling for lumber for homes. And in 1863 the Mississippi saw such drives of logs as it had never been a witness to before.[22] Wages for loggers were on the increase, evidence that the industry was making progress. In the winter of 1870, four thousand men and two thousand horses and oxen went into the woods of Minnesota. Lumber did have a setback in the panic year of 1873, but in 1874 loggers on the Mississippi found themselves hewing down the tall pine north of Grand Rapids.[23] In 1878 the first mill at Cloquet began its work, and the Duluth district was modestly carrying on logging.

Improvements were being made in order that production might meet the market demand. The passing of the pioneer stage of logging cannot be precisely dated, for the change depended to a considerable extent on whether a given logging establishment was that of a small owner, or of a jobber, or of a man of "big business." It was in the 1870s that the more primitive methods of logging began to disappear, however. The one-room Maine shanty was passing, and in its place was coming a good-sized lumber camp with perpendicular sides, which was warmly built and lighted with windows. The new camp housed from fifty to eighty men.

Sometimes a partition separated the eating and sleeping quarters; often camps were constructed with these quarters in separate buildings. Men no longer slept on the floor, but in bunks with mattresses filled with hay, straw, or perhaps balsam boughs. The bunks were single, or double, or treble, depending upon the size of the camp. They were arranged like berths in a Pullman car. With his turkey or his tussock, the bag which held his possessions, under his head, the lumberjack rested well after the day's labor, only to be called again before the light of another day. There was no mistaking the call of the shanty boy, later known as the bull cook, when he blew the camp horn in the morning. The horn was made of tin and it was five feet long. Its din was followed by another, the call of "Daylight and the swamp boys — roll out!" or "Roll out, daylight in the swamp." [24] Perhaps the most original of calls was one used on the St. Croix, "Roll out, tumble out, any way to get out. This is the day to make the fortune." [25] Surely a stimulus for any lumberjack! It caused the sleeper "to tremble and start from the land of dreams to the land of pork and beans," wrote a would-be poet in 1875.[26]

The first ray of light sent the lumberjack to work. The teamster was up at four. His day was long, but he was of the upper caste in the hierarchy of lumberjacks. His wage compared with that of the cook, and was lower only than that of the foreman. The teamster drove thousands of feet of logs in a single load with two, four, or six horses over the iced boulevards that were introduced into Minnesota by Michigan lumbermen. He had a daredevil's job; one accident, and he was forever gone from the list of able teamsters. The "road monkey" or "hayman on the hill" was of importance to the teamster, for it was the business of the road monkey to put hay or sand on the very steep places to be traversed by the teamster.[27] If he failed in his work, a dangerous accident might ensue.

Each man had his job and at break of day each was in his place.

"The sharp ring of well plied axes, the crash of falling trees, and the see-saw clang of cross-cut saws . . . the rattling of chains and the crunching of snow" all made up a scene of busy toilers whose work went steadily on until the bull cook — who during the morning had supplied wood and water for the men's shanty, had washed the roller towel, cleaned the lamp, and swept the floor — blew his big horn for lunch. The noon meal was nearly always eaten in the open, for sometimes the woodsmen were several miles from camp. In a big box on a homemade sleigh drawn by a horse came the food for the big, husky, hungry woodsmen. The beans froze on their tin plates. Their whiskers froze too, though they ate around a big open fire. Then more sharp ringing of well-plied axes until dark and their day was done. Work from daylight to dark was the lot of a lumberjack. No six-hour day, no eight-hour day for him! [28] The lumberjack took pride in hard work. Every sawyer, every teamster, every undercutter, reported to the clerk the number of feet of heavy timber he had handled during the day. Competition was keen.

The lumberjack had respect for physical prowess; he was proficient; he was trustworthy, generous, and dependable. He pitted red blood against a hard job. He was noted for his generosity; he would contribute toward a hospital or funeral bill of any fellow worker, though he were someone almost unknown.[29] They had a code, these lumberjacks, and it was a chivalrous one.

At the end of a day the lumberjacks went home to partake of the cook's good meal. The cook — and what a man was he — second to none in the camp except the foreman! He was the major-domo whose precinct no one dared to invade.[30] It was good business, too, to stand well with the cook, for it was quite likely that somewhere he had a bit of toddy stored. In the cook's domain the bean hole had gone and the big cookstove had taken its place. The food had improved greatly. Better facilities brought better supplies. Fresh meat and mashed potatoes had been added to salt pork and beans; pound cake, rice pudding with raisins, vegetables, hot biscuits, and pies of many varieties were served to the men.[31] The prune, called in camp parlance the "loggin' berry," seemed to rank high. Blackstrap had been replaced by brown sugar, and after 1890 white sugar took the place of brown.

The Stone-Ordean-Wells Company of Duluth, a wholesale grocery firm, sold the lumber concerns of the nineties ten-pound cans of peaches, plums, and pears. Oleomargarine was used almost always in place of butter — five thousand pounds of it was the usual order for a hundred men for two hundred days. Alger, Smith and Company of Duluth, a Michigan lumber firm that removed to Minnesota in the nineties, bought on the average 365 sacks of beans a year, and a sack weighed 165 pounds. Thus beans were still a good old stand-by. The annual tobacco and snuff bill of the same concern alone amounted to $25,000. And the grocery bill paid by that firm to the wholesale grocers mentioned above was about $250,000 annually during the period of its greatest activity in 1898 and 1899. "Has anything replaced the business which the logger gave you?" the writer asked Mr. J. Edgar Willcuts, who had charge of the supplies sent to loggers for Stone-Ordean-Wells. "Nothing," he said, "nothing. Those were the good old days." [32]

But to return to the lumberjack. On Saturday night a stag dance would probably take place; men with handkerchiefs around their arms played the part of women. Or by chance there was a squaw dance.[33] Music — such music as there was, and it was not all bad for one finds comparisons to Camilla Urso and Ole Bull — was usually furnished by a fiddler, who was as necessary in the lumber camp as the ox teamster, or perhaps by someone who played the mouth organ or the accordion. But music there was. "Hot Bottom," "Shuffle the Brogue," and "Buy My Sheep" were favorite games.[34] Especially popular was "Buy My Sheep," whereby a greenhorn was initiated into the fraternity of lumberjacks. Some of the men amused themselves by singing songs of their own composition. These usually had an epic theme, recounting the heroism of some lumberjack, usually in their own camp. Perhaps one of the oldest that has survived is the "Pokegama Bear," composed in camp in 1874 by Frank Hasty.[35]

Come all you good fellows who like to hear fun,
    Come listen to me while I sing you a song;
Come listen to me while the truth I declare,
    I am going to sing the Pokegama Bear.

One cold frosty morning, the winds they did blow,
    We went to the woods our days work to do,
Yes, into the woods we did quickly repair,
    It was there that we met the Pokegama Bear!

One, Morris O'Hern, — a bold Irish lad,
    Went to build a fire all in a pine stub;
He rapped with his ax when he went there,
    When out popped the monstrous Pokegama Bear!

With a roar like a Lion, O'Hern did swear,
    Saying, "Run boys for God's sake, for I've found a bear!"
As out through the brush Jim Quinn did climb,
    Saying, "To hell with your bear, kill your own porcupine!"

Into the swamp old bruin did go,
    O'Hern and Hasty did quickly pursue,
As on through the brush those heroes did tear,
    To capture or kill the Pokegama Bear.

Old Bruin got angry — for Hasty did steer!
    He prepared to receive without dread or fear,
With his teeth firmly set and his ax in the air,
    He slipped and fell on the Pokegama Bear.

Out on the road old bruin did go,
    He thought that was better than wading in snow,
Yet little he knew what awaited him there,
    For fate was against the Pokegama Bear.

There was one, Mike McAlpine, of fame and renown,
    Noted for foot racing on Canadian ground,
He ran up the road, raised his ax in the air,
    And dealt the death blow to the Pokegama Bear.

When out to the camp old bruin was sent,
    To skin him and dress him it was our intent.
And we all agreed that each should have a share,
    Of the oil that was in the Pokegama Bear.

To the cook it was taken, the tallow fried out,
    Each man with his bottle did gather about,
When Hasty and McAlpine they both lost their share,
    Of the oil that was in the Pokegama Bear.

Then it was taken by cook and it fried,
    It was all very good it can't be denied,
It tasted like roast turkey, Bill Moneghan did swear,
    As he feasted upon the Pokegama Bear.

Now my song is ended, I am going to drop my pen,
    And Morris O'Hern, he got the bear skin;

Here is long life to you boys, and long growth to your hair,
  Since it is greased with the oil of the Pokegama Bear.

Stories relating vague rumors of dreadful beasts which the lumberjacks had met on the tote road formed no small part of the evening's entertainment. There was the "agropelter." That animal, infuriated by the invasion of his secret precinct, the great forest, was a terrible threat to the logger. From Maine to Oregon the lumberjack feared his uncanny stroke. This horrible animal found shelter in hollow trees, and anyone who was unfortunate enough to pass his abode was usually reported as killed by a falling limb. Only one human being is ever known to have escaped death when given a blow by this treacherous beast. He was a Minnesota lumberjack. Big Ole Kittleson, cruising on the St. Croix, was the hero. The "agropelter" dealt the blow, but the "limb was so punky" that it flew into bits on Big Ole's head. He got a good view of the vicious creature before it bounded into the woods.[36] Many such stories were told and retold by the lumberjacks. The men of that fraternity pass the palm for storytelling to the French-Canadian, who excels in superstition and imagination.

Nine o'clock was the usual bedtime for men in the camps; but on Saturday night, when games of chess or cards were played, the hour was usually later.[37] Cards were not allowed in some camps, and in some, gambling was forbidden except when tobacco was used as a stake. Sunday was "boil-up" day. This one day in the week was used by the lumberjacks to shave, to cut hair, and to clean clothes. A big lard can was placed over an open fire outdoors, and there each lumberjack in turn scrubbed and boiled his clothes. Then the men patched their clothes and sewed on buttons. Sunday night saw them early to bed, in preparation for another week of hard work.

In no sphere is the lumberjack so distinctly individual as in his mode of expression. His environment is the source from which his peculiar vocabulary comes, and his phrases are quite unintelligible to anyone not of his fraternity. A woodsman over eighty years of age, who was found by the writer planting potatoes, made her realize how unfamiliar was the woodsmen's tongue. She knew she could not spell the words, and she had no notion of the meaning of some of the queer terms that the lumberjack's Irish tongue sputtered so easily. When the writer asked him what certain terms means, he laughed and said, "Well you're having the same trouble as did a Sister who used to take care of our boys in the hospital at Duluth." Such was his story: A certain top-loader had had his leg crushed by a log. The nun had inquired just how so serious an accident could have happened. The lumberjack replied: "Well, Sister, it happened this way. I dropped in at one of the Sawyer Goodman Company's camps and as I was the first 'gazebo' who came down the 'pike' and the 'push' needed men, he put me to work 'skyhooking.' The first thing the 'ground-hog' did was to send up a 'blue.' I hollered at him to throw a 'Saginaw' into her but he 'St. Croixed' her instead. Then he 'gunned' her and the result was I got my stem cracked." [38] Every term has its meaning. The woodsman's special vocabulary numbers about three hundred words and is both picturesque and significant.[39]

The business of logging grew. By 1900 no state in the union could compete with Minnesota in this domain. In the quantity and value of timber produced the state surpassed all others. A larger amount of capital was invested in logging in Minnesota than in any other state. Indeed, the capital invested per establishment was nearly double that of Wisconsin or California, Minnesota's nearest competitors. Minnesota likewise employed twice as many men in its camps as were employed in camps in any other state.[40]

In recent years the Maineite, the Canadian, the German, and the Scandinavian have been replaced by the Russian, the Finn, and other Europeans. The simple go-devil in time gave way to the giant steam overhead skidder, which grabs in its claws the logs that once were lifted by the masterful arms of the lumberjack. As in other industries, machine power has replaced manpower in the logging business. In 1900 the Rum and St. Croix rivers could no longer boast the largest logging camps in the state. They had shifted far into the northland, to Beltrami, Itasca, and St. Louis counties, where fifteen to twenty thousand men logged during the cold winter months.[41]

The lumber industry reached its height in the early years of the present century. In 1837 Franklin Steele and six half-breeds cut white pine in Minnesota. In 1912 about forty thousand lumberjacks logged in its forests.[42] Many of them cut logs for the largest white pine mill in the world — that at Virginia. Today the mill is gone. So is the lumberjack. This young giant, strong and wild in body and spirit, rough in dress and manner, belongs to the past. His stories, his songs, his language, his mode of dress, and his manner of living should be carefully recorded, for they are of interest to the historian. As a part of the group that helped to lay the basis of the state, he deserves to be studied. He is the hero of the drama of the pine forest, a drama that has now ended in Minnesota.

Minnesota, Montana, and Manifest Destiny

HELEN McCANN WHITE

WHILE LUMBERMEN from the East were moving to the Minnesota pineries, other ambitious Minnesotans were casting their eyes farther west. In the 1850s and 1860s they beheld visions of an economic empire based on the gold of the Rockies, the fertile plains of Dakota and Saskatchewan, and the trade of the Pacific. The story of this dream of empire and the daring efforts that were made to realize it is told in the following article. It was published in June, 1962 (volume 38) and received the Minnesota Historical Society's Solon J. Buck Award as the best article of the year in which it appeared. Helen McCann White served as manuscripts assistant on the society's staff from 1937 to 1941. Since then her husband's foreign assignments for the United States government have taken her and her family virtually around the world. In 1964 she received a grant from the society to complete her work, begun in 1944, on a volume of documents relating to the wagon train expeditions from Minnesota to the gold fields of Montana in the 1860s.

IN THE SUMMER of 1862, Minnesotans were in the vanguard of fortune hunters who migrated to new gold fields of the northern Rocky Mountains. Drawn west by news of rich discoveries in the Salmon River region of present-day Idaho, they turned off the trail to prospect in what in 1864 became Montana Territory. In the period between 1862 and 1868 unnumbered hundreds of them, hearing the magic word "gold," loaded their wagons, hitched up the oxen, said goodbye to Minnesota, and headed west for Bannack, Virginia City, and Helena, in the Eldorado of southwestern Montana.

Gold alone, however, cannot explain the significance of Montana in the minds of frontier Minnesotans. A fascination with the area was widespread among those who stayed at home as well as those who went. Shakopee, Mankato, Winona, and St. Cloud held mass meetings to hear wagon train leaders speak of Montana and discuss ways of going to the mines. The Anoka Library Association, the Minneapolis Lyceum, and the Minnesota Historical Society in St. Paul scheduled lectures on Montana, as did chambers of commerce and boards of trade in various other places. These local citizens' groups adopted memorials to government officials in support of a variety of projects they hoped would be helpful to the development of both Minnesota and Montana. Their proposals were forwarded to the state capital and to Washington. Newspapers of the state at once reflected and fostered this Montana enthusiasm by reporting on proposals for legislation, publishing dispatches from the gold fields, and printing news and gossip from neighbors who had migrated there. Their columns left the impression that every emigrant who went from Minnesota or through Minnesota to the west had contributed to the long-range interests of the state.[1]

While a few writers saw Montana only as a land where individual fortunes could be made, others perceived the wide-ranging benefits which the gold fields could generate for Minnesota. Immediate gains from the outfitting trade were apparent. In addition, profits could be expected from increased military activity on the northern plains, occasioned by the emigration across Indian lands. Beyond the plains, these visionaries saw the beginnings of a trading area that would look to Minnesota for supplies and capital. Sensitive to the promise of this expanding empire, these writers encouraged Minnesotans to go west and button Minnesota to the sleeve of the gold regions.

Another group of dreamers had a still larger vision. Newspapers of the territory and the state during the 1850s and 1860s revealed a global view of Minnesota's manifest destiny. Their columns expressed the belief that the gold fields were but a way station on a destined line of communication between Minnesota and the Orient. To this group the state's dreams of empire were not limited to the western regions of the North American continent. Roads to the new gold fields, when extended to the Pacific, would become the route of a future railroad connecting Minnesota with Puget Sound and the trade of the Orient.[2]

In the opinion of some of Minnesota's most articulate boosters the state's greatest resource was its unique geographical position at the heart of the North American continent. Its capital city, St. Paul, was located on the forty-fifth parallel, halfway between the equator and the North Pole — a circumstance of symbolic and almost mystical meaning for some writers. Within the state's borders were the headwaters of the Mississippi River, then at the height of its importance as the country's great inland waterway. To the north Minnesota shared a boundary with British America and commanded the source of the Red River of the North, a navigable stream leading to Winnipeg and the rivers flowing into Hudson Bay. At the head of Lake Superior, Minnesota stood at the terminus of an inland waterway which dreamers even then believed would bring ocean vessels from the Atlantic into the heart of North America. Thus situated on natural avenues of commerce to the east, the south, and the north, Minnesota needed only a connection with the Pacific to place it in easy communication with the whole northern hemisphere.[3]

Climate became an important consideration in this global vision. It was true that winters were severe and the northern waterways were frozen over half the year. It was also commonly believed in the mid-nineteenth century that the northern latitudes of Minnesota and the plains to the west were inhospitable to settlement or gracious living. But the global dreamers turned attention from latitude to isotherms and reasoned away the bugbears of snow and ice with the help of two men — Alexander von Humboldt and Lorin Blodget. Pointing out that the climate of a region is influenced by configuration of the surface, humidity, prevailing winds, and altitude, as well as by distances from the equator and the poles, Humboldt developed the concept of isothermal lines connecting points of equal average temperatures. Maps drawn by Blodget placed Minnesota and much of the northern plains region in an isothermal zone of temperatures ranging from thirty-two to fifty degrees. This zone extended around the globe in the northern hemisphere and embraced the areas of greatest settlement and human enterprise. Because a high civilization flourished in this zone, it was asserted that the climate was therefore particularly conducive to the health and happiness of the human race. The exhilarating conclusion to be drawn from such reasoning was that human enterprise would thus inevitably expand and flourish in Minnesota and the unsettled area to the west.[4]

During the 1850s the belief in Minnesota's future greatness was further strengthened by the expansion of transportation routes and means of communication. The survey of a northern railroad route to the Pacific conducted by Isaac I. Stevens in 1853 first fired the hopes of expansion-minded Minnesotans, and these were given further impetus by the completion of a rail line to the Mississippi River at Rock Island, Illinois, in 1854, the opening of the Sault Ste. Marie Canal in 1855, and the extension of telegraph service to St. Paul in

1860. In 1859 the building of a stage road from St. Cloud to the Red River and the beginning of steamboat navigation on that stream projected the state's line of communications far to the north and west.[5]

Around the world in the northern hemisphere, Minnesota's global dreamers saw a corresponding expansion of people and lines of communication which they felt supported their dreams of Minnesota's destiny. The premature opening in 1858 of the Atlantic cable, a joint British-American venture, was hailed as a major stride toward linking the markets of Europe and America and occasioned a large public celebration in St. Paul. An aroused British interest in western Canada encouraged Minnesotans to think either of beating the British to the Pacific by railroad or, if that were impossible, of somehow tying British enterprise to Minnesota, either by the logic of geography or by practical business arrangements. In Russia the visionaries saw a country which was expanding into a frontier region similar to the northern plains of the United States and extending its commerce and civilization toward the Pacific. The opening of Japan to trade following the expedition of Commodore Matthew C. Perry in 1852–54 was greeted by the *Pioneer* as "one of the great achievements of the nineteenth century."[6] The results of Perry's trip appeared even more promising when scientific information which had been gathered concerning the Japanese Current was made public. This pointed to advantages in a great circle sailing route from the Orient across the Pacific to Puget Sound and caused one Minnesota booster to rhapsodize that "even the broad currents of the Pacific enter into the conspiracy of natural and human agencies for building up this great Northern Highway to the Indes."[7]

In spite of the "sublime combination of causes which seems to sum up the energies of half the globe to build a railroad from Puget's Sound to St. Paul," there remained nearly two thousand miles of unsettled wilderness to span.[8] The financial collapse of 1857 discouraged promoters, as did the threatening shadow of the approaching Civil War. In this setting, the discovery of gold in the northern Rockies was indeed fortuitous, and the molders of Minnesota's destiny were not slow to take advantage of it.

Already it had occurred to these men that emigrant routes opened over the northern plains could become channels of communication between the Mississippi and the Pacific and would encourage settlements along the way which would eventually support a railroad. They had no doubt that a wagon road would serve as an "entering wedge" for the iron horse. This idea prompted the *Pioneer and Democrat* to remark as early as December 17, 1856, that an "emigrant road becomes of far greater importance to the people of Minnesota, than attaches to it merely as a wagon road through our Territory to the Pacific."

Attempts in 1857 to open a route through Dakota and Wyoming to California and in 1859 to establish a northern route through Saskatchewan to the Fraser River had both fallen far short of Minnesota expectations.[9] In January, 1862, however, Congress — spurred to action by the great interest in the new gold fields and conscious also of the need for increased gold supplies to finance the Civil War — appropriated $25,000 "for the Protection of Overland Emigrants to California, Oregon and Washington Territory."[10] Late in April Minnesota Representative Cyrus Aldrich, accompanied by Senator James W. Nesmith of Oregon, called on Secretary of War Edwin M. Stanton. They asked him to earmark some of the appropriated funds for emigrants traveling over the northern plains. Stanton agreed and designated five thousand dollars for protection on the route surveyed by the Stevens expedition.[11]

Aldrich was only one of the many Minnesota politicians and business leaders who were dedicated in varying degrees to the vision of the state's manifest destiny. Probably the best known and most articulate spokesman for Minnesota expansionism was James W. Taylor, a lawyer who was at that time a special agent of the treasury department. His interest in western British America — looking toward the annexation of that region to the United States — had already earned him the sobriquet "Saskatchewan," and his talents as a scholar, lecturer, politician, and skilled writer had long been employed in disseminating information and ideas about the importance of the northern plains.[12] He was ably seconded by others, including Joseph A. Wheelock, Minnesota's pioneer statistician and editor of the influential *St. Paul Press.* If, however, these were the movement's men of thought, its man of action was James Liberty Fisk. To him fell the task of guiding emigrants across the plains and mounting a propaganda offensive in support of the route.

A twenty-six-year-old Irishman from White Bear Lake, Fisk had worked as a raftsman, farmer, carriage maker, and newspaperman. In 1857 he had accompanied the expedition headed by William H. Nobles which had tried without success to build a wagon road from Fort Ridgely to South Pass. Somewhat later he had served as secretary of the Dakota Land Company, a firm organized to promote settlement along the road. An intelligent, goodhearted, generous, and impulsive man, he had the Gaelic "gift of gab" and a strong tendency to rationalize himself out of most predicaments. He was a loyal friend, an energetic enemy, a dead shot with rifle or pistol, and a frontiersman of experience.[13]

On May 29 Fisk received a commission as captain in the quartermaster corps of the United States Army and instructions to enlist and equip a body of fifty men to protect emigrants on the northern route "not only against hostile Indians but against all dangers including starvation, losses, accidents, and the like." He was to appoint a rendezvous at Fort Abercrombie on the Red River, give notice of his plans through newspapers and handbills, and hire in addition to the protective escort such assistants as a secretary, guide, interpreter, physician, and wagon master, as well as teamsters, herders, and cooks. The duties of the escort were to end at Fort Benton, the eastern terminus of a military road connecting the Missouri and Columbia rivers, which had been constructed by Lieutenant John Mullan in 1859–62. Because army crews were still at work on the road, and because the Indians of the far Northwest had been peaceable for some years, the war department no doubt felt that emigrants were safe beyond that point. Fisk was further instructed, however, to proceed over the Mullan road as far as Fort Walla Walla, sell his government property, and return home by way of Panama.[14]

The lateness of his appointment left Fisk little time for preparation. In fact, one group of gold seekers, too impatient to wait for the government's "tardy agent," had already gone on ahead. Gathering at Fort Abercrombie at the end of May, they had formed a train of some seventy persons and designated Thomas A. Holmes their military captain, secretary, treasurer, Indian interpreter, and sergeant of the guard. Holmes, described by Taylor as "a representative man of the Northwestern frontier," had been a fur trader, townsite promoter, and a member of the Minnesota territorial legislature. His own estimate of his talents was summed up in the statement that though he could not sign his name, he could "skin a muskrat quicker than an Indian." [15] He was well equipped for the task set for him and led the train safely across the plains on an old fur-trade route that followed close to the forty-ninth parallel as far as the Montana border, and picked up the Stevens route in the valley of the Milk River, eventually turning south to Fort Benton.[16]

Fisk meanwhile had arrived in St. Paul on June 4 and made his first announcement to prospective emigrants in the *Pioneer and Democrat* of June 7. He was able to hurry preparations by recruiting his military escort from among the emigrants themselves, and for officers he secured friends, acquaintances, and persons recommended by Minnesotans promoting this emigrant project. Among the latter were Nathaniel P. Langford, a brother-in-law of Taylor, and Samuel R. Bond, who served as secretary and journalist of the expedition. By a stroke of good fortune he also secured the services of Pierre Bottineau, who had guided the Stevens expedition and probably knew the northern plains as well as any man in the Northwest.[17]

On June 16 members of Fisk's expedition set out from St. Paul. Joined by emigrant wagons along the way, they pushed north to St. Cloud and then out the Sauk Valley, following the stage road to Fort Abercrombie. The Fourth of July was celebrated at the fort, and there Fisk met other emigrants who had been waiting for his arrival. A nose and wagon count revealed 117 men, 13 women, 53 wagons, 168 oxen, 17 cows, 13 saddle horses, 14 team horses, and 8 mules. The train was made up largely of Minnesotans, almost half of them from Hennepin County.[18]

They left Fort Abercrombie on July 7, 1862, a fair summer day on the plains. Following the Stevens route, with Stevens' guide ahead of the train as far as the Missouri at Fort Union, and with a copy of Stevens' report stowed away in one of the officers' wagons, the train reached Fort Benton without serious mishap in the first week of September. There Fisk's duties were officially ended, but since he had been instructed to sell his equipment at Walla Walla, and must necessarily follow Mullan's road to that point, the emigrants asked him to travel on with them on an informal basis. So the expedition continued much as it had before until it came near the valley of the Prickly Pear not far from present-day Helena. There a small party turned off to prospect. The specimens of gold they found persuaded a large number of others to stop at Prickly Pear instead of going on to Salmon River.[19]

Several small ceremonies marked the breakup of the train on September 22. The officers of the expedition were entertained at a table "decked with a fine white tablecloth and snowy napkins" and "loaded with viands." As Fisk and the others prepared to leave, the emigrants gathered around the flag wagon and presented the leader with a testimonial, signed by all members of the train, expressing their appreciation for his services in guiding them safely across the plains. After hearty cheers, general handshaking, and kissing of the ladies, Fisk and his small group moved on, leaving some eighty-two members of the party at Prickly Pear.[20]

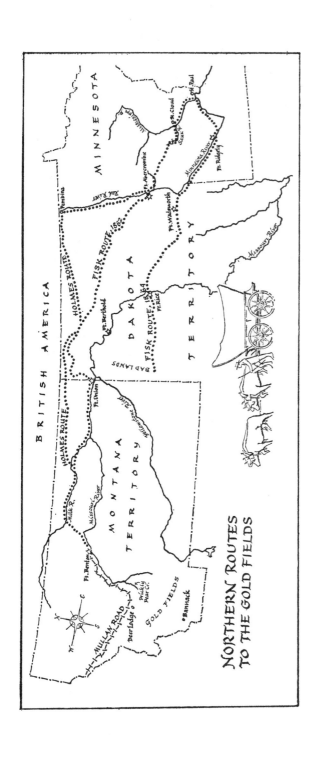

NORTHERN ROUTES
TO THE GOLD FIELDS

A few days later in the Deer Lodge Valley the last of the Minnesota emigrants departed to seek their fortunes in the mining region. Three wagons and fourteen men of the escort remained to accompany Fisk to Walla Walla.

It had been from every point of view a highly successful venture, and Bond, the journalist, could not resist predicting on the closing page of his report that "the greater portion of future emigration from the northwest to the gold fields . . . will pursue the general overland route over which we passed . . . and that the whole route will, before many years, be marked by a continuous line of settlements, which the country is fully capable of sustaining." [21] In St. Paul the *Daily Press* described the gold seekers of 1862 as "a victorious army . . . sent forth by Minnesota to clear the path of emigration and commerce to the Pacific." [22]

Before spring a full-scale campaign had been launched to gain support for Minnesota's new highway to the Pacific. The official report of Fisk's expedition was published early in 1863, and following it appeared a handbook for emigrants, the second of three accounts of northern overland expeditions to be published over Fisk's name. It contained a lyrical description of the gold region in the newly formed territory of Idaho, soon to become Montana. In addition to untold mineral wealth, Fisk assured would-be settlers that the area had a mild and healthful climate, particularly in the south and to the west, "in accordance with the well-known fact that the isothermal line, or the line of heat, is farther north as you go westward from the Eastern States toward the Pacific." [23]

In addition to his publications Fisk's propaganda efforts included numerous speeches, conferences with chambers of commerce, military leaders, and members of Congress, and he even joined the Minnesota Congressional delegation in 1864 in a call on President Lincoln at the White House.[24] By 1866 the captain had set up information and recruiting offices in various cities from which he carried on correspondence with people interested in traveling to the gold fields over the northern plains. Indeed, his publicity was so effective that one of the overland trails — approximately the Stevens route — came eventually to be known by Fisk's name. One critic compared his tales of the West with such "monstrous but pleasing and ingenious fictions" as those in which figure Sinbad the Sailor, Gulliver, and Baron Munchausen.[25]

As the campaign gathered momentum, handbills, circulars, and maps were issued describing the gold fields and the routes to them and telling prospective emigrants where parties were being organized and when they planned to start west. The famous "Rubber Stamp Map" of the Northwest — so called because the name of the new territory of Montana was inserted with a rubber stamp after the map had come off the press — was issued in 1864 by Daniel D. Merrill, a St. Paul bookseller, together with a circular for gold-field emigrants. Such literature was an important feature of the campaign, because few of the standard guidebooks for western travelers contained information about the northern plains.[26]

Newspapers reported the comings and goings of emigrants and promoters and carried announcements of the places and times of rendezvous set by various parties. They described in great detail the immediate benefits that might be expected by the upper Midwest in the form of increased commerce and trade with the gold-field settlements, and repeatedly emphasized the long-range significance of communication with the Pacific Coast. Local businessmen's organizations pledged financial support for the routes, and some companies prepared to send wagonloads of goods over the trails for sale at the mines. Eastern capitalists were urged to invest in townsite or mining companies, or to finance expeditions to settle mining towns. Despite tempting descriptions, little Eastern capital seems to have been attracted.[27]

The spearhead of the campaign, however, was the effort to secure government assistance. In Congress such men as Asahel W. Hubbard and James F. Wilson of Iowa and Ignatius Donnelly, Morton S. Wilkinson, William Windom, and Alexander Ramsey of Minnesota supported bills for the protection of overland emigration, for the surveying, construction, improvement, and marking of wagon roads, and for the establishment of post and express routes across the northern plains.[28] Though loath to provide funds for the building of wagon roads, Congress did follow up the successful Fisk expedition of 1862 with appropriations in 1863 and 1864 for military protection of emigrants on the Fort Benton route. Fisk was again appointed to superintend emigration and organized expeditions in both years. Because of drought and Indian unrest in 1863 only a small group ventured west and the expedition of 1864 was attacked by Indians and forced to turn back.[29]

Although the government did not directly sponsor any other emigrant expeditions over the northern plains in the 1860s, the army did in fact give military protection to privately organized trains. The extent of this protection varied considerably from year to year, but all the northern overland trains of the 1860s, except that led by Holmes in 1862, received assistance of one kind or another from the army.

In some cases the help took the form of military escorts; in others, the amount and type of aid depended on the state of Indian affairs at the moment, or the whims of the officers in charge of forts along the routes. Some emigrant trains took advantage of the army's campaigns against the Sioux and traveled with various military units in their marches across the plains.[30]

After his failure in 1864, Fisk was unable to secure further government funds. In 1865 he was also unsuccessful in efforts to organize a private expedition, but the summer of 1866 found him at the head of the largest and last train he was to conduct across the plains. Meanwhile other groups that made the trek under varying degrees of danger and difficulty included a second train led by Holmes in 1864 and a third in 1866. In 1867 Captain Peter B. Davy headed an expedition. Altogether it is estimated that in these trains some fifteen hundred people crossed the northern plains.[31]

Not satisfied with these limited results, Minnesotans proposed another elaborate scheme. Under the guise of a contract to carry the mails from St. Paul to Helena, they hoped to have the government underwrite the opening of an improved wagon road, complete with stations, bridges, and ferries, which would, as the *St. Paul Weekly Pioneer* of April 12, 1867, put it, "enduce the immigration and travel between the States and Montana, through Minnesota, with their accompaniments of capital and trade." Unfortunately the firm which received the contract was interested only in carrying the mail and had no plans to build a road or improve the route. The service was ill performed, Indians harassed the messengers, and, it was said, the riders used the newspapers for fuel and the letters for cigar lighters. The mail contract was dropped and hopes for a wagon road died.[32]

Though the Montana mines of the 1860s were among the world's richest placer mines, the deposits accessible by "pick and pan" methods were quickly exhausted and with them disappeared the opportunities for individual prospectors with little capital to invest. This fact, together with the opening in 1869 of the Union Pacific Railroad and continued Sioux hostility, ended migration to Montana over northern routes. But the dream of a northern railroad that would link the Great Lakes and the headwaters of the Mississippi with the Pacific and thus put the center of the continent in touch with the two oceans survived. Eventually not one but three railroads reached across the northern plains of the United States, and the present-day traveler who journeys from Minnesota to Montana on these railroad lines follows the northern emigrant trails at many points.

Social and Economic
Effects of the Civil War

LESTER B. SHIPPEE

THE SIGNIFICANCE of the Civil War in American history has become a commonplace, and volume after volume on the conflict continues to roll from the nation's presses, testifying to the topic's perennial fascination for historian and reader alike. The following wide-ranging discussion appeared during World War I in the second volume of Minnesota History *(May, 1918), long before the tide of publications on the subject had reached its present flood proportions. That it has stood for almost half a century speaks well for the perspicacity of its author, Lester B. Shippee, who pointed up some often neglected aspects of an event that occupied a central place in the development of an expanding urban and industrial nation. Shippee's special field of interest was American diplomatic history; his last major work, published in 1939, was entitled* Canadian-American Relations, 1849–1874. *As a member of the history faculty in the University of Minnesota from 1917 until his death in 1944, he was a dedicated teacher and writer. At the time of his death he was president of the Minnesota Historical Society.*

NO PEOPLE can pass through a period of abnormal existence without some modification of its fundamental institutions, more or less profound.[1] Even though the period of abnormality be short and the ruffling of the surface of things apparently insignificant, the path of the destiny of that people takes a new turn and never can affairs be put back upon the old footing. Wars rank among the most potent of modifying influences. Nevertheless all wars do not equally produce immediate and perceptible changes in the life of a nation. While more spectacular and politically significant, the American Revolution did not remold the lives of the people of the United States as did the titanic European struggle to eject Napoleon, wherein the War of 1812 was one of the closing chapters.

The Civil War in the United States has been, down to the present conflict [*World War I*] in which we are engaged, the most momentous and the most highly significant armed struggle which has wrenched our people out of the beaten track. Leaving out of consideration the political effects of this strife as well as the legal and social results of putting an end to domestic slavery, the student of the period of the war and the years immediately following perceives the rise of new forces in the social order and the submergence of older factors. All portions of the Union, however, were not equally affected. The South, obviously, was most radically modified, both during the war and in the following reconstruction period. Yet the North by no means emerged from the contest unchanged, although it was but little affected by the ravages of contending armies and subject to nothing of the blighting economic depression which spread its pall over all the seceding states.

In April, 1861, the industrial organization of the North was attuned to peace. For four years preceding the fall of Sumter the country had been slowly emerging from the hard times following the panic of 1857, and, but for the political cloud on the horizon, everything appeared propitious for a new era of prosperity. Factories turned the product of the southern cotton fields into cloth, while mines were sending to the smelters the ore which would yield metal for all the varied industrial demands of an age of steam. Better prices and ample labor stimulated the farmer to produce the foodstuffs and raw products which a reviving industry demanded, while good wages made the laborer's position better than anywhere else in the world. To be sure, there were flies in the economic ointment; mutterings about the railroads were later to become articulate; the germ of the subsequent disputes between labor and capital could be discerned by a keen observer; and there were some who questioned whether there might not come a time of reckoning with the problems growing out of the concentration of population which accompanied the factory system. Nevertheless, if the troublesome issues arising from slavery could be compromised away, as had been the case so many times before, it was possible to face the economic future with confidence.

When it was realized, however, that the war was to be something more than a holiday excursion to Richmond, the future began to appear less rosy. The stopping of the cotton supply caused the mills of the North to slacken their activities. Soon, when the accumulated stock of fiber was exhausted, the hum of the spindles nearly ceased, and, while some operators attempted to keep their employees busy with repairs, improvements, and extensions for a time when normal conditions should be restored, many of them were obliged to shut their doors and see their help drift off into other work. Frantic efforts were made to substitute other fibers, but little success attended these endeavors. Hopes were raised high when portions of the southern coast fell before the exploits of the Union armies and navy, only to be dashed by the meagerness of the bales obtained. Even when New Orleans was captured, only a small amount of cotton was secured. To be sure, a little trickled through the lines in exchange for articles needed in the South, even for war munitions in some cases, and this was sold to manufacturers, or more often to speculators, at rapidly mounting prices. Cotton fabrics became so scarce that silks from the Orient could be obtained more easily and more cheaply.

If cotton manufacturing had been dealt a staggering blow, many other industries were inordinately stimulated. All sorts of supplies for the armed forces were in great demand; the metal industries were rushed to capacity; cloth for uniforms was desired in such quantities that the millowner stilled for a time his incessant plea for protection and yet more protection. The cry for wool made sheep raising upon the barren hills of northern New England profitable once more, and hundreds of hitherto almost worthless farms were turned into paying sheepwalks. Shoddy came into its own, even though soldiers in the field complained that their uniforms dropped to pieces in a few weeks. Shoes and boots for the army gave an impetus to factory production of these articles which was now possible because of an adaptation of Howe's sewing machine. Leather soared and cattle raising throve.

Whatever surplus of labor was loosed upon the community by the stopping of a few industries was rapidly absorbed by the extraordinary demands in other branches, and soon the cry of shortage in the labor market was heard. This appeal became more insistent as the armies grew and absorbed thousands of young men. Yet, when it is considered that the Union forces were made up principally of boys in their teens and young men in their early twenties, it can be perceived that the greatest part of the labor power of the country was not turned from productive to destructive activity. Two factors, moreover, served to relieve the labor situation: the substitution of women for men workers, and the use of laborsaving machinery. It was at this time that women began in large numbers to take positions hitherto almost exclusively filled by men; the schoolma'am ruled in the place of the schoolmaster, and the female clerk, it was discovered, was as efficient as her brother. Whatever was gained in the economic struggle by women during the war was not relinquished at its close, and furthermore a great impetus was given to the demand for women's equal rights, economic, social, and political.

But if the transition advanced materially the cause of women in certain aspects, it brought other and sadder changes. The need for ready-made clothing stimulated sweatshop methods. Hundreds of women, old and young, pushed to the wall by mounting prices and by the removal of male wage earners, eked out a bare living sewing for army contractors and subcontractors at the scantiest of wages. Again Howe's invention, made practicable just before the outbreak of the war, contributed both to rapidity of supply and to heartbreaking toil.

It was in the agricultural field, however, that machinery as a substitute for manpower made itself most evident. The armies had to be fed as well as clothed; not only that, but ample allowance had to be made for the inevitable waste which attends military operations. Without the mowing machine, the horse rake, and the reaper it is impossible to conceive how the armies or the civilian population could have been fed, or a surplus of wheat raised and sent abroad to help maintain the credit of the United States in the mart of the world. To laborsaving devices, more than to any other one cause, was due the tremendous increase in the production of foodstuffs in the fields of western New York and Pennsylvania, and of the Northwest. Still, machines could not take the place of human labor entirely, and while the agricultural West raised no such complaint of shortage of labor as did the manufacturing East, women had to work in the fields to sow and harvest the crops, particularly in the last two years of the war when the draft was garnering in a constantly increasing number of youths.[2]

It was not enough to produce the food and the other raw products. They had to be transported to the front, to the manufacturing centers, and to the seaboard for export. One of the decisive adverse factors with which the Confederacy had to contend was a most inadequate railroad system, constructed wholly from Northern and European materials, while one of the elements contributing to Union success was a network of lines which not only connected the interior with the seaboard but linked remote communities with the business centers of the North.[3] In the later period of the war some portions of the South were on the verge of starvation while others had an unusable surplus of food; Lee's army, for instance, was destitute in Virginia when Alabama had all the necessaries in abundance. On the other hand, after it had been gathered at the primary distributing centers by rail or by river boat, the wheat of Minnesota, Iowa, Illinois, and Wisconsin poured into New York from Milwaukee and Chicago either by rail or by the Great Lakes and the Erie Canal.

The railroads were not slow to realize that they held the whip hand. Prior to the war Atlantic ports competed with New Orleans as outlets for the products of the upper Mississippi and the Ohio; long usage gave the southern port advantages not easily overcome. When, however, the Confederate government realized that the Northwest was going to throw its lot with the Union, the Mississippi was closed, and traffic had to be diverted to the welcoming but not necessarily benevolent competitors. They were not averse to making all possible use of their commanding position, to the end that the farmer could complain that an unduly large portion of the fruits of his labor was absorbed in transportation charges. In no small degree did this extortion add to the already existing dissatisfaction with railroad treatment and precipitate the "Anti-Monopoly" revolt which came at the close of the war as a precursor to the Granger agitation and legislation of the early seventies.[4]

Not content with the added tonnage and consequent receipts which the closing of the river gave them, the railroads took steps to throttle local river transportation. Wherever the rails tapped a territory which was also served by river boats, cut rates forced the cheaper carrier to lay up, except where a persevering independent continued to carry on a precarious business. Moreover, all possible steps were taken to divert to rail points traffic which logically should have sought noncompetitive river facilities. At a time, then, when one would expect that traffic on the upper river and its affluents should have shared in the benefits of war commerce, there came a falling off. For instance, in 1862 St. Paul had the largest number of boat arrivals during the war (1,015) exceeded only by those in 1857 and 1858 (1,026 and 1,068). Thereafter the decline which ensued was continued with occasional spurts of renewed life. What was true of St. Paul obtained at the ports on the smaller streams.[5]

Minnesota necessarily shared in the economic transition which affected the whole Northwest. Yet, inasmuch as Minnesota was still in the midst of her pioneer endeavors, it is difficult to determine with any precision just what should be charged to war conditions and what to a continuing primitive stage of development. When territorial status was proclaimed in 1849 fewer than 5,000 souls lived in Minnesota, but such was the rush to virgin lands that the census of 1860 disclosed a population of 172,022. The next five years saw this number nearly doubled, but in the five years following the war a smaller proportionate gain in population was made than in the war era. There were 250,099 persons in the state in 1865, in 1870 there were 440,076. Nevertheless this was an average annual increase of 15.19 per cent, and in the decade from 1860 to 1870 only Nebraska and Kansas had higher rates of increase.[6]

The war did affect the relative proportions of males and females. Whereas in a normal community which has passed through the earlier formative stages the number of females is slightly in excess of the males, in 1860 Minnesota's male population exceeded the female by 8.22 per cent; in 1870 this disproportion had somewhat disappeared for the males were only 6.84 per cent more numerous, yet the state census of 1865 showed that the females were outnumbered by but 5 per cent. In the census returns after 1870 the approach to a normal relation of the sexes demonstrated that pioneer days were rapidly becoming a thing of the past.

As a result of the inpouring of people, despite the ample response of Minnesota to Lincoln's calls for soldiers, there was no such dearth of labor as was experienced, for instance, by her neighbor, Wisconsin. Late in 1863 and during 1864, when more plentiful money accompanied renewed activity, especially in railroad construction and in lumbering, there is some evidence that there was a heavier demand for labor, yet nowhere does there seem to have been such a shortage as was experienced in the agricultural and lumbering states east of the Mississippi. Again, while wages increased somewhat between 1861 and 1864, the average for common laborers in the latter year was not as high as in Wisconsin.[7]

In common with all the rest of the United States the increase in wages was not at all proportionate to the rise in prices of all sorts of commodities. There was nothing unusual in the way that prices of necessaries soared during the war; similar phenomena have been observed among every people engaged in a great armed struggle. Nevertheless, large amounts of fiat currency issued by the United States served to aggravate the prevailing tendencies. In the West, however, the greenback was not looked upon with the disfavor it encountered in the older portions of the Union. Contrasted with the depreciated notes of state banks, the United States note was indeed the "best money" the West had ever known, and to the local economist there was in it no evil except its limited amount.

State banking, which was usually accompanied by secured and

superabundant note issues, forms one of the least pleasing features of the early history of most of our frontier states from the beginning of the century down to the time the national banking act began to operate in full force. Minnesota had not escaped the prevailing passion and had sought to eke out the scanty supply of specie trickling into her commercial channels by authorizing banks to issue upon securities regarded by outsiders with suspicion and not sound enough to prevent great depreciation. The war, however, did not produce so much added disturbance in the exchange value of notes secured by railroad bonds as it did in Wisconsin and Illinois where bonds of southern states had been largely used as a guaranty. In fact, after a time, the war proved a blessing so far as Minnesota's currency situation was concerned. Not only did the greenback afford relief, but the state banks chartered during the war based their issues upon state and national bonds of one sort or another and so inspired a confidence which had been almost lacking previously. But no greater alacrity to take advantage of the national banking act of 1863 was shown by banking interests in Minnesota than was the case in other states. Many new state banks were incorporated, but only two national banks had received charters before Congress in March, 1865, forced all banks of issue to enter the new fold or go out of existence.[8]

While relief had come by 1863, the previous two years had been a period of great money stringency in the state. Specie disappeared from circulation as it did all over the United States; money was almost impossible to obtain and exorbitant rates of interest were charged.[9]

Investigation of the agricultural phase of war economics in Minnesota is complicated by the difficulty of determining whether the truly remarkable progress exhibited by the state was a result of the war or came in spite of the war. Undoubtedly there would have been a great development under normal conditions, for, prior to the outbreak of hostilities, the earlier steps had been taken and the temporary setback produced by the panic and hard times had been overcome. Untouched lands have ever tempted man to exploitation, and Minnesota's millions of fertile acres have proved no exception to the rule. On the other hand the high prices of wheat and other grains unquestionably stimulated production. Despite the Indian outbreaks and a devastating drought in 1862 and 1863 the wheat harvest advanced from 5,101,432 bushels in 1860 to 9,475,000 bushels in 1865. As the assistant secretary of state remarked in his annual report, "the development of agriculture kept even pace with the population." Moreover, a high yield per acre encouraged more men to sow wheat.[10]

The new homestead policy of the federal government added to the total available public lands open to settlement. These were already extensive for, in addition to the school and university lands and swamp lands which had been donated to the state and territory, enormous grants for railroad purposes, amounting eventually to nearly twelve million acres, were open to purchase or to pre-emption. In 1863 a total of 463,296 acres was taken up; this amount increased in 1864 to 665,750, and in 1865 to 804,982 acres. After the close of the war this rate of increase was not maintained; in 1866 a smaller acreage passed into private hands than in the previous year, and in 1869 there was only a slight increase over 1865. *Post-bellum* depression and poor harvests in these two years in part explain the falling off.[11]

Minnesota was not unaffected by the prevalent stimulus which was given to certain activities. Naturally those related to some branch of husbandry received the greater attention. Attempts were made to find substitutes for the cane sugar and molasses which could no longer be obtained from Louisiana. Sorghum was the most promising of these substitutes, and it was tried out on a considerable scale. While this plant yielded a syrup of good quality, all efforts to cause it to crystallize into sugar proved fruitless. It was thought that tobacco might be raised and so free the North from dependence on the South for this article, but no very serious attention was given the crop during the war. It was not until the period of high prices in 1868 and the years immediately following that farmers of the Northwest believed there were sufficient prospects of a paying crop to invest much time or money in its growth.[12]

Wool, however, was in a different category. The high price of this commodity early stimulated the Minnesota husbandman to try his luck at supplying a portion of the demand in the hope of securing a share of the enormous profits of the successful sheep raiser. The number of sheep in the state in 1864 was slightly over 97,000. Importations and natural increase sent this number to 193,045 in 1866. The high expectations were not realized, however, for in 1869 the number of sheep in the state had fallen to 135,450, while the next year saw another decrease. A report of the state department said, "It will hardly be claimed that even the more moderate expectations respecting the growth of wool have been justified by the results yet obtained; and it is undeniable that this important interest has experienced a serious decline, and labors today under great depression."[13] Experience proved that the lateness of the spring in this northern climate caused the lambing season to come too late for the best development of flocks, and men soon drew out of this branch of husbandry as rapidly as they could.

Next to agriculture, lumbering received the strongest impetus from the war. In common with Wisconsin and Michigan, Minnesota possessed vast resources in standing timber, of which the white pine covering much of the northern portions of this section was considered most valuable. In 1863, after a depression in the first years of the war which was more seriously felt in Wisconsin where greater development had already taken place, the prices of lumber began to jump and continued to rule high. In 1864 the pineries of Minnesota, like those of western Wisconsin, were precluded from taking advantage of the price of twenty-three dollars a thousand in Chicago by the unusually low water in the branches of the upper Mississippi; but the next year saw a different situation and millions of feet were floated down to market. Peace brought a great slump in the lumber market, and it was not until 1867 that reviving conditions pushed the price even higher than it had been during the war.[14]

The 1850s had, down to the panic, been a boom period for lumbermen, signalized by the concentration of thousands of acres of valuable timberland in the hands of a few operators. The fraudulent use of half-breed scrip, among other means, had contributed to the alienation of much public wealth.[15] During the war a stop was put to this easy method of appropriating the public's wealth, but in 1868 a more complaisant secretary of the interior opened the door again and the merry scramble was resumed. Railroad lands, too, offered an opportunity to the energetic and not-too-scrupulous lumberman, which, coupled with an easy attitude on the part of state officials, further served to build up enormous holdings. A single illustration, by no means extreme, serves to indicate what opportunities lay open to the astute. The firm of Hersey, Staples, and Bean (Hersey, Staples, and Hall after 1866) was organized in April of 1861. When the partnership was dissolved in 1875 each of the three associates was able to take as his third of the accumulated holdings a hundred thousand acres of timberland. Co-operation of state officials, as well as local agents of the federal government, with favored lumbermen also aided the latter, not only to secure the land itself, but, in some cases, to allow cutting of timber at a more than reasonable valuation without the necessity of buying the soil which grew the trees. This was a variant of the scrip frauds.[16]

The war both retarded and promoted the construction of railroads in Minnesota. When the vast land grant to the prospective state was made by Congress in 1857 for the purpose of forwarding the building of lines which should connect distant points with the more settled portions and also link Minnesota up with her neighbors, everybody looked to a period of prosperity even more intense than that which had existed in the preceding few years. But the panic in the same year spelled doom to such anticipations. Although the land was granted to companies, it was impossible to secure sufficient money for construction either in the East or in Europe. Land was a drug on the market. State bonds were issued to the chartered companies as the grading of successive strips of roadbed was completed. These were formally like other bonds, but in the minds of the people who had amended the state constitution so that the "credit" of the state might be loaned they were merely a form, for it was intended that the railroads themselves should pay the obligation. New York capitalists, moreover, looked askance at any kind of new securities, especially those which had to do with new enterprises whose returns were problematical. The net result was the defaulting of the railroad companies, while Minnesota had a few score miles of poorly graded roadbed to show for an obligation of over two million dollars known as the "Five Million Loan." The retraction of the amendment of 1858 and a regrant of the lands to newly organized companies in 1861 and 1862 brought the completion of only ten miles of track, and this was the situation when the war had gone on for a year.[17]

The regrant of lands and privileges which the old companies had forfeited, together with easier money, injected some show of life into railroad enterprises, and when 1863 closed there were fifty-six and a half miles ready for operation. The following year saw over thirty miles added and at the end of 1865 over two hundred miles of railroad existed in the state.[18] But to counterbalance this was the alienation of thousands of acres from the public domain, as well as the specter of that "Five Million Loan," which was to come up year after year until the ghost was finally laid in 1910.[19]

Except in flour milling and in the manufacture of lumber, Minnesota did not share in the industrial burst of the northern states during the war. Even in these lines, while the proportional increase was impressive, the absolute results were not correspondingly great. The total number of manufacturing establishments rose from 562 in 1860 to 2,057 in 1870, yet the capitalization of all these concerns was only $11,806,738.[20] Nevertheless, this showing was not bad for a pioneer state so young as Minnesota, even though the major portion of the increase came in the last half of the decade. Milling of flour and the primary processes of lumber manufacture accounted for more than half the total capital invested and nearly half the number of establishments, while these two lines gave employment to approximately one-third of the persons engaged in industrial pursuits. Some beginnings are seen in the fabrication of sashes, doors, and blinds, furniture, machinery, agricultural implements, carriages and wagons, harness, and a few other articles.

After Lee surrendered in 1865, it took a little time for a society grown accustomed to war conditions to adjust itself again to peace. A temporary economic stagnation accompanied the return of the armies to everyday existence. This slackening was, however, of short duration. The world marveled at the ease with which a million men who had just laid aside their arms could be absorbed into the economic life of the community, causing scarcely a ripple upon the surface of the social fabric. Minnesota, in common with the rest of the states of the West, was an important factor in the process. Her vacant and inviting lands, which could be obtained for a trifling cash investment plus a large amount of energy, fortitude, and patience, stood ready to receive all those who were unwilling to return to their old homes to try to fit themselves into a situation which had grown strange in their absence. The population of the state increased between 1865 and 1870 by nearly two hundred thousand, while the taking up of railroad, state, and federal lands kept even step with the march of the inpouring flood.[21]

It was not, however, returning soldiers alone who swarmed to Minnesota. Up to 1865 the population elements of the state were not much dissimilar from those of her neighbors of the Northwest, or for that matter, of the whole North. In 1860 something over two-thirds of the inhabitants were of native birth. Those of foreign birth, who totaled 58,728, were mostly Irish, Germans, English, and British Americans, just about the same racial elements to be found anywhere from New York to the Mississippi. In 1864 the legislature enacted a law to "organize a system for the promotion of immigration to the State of Minnesota" in order to offset the further drain which might be anticipated on account of the war, as well as to secure settlers for the waiting prairies. Pamphlets in the English, German, and Scandinavian tongues were printed and spread broadcast to picture the possibilities of the region as well as to remove many misapprehensions as to the soil and especially the climate. Beginnings of Scandinavian immigration had been made as early as the late 1850s, but in 1860 this element comprised less than 12,000 of the 172,000 people in the state. These, like the Germans, had for the most part moved on from Wisconsin. But the seed had been planted.

The watering came when a board of immigration was created in 1867, with Hans Mattson its secretary. Mattson held the position of land agent for one of the railroads which traversed some of the most desirable portions of the state, hence he was able to give definite directions as to favorable points for settlement.[22] Perhaps to this man, more than to any other one factor, is due the great Scandinavian migration to Minnesota. In 1870 Swedes, Norwegians, and Danes comprised thirteen and one-half per cent of the population and had already begun to impress upon the state an indelible mark. In 1860 there had been only half as many Scandinavians as there were in Wisconsin; by 1870 Minnesota had over 59,000 as against Wisconsin's 48,000. The Swedes alone were pressing close to the lead of the Irish, and in a year or so overtook and passed this element. Only the Germans could rival the Scandinavians and even they comprised but 48,457 souls as against 59,390.

When men return to the primitive passions brought by war there is necessarily a loss of much of the hardly won refinement which can be a product of peace alone. How long after the struggle there will be seen the results of this relapse is a matter difficult of determination. All students of the Civil War, however, have noted that the years immediately following 1865 presented an unusual number of examples of low public morality. This was the period when the Whisky Ring was profiting at the expense of the federal government, and when federal officers connived at gross irregularities as well as shared in the profit. The Crédit Mobilier not only was an example of "high finance" in railroading, but it served to blast several public careers as well as to sully the reputations of prominent men who were not completely overwhelmed by the public wrath which followed exposure. The manipulations of the Tweed Ring in New York, aided by its intimate relation with certain Wall Street interests, exemplify in an exaggerated degree, perhaps, the degradation into which most of the larger municipalities had fallen.[23] The whole civil service of the United States had become so honeycombed with corruption and inefficiency that the reform element of the Republican party could, in its campaign from 1870 to 1872, urge with great force the need of a complete house cleaning. The old guard itself could not present any defense and was forced to adopt at least in form the principles of the reformers.

It would be easy to say, of course, that all this array of horrible examples, which was exposed to view in investigation after investigation from about 1870 on, could be paralleled at many other times in the history of this country or of other nations. It might be said that every now and then a people has a spasm of reforming zeal and while in this mood can find evidences of corruption and laxity if it looks with sufficient care; that the period, say from 1872 to 1875, was just one of these periods. Furthermore it might be added that a panic followed by hard times is likely to produce soul searching on the part of a stricken population; religious revivals vie with judicial and legislative investigations.

Still this does not wholly dispose of the case. Not alone in the United States after the Civil War, but in Germany after the Franco-Prussian War, for instance, keen observers noted a recklessness, an abandon, which characterized the economic and social life of the people. Everybody was enjoying good times, nobody was interested in counting pennies or in inquiring too carefully into the doings of his neighbor so long as his own particular activities were not interfered with. In such times the public official who inclined to make the most of his position could pursue his course without much fear of interruption, while the man who desired to remain honest was sorely tempted when he perceived the ease with which he, too, might profit in the way others were doing. There is no doubt that the later years of the war and those immediately following were permeated with this spirit, and that public opinion was generally inclined to laugh at the "smart" man more than to be indignant at pilferings or gigantic steals. Our civilization is too thin and too recent a veneer to stand much hard rubbing, and war rubs hard. Moreover, the veneer cannot be renewed immediately after the struggle ends.

Did Minnesota experience any of this general laxity which followed the war? If evidences are found shall they be attributed to a continuation of pioneer times, when there is a certain lack of regard for the finer products of civilization, such as the perception of more delicate degrees of public morality; or shall they be accounted for by the fact that Minnesota shared with the rest of the conquering North in a debauch of moral letdown? It would be hard to give a categorical answer to such a question. It may be said, however, that the late 1860s and the early 1870s saw a sufficient development of Minnesota to warrant confident belief that the worst aspects of the pioneer stage ought to have been things of the past. Nevertheless there are many indications that a deplorable laxity, if nothing worse, permeated the community and manifested itself in various irregular transactions.

One of the most spectacular of the revelations enjoyed by the newspaper-reading public was that attending the Seeger investigation and impeachment. It must be said at the outset that the legislature of Minnesota, by paying the state treasurer a salary of only one thousand dollars a year, actually, if not deliberately, encouraged all sorts of irregularity. It appeared that for years before this investigation, which came in 1873, the state treasurer was accustomed to "loan to and let bankers and business firms have the use of large sums of the State fund" as well as to draw upon the county treasurers for moneys not yet due and have personal use of such funds sometimes for many months. Furthermore the books of the treasurer's office were in such a condition that it was impossible to obtain an adequate idea of the financial status of the commonwealth. When there came a change in the treasurer's office, the new incumbent, who happened to be the father-in-law of the outgoing treasurer, concealed the fact that large sums belonging to the state were not actually turned over, although subsequently the deficit was made up.[24]

Such an opportunity as this to attack the party in power was not to be overlooked by the Democratic "outs," and this attack in turn provoked other revelations. It was discovered that county treasurers were also in the habit of failing to regard the distinction between the public funds and their own money.[25] They loaned the county's money to banks and other business firms and, in some instances at least, received the interest themselves. It was further charged that sometimes bank officials had exerted themselves to secure the election of a particular man as county treasurer, and if the campaign proved successful, the bank was not the loser. And then, when a leading Republican paper could seriously argue that nobody would convict a man for shielding his son-in-law, there is evidence that the standard of public morals was not overly high, to say the least.[26]

The disclosures made in 1873 were followed by equally sensational ones the next year. Just before the Seeger investigation had lifted the lid, the *Saint Paul Daily Press* had reviewed the various departmental reports submitted to the legislature and, among other comments, took particular pains to felicitate the state upon the efficient service rendered by the state auditor. He "closes an administration," the *Press* remarked, "which has been substantially coextensive with the ascendancy of the Republican party in his State, embracing in its four official terms a period of twelve years, with a terse statistical record of the varied questions during that time of the more important departments of the State Government under his control, which will form an enduring memorial of the general economy, prudence and beneficence which have, on the whole, characterized the management of State affairs by the Republican Party, and of Mr. McIlrath's own conspicuous and honorable share in its marked successes." [27]

The McIlrath investigation of 1874 demonstrated the truth of the statement made by the *Press* about the "conspicuous" share of the late state auditor. It was found that the auditor, in performing his functions as land commissioner, had been in the habit of accepting notes secured by a lien upon logs cut instead of cash payments for timber sold to lumbermen. In many instances before any payment was made the logs would have been disposed of. He sold timber at far below the market price; he connived at agreements among prospective purchasers of standing timber whereby there was no competition in bidding; he had kept in his own name and had received the interest on bonds purchased with money from the school fund, although eventually the bonds were credited to the fund. All the accounts of these, as well as other transactions were kept in such an ill-ordered manner that McIlrath himself testified before the investigating committee that he could not explain them. In all a sum of not less than one hundred thousand dollars was unaccounted for, as a result of "irregularities" beginning at least as early as 1866. In addition to the above, McIlrath had acquired, in 1868, an interest in a firm which entered into a contract with the state for the purchase of the right to cut timber on some thousands of acres of university lands. It is no wonder certain lumbermen were anxious for the re-election of McIlrath at a time when some opposition seemed to be developing, especially when it is considered that, in addition to reasons which may be suspected from the foregoing statements, there had never been a prosecution of trespassers upon the state timberlands during his incumbency. As a matter of fact, the committee found that "extraordinary inducements were held out to parties to cut timber as trespassers." [28]

Give all allowance possible to frontier conditions, grant every excuse to the men engaged in the task of opening a new land, and still there remains evidence of a sadly deficient sense of public morality. When we find all over the North similar conditions which cannot be explained by primitive necessities, the conviction grows that there was something abnormal in the atmosphere. Add to this the testimony of men high in the public estimation of the time, as well as the word of those who have sought an explanation of the social phenomena of that day, and the naïve confessions of that sanctimonious old railroad pirate, Daniel Drew, and it is impossible to conclude that some portion of the explanation is not to be found in the war and its aftermath.[29]

If the Civil War teaches that such a social cataclysm stirs the mud in the depths of the pool, it also reveals the fact that men are stimulated by it to re-estimate all social values. Alongside the loosing of the baser propensities of mankind there comes a renewed interest in many of those problems whose roots have been slowly entwining themselves about the inmost parts of our social structure. From 1865 down to the panic of 1873 the labor world was shaken by notable convulsions. Unionism, which had had a precarious existence up to the time of the war, advanced with remarkable strides. Educational questions, including the problem of the education of women, were receiving new attention. The temperance movement gained a wider following. The same stimuli that induced reflection along these lines served in time to turn thought to the corrupting sores which had developed in the social body. Those who would renovate an educational system or seek to find the true relations between capital and labor were not long content to tolerate in silence those blots upon our political organization which anyone could perceive if he stopped to observe.

In times like these one naturally desires to learn whether it is possible to draw upon the experiences of the 1860s for guidance in our present crisis and in the years which are to follow the war of 1917. Unfortunately, perhaps, it appears that general conditions are so dissimilar that little of a positive nature can be found. Among the more striking differences may be noted the fact that the Civil War in no way depleted the world's accumulated store of products as the present war is doing. The South was impoverished by the conflict and even yet has not recovered all the ground lost, but the resources of the North were not drained to an appreciable extent. This was due in part to the fact that so great a portion of the country was as yet untouched. Natural resources undreamed of in 1865 were to be discovered as the years passed, as, for example, the iron mines of Minnesota. Even more it was due to a failure to destroy on such a colossal scale as that on which the world now destroys.

America, after the close of the Civil War, offered to the people of the world an opportunity unequaled elsewhere. Migration on an unprecedented scale, arrested temporarily by economic depression in the 1870s and again in the 1890s, sent workers to develop untouched possibilities. When the present war closes, America will no longer be the outlet for the land-hungry people of Europe. Some less desirable remnants of land will be found here and there, but, except in parts of Canada, the land will not be given away to the asker. Furthermore, it is even a question whether there will not be a reverse process. There are indications that there may be a movement back to Europe which will most decidedly affect our future social and economic life.

The Civil War does not help us to see our path in matters of collective control of transportation, food, fuel, manufactures, or in any of the vital problems with which we are now grappling under abnormal conditions but which we shall find ourselves unable to drop the moment peace is declared. We shall find that we have clasped the handles of an electric machine the current of which will paralyze our efforts to relax our muscles. The world has gone far since 1865 in its ideas of the relation of the individual to the community.

There is, however, one ray of light which the earlier war and its effects throw upon existing and future problems. The partial economic emancipation and consequent general advance in status gained by women during the rebellion was not lost when peace came. It can confidently be stated that what is being gained now will be retained; not only that, but it will serve as another steppingstone toward political, social, and economic equality with men. We shall not go back.

Could we predict with equal confidence along other lines it would be possible to guide our activities today in such a manner that the grosser blunders might be avoided. But, after all is said and done, about the extent of safe prophecy is this: war, under modern conditions, unsettles many if not most of our institutions; it is as futile to dream of getting back to the world in which we lived before 1914 as it is to believe we are in the last month by failing to tear a leaf from the calendar. Nevertheless, it will be the aim of many people to execute just this reverse. If the Civil War brings home the lesson that it caused men to modify their course and that when it was ended society was marching in a somewhat different direction than it had been before, then it is possible to keep in mind that the same thing will be true when this war ends, with this sole qualification: there can be no comparison in the magnitude of the change.

Rivalry for a River:
The Twin Cities and the Mississippi

LUCILE M. KANE

THE EARLIEST and the largest urban growth in Minnesota took place on the banks of the Mississippi; as a channel of commerce the river created St. Paul, and as a source of power it built Minneapolis. Lucile M. Kane, who here discusses the early rivalry between the two urban centers for control of the river's benefits, has in preparation a book on the industrial development fostered by the Falls of St. Anthony. This article appeared in December, 1961 (volume 37) as a by-product of her larger study. Miss Kane is curator of manuscripts on the staff of the Minnesota Historical Society, a post she has held since 1948. She is the author of numerous articles which have appeared in Minnesota History *and in other scholarly journals, and she is the editor and translator of the journal of Philippe Régis de Trobriand which was published under the title* Military Life in Dakota *(1951).*

DURING THE LONG YEARS Minneapolis and St. Paul have sparred across the city limits, their rivalry has been spiced by many a bitter controversy. No contention in the nineteenth century aroused more violent passions than that which developed over the utilization of the Mississippi River between the Falls of St. Anthony and Fort Snelling. This turbulent and shallow stretch of water deterred steamboats from reaching Minneapolis and in its swift descent formed a water-power site coveted by St. Paul.

Each city aspired to share in the gift nature had bestowed upon the other. Minneapolis owed its manufacturing supremacy in the Northwest to the cataract where the Mississippi dropped over a jagged limestone ledge to form the Falls of St. Anthony; but manufacturing was not enough to satisfy its metropolitan ambition. It wished to be a center for trade as well as industry, and to realize this dream it sought to secure the same direct access to river navigation that St. Paul had long enjoyed.

230

Ironically, it was the falls that had created the barrier between Minneapolis and unimpeded navigation. Centuries before the city was founded, the falls had been located in the vicinity later overlooked by Fort Snelling. Through years of erosion they had retreated upriver, leaving behind them a trail of boulders and sand in the channel. The river was most treacherous in a two-mile passage just above Meeker Island. Here the swift waters continued a descent begun at the falls, forming rapids that frightened the most intrepid steamboat captains. Into the caldron, the cataract, still retreating, dropped an annual load of rock and sand, until the water-power companies which controlled the falls in the 1860s built a shield to prevent further erosion and hold the ledge in place.[1]

Bountiful nature, while endowing Minneapolis with water power, gave the gift of navigation to St. Paul. As head of practical river transportation, St. Paul developed into a commercial city — the focal point for transshipment of goods to Minneapolis and other parts of Minnesota. But St. Paul, too, had a metropolitan dream that could not easily be satisfied. It aspired to become a great manufacturing city as well as a trade center; and it believed that this goal could be realized if it were to secure possession of the water power in the rapids below the Falls of St. Anthony.

The first phase in the struggle centered on navigation. Minneapolis and its sister town, St. Anthony, embarked in the 1850s on a crusade to snatch from St. Paul its position as head of river transportation. They focused their attention on two contradictory objectives: The first was a stubborn argument against facts, for they sought to prove that the river was indeed navigable almost to the falls. The second was a campaign to remove the boulders from the stream below the falls and construct locks and dams that would carry boats past the obstructions into a Minneapolis harbor.

To support their assertion that the river was indeed navigable, the towns sponsored several enterprises designed to bring steamboats to their doors. A group of St. Anthony men in 1849 joined with Stillwater citizens to form a company that would run a steamboat between the Falls of St. Anthony and the falls of the St. Croix. They planned to use a shallow-draft steamer, capable of running "any place where it is a little damp."[2]

The falls-to-falls steamer service seems not to have materialized, but the eager towns were just beginning the struggle. In 1850 a group of citizens offered the "Lamartine" a two-hundred-dollar premium to make the trip from St. Paul to the falls. The historic run was a gala occasion. Pleasure parties accompanied by a military band boarded the boat at St. Paul and Fort Snelling. The "Lamartine" proceeded easily to Steele's Landing, just below the falls. There the churning rapids halted its progress. When the engines could make no more headway against the powerful current, the boat was moved a few more lengths towards the falls by means of a hawser fastened to the rocky cliffs and attached to the capstan on the boat. For several moments "the beautiful little steamer was forced up the billows of the mighty cataract, where boat, bark or birch canoe had never floated before." [3]

An officer from Fort Snelling who was on the "Lamartine" asserted that there "is no doubt *now* about the head of navigation." [4] Citizens of St. Anthony and Minneapolis seemed to agree with him, for when other boats followed the "Lamartine," they prepared for an extensive commercial business. The *St. Anthony Express* of June 28, 1851, exultantly informed its readers that "the Lamartine, Wayne, Dr. Franklin No. 2 and the Nominee have all witnessed the spray of the dancing waters of our own beautiful falls," and triumphantly proclaimed that "St. Anthony is the head and foot of navigation."

Despite these victorious declarations, Minneapolis and St. Anthony found they had to coax steamboats into their limits. They offered bonuses and funds for insurance to captains who agreed to make the trip; they built warehouses at the foot of the swift rapids; they made agreements with captains and steamboat lines, promising them exclusive cargo rights; and they organized companies with boats dedicated to the falls trade. [5]

When traffic to the falls remained a trickle while hundreds of steamboats crowded the levees at St. Paul, some observers were inclined to blame the malevolence of the rival city. According to the *Express,* St. Paulites talked so much about the dangers of rapids and boulders that captains believed "there is danger in coming here which does not exist," and insurance companies levied an additional charge on boats journeying to the falls. "St. Paul," the *Express* stated, "has everything at stake, and when it is once settled . . . that this is the true head of navigation, the CITY(?) of St. Paul will retrograde to a modest little village, — grass will grow in the now crowded, and busy Exchange; the owls will build their nests in City Hall." St. Anthony, head of navigation as well as possessor of water power, would be both the commercial and manufacturing center of the Northwest. [6]

Witnessing the struggle of its rivals, St. Paul struck an attitude of amused tolerance. In a typical story, a St. Paul organ declared, "Our neighbors are blessed with credulity, but we fear they lack the faith that removes mountains, sand-bars and boulders; and that shoves a three foot keel up a stream that runs nine miles an hour over ledges and beds of gravel but ten inches under the surface." [7]

Despite their seemingly blind belief that the river was navigable, the towns at the falls did not really ignore the boulders. Nor did they rely altogether upon faith: their citizens in the early 1850s raised money to remove the obstructions. Typical sons of the frontier, these men began as early as 1852 to solicit assistance from the federal government to supplement the few thousands they had collected. In that year the *St. Anthony Express* urged the territorial delegate to introduce into Congress a bill for river improvement below the falls, and citizens placed in his hands a petition to that effect which he presented to the House. The territorial legislature forwarded memorials calling for river improvement in 1855 and 1856, and the state legislature transmitted others in 1858 and 1861. [8]

The second phase in the struggle to bring navigation to the falls opened in 1857, when a group of Minneapolis men headed by Bradley B. Meeker organized the Mississippi River Improvement and Manufacturing Company. Chartered for fifteen years with a capital stock of two hundred thousand dollars, the company was empowered to build a lock and dam and create water power. [9] The launching of the company brought within view the partial realization of a project the *Express* had advocated two years earlier, when it proposed the construction of two locks and dams, one near Meeker Island and another at the falls, to bring navigation "into the heart of this city." The editor claimed that the "water power obtained from these dams, will pay for the construction, and the future growth of the business of the Territory is not more certain than that they will be built." [10]

The lure of profits from water power, however, was not strong enough to push the new company into immediate action. From 1857 to 1865 its owners fought a delaying action to extend the two-year limit the legislature had placed upon completion of the lock and dam. They succeeded in 1858 in securing an amendment to the charter extending the limit to four years, and in 1865, they obtained a further five-year extension. Later the same year the company began a campaign to secure from Congress a grant of public lands that would enable it to build the lock and dam. It forwarded a memorial to Congress, and early in 1866 the Minnesota legislature sent a similar petition. The legislature requested that Congress grant the land to the state, which would then give portions to the company as work on the lock and dam progressed. [11]

The appeal of the legislature was based upon the need for navigation improvement. It reviewed the earnest efforts made by citizens at the falls to improve the river before the panic of 1857 and the Civil War had put an end to their enterprise. "In consequence of these delays and public disasters," it stated, "navigation . . . has receded some sixteen miles, to St. Paul, where all the freight destined to these cities . . . and the vast regions north and west dependent on them for their goods and groceries, must break bulk and be carried on cars or wagons to their destination." The memorial carefully soft-pedaled the company's right to develop water power as "incidental" to the chief purpose of improving navigation. Since the "inexhaustible" water power controlled by the Minneapolis Mill Company and the St. Anthony Falls Water Power Company at the falls was sufficient to supply demands for years to come, it argued, the Mississippi River Improvement and Manufacturing Company "cannot now look to the incidental advantage of using the water as any adequate return for their labor and capital." Since the company's charter required it to lock boats and rafts free of charge, it was left without any immediate return for improving navigation on a public waterway.[12]

Meeker and his associates forwarded copies of the two memorials to Ignatius Donnelly, representative in Congress from the district which included both Minneapolis and St. Paul, and appealed to him to carry the land-grant bill through the House. The preliminary strategy, they assured him, had been excellent. Foreseeing St. Paul opposition, Minneapolis men had secured support for the memorial from St. Paul representatives in the state legislature by endorsing a request for river improvement between the capital city and St. Louis.[13]

Opposition, Meeker and his friends warned Donnelly, would come not from St. Paul interests, but from the two companies which controlled the water power at the falls. Richard Chute, one of the owners of the St. Anthony Falls Water Power Company, would be an outspoken opponent, Meeker felt, while the owners of the Minneapolis Mill Company, which possessed the water power on the west bank, would be divided. Meeker predicted that Cadwallader C. Washburn and his brother, William D., would oppose the bill, while Dorilus Morrison, who was one of the incorporators of the Mississippi River Improvement and Manufacturing Company, as well as a part owner of Minneapolis Mill, would support it. He went on to point out that the influence of the Washburns would be particularly dangerous, for their brother, Elihu B. Washburne, was himself a member of Congress.[14]

In the early months Meeker and his associates clung to a small hope that Morrison's influence would rally the Washburns to support the bill. But the hope soon faded. On February 14 Meeker sent a strong warning to Donnelly. William D. Washburn, he reported, had attempted to get control of the company's stock; failing in this, he had thrown his strength against the bill. "Their fear is," Meeker wrote, "another water power that might result *incidentally* from our effort to get Boats to the Falls of St. Anthony." In view of the narrow perspective the water-power companies took, he warned that Donnelly must beware of the Washburns and of the "slippery" Richard Chute.[15]

The opposition, Meeker believed, would employ two lines of attack to defeat the land-grant bill. One would be an attempt to discredit the company by pointing to its nine years of inactivity. For this argument Meeker had a ready answer. "For the past five years," he wrote, "we have been in war and desolation   The four preceding years were noted for commercial and financial disaster. Who in the West could make any considerable improvements even in matters of less undertaking?" The second stratagem, more devious than the first, Meeker termed *"Washburne through out."* The heart of the alleged black scheme was to block the land-grant bill, push through another providing for a survey of the upper Mississippi River, and then control the investigators' report. The scheme was born in the fertile brain of Richard Chute, Meeker claimed, and the supporters of the bill "don't want it nor do we ask it."[16]

The Washburns did not go unscathed in their program to block the improvements Minneapolis had so long desired. Ex-Governor Stephen Miller advised Donnelly on how to confound Elihu. "I am told," he wrote, "that Mr. Washburn [*sic*] of Ill. is opposed to this measure. This comes with an ill grace from that quarter, as his brothers are heavy stock holders in the Minneapolis Water P. Company. I learn that he is asking for appropriations for divers improvements in Ill and Wisconsin, and his thunder should be silenced by hostility to his pet improvements, until he consents to do justice to us."[17]

Meeker accosted William D. Washburn on a Minneapolis street. In the argument which followed, he denounced him for opposing a measure of such great importance to the community because "it *might* make water-power which that interesting family of patriots could not control." Describing the incident to Donnelly, he added: "In the *Democratic* vernacular, I gave him 'Hell.' "[18]

In their eagerness to keep Donnelly active in the cause, Meeker and his associates proffered tempting fruit of political support and financial reward. Donnelly, who faced a campaign for re-election in

1866, was promised the backing of men who had never before labored for him. Block the men from the water-power companies in their infamous purpose, Meeker urged in a letter dated March 29, 1866, "and you will have the support of men in your next Campaign that will take a pleasure in defeating these *sneaks*." Triumph in securing the grant, and "the *Devil in arms* could not prevent your carrying *Hennepin County*." The suggestion of financial reward was less direct. Dr. Hezekiah Fletcher, a stockholder in the company, wrote Donnelly that in accordance with their understanding, he had subscribed to twenty thousand dollars in stock, "half of which you could have at any future time." Senators Daniel S. Norton and Alexander Ramsey, and Representative William Windom, he claimed, "are situated in just the same way." Meeker, reporting to Donnelly that would-be supporters had been importuning him for stock in exchange for "influence," stated that he was saving the stock he controlled "for those who *can* and will help the cause." Since no company records are available, it is not known whether company members rewarded any of the Congressmen with shares in the enterprise.[19]

True to the cause, Donnelly sponsored the land-grant bill in the House. It was read twice, then referred to the committee on public lands. The predictions of its proponents proved accurate, however, and the measure was lost, while a provision for a river survey was passed as part of the rivers and harbors bill. Donnelly did not oppose the latter action. He was, in fact, among its foremost advocates when it came before the House. "The importance of the work contemplated in such a survey," he declared, "cannot be overestimated. It would carry the navigation of the Mississippi river up to the foot of the great falls of St. Anthony and make continuous navigation in an almost direct line north and south from that point to the Gulf of Mexico. The head of such a mighty valley cannot be unimportant. Around it are already clustering great cities — St. Paul . . . and the twin cities of Minneapolis and St. Anthony, possessed of the greatest manufacturing facilities to be found in the entire Mississippi valley; and where already the hum of woolen and cotton mills is heard, with the clatter of innumerable lumber mills. . . . It is right and just," he continued, "that the navigation of the great river should reach to the very foot of the falls and receive the cargoes of its floating palaces from the very doors of its factories."[20]

When General George K. Warren of the United States Army engineers organized his forces for conducting the survey, the company's advocates might well have believed their fears that the water-power in-

terests would influence the report were well founded. Meeker had recommended that the job of conducting the actual surveys between
Fort Snelling and the falls go to Gates Johnson, an engineer from St.
Paul. Johnson, Meeker observed to Donnelly, knew "every foot of
the River from here to St. Paul," was acceptable to the city of St. Paul
"and perfectly to *our company*. He is qualified *eminently*. He is prepared to go right at it. He is a friend of *yours* and our enterprize."
The appointment, however, went not to Johnson, but to Franklin
Cook, engineer of the Minneapolis Mill Company. Cook did not mask
his association when he applied to Donnelly for support in getting the
appointment. He stated that he had been employed by the water-power
company as engineer for several years, and he included among his references Cadwallader C. Washburn and Hilary B. Hancock, agent of
the company.[21]

Meeker's fear that the report would be tailored to defeat his project proved groundless. When it was in preparation late in 1866,
Meeker himself stated that the conclusions were "all that the friends
of navigation to this place could wish." Cook recommended a lock
and dam at Meeker Island, after the completion of which other locks
would be required "to elevate boats eighty feet in order to pass into
the level above the mill-dam." Only the first project was recommended
for immediate action. Its cost would be $230,665.48, Cook estimated,
but its benefits to trade, commerce, and manufacturing at the falls
would be immense.[22]

Cook's report removed the last obstacle to legislation, and Minnesotans lauded it. Newspapers published extracts from the report and
commented on the benefits the lock and dam would bring. "Now friend
Donelly [*sic*] put your Shoulder to the wheel," Meeker wrote in a
mood of jubilation, "and give us such a lift as old Hennepin gave
you." [23]

Both "friend" Donnelly and Senator Ramsey put their shoulders to
the wheel. Under their sponsorship, Congress passed a bill in 1868 providing for a grant of two hundred thousand acres of land to the state
of Minnesota. The bill included several restrictions. Not more than
one section was to be chosen from any single township, and government engineers were to supervise construction of the lock and dam.
If the work was not completed within two years after the legislature
had accepted and disposed of the grant, the lands were to revert to the
United States. The lands would also revert if before the completion
of the lock and dam Congress were to appropriate money sufficient for
their construction.[24]

Minneapolis rejoiced when Congress passed the land-grant bill. "A dam and lock at Meeker's Island," stated the *Minneapolis Daily Tribune* on June 7, 1868, "will be of immense importance to Minneapolis, as it will make St. Anthony Falls in reality the Head of Navigation on the Mississippi, and transfer the commercial *prestige* of this upper country from St. Paul to the 'Magnet.' It will also give us another Water Power, just below the city limits, nearly equal in volume to that at the Falls, proportionately increasing our manufacturing facilities. With our city the head of navigation on the Mississippi, and seventy-five per cent added to her already magnificent resources in point of manufacturing capacity, who will longer dispute that Minneapolis is the real 'Seat of Destiny' in the Northwest?"

No one could question the fact that the building of the Meeker Island lock and dam would make Minneapolis the head of navigation. But, in announcing that Minneapolis would possess a new water power, the *Tribune* had ignored transactions that shifted control of the company from Minneapolis to St. Paul. If the citizens of Minneapolis were unaware of this, they had only to read the triumphant announcement in the *St. Paul Daily Dispatch* of June 6 that passage of the bill "secures to St. Paul a water power equal to St. Anthony." The water, stated the *Dispatch,* "will be conducted by canal to St. Paul. It will furnish hydraulic capacity of sufficient power to drive mills and turn spindles enough to make St. Paul one of the largest manufacturing cities on the continent."

In announcing that St. Paul had secured a water power, the *Dispatch* was right, for on the great day when Congress enacted the land-grant bill, St. Paul men were in control of the Mississippi River Improvement and Manufacturing Company. How did Minneapolis let slip a water power within its limits that would nourish the manufactures of a rival city? How did St. Paul execute the coup when Minneapolis had already paid a price by supporting the memorial for downriver improvements?

Rumblings had begun early in 1866. On a visit to St. Paul, Dr. Fletcher was surprised to learn that leading citizens had become very much interested in the success of the land-grant bill then before Congress. Their "very unexpected" reasoning was that "if they can have a water power half way to St. Paul it will become a St. Paul institution." In this fertile soil, Meeker had cultivated the seeds of compromise that would gain for his bill the support of St. Paulites. Holding confidential interviews with leading businessmen, he found that they would indeed be willing to trade "a few Boats for a great Water power." The exchange was accomplished on February 7, 1867, when Meeker sold the company for twelve thousand dollars to Horace Thompson, Dominic W. Ingersoll, Russell Blakeley, Henry H. Sibley, and other St. Paulites. Although he held in secret stock for himself and his friends, the company became a St. Paul firm.[25]

After the announcement of the sale, a torrent of comment flooded the columns of St. Paul and Minneapolis newspapers. The *State Atlas* (Minneapolis and St. Anthony) declared on February 13, 1867, that the "sharp ones" who were the buyers were "blustering a good deal about the magnitude and future value of their purchase." There was nothing to prevent St. Paul capitalists from investing at the falls, said the *Atlas*, but "it looks to us like a quiet acknowledgement that if the mountain won't come to them, they must come to the mountain. When they get their 'big factories, mills, &c.' in operation, we can easily extend our city limits so as to include them within our growing city. Of course this will be acceptable to them as they will feel that they have at last, got into a city that *does* grow — at the true 'head of navigation.'"

The *Minneapolis Tribune,* on May 26, a few months after the sale took comfort from the fact that the new owners had as yet done nothing to improve the power. "Owing to various reasons obvious to practical businessmen," stated the journal, "the earth has not yet been rent asunder and the Mississippi river invited to change her base and flow through an artificial channel, beset with over and undershoot wheels, by means of which the power is to be furnished to St. Paul to manufacture for the world. The whir of millions of spindles and the ceaseless roar of our vast manufacturing establishments, is not yet *heard.* Not a wheel turns, not a spindle whirs. . . . It takes time, thought, co-operation and capital to develope this vast water power, which now flows by the feet of our city, helpless, useless, except that it does to float a few boats and furnishes cheap transportation for some lumber mills in operation at remote villages, like St. Anthony and Minneapolis."

The *Minneapolis Chronicle* betrayed a tone of annoyance in commenting that the city was not jealous of St. Paul, which was welcome to a little water, whether obtained through "a straw, or a fifty-foot canal, or by a hose." What it did object to was the "blowing" and "blasting" of the *St. Paul Press,* whose "counting the chickens before they are hatched is rather 'hifaluten' and looks too much like a female of bad reputation boasting of her virtue."[26]

At first St. Paul newspapers were restrained in their expressions of triumph. The *Press* maintained on February 15, 1867, that St. Paul's true interest was "to promote the development of manufactures at the falls and at all available points in her neighborhood." St. Paul citizens, in furnishing capital to develop the Meeker Island property, showed "another evidence of the generous and unselfish enterprise which has always characterized our citizens. They act upon the sound maxim that their own prosperity depends upon that of their neighbors, and that they can help themselves so effectually in no other way as by helping others."

This Olympian level was soon abandoned, however. Piqued by the belittling sneers of the Minneapolis newspapers, the *Press* unloosed its bolts. Minneapolis, of all cities, it maintained, should have an appreciation of what water power could do. The *Chronicle* had accused the *Press* of having water on the brain after the Meeker sale, but the latter observed that "The *Chronicle* has mistaken the diagnosis of our disease. Our impression is that we have a *cataract in our eye*." [27]

And what could water power do for St. Paul? By digging a canal from the Meeker Island site to locations within the St. Paul city limits, the *Press* maintained on April 23, 1867, St. Paul would possess the very resource that made Minneapolis a great manufacturing center. And St. Paul would have even more than its neighbor, for the enterprise would engraft "one of the finest water powers in the world" upon "the actual head of navigation of one of the grandest rivers in the world."

Pre-eminent in both trade and manufactures, St. Paul would be the leading city in the Northwest, and unique among cities in the world. "We believe," stated the *Press*, "there is no instance on this continent, or on the other, where a valuable water power is associated with a great commercial centre. Manufacturing towns, based on water power, are almost universally . . . inland places, at more or less distance from those great lines of water transit, which are the indispensable bases of great commercial centres. Such water powers are very often found in the close neighborhood of commercial cities, and the manufacturing towns built up thereon, are necessarily secondary and tributary to their commercial neighbors." When the St. Paul water power is developed, the paper went on to boast, "we shall be able to compete 'with all the world and the rest of mankind.'" [28]

It looked in 1868 as if St. Paul had won the new water power and Minneapolis must comfort itself with the capture of navigation. But canny Minneapolitans made a bold stroke to appropriate both benefits from the Meeker Island project. The land-grant bill had passed and St. Paulites were in control of the Mississippi River Improvement and Manufacturing Company; however, the provisions of the bill actually gave the land to the state of Minnesota. By legislative enactment, the state was then to pass the grant to a company that would build the lock and dam.

When Congress adopted the measure there was only one company in a position to receive the grant, but Minneapolitans quickly changed this situation. On January 25, 1869, a group of men representing the water-power firms and manufacturing and real-estate interests in Minneapolis and St. Anthony incorporated the Mississippi River Slackwater Navigation Company. Capitalized at three hundred thousand dollars, the organization had as its purpose the improvement of navigation and creation of hydraulic power by erecting locks and dams "at or near" Meeker Island. Among the incorporators were several men who had been among the original members of the rival group.[29]

The first meeting of the new company, held in the rooms of the Board of Trade, was a busy one. Books were opened for stock subscriptions. In the election of officers, Dorilus Morrison was made president, Wilson P. Westfall, vice-president, Edward Murphy, secretary, and Rufus J. Baldwin, treasurer. The most important business of the evening was the appointment of a special committee "to look after proper legislation in regard to the improvements at Meeker Island, and building of the lock and dam and the further disposition of the land grant for the same."[30]

The new company, however, could not marshall enough influence to win the land grant. The legislature, in an act approved by the governor on March 6, 1869, awarded the land to the Mississippi River Improvement and Manufacturing Company. The grant, made in the form of an amendment to the company's charter, stipulated that the company spend a minimum of twenty-five thousand dollars for materials and labor by February 1, 1871, and complete the work within the time limit Congress had prescribed. It provided further that in case the company failed to carry out the provisions, its rights and privileges were to be forfeited to the state. The legislature would then be free to grant them "to any company or individuals who will undertake the construction of said lock and dam."[31]

Favored by every benefit it had requested, the Mississippi River Improvement and Manufacturing Company still did not start construction. In August, 1870, only a few months before the expiration of the time allowed for beginning the work, the cities at the falls became restive in the face of the company's inactivity. The *Minneapolis*

Tribune, investigating the cause of the delay, found that it was attributed to the refusal of Congressman Eugene M. Wilson to sponsor legislation giving the company ten years in which to complete the work. "We think that Congressman Wilson did perfectly right in this matter," stated the *Tribune,* "and we further think that a request for a postponement of this improvement for ten years [is] a graceless and unreasonable prayer, if it is not rather to be regarded as a formal announcement, that they did not intend to carry out the will of Congress and the Legislature at all." [32]

The company saved its grant by hurriedly spending twenty-six thousand dollars for labor and materials late in 1870 and early in 1871. Instead of beginning actual work on the lock and dam, however, it requested another boon from Congress. The company wanted an amendment to remove from the act the provision that not more than one section of land could be selected from any township. On December 12, 1870, Ramsey introduced into the Senate a bill which allowed the selection to be made anywhere in the state, and Representative Wilson introduced the same measure into the House on the same day. The bill, which lost in the 1870–71 session, was reintroduced in 1872 by Senator Ramsey and Representative Mark Dunnell. Again it failed to pass. [33]

The attempt of the Mississippi River Improvement and Manufacturing Company to secure the amendment catapulted the Twin Cities into a brief but bitter furor. In exchange for their support of the amendment before Congress, Minneapolitans demanded that the St. Paulites hand over to them a controlling interest in the company, and the St. Paul owners acceded to their request. William S. King of Minneapolis, who was then a member of Congress, justified the demand by reasoning that "the act of 1868 was passed for the benefit of the community at the Falls, and with the intention of giving us facilities on the river equal to those enjoyed by St. Paul." He contended that "it was unnatural and unreasonable to make St. Paul men the custodians of such a trust, when it was well known that they would prefer to have the Mississippi run into a cave at Fort Snelling and disappear forever from sight, to having navigation brought to the Falls." [34]

But at this point, with the control of the company again in Minneapolis hands, a curious event took place. During the months in which Congress was considering the amendment, a furious debate broke out in Minneapolis. Now that the situation was about to be made propitious for the construction of the lock and dam, it became painfully evident that some Minneapolitans did not want them. In violent debates in the rooms of the Board of Trade, businessmen assailed one another in language, that in the words of a newspaper reporter, produced a "scene." At one point, when the discussion became heated, one of the directors of the board, "took the helm, and carried the vessel safely over the rapids." [35]

Arguing against support for the amendment were the familiar names of water-power company owners who had fought the 1866 land-grant bill — William D. Washburn and Richard Chute. Joining them were sawmill operators and boom company proprietors, such as William W. Eastman, John Martin, Sumner W. Farnham, James A. Lovejoy, and Joel B. Bassett. Urging passage of the amendment were stockholders in the Mississippi River Improvement and Manufacturing Company, long-time proponents of river navigation, and business leaders of the city. Among them were William E. McNair, Eugene M. Wilson, William S. King, Edward Murphy, and Isaac Atwater. Dorilus Morrison, in 1872–73 as in 1866, stepped out of the ranks of the water-power owners and took his stand with the advocates of the Meeker Island project.[36]

From the confused and heated language of the debates, several arguments against the venture emerged. Water-power owners of the falls feared the competition of a new site at their very doors and deemphasis on their requests for federal funds to preserve the Falls of St. Anthony; owners of the boom below the falls opposed the plan because establishment of sawmills near Meeker Island would obligate them to keep the river open for log driving; and sawmill owners at the falls saw an end to their practice of dumping sawdust into the river. Other opponents of broader vision advanced a more valid argument. Improvement of the Mississippi River for navigation, they maintained, was an obligation of the federal government, not of a private corporation subsidized by the government. Moreover, the selection of the Meeker Island site for the lock and dam was not based upon sound engineering, as the best location for a navigation dam was near the University of Minnesota.[37]

After the bill introduced in the 1872–73 session of Congress was lost, the debates over the scheme diminished. Fitfully, however, like an unforgettable theme, the subject returned for consideration. In 1874, the St. Paul Chamber of Commerce appointed a committee to investigate the possibility of carrying water from Meeker Island to St. Paul through an aqueduct. At that time (April 21, 1874) the *Minneapolis Tribune* generously conceded that Minneapolis had all the water power it could use "and St. Paul is welcome to all that she can borrow from Meeker's dam."

In 1879, when citizens in St. Paul and Minneapolis were discussing the possibility of consolidating the two cities, a St. Paul man suggested that the Meeker dam development might weld the union. He submitted that "the creation of another water power vaster than that at the falls" would draw to the area "a dense population between the two places that would cement them into one great city."[38]

Another flurry of excitement came in 1882, when the *Minneapolis Tribune* announced on October 29 that the Mississippi River Improvement and Manufacturing Company, revived by a new group of St. Paul and Minneapolis capitalists, was ready to take hold of the project abandoned ten years before. The *Tribune* declared that since the company had not relinquished the land grant, it was still effective. The development, the capitalists predicted, would create twenty thousand horsepower, which would be used by a variety of manufacturing enterprises that would spring up in the area. They planned to begin work in the fall of 1882 and to spend half a million dollars on the project. Again, however, only silence followed the announcement of plans for action.

In 1890 came the final move to revive the Meeker dam project — an effort that kindled anew the rivalry of the two cities for its possession. The incident was touched off by an announcement that the financier and railroad magnate, Henry Villard, had cast "his practical, money-making eye" upon the Meeker Island site. Villard, it was reported, intended to enlist the support of St. Paul and Minneapolis capitalists in developing the site for hydroelectric power to light the two cities, to propel streetcars, and to power machinery. With the prospect for the revival of the old project under the sponsorship of a powerful businessman already heavily interested in St. Paul electric utilities, the Twin Cities again took up their quarrel over which would control the power. This time Minneapolis was the aggressor, for its spokesmen demanded that in exchange for their city's support St. Paul relinquish part of the midway district that would be benefited by the power.[39]

Minneapolis need not have wasted its energies in this last fling at St. Paul over the Meeker water power. When Villard in April, 1890, spoke to the Twin City Commercial Club about his plans for developing electric light and power in the area, he responded to pressures for comment on the Meeker power. He regretfully informed his audience that the engineer he had engaged to investigate the project had submitted a negative report. The power potential, the engineer found, was more nearly six thousand to seven thousand horsepower than the twenty-five thousand represented to Villard. Costs, the investigator reported, would run higher than anticipated, and at least three separate companies claimed property rights in the area. In December Villard made the announcement that he had decided definitely to abandon the scheme.[40]

While talk of the Villard project was still enlivening meeting rooms in the Twin Cities, the third phase in the development of the river between Fort Snelling and the falls had already begun. The St. Anthony Falls Water Power Company, an old opponent of the Meeker dam scheme, in 1890 announced plans to erect on its property above the island a dam and powerhouse for producing hydroelectric power. Between 1895 and 1897 it built an installation whose yield of ten thousand horsepower was eventually leased to the Twin City Rapid Transit Company.[41]

The federal government had recognized as early as 1873 its obligations for improving navigation and in that year had appropriated twenty-five thousand dollars for a lock and dam, contingent upon the release of the existing land grant. It finally took up the project in the 1890s. In its first plan, the government scheduled two locks and dams, one located near Meeker Island and the other near the mouth of Minnehaha Creek. Construction on the former installation was begun in 1899 and completed in 1906. The second was begun in the same period. In 1909, however, before the Minnehaha dam was completed, the government changed its plan. A board of engineers appointed to investigate the matter in that year decided it was advisable to have one high dam instead of two lower ones, in order to secure a deeper channel and combine water power with navigation. To carry out the plan, they converted the Minnehaha project into a high dam with a lift of thirty feet, which was opened for navigation in 1917.[42]

The lock and dam built near Meeker Island proved to be an embarrassment to the government — a "shocking blunder" some called it. Since over a million dollars had been spent on it and on preparations for the Minnehaha installation, it weighed heavily on the minds of the engineers responsible for the decision. Yet abandoned it was in 1912, and part of it was subsequently demolished.[43]

The decision to build a high dam that combined water power and navigation touched off another struggle between St. Paul and Minneapolis, but though each sporadically accused the other of plots to grab the water power, they did seem disposed to settle the question peace-

fully. "Let them resolve," one editorial writer declared, "that no longer shall that gorge stretch between them, a melancholy example of
splendid opportunities wasted by small jealousies; but that all the
good shall be won from it that Providence meant when it directed the
planting of two great cities on its borders." [44]

For a time the cities worked closely together to win the power
rights from the government for municipal use rather than allow them
to fall to private companies. In 1911, they, with the University of
Minnesota, incorporated the Municipal Electric Company. Its charter,
however, did not enable it to issue the bonds necessary to build a power
plant. St. Paul, then, through the Greater St. Paul Committee, directed its attention to obtaining the power for St. Paul and invited Henry
Ford to build a plant in the city to use it. Although Minneapolis
clung to the idea of joint municipal use, the government in 1923 supported St. Paul when it granted the license to Ford.[45]

With the completion of the high dam, navigation was carried into
Minneapolis as far as the Washington Avenue bridge, where the city
built a harbor. The high dam was no sooner completed, however, than
Minneapolis again took up its campaign to bring navigation into the
very heart of the city. The situation at the time, one advocate claimed,
was "comparable to having a road stop at the edge of town." The
plan for the "Upper Harbor," as the project was dubbed, included
two locks between the high dam and the falls, and a canal around the
falls on the west side of the river.[46]

Through the 1920s, 1930s, and 1940s, Minneapolitans devoted to
the scheme bombarded Congress with requests for appropriations.
There is no space within the scope of this article to detail the tortuous
story — the false starts and frustrated plans, and the bitterness engen-
dered between dissident elements within Minneapolis and between the
Twin Cities. At long last, in 1950, work on the lower installation was
begun. It was completed in 1956, and in 1959 the government began
the upper lock at the falls, scheduled for completion in 1963.[47] *

When work began on the lower lock and dam, one event recalled the
Meeker dam scheme, long obscured in the shades of the past. The St.
Anthony Falls Water Power Company had years before built a dam
for power generation only, and the early government installations had
been dedicated solely to navigation. In 1958 the two purposes were
combined when the company abandoned its "lower dam" to use the

* The lock and canal were opened on schedule. First through the new installations was the tugboat "Savage," which made the trip on September 21,
1963. *L.M.K.*

government dam built slightly downstream. Here was realized, after a hundred years, an installation contemplated by Bradley B. Meeker when he organized his ill-fated company to bring navigation into Minneapolis over the treacherous waters and at the same time capture power from the river rushing down from the Falls of St. Anthony.

A more ironic twist in retrospect, perhaps, is that neither Minneapolis nor St. Paul had been as dependent on the river as they once thought they were. Without water power until the 1920s, St. Paul had developed its manufactures nonetheless. And Minneapolis, deprived of navigation until the twentieth century, had acquired a wholesaling business which overshadowed that of St. Paul. Both were the commercial-industrial cities they had dreamed of becoming, and together in relative peace, they formed a double-headed metropolis supreme in the Northwest.

The Rise of Organized Labor in Minnesota

GEORGE B. ENGBERG

WITH THE GROWTH of an urban working force came the first experiments in modern industrial unionism. The birth of unions in Minnesota during the nineteenth century is described by George B. Engberg in the following article, which appeared in December, 1940 (volume 21). The author, who is professor of history in the University of Cincinnati, was in the vanguard of historians to become interested in labor on the local scene. Since this article appeared fifteen years ago, the field has received additional attention from Mr. Engberg and others, and a book-length History of Labor in Minnesota *by George W. Lawson was published by the Minnesota State Federation of Labor in 1955.*

BEFORE AN AREA can become a field for labor organization, it must have an urban population in which wage earners form a group large enough to be conscious of their potential power. In Minnesota, the first labor unions were formed during the territorial period, in the 1850s, and at least one group of workers not only organized before the Civil War but went so far as to affiliate with a national organization.

The population of Minnesota, about six thousand in 1850, increased very rapidly after the Civil War. The growth was most pronounced in the decade of the 1880s, when the number of people in the state jumped from 780,733 to 1,310,283. The growth of Minneapolis and St. Paul closely paralleled that of the state, though the latter had about ten times as many people as either city. The Twin Cities are the center of this story because it is there that organized labor has played its most prominent Minnesota role. The population of St. Paul, a struggling town of 1,100 in 1850, with a fifth of all the white inhabitants of the territory, increased nearly a thousand per cent in the next ten years, and then doubled each decade until 1890, when the census

248

showed an increase of more than three hundred per cent over the figures for 1880. Minneapolis started later, but, after absorbing St. Anthony in 1872, it passed St. Paul in the next census and went on to become the state's leading commercial and industrial center in the period of exceedingly rapid growth of the 1880s.[1]

In spite of the fact that Minnesota was overwhelmingly rural, manufactures did develop and a wage-earning group, which felt that it had interests distinct from those of the employers or of the farmers who formed the bulk of the population, appeared. The gross value of manufactured products in Minnesota rose from $58,300 in 1850 to over $76,000,000 in 1880 and $192,000,000 in 1890. The average number of employees engaged in manufacturing went from 63 in 1850 to 21,247 in 1880 and 79,629 in 1890; while the total wages increased from a paltry $18,540 at the mid-century point to over $8,000,000 in 1880, and then catapulted to $38,000,000 in 1890. This industrial progress was faster than that of most other states, for the rank of Minnesota in number of employees rose from thirty-fifth in 1850 to fifteenth in 1890.[2]

The two principal Minnesota manufacturing industries in 1880 were flour milling, which accounted for about fifty-five per cent of the machine-made products, and lumbering. The employees in flour mills and sawmills were not among those who organized in the early years, however, and smaller industries were the leaders in the adoption of collective bargaining methods. The small industries which had over a thousand employees each were agricultural implements, brickmaking, carpentry, and men's clothing. Others having at least five hundred employees which became the base for labor organization included boots and shoes, cooperage, foundry, masonry, and the making of sash, doors, and blinds.[3]

Early industrial development in Minnesota was hampered by the lack of transportation facilities, for it was not until the 1860s that the first railroads were built in the state, thus releasing it from dependence on watercraft, wagons, and picturesque Red River carts. Railroad construction, which had been fairly rapid in the years immediately preceding the panic of 1873, was almost at a standstill during the middle 1870s, but it picked up during the next decade to give the state nearly 5,400 miles of track by the summer of 1890. With railroad growth came a more rapid development of manufacturing.[4]

The presence of a labor problem was officially recognized during the first year of the state's existence. At its first session in the summer of 1858 the legislature passed a law prohibiting children under eighteen and women from being employed more than ten hours a day in factory work in the absence of a contract making other provisions.[5] Although this law was vitiated by the contract provision, it did recognize the existence of labor problems. In the same session, a bill to protect laborers on railroads and public works was introduced but failed to pass.[6]

That there was a labor problem as early as the fall of 1854 is illustrated by the fact that the journeymen tailors of St. Paul struck for higher wages. The strike appears to have lasted at least two days, but no record has been found of its outcome.[7] Such a strike is not necessarily proof of permanent organization, but it at least indicates organized activity on the part of laboring men and the probability that some temporary group had been formed to deal with a specific problem facing the trade. On the other side of the employer-employee ledger, it is only fair to note that as early as 1855 and 1856 St. Paul storekeepers were agreeing to close their places of business at the early hour of 7:00 P.M. In thus limiting the hours of work, they achieved an end which clerks later organized to obtain.[8]

Successful unionization in Minnesota started among the printers, members of a skilled trade which had a record of organized activity in the United States running as far back as the Declaration of Independence. On December 20, 1856, a St. Paul paper announced that the local printers intended to celebrate the birthday of Benjamin Franklin, but within a week their attention was turned to more ambitious plans when a notice appeared calling a union meeting. It was signed "R. Bradley, Pres't." and "A. P. Swineford, Sec'y," indicating some previous organization, unless the officers were self-appointed. The success of the meeting is indicated by an announcement, which appeared a few days later in identical form in four St. Paul papers, stating that the organization of a printers' union had been perfected at a meeting on December 30. A constitution and bylaws were adopted and permanent officers were elected for a term of one year; the naming of four officers and five directors indicates a minimum of nine members. The birth notice concluded with the claim that the organization "may now be considered one of the city's permanent institutions." [9]

Shortly after its organization, there was some friction between the new union and Thomas M. Newson, editor of the *Minnesota Times*. Two journeymen left Newson's establishment, either because, as he said, they were discharged, or because, as J. Q. A. Ward, a union official, stated, the union ordered them to leave.[10] Wide recognition was not obtained until 1858, the year often given as the date of the organization of the St. Paul local, probably because it marks the entrance into the National Typographical Union. That entrance had been delayed by the negligence of the national secretary-treasurer. The union convention of 1858, however, ordered the issuance of a charter to the St. Paul group and named J. M. Culver of the new Union No. 30 to the national executive committee.[11] In the spring of 1858 another clash occurred between Newson and the union over the question of wages; charges and countercharges in the *Minnesotian* indicate that the union had at least twenty members at the time. Newson declared for a non-union shop, and the union began a publicity campaign by running for several months a formal notice certifying to its existence and good standing in the other three papers of the city.[12]

The printers of Minneapolis and St. Anthony, not to be outdone by those living downstream, soon organized their own union and received a charter dated September 10, 1859, from the national organization. This charter, now in the collections of the Minnesota Historical Society, named eleven men as the applicants, gave the union the number 42, and located it jointly at St. Anthony and Minneapolis. This group of typographers was either less ambitious for publicity or it was faced with less sympathetic publishers than the St. Paul men, for it failed to receive notice in the *Falls Evening News* during September and October, 1859. D. L. Payne of Minneapolis was made a member of the union's national executive committee for 1860–61, thus giving recognition to the new group.[13]

Neither of the printers' unions was able to survive the strain of the Civil War period; in 1864 the national convention dropped both locals because of failure to report for at least two years. The St. Paul group recovered first; its charter was reissued in 1870, and one of its members was appointed to the national committee each year until 1874. The Minneapolis group was rechartered in 1873 and was likewise given representation on the national board. Both locals were listed in the city directories, a testimony either to their courage or to their general acceptance by the community.[14]

Tailors and printers were not, however, the only Minnesota craftsmen who were conscious of the advantages of collective bargaining during the 1850s. In the summer of 1858 the citizens of St. Anthony were disturbed by several hundred lumber workers, who met to discuss means of collecting wages due. Some favored violent action, but moderation prevailed and a committee of twelve workers was appointed to carry an ultimatum to their employers stating that if payment was not made by the following Wednesday the boom would be cut loose and the logs taken downriver and sold. Since no further notice of the difficulty appears, it may be concluded that a harmonious settlement was reached.[15] But this was an isolated case, and the continuous labor movement in the state cannot be said to have started before 1867. Minnesota apparently had no connection with the National Labor Union, which had its first convention in 1866, or with the eight-hour movement of the same period, led by Ira Steward.

There is evidence that the Minnesota labor movement continued to gain strength in the late sixties. In June, 1867, the workers engaged in the construction of the school for the deaf, dumb, and blind at Faribault quit work because of some difficulty with a subcontractor. About the same time fifty-two Germans in Minneapolis formed a workingmen's society with the objectives of finding employment for all members and of supporting themselves and their families; this group was a mutual benefit organization with nationality as the principal basis for membership, rather than a labor union in the usual sense of the term. There is some indication that the St. Paul plasterers organized in 1867, but definite proof is lacking.[16]

- In the following year, unions appeared in two or three other industries. The Journeymen Cigar Makers' Protective Union, No. 98, of St. Paul drew up and published a *Constitution and By-laws* which provided for a three-year apprenticeship period, monthly meetings, the semiannual election of officers, a ten-dollar initiation fee, and dues of fifty cents a month. A quorum requirement of nine gives some indication of the size of the local.[17] In September, 1868, about seventy-five Minneapolis and St. Anthony coopers, upon whom the flour mills were dependent for barrels in the days before the widespread use of cloth and paper sacks, struck for a fifteen per cent wage increase. The action was promoted by two unions, but failed when two of the leaders were arrested while directing a march on a nonunion shop. There is some evidence that the Marine Engineers Beneficial Association No. 78 of Duluth also was organized in 1868, but conclusive proof is not available. The mechanics of Minneapolis must have organized about this time, as their initial ball was held in February, 1869.[18]

During the early 1870s labor organization gained momentum, with an increasing number of strikes and new unions. For the year 1870 at least seven strikes can be traced through Minnesota newspapers; among the strikers, whose chief demands usually concerned wages, were telegraphers, coopers, railroad laborers, sawmill workers, and bricklayers. The locations of both strikes and new unions indicate that laborers were stirring in smaller towns outside the Twin Cities; unions organized at Lake City and Farmington admitted members without reference to their respective trades. Fifty voters were present at the organization meeting of the Lake City group and adopted a constitution declaring their object to be "to protect the interests of the laboring man against all encroachments of whatever form or nature." Political discussion was to be barred, though corrupt officeholders, political rings, and moneyed monopolies were listed as enemies; the initiation fee was set at twenty-five cents and weekly dues at five cents; and Monday and Friday were designated as regular meeting nights. The Lake City newspaper adopted an attitude contrary to that of most contemporary papers and urged every laboring man to join the union.[19]

In 1871 a serious outbreak occurred among the construction workers on the Northern Pacific Railroad, but quiet was restored when the ringleaders were arrested and sent to Fort Ripley. Some of the other participants were set at liberty when they paid their share of the damages. The predominant nationality group of New Ulm came to the fore in 1873, when it organized the Arbeiter Verein. According to its articles of incorporation, its purposes were the elevation of workmen morally and intellectually, mutual aid and assistance to members under affliction, and the maintenance of a library and hall.[20]

John Lamb, Minnesota's first commissioner of labor, said in his initial report to the legislature in 1888 that the labor movement had its beginning in Minneapolis in 1872.[21] The basis for this statement is not very clear, since it appears that at least four unions had been started in Minneapolis before 1872, that none was established in that year, and that three were organized the following year. In addition to the rechartering of the typographical union in 1873, there is some evidence to indicate the formation of a general workingmen's union and also the unionization of tailors and locomotive engineers. A millers' union that was holding regular semimonthly meetings in 1874 may have been organized earlier; the fact that its corresponding secretary was a miller at the Washburn B Mill indicates that this was not entirely an employers' organization.[22]

In St. Paul the iron molders may have organized as early as 1872, but evidence for a definite statement is not available. There are several reasons for confusion about the organization dates of unions. Many groups found secrecy not only desirable, but absolutely necessary to their existence. A great number of unions did not maintain a continuous existence and dates of reorganization are often confused with the dates of original organization; the point at which a subsequent union in a trade becomes a new union rather than a reorganization of the original is often almost impossible to determine. The inaccurate memories or carelessness of union secretaries, slipshod newspaper reports, and conflicting official records do not make the solution of the problem any easier.

Some St. Paul leaders had ambitious plans when they formed the Workingmen's Association No. 1 of the United States in 1873; the constitution and bylaws opened the organization to all workingmen of eighteen or more years who depended chiefly on physical labor for their livelihood. The following year the Butchers Mutual Benefit Society of St. Paul was incorporated for the purpose of establishing sick and disability aids.[23]

The railroad brotherhoods have long been famous for the effectiveness of their organization and the high quality of their membership. The first groups formed in Minnesota were brotherhoods of engineers. The Brotherhood of Locomotive Engineers No. 102 of Austin, founded in 1870, is the oldest labor organization in the state with a record of continuous existence. In 1872 division No. 150 was organized in St. Paul. Its articles of incorporation, filed in 1875 and stating that its purposes were to advance the interests, increase the proficiency, and further the improvement and happiness of the members, were gentle enough not to cause alarm, but sufficiently general to allow definite organized action if such became desirable. In 1873 divisions were established at Minneapolis and Staples. The latter group, which was named the Brainerd lodge, is sometimes listed as located in that city. The home of some brotherhoods varied from year to year, probably with the addresses of the officers, who were members of a highly mobile group.[24]

On the periphery of organized labor there are usually many groups composed of laboring people, or dependent upon them for financial or political support, whose main object may or may not be the advancement of the cause of labor. Building and loan associations, composed of laboring people to a considerable extent, began in St. Paul as early as 1869, and during 1874 three were founded in Minneapolis. The very active Ancient Order of United Workmen was a workingmen's organization chiefly in title, for its purposes were mainly insurance and social activity.[25]

Laboring groups, particularly in their infancy, have often found it difficult not to become involved in politics. The Minnesota groups were no exception, although they may have profited by some of the sad experiences of earlier groups in the East. In the legislative elections of 1870 certain candidates were listed as "Labor Union" candidates. The prime leader in the attempt to unite the farmers and laborers of Minnesota into a political group was Ignatius Donnelly. In 1873, when hard times were descending, he tried without much success to co-ordinate the forces of industry and agriculture behind his reform program. In a pamphlet entitled *Facts for the Granges,* he urged farmers to follow the lead of mechanics in organizing, and reported a convention at Brownsdale which favored a union of farmers and laborers and called a "Farmers' and Laborers' Convention" for September, 1873. This clarion call does not appear to have had a decided effect on the forces of organized labor, although it helped to bring about the organization of the short-lived Anti-Monopoly party.[26]

Minnesota industry stagnated in the 1870s along with business throughout the nation. The financial depression following the panic of 1873, the deflation of the national currency, and the five-season grasshopper scourge which started in 1873 all helped to stop the wheels of the Minnesota factories. Labor organization suffered all over the country during this period, and it is not surprising that after the boom of 1873, only two new Minnesota unions were formed in 1874 and none in 1875, the only year after 1871 of which that may be said. But 1876 marked the beginning of a recovery in labor organization, although general business prosperity did not return until later in the decade. Throughout the nation very few of the trades assemblies of the sixties survived the depression of the following decade, but the years after 1876 saw a rapid growth in the number of local trade unions both in Minnesota and in the rest of the nation. The rate of growth was fairly constant until about 1884, when the Knights of Labor became exceedingly active.[27]

— In 1880, according to the census of that year, Minnesota had 21 trade societies out of the 2,440 in the whole country, a number which gave the state a rank of twentieth among the thirty-nine states and the District of Columbia. Nine of the Minnesota unions were railroad brotherhoods of engineers or firemen, and the others were composed of workers in manufacturing or mechanical pursuits, with three coopers' unions forming the largest trade group.[28] The number of strikes, which serves as a relatively accurate index of labor activity, rose sharply in Minnesota in the 1880s. Whereas only about fifteen strikes may be traced through St. Paul papers from 1849 to 1881, there were about seventy from 1881 to 1884; of these nearly half were ordered by unions, and half were mainly for the purpose of procuring wage increases. Minnesota employers of the period rarely used the lockout, an instance in 1883 being the only one in the first half of the 1880s.[29]

St. Paul was the chief center of union activity during the early eighties. In spite of the reorganization of 1870, the members of the Typographical Union No. 30 were unable to hold their group intact during the strain of the next few years. The present organization in St. Paul dates back to the spring of 1882; it reported 85 members for that year and 133 two years later. The great mobility of the printing trade at the time is indicated by the fact that in 1884 the local admitted 203 new members and 180 withdrew by card. In 1883 and 1884 the union had trouble with the managers of the *St. Paul Globe* about wages and the closed shop principle.[30] The German-speaking element in the city had its own newspaper, the *Volkszeitung,* and the printers in turn had their own union, the German-American Typographia. Since this local went through at least one reorganization, its original date is not clear, but it existed as early as 1878, when its members participated in both a ball and a strike. This early strike was a result of a union demand for the wage scale set up by the national office in New York, and it thus forced recognition of one of the major problems faced by local unions with national connections. The printers were willing to accept a compromise wage agreement, pending approval by the parent organization; but when the approval was denied, they struck for the full union scale. The manager of the office agreed to a pay restoration, but could not swallow a limitation on his power to dismiss workers as he pleased. A pressmen's union also was functioning as early as 1883, and had twenty-five members the following year.[31]

During the early eighties the building tradesmen of St. Paul became union conscious. The masons, who were the first in line, incorporated the Bricklayers Benevolent Union No. 1 in 1881 for mutual protection, mutual aid in times of sickness and death, the securing of a fair and just remuneration for their labor, and the improvement of their skill. Any bricklayer of good moral character who would pay the three-dollar admission fee and the twenty-five-cent monthly dues was eligible for membership. The establishment of branches throughout the state was contemplated, but about two months after incorporation the major attention of the members was probably taken up by an unsuccessful strike for a closed shop. A strike the following year also was unsuccessful, but the influx of Chicago union men helped to maintain the union spirit.[32] The plasterers, feeling the urge to co-ordinate their activities about the same time, filed articles of incorporation of the Plasterers Protection and Benevolent Union over the signatures of twelve members. Trouble crept in, however, and an attempt was made to organize again in 1883, and finally in 1884 a membership of fifty-six was definitely reported. Other building groups that organized unions were the stonecutters in 1878 or 1880, the plumbers in 1882, and the carpenters in 1883. The latter incorporated two years later. It is interesting to note that the plumbers were able to boost their wage twenty cents a day and cut the hours of work on Saturdays from ten to nine.[33] Members of various miscellaneous craft groups also organized in St. Paul at this time. The Cigar Makers' International Union of America No. 98 enrolled over two hundred members, but failed in its strike against the employment of girls because there was an abundance of labor available. The Minnesota Cooks, Pastry Cooks, and Confectioners Association incorporated in 1881, but Bakers Union No. 21 apparently took its place three years later. Most of the original officers of the Journeymen Tailors Self-Protection Society were Scandinavians. Railroad engineers, firemen, and conductors, after organizing their locals, sent representatives to the St. Paul Trades and Labor Assembly. Among the other groups which organized were the boilermakers, stationary engineers, iron molders, shoemakers, and telegraphers. The general labor unions formed in St. Paul did not continue long; one founded in 1873 was followed in 1878 by a Workingmen's Union organized with the help of a similar Minneapolis group. At the first regular meeting 120 members were registered, and a month later a meeting of the group filled the old Ramsey County courthouse. Its purpose was the discussion of political matters and city bonds for a proposed bridge to tap the trade area beyond Fort Snelling and thus prevent Minneapolis from monopolizing the business of the section. Such action reflects the fact that both employers and employees were admitted to membership upon the payment of a ten-cent fee, and indicates that the organization was more nearly a chamber of commerce than a labor union. Yet it did condemn a rather common device used by employers to reduce wages — that of publishing reports that work was plentiful in order to attract laborers.

At least two Minneapolis unions either survived the economic storms of the middle seventies or recovered very rapidly. The typographers admitted nineteen members during 1877, bringing their total to thirty-one, and their union continued to grow until in 1882 it had a hundred members. Beginning in the latter year a deputy was appointed from Minneapolis to encourage the formation of more local unions. Strikes for the union scale of wages in 1882 and 1883 were not successful, and in one controversy the union declared the strikers in error and ordered them back to work. The coopers stepped across municipal boundaries in 1878 to meet with the St. Paul Workingmen's Association, and in 1884 they prosecuted two strikes, the second of which was successful and brought congratulations from the St. Paul Trades and Labor Assembly. A bootblacks' union, started in 1878, raised the price of shoeshines to ten cents on Sundays, twice the regular weekday rate. The cigar makers and iron molders both organized in 1880 and won and lost strikes in the years following. The boilermakers and the stonecutters were also unionized about 1880. Among railroad men, the Minneapolis firemen and conductors added their groups to that of the engineers.[34]

A Workingmen's Union, which may have been the one formed in 1873, took an active part in municipal politics in 1878 and lasted at least until 1880. Its president, Chauncy W. Curtis, had been active in the coopers' union and in co-operatives, and he was to take a leading part in the future Knights of Labor. The union demanded an examination of the county books; sent a petition to Congress signed by over two thousand members asking for an income tax, the repeal of the resumption act, the abolition of the national banking system, and monetary reform; requested a state bureau of labor statistics; and promoted an independent political movement, the endorsed candidates of which were defeated. The organization forbade union members to take the jobs of striking construction workers; it forced employers to stop the practice of withholding twenty-five cents of the daily wage in order to keep employees from leaving; and it sent representatives to the funeral services for the unidentified victims of the Minneapolis flour mill explosion of 1878. On one occasion, members of the union listened to an address by the indomitable Ignatius Donnelly on the subject of the whole labor problem. The hostile *St. Paul Pioneer Press* predicted that the union would not last three months, but the friendly *St. Paul Globe* came to its defense by maintaining that it was not communistic.[35]

The belief that co-operation among the various unions in a city was desirable took hold relatively early in the United States and resulted in the organization of groups usually known as city centrals, trade and labor assemblies, or councils. A central co-ordinating and liaison body of which unions and not individuals were members could serve many obvious purposes in the attempts of laborers to improve their lot. It was necessary to have a group of well-established unions, a recognition of the need of centralized effort, and proper leadership before significant steps could be taken. These conditions did not exist in combination in either of the Twin Cities until the 1880s, the decade that marks the establishment of stronger and more widespread Minnesota labor organization.

The minutes of the St. Paul Trades and Labor Assembly give a fairly complete picture of its work, beginning with its organization on November 12, 1882, by thirty-five delegates from five unions and two Knights of Labor assemblies. At its second meeting two weeks later, the assembly adopted a constitution, bylaws, and established an order of business. It ruled to admit three delegates from unions which had fewer than fifty members and to allow one more for each additional twenty-five members, and it elected officers to serve for terms of six months. The assembly heard discussions on a wide variety of topics at its semimonthly meetings; business conditions, the progress of strikes, prospective unions, the union label, and political subjects were all in order. The union representatives took action in calling mass meetings, black-listing or boycotting unfair employers, persuading legislative candidates to pledge themselves to oppose convict labor, and encouraging the formation of new unions. Socially, the group promoted a picnic and held an annual ball. The St. Paul organization attempted to prevent improper presentation of the case of labor to the public by making plans to operate a page in the Sunday *Herald*. Although at least five groups in addition to the original seven sent delegates to the assembly during its first two years, there were periods when the organization not only languished, but even gasped for breath; it did maintain its existence in spite of the fact that it went as long as four months without an officially recorded meeting.[36]

The Minneapolis Trades Assembly, which probably was organized in September, 1883, also went under various other names — the Minneapolis Labor Council, the Minneapolis Trades and Labor Council, and the Trades and Labor Assembly of Minneapolis and Hennepin County. The leaders of the group were men who were prominent in many phases of city and state labor affairs; John Lamb, later state commissioner of labor, served as statistician. The assembly may have served as a sounding board for the general discussion of public questions by the Knights of Labor, whose sessions were otherwise secret, but it did include craft unions as well in its rather loose organization.[37]

In the area outside the Twin Cities unions became increasingly numerous as the population grew and was able to support manufacturing and railroads. Proximity to the comparatively large metropolitan center does not seem to have been a great stimulus to unionism, as only two towns within a fifty-mile radius of the Twin Cities had unions. The union coopers of Red Wing were dismissed in 1878 because they threatened to strike and an unidentified Union No. 1 drew up a declaration of principles which came into the possession of the Minnesota

Historical Society sometime previous to 1888. The Stillwater molders were very busy in 1883 with meetings, a dance, and a wage strike.[38]

In the fertile southern part of the state, railroad unions were numerous, for it was there that much early railroad development took place. Austin followed up on an early start by the formation of the Brotherhood of Locomotive Firemen and Enginemen No. 126 in 1882, but Waseca was already on the scene with unions of engineers, firemen, and conductors. In Winona the trainmen may have organized in 1883, but a stationary engineers' union had been formed the preceding year. This thriving river city also had a branch of the United Laborers Association of the United States, which had its home office in Chicago even though it was incorporated under a Minnesota law in 1884 for the mutual benefit of the laboring classes and for the purpose of combating the evils of capitalists, monopolies, and corporations, of which latter it was one. The cigar-making trade prospered for a time, particularly in Winona and St. Peter, where the unions won and lost strikes.

In the northern and western parts of the state, the forces of labor found several centers about which to rally. The granite cutters probably organized at St. Cloud and Ortonville in 1877. The St. Cloud union was active in promoting strikes, reporting nine stoppages in the three years from 1881 to 1883. In 1882 the Moorhead printers organized Typographical Union No. 186, probably a branch of a union at Fargo, North Dakota, and it immediately lost a strike for higher wages. The railroad brotherhoods added several unions — the Montevideo conductors in 1882 or 1883, the Dilworth engineers and Crookston-Barnesville firemen in 1883, and the Staples conductors and Melrose trainmen and firemen in 1884. The Duluth longshoremen reportedly won a wage strike in 1883, although their union was supposedly not organized until the early nineties. In other trades, the carpenters of Morris requested incorporation of Union No. 41 of the Brotherhood of Carpenters and Joiners of America in 1883, and the Brainerd iron molders were unionized between 1884 and 1886.[39]

By 1884 at least seventy-three unions had been organized in Minnesota — seventeen in Minneapolis, twenty-seven in St. Paul, and twenty-nine in other centers. Such growth indicates a substantial amount of labor organization activity. Even though many of the early Minnesota unions were short-lived, there is evidence that the leaven of unionism spread through much of the state before the labor boom of the middle eighties, which came with the flowering of the Knights of Labor.

The People of the Mesabi Range

JOHN SIRJAMAKI

*THE OPENING of the Mesabi Range in the 1890s added a new ele-
ment to Minnesota's economy. It also brought fresh waves of immigrants who quickly joined the state's labor force. Serious historical
studies of Minnesota's iron country and the complex industry it supports have as yet been few — a fact that enhances the importance of
this article by John Sirjamaki. It appeared in September, 1946 (volume
27), and was drawn from an unpublished Ph.D. thesis on the history of
the Mesabi communities, submitted at Yale University in 1940. Mr.
Sirjamaki is now professor of sociology in the State University of New
York at Buffalo.*

THE MESABI RANGE was a great expanse of forests and swamps in
northeastern Minnesota when, in 1890, iron ore was discovered near
what is now the thriving village of Mountain Iron. This first find of
ore led, with later surveying, to the uncovering of vast ore beds along
the southern slope of a range of low-lying hills which stretch in a flat-
tened S-curve some eighty miles in length and two to ten miles in width
in a general northeast-southwest direction. In 1890 the area of the
Mesabi, some seventy miles northwest of Duluth, was enveloped in
wilderness. The Duluth and Iron Range Railway, which ran between
Two Harbors and the Vermilion Range, skirted the range at the village
of Mesaba, far to the east of the newly discovered deposits. At the
west end of the range, lumbermen steadily pushed their operations up
the Mississippi and Swan rivers after 1870, but by 1890 they had not
yet reached the section in which the ores were first discovered.

Unsettled and isolated until the discovery of ore, the Mesabi Range
came to quick life after 1890. The digging of iron ore began in a high
pitch of mining fever; companies were organized to mine the ore deposits, men moved into the area to seek new jobs and possibly acquire
wealth, and mining camps and villages were laid out to care for the
influx of population. In 1892 the first shipment of ore was made from

261

the Mountain Iron mine; in the next year nine mines made shipments; and there were eleven in 1894, with a total tonnage of one and three-quarter millions.[1] By 1895 the Mesabi had attained its present reputation as the most productive of all the Lake Superior ranges. The increase in population was in keeping with the rapid expansion of ore output. In 1892 some fifteen hundred men were reported as actual or prospective workers on the range. In 1895 six villages and seven townships reported a total population of 8,870. Five years later the population of the Mesabi communities reached 15,000 and they had 65,000 inhabitants in 1910.[2]

The people who were attracted to the Mesabi mines were predominantly of foreign stock, and they represented a confusing array of immigrant groups. In the first wave of people to the range in the 1890s were Americans; English from Cornwall; English, Scotch, Irish, and French from Canada; Scandinavians; and Finns, as well as some Slovenes, Italians, Bohemians, Poles, and Lithuanians. After 1900 Slavs and Latins began to arrive in considerable numbers. They included Slovenes, Croats, Serbs, Montenegrins, Italians, Bulgarians, Greeks, Poles, Russians, and others. At the height of the influx of population to the range about 1910, there were at least thirty-five minority groups of sufficient size to be identified; scattered individuals were present from a handful more.

The story of the diverse immigrant groups who settled on the range and worked in the mines, as well as that of the paths they followed in traveling to the Mesabi communities, reflects in graphic profile the way a colorful section of northern Minnesota was peopled.[3]

The sources of population on the range may be grouped as follows: an early labor force recruited from the older ranges of the Lake Superior area, principally from the upper Michigan peninsula; desertions, mainly of marginal workers, from the lumber operations in the area of the range; direct immigration from Europe; indirect migration of Europeans from other areas or cities of first settlement in the United States; and labor agents, employment offices, and advertising, which were used to a limited degree.

By 1890, when the Mesabi deposits were discovered, the older Michigan ranges had already developed a mixed population which came to be the prototype of that of the Mesabi communities. The Marquette Range, which first shipped iron ore in 1854, was developed principally by miners from Cornwall. Until the middle 1860s the Cornishmen were virtually the only miners of the Marquette district, but the Irish began to move in then, and the two groups furnished, not without bitter rivalry and conflict, the labor forces of the mines. At the same time the earliest Scandinavians and Finland Swedes filtered into the district, as well as some French Canadians and Germans. Finns began to arrive in numbers after 1880, primarily from the provinces of Oulu and Vaasa. Other ethnic groups went to Michigan in later decades; they included Slovenes, Italians, Poles, Bohemians, and Slovaks. By the middle of the 1890s the population of the Michigan ranges was marked by an ethnic confusion.[4]

From this conglomerate population were drawn the initial recruits for the Vermilion Range operations in Minnesota, which began in 1882 when the Minnesota Iron Company was organized by Charlemagne Tower and his associates. Native Americans, Cornishmen, Irish, Scandinavians, Finns, French Canadians, and Germans comprised the larger groups, but Italians and Slavs were also represented. In the main, the population was drawn from the countries of western and northern Europe.[5]

When mining operations got under way on the Mesabi, the first and main source of labor was from the older ranges of the Lake Superior area. This remained true during the entire first decade of activities. Companies which owned mines in Michigan as well as in Minnesota were particularly able to shift employees to the Mesabi operations. This was especially true during the latter part of the 1890s, after the numerous, small, and often speculative companies of the earlier years had disappeared into the consolidation of companies under the control of the great steel furnace corporations.[6] A small but steady flow of men moved from the Michigan mines to the Mesabi after 1892; the economic hardship that accompanied the depression of 1893 made many companies willing to send their men to Minnesota, or caused the men to go voluntarily. They hoped for employment in the mines, but they were prepared to work in the forests as lumberjacks if necessary. From Duluth, Superior, and other cities or areas in Minnesota and Wisconsin went men to look for work or for business or professional opportunities in the new Mesabi villages. A constant shuttling to and fro between the Mesabi and near-by Vermilion ranges also occurred.

Of the early labor force on the Mesabi, the most skilled and experienced were the Cornishmen (known locally as "Cousinjacks"), who had learned to mine in the tin mines of Cornwall and had worked in Pennsylvania before migrating to the Michigan ranges. They not only furnished a large body of miners, but the main supply of mine bosses as well. By the turn of the century, however, they had been largely displaced by Scandinavians and Finns, and had moved on in large numbers to mine in the Rocky Mountain area. Those who remained were mine captains and shift bosses.

The Swedes comprised the largest group of the Scandinavians to settle on the Mesabi Range. Norwegians came next, but they were much fewer in number than the Swedes, while the number of Danes and of Icelanders never was large. Probably more than a fourth of those classified as Swedes were Finland Swedes, who, although they spoke the Swedish language, had emigrated from Finland and maintained a separate identity from the true Swedes.[7] Early settlers of the area reveal that the Swedes came predominantly from the southeastern provinces of Sweden, including Gotland, Göteborg och Bohus, Skaraborg, Kronoberg, Halland, Värmland, and Älvsborg. The Finland Swedes lived along the Finnish seacoast from Hanko to Turku; most of the range group came from the province of Vaasa, and more specifically, from Österbotten. Norwegian immigrants appear to have come from the southeastern provinces of Norway — Akershus and Buskerud — and from along the seacoast from Bergen to Nordland. The Danes and the Icelanders came from scattered areas rather than from specific centers in their countries.

Like the Finns who mined in Michigan, those of the Mesabi Range were predominantly from the southwestern agricultural provinces of Vaasa and Oulu. After 1900, immigrants began to come from other parts of Finland, notably from cities such as Helsinki, Turku, and Viipuri in southern Finland.

Immigration from the British Isles to the Mesabi district appears to have been indirect for the most part. Most of the English-speaking groups were derived from Canada rather than from Britain. They include the Canadian English, Scotch, and Irish, and intermixtures among them — people who have maintained a separate identity from the Cornishmen and have never been intimate with them. The Canadian groups came from eastern Ontario and Quebec; from the latter province came also the Canadian French. There was no direct immigration from France. The Canadians originally went into the United States as lumberjacks, many of them crossing the border at Detroit. They worked in the Michigan and Wisconsin forests during the winter months, and returned to Canada for the summers to work on their own farms. Over a period of years many of these people settled permanently in the United States. Generally they remained with the lumber companies, moving into Minnesota after the Michigan and Wisconsin forests had been cut. In general, they were quickly accepted and treated as native Americans.

The early Slavic movement to the Mesabi Range occurred mainly from the Michigan and Vermilion ranges, and included Slovenes, Poles, Bohemians, Slovaks, and others. Of these groups only the Bohemians and Slovaks failed to increase considerably in number after 1900. They were drawn from the provinces of Bohemia and Moravia, and from Hungary in what was then Austria-Hungary. German and Russian Poles comprised the early Polish group, the German Poles having emigrated from the provinces of Posen and Silesia, while the Russian group came mainly from the vicinity of the cities of Warsaw and Lublin. These two groups of Poles did not associate intimately with one another, and they tended to refuse identification with the Austrian or Galician Poles, who went to the Mesabi after 1905. Most of the Italians on the range in the 1890s were from northern Italy.

The lumber industry attracted Germans to the Mesabi Range, as well as groups of Irish, French Canadians, Scandinavians, and Finns. When ore was discovered in 1890, the lumber companies were already cutting timber on the upper reaches of the Mississippi River, and additional operations were begun near the newly laid-out range villages. Virginia became the center of considerable lumbering activity. From the woods it was easily possible for men to transfer to the mines. Not many Germans, however, became miners. They usually remained with the lumber concerns, often as saw filers or other craftsmen. But in the interflow between mine and woods employment during the first decades of range history, the mines generally won out. Lumber operators who were interviewed felt that the professional lumberjacks did not as a rule forsake the woods for the mines; those who became mine workers were marginal laborers, and most of them were recent immigrants who accepted the work that paid the highest wages.

Members of the minority groups obtained jobs in the Mesabi mines according to their previous experience and their ability to speak English. As the most skilled miners, the Cornishmen became the first mine captains and shift bosses, although in later decades mine officials were recruited elsewhere, particularly from the Scandinavian, Finnish, Slovene, and Italian groups. The skilled labor required of steam shovel operators, locomotive crews, and craftsmen, as well as of office workers, was performed by Americans, Cornishmen, Irish, and French Canadians. Mine crews were made up of Scandinavians, Finns, Slovenes, Italians, and other groups. Relatively few of the Canadian English, English, and Scotch became miners. They were business and professional workers in the range communities, or they remained in the employ of the lumber companies.[8]

By 1900 the older ranges could no longer furnish labor sufficient for the Mesabi mines. The demand for labor continued to increase, however, and it became urgent as new mines were opened and stripping and open-pit operations expanded in volume. The Mesabi Range was far removed from the main labor markets of the country, and it was difficult to entice workers to such distant mining settlements. Range newspapers of this period reflected the dearth of labor which confronted the mine operators. "Owing to the scarcity of men on the Iron Ranges," a typical news item of 1899 reads, "mining company officials are advertising in other parts of the country for miners. An additional 1,000 men can find work on the Mesaba and Vermilion Iron Ranges at the present time with the demand promising to be greater when the shipping season opens the latter part of the month." [9]

Immigration from Europe, rather than the conscious efforts of the mining companies, however, solved the labor problem. In the decade following 1890, the ranks of the foreign born on the Mesabi increased slowly as the result of direct arrivals from abroad, but after 1900, when the total volume of European immigration to the United States reached flood proportions, the flow of population to the range communities quickened. The immigrants in the Mesabi villages sent letters and money to those who had stayed behind, and thus publicized the range in far-off European settlements. Members of each ethnic minority group acted as magnets to attract their countrymen. Immigrants who might have settled elsewhere in the United States went to Minnesota, where they could be helped to jobs by persons already employed and happy to intercede for them with "the boss." Furthermore, the mining companies, which could use unskilled labor, put the men to work immediately. Since immigration after 1900 came preponderantly from southeastern Europe, the Mesabi communities received increased proportions of the Yugoslav and Italian groups, although accretions continued for the Scandinavian and Finnish colonies.

Many foreign-born workers migrated to the Mesabi Range from cities or regions where they had first settled in the United States. This was particularly true of the Slavic groups, who paused to work in Pittsburgh, Wilkes-Barre, Cleveland, Chicago, and other cities. During periodic layoffs they found their way to the range, attracted there by friends or relatives who reported in letters the booming condition of the Minnesota mines. Most of these people had not been long in other areas. A study of the employees of the Oliver Iron Mining Company on the Mesabi and Vermilion ranges was made in 1907. It showed that of 12,018 employees 84.4 per cent were foreign born; half of the latter, or 49.3 per cent, had resided in the United States less than two years, and 12.4 per cent less than one year. Groups with the largest numbers who had been in America less than one year were the Montenegrins with 34.3 per cent, the Austrians with 16.6 per cent, the Croats with 14.9 per cent, the Slavs with 13.6 per cent, and the Slovaks with 12.8 per cent. Nationalities showing a high proportion of persons who had resided in the country ten years or more were the Irish with 87.7 per cent, the Scotch with 77.4 per cent, the English with 74.4 per cent, the Scandinavians with 48.4 per cent, and the Germans with 23.7 per cent.[10]

After 1905, when stripping operations became extensive on the range, resort was sometimes made to labor agents or labor exchanges to secure employees for work in the open pits. Labor agents, many of them Serbs or Montenegrins, were usually former miners who operated saloons or other businesses and had become leaders among their countrymen. They entered into contracts with the mining companies or the stripping concerns to deliver workmen, usually recruited from immigrant colonies in the eastern or central United States industrial cities. The labor agent arranged for their employment, and generally supervised their living accommodations, which were often in mining camps.

A *padrone* system appears, likewise, to have existed among some of the Serbs, Montenegrins, Sicilians, and possibly Greeks. The *padrone* was the labor agent or leader of a group of men who contracted with the mining companies for their employment as a unit. Usually he retained for himself the control of the camps in which his men were housed, and he made his income by boarding the men, and mulcting whatever he could from them or from the companies. This system was suitable for large construction operations where a big labor supply was needed, and it was used primarily for stripping jobs on the Mesabi. There is evidence, however, that underground mines occasionally secured men through *padrones*. They functioned between 1907 and 1912, and thereafter disappeared, since the need for their services no longer existed.

It does not seem likely that direct recruiting of immigrants in the European countries by labor agents for the mining companies was undertaken on a large scale. Some residents on the range were solicited to emigrate, but the persuasion was by agents for concerns in other areas. In August, 1907, Serbs and Montenegrins were shipped to the Mesabi Range by the local companies to break the strike of that year. The men were sent in boxcars to the range villages, where it is still recalled that, if they had not come directly from Europe, at least they had not stopped on the way long enough to wash the soil of their native land from their faces. Nevertheless, it is improbable that these people were direct recruits from Europe. More likely they were recent arrivals to the United States who were hired after they landed for shipment to the strike-bound Mesabi Range.[11]

After 1900 underground mining was done chiefly by Finns, Slovenes, Croats, and Italians, though some Poles, Slovaks, Bohemians, Lithuanians, Bulgarians, and others also were employed. Most of the Slovenes and Croats have continued in underground work; the others, however, have worked in open-pit operations as well. After 1905, when open-pit mining and stripping activities increased in volume and importance, the most recent immigrants found employment mainly in surface operations. Into this type of work went the Carpatho-Russians, Montenegrins, Serbs, Bulgarians, Romanians, South Italians, Galician Poles, Lithuanians, and Greeks who arrived in that period. They worked chiefly in track or lining gangs in the open pits or on the ore or earth dumps, where unskilled labor could be quickly trained and used.

Southeast Europeans gradually displaced the Scandinavians in the mines after 1900. Unlike the Cornishmen, who went to other parts of the country to continue as miners, the Scandinavians were pushed up rather than out of the industrial hierarchy on the Mesabi Range. They transferred to the skilled trades in the villages, where today they form the largest proportion of carpenters, masons, plumbers, and plasterers. The Scandinavians who have remained in mining are usually officials or craftsmen. During the first decade of the twentieth century, when the ore bodies on the range were being charted, they also formed the main labor force of the drill and exploration crews, since they were expert diamond and churn drill operators.

The earliest adequate census figures on the population components of the Mesabi Range area are those for 1905, when the fifth decennial state census was taken in Minnesota. In that year the Finns were definitely the largest ethnic group in the Mesabi population, with the Scandinavians, Canadians, and Slavs comprising other major elements. Listed as Austrians in the census were the Slovenes and Croats; few German-speaking Austrians have gone to the range. Although a substantial Slavic immigration occurred after 1905, the group was by no means small in that year.[12]

Of the Yugoslav groups in the Mesabi area, the largest was the Slovene. The range contingent was derived chiefly from the province of Carniola, with lesser numbers from Styria, Coastland, and Carinthia.

Slovenes were present from the early years on both the Vermilion and Mesabi ranges, and they therefore set up currents of immigration from Europe before 1900. Cleveland, which has a large concentration of Slovenes, was a stopping place for many before they went to the Mesabi. After the Slovenes, the Croats formed the next most numerous group of Yugoslavs on the Mesabi. The two groups have generally been identified because of a common Roman Catholic bond, although they have not always lived in harmony. The Croats emigrated from the provinces of Slavonia, Croatia, and Dalmatia. Many of them stopped first in the industrial cities, mainly about Pittsburgh, before venturing to the Mesabi. The Serbs and Montenegrins, who are identical ethnically with the Croats but are members of the Greek Orthodox church, came from the provinces of Croatia, Bosnia, and Herzegovina. The numbers from the kingdom of Montenegro have apparently never been large.

The Russians of the range are Little Russians, also known as Ukrainians or Ruthenians. They came mainly from the Carpatho Mountain district in eastern Galicia, which before 1918 was a province of Hungary. The number of Russians who emigrated from Russia was small, the most extensive group having come from Kiev. From Galicia also came a large group of Poles, who were listed in early census reports as Galician or Austrian Poles. These two groups appeared on the range after 1905. Before going there many of their members had stopped in Russian or Polish colonies in Wilkes-Barre, Buffalo, Pittsburgh, and other cities.

Italians on the range in the 1890s were mainly North Italians, drawn from the provinces of Piedmont and Lombardy in Italy and Tyrol in Austria. After 1905 the Italian emigration came from virtually all the Italian provinces, with the largest representations from Piedmont and Marches. North Italians have, however, remained numerically superior to those from the south.

From Russia as it existed before the First World War came Finns, Finland Swedes, Poles, Jews, and Lithuanians. The two latter groups came after 1905 from approximately the same areas — the provinces of Kovno and Vilna in Lithuania. Thus most of the Mesabi Range Jews are Lithuanian Jews; only small numbers have come from the Polish or Russian sectors of Russia or from other European countries. In the early 1890s there were Jewish businessmen on the range who had moved from such near-by cities as Duluth and Superior, where they were engaged earlier in retail enterprises. On the range they entered business or the professions.

Substantial numbers of Greeks and Bulgarians emigrated from Macedonia at a time when that province was still controlled by Turkey. Those who came from the Grecian mainland and islands appear to have had no definite centers of emigration. They were the latest group to arrive on the range, settling there chiefly after 1910, and going there usually after initial employment on the railroads running to the area. The Bulgarians, who arrived after 1907, worked in surface operations. Romanians were present on the range in numbers for some years after 1907, but they have since disappeared from the area almost entirely. Small groups came also from Belgium, the Netherlands, Switzerland, Spain, Turkey, Mexico, Syria, Argentina, and other countries.

The immigrant movement to the Mesabi came to a standstill with the outbreak of World War I. Before that conflict, however, immigration had slackened considerably. After 1912 the Balkan wars drew large numbers of immigrants back to Europe for military service. Among them were Montenegrins, Serbs, Bulgarians, Greeks, and Romanians. The Montenegrins, who were chiefly young, single men in the prime of life and imbued with an intense patriotism for their native land, left en masse, going in such large numbers that their large range population was reduced to a nominal fraction.

The movement away from the Mesabi Range was accelerated, also, by the depression of 1914–15, which was caused in part by the uncertainties of the opening year of World War I and the temporary loss of foreign markets. The range was particularly hard hit, and as a result men began to drift away to other sections of the country in search of employment. After the war, the usual movement of immigrants returning to Europe, which was always notable in the Mesabi communities, was resumed. In addition, there were many immigrants who left because love for their native soil made them eager to participate in building up such European countries as Yugoslavia, Finland, Poland, and Lithuania, which gained their independence as a result of the war.

During the boom war years of 1916 to 1918, the mining companies were compelled by a temporary shortage of labor to begin a program of mechanization of mine and pit operations. The machines and mechanized processes then introduced proved immediately rewarding to the companies, and they were retained and extended in the years following, with the result that since 1920 there has been a steadily decreasing need for labor on the Mesabi Range. This has resulted in a continuous drift of workers away from the range. After 1920 some ethnic groups disappeared almost entirely from the area. The colonies of Romanians, Bulgarians, Montenegrins, Greeks, and

Slovaks faded away, and only a few members of these groups remain on the Mesabi. The number of Irish, Norwegians, French Canadians, and others has been materially reduced. The range population of 1946 is dominated by a smaller number of minority groups, of whom the Finns, Yugoslavs, Italians, Scandinavians, Poles, English, and Canadians are the most numerous.

With the passage of years the proportion of immigrants in the Mesabi population has steadily diminished. In 1900, half the residents were foreign born; in 1940, the proportion had dropped to twenty per cent, as indicated by the federal census of that year. The immigrants and their children, however, constitute eighty-five per cent of the total population. Today the American-born children of the immigrants are the adults of the Mesabi communities, and they carry on after their parents. From twenty-five to thirty-three per cent of these immigrant young have intermarried with members of other minority groups.[13] The range is actually a melting pot, and by the time a third generation appears there, the ethnic identity of most of its members will be obscure or unimportant. Interest in ancestry will then be more one of curiosity than of concern with ethnic origins.

The Persistence of Populism

JOHN D. HICKS

LIKE THE URBAN WORKING MAN, the farmer felt the weakness of his bargaining position as the subsistence economy of the frontier gave way to dependence on cash crops and the world market. Aggravated by crushing farm debt and falling prices, waves of agrarian protest swept the Middle West and reached a climax in the Populism of the bitter 1890s. One of the foremost historians of this period is John D. Hicks, whose pioneering study of The Populist Revolt *was published in 1931. Mr. Hicks was the principal speaker at the annual meeting of the Minnesota Historical Society that year, and his address was published in the March issue of* Minnesota History *(volume 12). The paper that follows subsequently appeared, with suitable annotation, as a chapter in* The Populist Revolt. *It has frequently been cited as a classic statement of the interpretation which finds in Populism the roots of twentieth-century reforms culminating in the New Deal. At the time of its original publication, Mr. Hicks was dean of the college of arts and sciences in the University of Nebraska. He is now professor emeritus of history in the University of California, Berkeley. His later work includes a study of* Agricultural Discontent in the Middle West, 1900 –1939 *(1951), written in collaboration with Theodore Saloutos.*

EARLY IN 1890, when the People's party was yet in the embryo stage, a farmer editor from the West set forth the doctrine that "The Cranks Always Win." As he saw it, "The cranks are those who do not accept the existing order of things, and propose to change them. The existing order of things is always accepted by the majority, therefore the cranks are always in the minority. They are always progressive thinkers and always in advance of their time, and they always win. Called fanatics and fools at first, they are sometimes persecuted and abused. But their reforms are generally righteous, and time, reason and argument bring men to their side. Abused and ridiculed, then tolerated, then respectfully given a hearing, then supported. This has been the gauntlet that all great reforms and reformers have run, from Galileo to John Brown."

272

The writer of this editorial may have overstated his case, but a backward glance at the history of Populism shows that many of the reforms that the Populists demanded, while despised and rejected for a season, won out triumphantly in the end. The party itself did not survive, nor did many of its leaders, although the number of contemporary politicians whose escutcheons should bear the bend sinister of Populism is larger than might be supposed; but Populistic doctrines showed an amazing vitality.

In formulating their principles the Populists reasoned that the ordinary, honest, willing American worker, be he farmer or be he laborer, might expect in this land of opportunity not only the chance to work, but also as the rightful reward of his labor a fair degree of prosperity. When, in the later eighties and in the "heart-breaking nineties," hundreds of thousands — perhaps millions — of men found themselves either without work to do, or having work, unable to pay their just debts and make a living, the Populists held that there must be "wrong and crime and fraud somewhere." What was more natural than to fix the blame for this situation upon the manufacturers, the railroads, the moneylenders, the middlemen — plutocrats all, whose "colossal fortunes, unprecedented in the history of mankind" grew even greater while the multitudes came to know the meaning of want? Work was denied when work might well be given, and "the fruits of the toil of millions were boldly stolen."

And the remedy? In an earlier age the hard-pressed farmers and laborers might have fled to free farms in the seemingly limitless lands of the West, but now the era of free lands had passed. Where, then, might they look for help? Where, if not to the government, which alone had the power to bring the mighty oppressors of the people to bay? So to the government the Populists turned. From it they asked laws to insure a full redress of grievances. As Professor Frederick J. Turner puts it, "the defenses of the pioneer democrat began to shift from free land to legislation, from the ideal of individualism to the ideal of social control through regulation by law." Unfortunately, however, the agencies of government had been permitted to fall into the hands of the plutocrats. Hence, if the necessary corrective legislation were to be obtained, the people must first win control of their government. The Populist philosophy thus boiled down finally to two fundamental propositions: one, that the government must restrain the selfish tendencies of those who profited at the expense of the poor and needy; the other, that the people, not the plutocrats, must control the government.

In their efforts to remove all restrictions on the power of the people to rule, the Populists accepted as their own a wide range of reforms. They believed, and on this they had frequently enough the evidence of their own eyes, that corruption existed at the ballot box and that a fair count was often denied. They fell in, therefore, with great enthusiasm when agitators, who were not necessarily Populists, sought to popularize the Australian ballot and such other measures as were calculated to insure a true expression of the will of the people. Believing as they did that the voice of the people was the voice of God, they sought to eliminate indirect elections, especially the election of United States senators by state legislatures and the president and the vice-president by an electoral college. Fully aware of the habits of party bosses in manipulating nominating conventions, the Populists veered more and more toward direct primary elections, urging in some of their later platforms that nominations even for president and vice-president should be made by direct vote. Woman suffrage was a delicate question, for it was closely identified with the politically hazardous matter of temperance legislation, but, after all, the idea of votes for women was so clearly in line with the Populist doctrine of popular rule that it could not logically be denied a place among genuinely Populistic reforms. Direct legislation through the initiative and referendum and through the easy amendment of state constitutions naturally appealed strongly to the Populists — the more so as they saw legislatures fail repeatedly to enact reform laws to which a majority of their members had been definitely pledged. "A majority of the people," declared the Sioux Falls convention, "can never be corruptly influenced." The recall of faithless officials, even judges, also attracted favorable attention from the makers of later Populist platforms.

To list these demands is to cite the chief political departures made in the United States during recent times. The Australian system of voting, improved registration laws, and other devices for insuring "a free ballot and a fair count" have long since swept the country. Woman suffrage has won an unqualified victory. The election of United States senators by direct vote of the people received the approval of far more than two-thirds of the national House of Representatives as early as 1898; it was further foreshadowed by the adoption in a number of states, beginning in 1904, of senatorial primaries, the results of which were to be regarded as morally binding upon the legislatures concerned; and it became a fact in 1913 with the ratification of the seventeenth amendment to the Constitution. The direct election of president and vice-president was hard to reconcile with state control of the election machinery and state definition of the right to vote, hence this reform never caught on; but the danger of one presidential candidate receiving a majority of the popular vote and another a majority of the electoral vote, as was the case in the Cleveland-Harrison contest of 1888, seems definitely to have passed. Late elections may not prove that the popular voice always speaks intelligently; but they do seem to show that it speaks decisively. In the widespread use of the primary election for the making of party nominations, the Populist principle of popular rule has scored perhaps its most telling victory. Benjamin R. Tillman urged this reform in South Carolina at a very early date, but on obtaining control of the Democratic political machine of his state, he hesitated to give up the power which the convention system placed in his hands. At length, however, in 1896 he allowed the reform to go through. Wisconsin, spurred on by the La Follette forces, adopted the direct primary plan of nominations in 1903, and thereafter the other states of the Union, with remarkably few exceptions, fell into line. Presidential preference primaries, through which it was hoped that the direct voice of the people could be heard in the making of nominations for president and vice-president, were also adopted by a number of states, beginning with Oregon in 1910. Direct legislation by the people became almost an obsession with the Populists, especially the middle-of-the-road faction, in whose platforms it tended to overshadow nearly every other issue; and it is perhaps significant that the initiative and referendum were adopted by South Dakota, a state in which the Populist party had shown great strength, as close on the heels of the Populist movement as 1898. Other states soon followed the South Dakota lead, and particularly in Oregon the experiment of popular legislation was given a thorough trial. New constitutions and numerous amendments to old constitutions tended also to introduce much popularly made law, the idea that legislation in a constitution is improper and unwise receiving perhaps its most shattering blow when an Oklahoma convention wrote for that state a constitution of fifty thousand words. The recall of elected officials has been applied chiefly in municipal affairs, but some states also permit its use for state officers and a few allow even judges, traditionally held to be immune from popular reactions, to be subjected to recall. Thus many of the favorite ideas of the Populists, ideas which had once been "abused and ridiculed," were presently "respectfully given a hearing, then supported.".

Quite apart from these changes in the American form of government, the Populist propaganda in favor of independent voting did much to undermine the intense party loyalties that had followed in the wake of the Civil War. The time had been when for the Republican voter "To doubt Grant was as bad as to doubt Christ," when the man who scratched his party ticket was regarded as little if any better than the traitor to his country. The Farmers' Alliance in its day had sought earnestly to wean the partisan voter over to independence. It had urged its members to "favor and assist to office such candidates only as are thoroughly identified with our principles and who will insist on such legislation as shall make them effective." And in this regard the Alliance, as some of its leaders boasted, had been a "great educator of the people." The Populist party had to go even further, for its growth depended almost wholly upon its ability to bring voters to a complete renunciation of old party loyalties. Since at one time or another well over a million men cast their ballots for Populist tickets, the loosening of party ties that thus set in was of formidable proportions. Indeed, the man who became a Populist learned his lesson almost too well. When confronted, as many Populist voters thought themselves to be in 1896, with a choice between loyalty to party and loyalty to principle, the third-party adherent generally tended to stand on principle. Thereafter, as Populism faded out, the men who once had sworn undying devotion to the Omaha platform were compelled again to transfer their allegiance. Many Republicans became Democrats via the Populist route; many Democrats became Republicans. Probably, however, most of the Populists returned to the parties from which they had withdrawn, but party ties, once broken, were not so strong as they had been before. The rapid passing of voters from one party to another and the wholesale scratching of ballots, so characteristic of voting today, are distinctly reminiscent of Populism; as are also the frequent nonpartisan ballots by which judges, city commissioners, and other officers are now chosen wholly without regard to their party affiliations.

In the South the Populist demands for popular government produced a peculiar situation. To a very great extent the southern Populists were recruited from the rural classes, which had hitherto been politically inarticulate. Through the Populist party, the "wool hat boys" from the country sought to obtain the weight in southern politics that their numbers warranted but that the "Bourbon" dynasties had ever denied them. In the struggle that ensued both sides made every possible use of the Negro vote, and the bugaboo of Negro domination was once again raised. Indeed, the experience of North Carolina under a combination government of Populists and Republicans furnished concrete evidence of what might happen should the political power of the Negro be restored. Under the circumstances, therefore, there seemed to be nothing for the white Populists to do but to return to their former allegiance until the menace of the Negro voter could be removed. With the Democratic party again supreme, the problem of Negro voting was attacked with right good will. Indeed, as early as 1890 the state of Mississippi, stimulated no doubt by the agitation over the Force Bill, adopted a constitution which fixed as a prerequisite for voting two years' residence in the state and one year's residence in the district or town. This provision, together with a poll tax that had to be paid far in advance of the dates set for elections, diminished appreciably the number of Negro voters, among whom indigence was common and the migratory propensity well developed. To complete the work of disfranchisement an amendment was added to the Mississippi constitution in 1892 which called for a modified literacy test that could be administered in such a way as to permit illiterate whites to vote, while discriminating against illiterate, or even literate blacks. The Tillmanites in South Carolina found legal means to exclude the Negro voter in 1895; Louisiana introduced her famous "grandfather clause" in 1898; North Carolina adopted residence, poll tax, and educational qualifications in 1900; Alabama followed in 1901; and in their own good time the other southern states in which Negro voters had constituted a serious problem did the same thing. Some reverses were experienced in the courts, but the net result of this epidemic of anti-Negro suffrage legislation was to eliminate for the time being all danger that Negro voters might play an important part in southern politics.

With this problem out of the way, or at least in process of solution, it became possible for the rural whites of the South to resume the struggle for a voice in public affairs that they had begun in the days of the Alliance and had continued under the banner of Populism. They did not form again a third party, but they did contest freely at the Democratic primaries against the respectable and conservative descendants of the "Bourbons." The Tillman machine in South Carolina continued to function smoothly for years as the agency through which the poorer classes sought to dominate the government of that state. It regularly sent Tillman to the United States Senate, where after his death his spirit lived on in the person of Cole Blease. In Georgia the struggle for supremacy between the two factions of the Democratic party was a chronic condition with now one side and now the other in control. Ex-Populists, converted by the lapse of time into regular organization Democrats, won high office and instituted many of the reforms for which they had formerly been defamed. Even Tom Watson rose from his political deathbed to show amazing strength in a race for Congress in 1918 and to win an astounding victory two years later when he sought a seat in the United States Senate. For better or for worse, the political careers of such southern politicians as James K. Vardaman of Mississippi, the Honorable Jeff. Davis of Arkansas and Huey P. Long of Louisiana demonstrate conclusively the fact that the lower classes in the South can and sometimes do place men of their own kind and choosing in high office. In these later days rural whites, who fought during Populist times with only such support as they could obtain from Republican sources, have sometimes been able to count as allies the mill operatives and their sympathizers in the factory districts; and southern primary elections are now apt to be as exciting as the regular elections are tame. Populism may have had something to do with the withdrawal of political power from the southern Negro, but it also paved the way for the political emancipation of the lower-class southern whites.

The control of the government by the people was for the thoughtful Populist merely a means to an end. The next step was to use the power of the government to check the iniquities of the plutocrats. The Populists at Omaha, when they were baffled by the insistence of the temperance forces, pointed out that before this or any other such reform could be accomplished they must "ask all men to first help us to determine whether we are to have a republic to administer." The inference is clear. Once permit the people really to rule, once insure that the men in office would not or could not betray the popular will, and such regulative measures as would right the wrongs from which the people suffered would quickly follow. The Populists believed implicitly in the ability of the people to frame and enforce the measures necessary to redeem themselves from the various sorts of oppression that were being visited upon them. They catalogued the evils in their platforms and suggested the specific remedies by which these evils were to be overcome.

Much unfair criticism has been leveled at the Populists because of the attitude they took toward the allied subjects of banking and currency. One would think from the contemporary anti-Populist diatribes and from many subsequent criticisms of the Populist financial program that in such matters the third-party economists were little better than raving maniacs. As a matter of fact, the old-school Populists could think about as straight as their opponents. Their newspapers were well edited and the arguments therein presented usually held together. Populist literature, moreover, was widely and carefully read by the ordinary third-party voters, particularly by the western farmers, whose periods of enforced leisure gave them ample opportunity for reading and reflection. Old party debaters did not tackle lightly their Populist antagonists, and as frequently as not the bewhiskered rustic, turned orator, could present in support of his arguments an array of carefully sorted information that left his better-groomed opponent in a daze. The injection of the somewhat irrelevant silver issue considerably confused Populist thinking, but, even so, many of the "old-timers" kept their heads and put silver in its proper place.

The Populists observed with entire accuracy that the currency of the United States was both inadequate and inelastic. They criticized correctly the part played by the national banking system in currency matters as irresponsible and susceptible of manipulation in the interest of the creditor class. They demanded a stabilized dollar, and they believed that it could be obtained if a national currency "safe, sound, and flexible" should be issued direct to the people by the government itself in such quantities as the reasonable demands of business should dictate. Silver and gold might be issued as well as paper, but the value of the dollar should come from the fiat of government and not from the "intrinsic worth" of the metal. It is interesting to note that since the time when Populists were condemned as lunatics for holding such views legislation has been adopted which, while by no means going the full length of a straight-out paper currency, does seek to accomplish precisely the ends that the Populists had in mind. Populist and free silver agitation forced economists to study the money question as they had never studied it before and ultimately led them to propose remedies that could run the gauntlet of public opinion and of Congress. The Aldrich-Vreeland Act of 1908 authorized an emergency currency of several hundred million dollars to be lent to banks on approved securities in times of financial disturbance. A National Monetary Commission, created at the same time, reported after four years' intensive study in favor of a return to the Hamiltonian system of a central bank of the United States; but Congress in 1914, under Wilson's leadership, adopted instead the Federal Reserve system. The Federal Reserve Act did not, indeed, destroy the national banks and avoid the intervention of bankers in all monetary matters; but it did make possible an adequate and elastic national currency varying in accordance with the needs of the country, and it placed supreme control of the nation's banking and credit resources into the hands of a

Federal Reserve Board, appointed, not by the bankers, but by the president of the United States with the consent of the Senate. The Populist diagnosis had been accepted and the Populist prescription had not been wholly ignored.

Probably no item in the Populist creed received more thorough castigation at the hands of contemporaries than the demand for subtreasuries, or government warehouses for the private storage of grain; but the subtreasury idea was not all bad, and perhaps the Populists would have done well had they pursued it farther than they did. The need that the subtreasury was designed to meet was very real. Lack of credit forced the farmer to sell his produce at the time of harvest when the price was lowest. A cash loan on his crop that would enable him to hold it until prices should rise was all that he asked. Prices might thus be stabilized; profits honestly earned by the farmers would no longer fall to the speculators. That the men who brought forward the subtreasury as a plan for obtaining short-term rural credits also loaded it with an unworkable plan for obtaining a flexible currency was unfortunate; but the fundamental principle of the bill has by no means been discredited. Indeed, the Warehouse Act of 1916 went far toward accomplishing the very thing the Populists demanded. Under it the United States department of agriculture was permitted to license warehousemen and authorize them to receive, weigh, and grade farm products, for which they might issue warehouse receipts as collateral. Thus the owner might borrow the money he needed; not, however, from the government of the United States.

In addition to the credits that the subtreasury would provide, Populist platforms usually urged also that the national government lend money on farm lands directly at a low rate of interest. This demand, which received at the time an infinite amount of condemnation and derision, has since been treated with much deference. If the government does not now print paper money to lend the farmer with his land as security, it nevertheless does stand back of an elaborate system of banks through which he may obtain the credit he needs. Under the terms of the Federal Reserve Act national banks may lend money on farm mortgages — a privilege not enjoyed in Populist times — and agricultural paper running as long as six months may be rediscounted by the Federal Reserve banks. From the Farm Loan banks, created by an act of 1916, the farmers may borrow for long periods sums not exceeding fifty per cent of the value of their land and twenty per cent of the value of their permanent improvements. Finally, through still another series of banks — the Federal Intermediate Credit banks, established by an act of 1923 — loans are made available to carry the farmer from one season to the next, or a little longer, should occasion demand; the intermediate banks were authorized to rediscount agricultural and livestock paper for periods of six months to three years. Thus the government has created a comprehensive system of rural credits through which the farmer may obtain short-term loans, loans of intermediate duration, or long-term loans, whichever his needs require, with the minimum of difficulty and at minimum interest rates. It would be idle to indulge in a *post hoc* argument to try to prove that all these developments were due to Populism; but the intensive study of agricultural problems that led ultimately to these measures did begin with the efforts of sound economists to answer the arguments of the Populists. And it is evident that in the end the economists conceded nearly every point for which the Populists had contended.

More recent attempts to solve the agricultural problem, while assuming the responsibility of the government in the matter as readily as even a Populist could have asked, have progressed beyond the old Populist panacea of easy credit. Agricultural economists now have their attention fixed upon the surplus as the root of the difficulty. In industry production can be curtailed to meet the demands of any given time, and a glutted market with the attendant decline of prices can in a measure be forestalled. But in agriculture, where each farmer is a law unto himself and where crop yields must inevitably vary greatly from year to year, control of production is well-nigh impossible and a surplus may easily become chronic. Suggestions for relief therefore looked increasingly toward the disposal of this surplus to the greatest advantage. The various McNary-Haugen bills that came before Congress in the 1920s proposed to create a federal board through which the margin above domestic needs in years of plenty should be purchased and held or disposed of abroad at whatever price it would bring. Through an "equalization fee" the losses sustained by "dumping" the surplus in this fashion were to be charged back upon the producers benefited. This proposition, while agreeable to a majority of both houses of Congress, met opposition from two successive presidents, Coolidge and Hoover, and was finally set aside for another scheme, less "socialistic." In 1929 Congress passed and the president signed a law for the creation of an appointive federal farm board whose duty it is, among other things, to encourage the organization of co-operative societies through which the farmers themselves may deal with the problem of the surplus. In case of necessity, however, the board may take the lead in the formation of stabilization corporations which under its strict supervision may buy up such seasonal or temporary surpluses as threaten to break the market and hold them for higher prices. A huge revolving fund, appropriated by Congress, is made available for the purpose, loans from this fund being obtainable by the stabilization corporations at low interest rates. There is much about this thoroughly respectable and conservative law that recalls the agrarian demands of the nineties. Indeed, the measure goes farther in the direction of government recognition and aid to the principle of agricultural co-operation than even the most erratic Allianceman could have dared to hope. Perhaps it will prove to be the "better plan" that the farmers called for in vain when the subtreasury was the best idea they could present. ￦

To the middlewestern Populist the railway problem was as important as any other — perhaps most important of all. Early Alliance platforms favored drastic governmental control of the various means of communication as the best possible remedy for the ills from which the people suffered, and the first Populist platform to be written called for government ownership and operation only in case "the most rigid, honest, and just national control and supervision" should fail to remove the "abuses now existing." Thereafter the Populists usually demanded government ownership; although it is clear enough from their state and local platforms and from the votes and actions of Populist officeholders that, pending the day when ownership should become a fact, regulation by state and nation must be made ever more effective. Possibly government ownership is no nearer today than in Populist times, but the first objective of the Populists, "the most rigid, honest and just national control," is as nearly an accomplished fact as carefully drawn legislation and highly efficient administration can make it. Populist misgivings about governmental control arose from the knowledge that the Interstate Commerce Act of 1887, as well as most regulatory state legislation, was wholly ineffectual during the nineties; but beginning with the Elkins Act of 1903, which struck at the practice of granting rebates, a long series of really workable laws found its way upon the statute books. The Hepburn Act of 1906, the Mann-Elkins Act of 1910, and the Transportation Act of 1920, not to mention lesser laws, placed the Interstate Commerce Commission upon a high pinnacle of power. State laws, keeping abreast of the national program, supplemented national control with state control; and through one or the other agency most of the specific grievances of which the Populists had complained were removed. The arbitrary fixing of rates by the carriers, a commonplace in Populist times, is virtually unknown today. If discriminations still exist as between persons and places the

Interstate Commerce Commission is likely to be as much to blame as the railroads. Free passes, so numerous in Populist times as to occasion the remark that the only people who did not have passes were those who could not afford to pay their own fare, have virtually ceased to exist, except for railway employees. Railway control of state governments, even in the old "Granger" states, where in earlier days party bosses took their orders direct from railway officials, has long since become a thing of the past. The railroads still may have an influence in politics, but the railroads do not rule. Governmental control of telephones, telegraphs, and pipelines, together with such later developments as radio and transmission of electric power, is accepted today as a matter of course, the issues being merely to what extent control should go and through what agencies it should be accomplished.

For the trust problem, as distinguished from the railroad problem, the Populists had no very definite solution. They agreed, however, that the power of government, state and national, should be used in such a way as to prevent "individuals or corporations fastening themselves, like vampires, on the people and sucking their substance." Antitrust laws received the earnest approval of Alliancemen and Populists and were often initiated by them. The failure of such laws to secure results was laid mainly at the door of the courts, and when Theodore Roosevelt in 1904 succeeded in securing an order from the United States Supreme Court dissolving the Northern Securities Company, it was hailed as a great victory for Populist principles. Many other incidental victories were won. Postal savings banks "for the safe deposit of the earnings of the people" encroached upon the special privileges of the bankers. An amendment to the national constitution in 1913, authorizing income taxes, recalled a decision of the Supreme Court that the Populists in their day had cited as the best evidence of the control of the government by the trusts; and income and inheritance taxes have ever since been levied. The reform of state and local taxation so as to exact a greater proportion of the taxes from the trusts and those who profit from them has also been freely undertaken. Labor demands, such as the right of labor to organize, the eight-hour day, limitation on the use of injunctions in labor disputes, and restrictions on immigration, were strongly championed by the Populists as fit measures for curbing the power of the trusts and were presently treated with great consideration. The Clayton Antitrust Act and the Federal Trade Commission Act, passed during the Wilson régime, were the products of long experience with the trust problem. The manner in which these laws have been enforced, however, would seem to indicate that the destruction of the trusts, a common demand in Populist times, is no longer regarded as feasible and that by government control the interests of the people can best be conserved.

On the land question the Populist demands distinctly foreshadowed conservation. "The land," according to the Omaha declaration, "including all the natural resources of wealth, is the heritage of all the people and should not be monopolized for speculative purposes." Land and resources already given away were of course difficult to get back and the passing of the era of free lands could not be stopped by law; but Theodore Roosevelt soon began to secure results in the way of the reclamation and irrigation of arid western lands, the enlargement and protection of the national forests, the improvement of internal waterways, and the withdrawal from entry of lands bearing mineral wealth such as coal, oil, and phosphates. At regular intervals since 1908 the governors of the states have met in conference to discuss the conservation problem, and this onetime dangerous Populist doctrine has now won all but universal acceptance.

It would thus appear that much of the Populist program has found favor in the eyes of later generations. Populist plans for altering the machinery of government with but few exceptions have been carried into effect. Referring to these belated victories of the Populists, William Allen White — the same who had asked, "What's the matter with Kansas?" — wrote recently, "They abolished the established order completely and ushered in a new order." Thanks to this triumph of Populist principles, one may almost say that in so far as political devices can insure it, the people now rule. Political dishonesty has not altogether disappeared and the people may yet be betrayed by the men they elect to office, but on the whole the acts of government have come to reflect fairly clearly the will of the people. Efforts to assert this newly won power in such a way as to crush the economic supremacy of the predatory few have also been numerous and not wholly unsuccessful. The gigantic corporations of today, dwarfing into insignificance the trusts of yesterday, are in spite of their size far more circumspect in their conduct than their predecessors. If in the last analysis "big business" controls, it is because it has public opinion on its side, and not merely the party bosses.

To radicals of today, however, the Populist panaceas, based as they were on an essentially individualistic philosophy and designed merely to insure for every man his right to "get ahead" in the world, seem totally inadequate. These latter-day extremists point to the perennial reappearance of such problems as farm relief, unemployment, unfair taxation, and law evasion as evidence that the Populist type of reform is futile, that something more drastic is required. Nor is their contention without point. It is reasonable to suppose that progressivism itself must progress; that the programs which would solve the problems of one generation might fall far short of solving the problems of a succeeding generation. One may not agree with the contention of some present-day radicals that only a revolution will suffice, and that the very attempt to make existing institutions more tolerable is treason to any real progress, since by so doing the day of revolution may be postponed. But one must recognize that when the old Populist panaceas can receive the enthusiastic support of Hooverian Republicans and Alsmithian Democrats, these once startling reforms have passed from the left to the right and are no longer to be regarded as radical measures at all. One is reminded of the dilemma that Alice of Wonderland fame encountered when she went through the looking glass. On and on she ran with the Red Queen, but "however fast they went they never seemed to pass anything."

"Well, in our country," said Alice, still panting a little, "you'd generally get to somewhere else — if you ran very fast for a long time, as we've been doing."

"A slow sort of country!" said the Queen. "Now, *here,* you see, it takes all the running *you* can do to keep in the same place. If you want to get somewhere else, you must run at least twice as fast as that!"

The Origin of Minnesota's Nonpartisan Legislature

CHARLES R. ADRIAN

WHEN THE POPULIST LEGACY of discontent passed to the Progressives of the early 1900s, the era witnessed a widespread reaction against political party machinery. A wave of governmental reform erupted throughout the nation. General dissatisfaction with the low moral standards of party politics in a period made famous by the muckrakers led to the suggestion that various offices should be filled by men elected without party designation. Minnesota in 1913 became the first state to extend the concept of nonpartisanship to its legislature. In an article published in the Winter, 1952, issue (volume 33), Charles R. Adrian describes how this unique and frequently criticized experiment came to be undertaken. The author is chairman of the department of political science in Michigan State University at East Lansing.

ONLY TWO STATES — Minnesota and Nebraska — select their legislators on a ballot without party designations. Minnesota's unusual arrangement dates from 1913 and is largely the result of a political accident — of a series of events strongly resembling a comedy of errors. Nebraska acquired its nonpartisan legislature more than two decades later, in 1934, when that state's lawmaking branch was completely reorganized.

In 1913, like most of the rest of the United States, Minnesota was affected by a reform movement in state and local government — a movement that spread the concept of "efficiency and economy" to national as well as state government. It was inspired by the successful example of the business corporation and by general disgust for the low moral standards that marked much political party activity about the turn of the century. Muckrakers had been exposing politicians, and as a result party prestige was very low.

The movement toward political reform, which reached its peak in the second decade of the twentieth century, urged such innovations as the primary election, proportional representation, a shorter ballot, concentration of responsibility in state administrative structure, the unicameral legislature, council-manager and commission government in cities, the initiative, referendum, and recall, and the nonpartisan election of certain public officials. Some reformers urged that judges and city and county officials should be chosen on a nonpartisan ballot. A few extremists went so far as to propose the use of nonpartisan elections in selecting all state officials.

When the thirty-eighth Minnesota legislature met in January, 1913, probably not a single member suspected that before the session ended the state would have a lawmaking body chosen without party designation. It was generally assumed that debate during the session would center about county option on the liquor question, industrial accident insurance, the desirability of the initiative, referendum, and recall, and the nonpartisan election of county officials.

Minnesota reformers had precedents for the nonpartisan ballot in electing county officials. Not only had California recently furnished an example, but the year before Minnesota itself had applied the nonpartisan principle to county superintendents of schools, officers of first-class cities, and state judges. Laws passed in 1912 by a special legislative session called by Governor A. O. Eberhart provided for the Minnesota changes. Five other states had previously removed the party label from their judicial ballots, and the move to "purify" this branch of government was in full swing. In four years, twelve states had adopted the plan.[1]

The nonpartisan principle was then extended to other areas of government. Reformers argued that local officials should be businesslike administrators, since there was no Republican way to gravel a road and no Democratic way to lay a sewer. California made all its district, county, township, judicial, school, and city officials nonpartisan. Other states considered extending the plan to the state superintendent of public instruction, university regents, local school officials, and city and village officials.

In 1913 Minnesota's political atmosphere was marked by many discordant elements and was further complicated by the wet-dry issue which transcended party lines. The Republicans who were rapidly becoming known as the dry party, were in complete command of all three branches of the state government.

In the organization of the 1913 legislature, the Senate was guided by Lieutenant Governor J. A. A. Burnquist of St. Paul, a dry Republican. After a close fight among the Republican elements, Henry Rines of Mora was chosen as the Republican candidate for speaker of the House. He was not a radical prohibitionist, but favored county option and pursued a middle-of-the-road policy. His solid reputation for honesty made him a natural choice for presiding officer — a man acceptable both to the drys and to the progressive Republicans.[2] This was an important asset in a period when the drys were regularly split between the county optionists, who favored leaving the liquor question to the voters of each county, and the prohibitionists, who would settle for no less than a completely dry state, and therefore opposed county option. When a vote was taken on the speakership, it resulted in 101 for Rines and 19 for Frank E. Minnette, a Democrat.

On February 7, 1913, Senator Julius E. Haycraft, of Madelia, a progressive Republican who was chairman of the Senate elections committee, introduced a bill to extend the nonpartisan provisions of the 1912 primary election act to include all judges and all city and county officers. He was convinced that the plan was sound and progressive, and the general feeling seemed to be that, although important and powerful party regulars opposed it, the bill was almost certain to pass.[3]

When the Haycraft bill reached the floor of the Senate on February 13, it was attacked from several angles by Senate leaders. F. A. Duxbury of Caledonia immediately introduced an amendment to eliminate the provision regarding all county officers except superintendents of schools. Joining him in the opposition was Senator A. J. Rockne of Goodhue County, a conservative and a long-time leader both in the Senate and in the Republican party. Rockne argued that political parties were necessary to the American system of government. The party system, he said, was anchored in the local community. Its elimination would destroy the roots of an important American institution. The Republicans, entrenched in all branches of state government, and powerful also in county and city government, had nothing to gain from a change in the party system. The Rockne group had little choice but to fight the bill on the Senate floor, since progressives controlled the elections committee. The Duxbury amendment, however, was voted down 34 to 20.

Backed by thirteen conservative party regulars, including Duxbury and George H. Sullivan of Stillwater, Rockne then conceived the idea that the proposal could be killed by adding members of the legislature to the list of nonpartisan officers. After conferring with Speaker Rines and being assured that the House would kill any such provision in its elections committee, on February 27 the Rockne group, represented by Frank Clague, proposed an amendment calling for the nonpartisan election of legislators.[4]

The proposal caught the Senate by surprise. Battle lines that had been forming slowly were altered and reinforced, for the bill now affected every member of the legislature. Senator Haycraft, as the author of the original bill, let it be known that he had not contemplated including state officers and that he was opposed to the altered plan. He, too, hurried to the speaker of the House, and received assurance that the bill would not pass if it included legislators, or that it would be so changed that a conference committee would become deadlocked over it.

In the Senate, progressives who had looked with favor upon the Haycraft bill were obliged to reconsider their position in the light of the maneuvers of the conservatives. Confusion seemed general. Regulars assumed that the Republicans favored the proposal. Some progressives evidently assumed that if a little medicine was good for the body politic, a lot of medicine should improve it. Other senators apparently felt that a vote for the bill would find favor with the voters at home. Besides, it was common knowledge that the bill was to be killed in the House. The Senate was more concerned with the bill's main proposal, which was intended to revise the primary law passed in 1912. Consequently, the Clague amendment passed by a vote of 35 to 22 almost without discussion, although only 21 senators actually favored the proposal. With only a few of the Rockne group opposing it, the amended bill was passed 53 to 8, and was then sent to the House.[5]

Senate File 412 was given a first reading in the House on March 1, 1913, and was referred to the elections committee, where it remained for nearly three weeks. During this period, the political significance of the bill received real consideration, and lobbyists went to work. Seeing the Republican party, which nearly always controlled the legislature, securely in the hands of the drys, the liquor and brewery interests quietly began to work for the bill in its Senate form. Lacking a majority in either house, the wets resorted to an ancient propaganda technique in order to advance the cause of the bill. Through Democratic Senator John Moonan and Republican Representatives G. W. Brown and H. H. Dunn, former speaker of the House, the wets let it be understood that they opposed any type of nonpartisanship, since only the drys could benefit from abolishing parties. Many drys rose to the bait.

Rural legislators, feeling that the proposal to put county elections on a nonpartisan basis was sure to win, feared that the whole burden of local political organization and support would fall on them. Unhappy at the thought of assuming this thankless task alone, many decided that a nonpartisan legislature would be a simple solution for their problem. City members had still another reason for becoming interested in the novel and unexpected Clague amendment. They had been troubled in recent elections by the growing popularity of the Socialist party in the poorer sections of large cities. Since the bill provided that only the names of the two candidates who received the largest votes in the fall primary could appear on the election ballots, city members thought this would be a way to get rid of the Socialist threat.

Still another group of representatives who became interested in the new plan were those who favored Theodore Roosevelt's Progressive party, which the legislature was considering legalizing. If this were to happen, the "Bull Moose" Republicans would be faced at the next election with the difficult decision of whether to run as Progressives or Republicans. In a legislature elected without party designation, this problem could be avoided. The bill appealed to still others as a *de facto* recognition of the breakdown of party lines that occurred in the previous session.[6]

Speaker Rines and Representative N. J. Holmberg, Republican chairman of the elections committee, led the opposition to the bill. They believed that the measure would destroy the vitality of political parties, which they regarded as necessary since they provided the opportunity for a "natural cleavage" on questions of public policy. They also argued that state officers would not be able to carry out party policy with a nonpartisan legislature.[7]

Some minority party members, apparently fearful of losing their identity, opposed the bill. The legislature contained a Populist, a Prohibitionist, and a Public Ownership member. Among them, only the Prohibitionist, Representative George H. Voxland, favored nonpartisanship. Some drys opposed the bill because they were skeptical of the wets' argument that Prohibitionist candidates would no longer draw votes away from dry Republicans if the nonpartisan bill were enacted. Apparently it occurred to some legislators who favored county option that they were entrenched within the larger of the major parties, and could make the state dry without altering the traditional legislative arrangement.

The elections committee reported the bill out on March 20 with the unanimous recommendation that it should pass after being amended to exclude from the nonpartisan ballot members of the legislature and all county officers except superintendents of schools. This was the form of the bill that had been promised Senator Rockne and his group, but the elimination of county officials was not acceptable to the progressive followers of Senator Haycraft.

The effects of lobbying and propaganda were fully evident when the bill was taken up by the House on a special order on March 27. During the debate, Republican Representative G. W. Brown of Glencoe moved to restore county officers and members of the legislature to the list of nonpartisan positions. According to the *St. Paul Pioneer Press* of March 28, Brown asserted that no partisan issues had been raised in the current session, and he assured his colleagues that none would be. Representative W. I. Nolan, a leader among House Republicans, made a substitute motion that only county officers be reinserted. This move would have restored the bill to its original form, but the amendment was defeated by an overwhelming 74 to 34 vote.[8]

According to the *Minneapolis Journal* of March 28, Representative G. B. Bjornson of Minneota, who favored making all state officers nonpartisan, held that such positions were not political in nature. "The governor," he explained, "is the state's official traveling lecturer." Representative Charles N. Orr of St. Paul pointed out that the Senate had extended nonpartisanship to the legislature in an effort to kill the bill, and that the action had not been sincere. He warned the House that affirmative action would not support the genuine attitude of a majority of senators. Representative Albert Pfaender of New Ulm, a Democrat, thought the Senate version of the bill excellent, but feared that nonpartisanship might be extended to the governorship.

When a vote was taken, the Brown amendment prevailed 71 to 39. Thirty-seven Republicans, one Democrat (Henry Steen, a wet), and one Public Ownership member voted against the measure.[9] Opposition came from progressives like Speaker Rines and Charles A. Lindbergh, Sr., as well as from conservatives such as W. I. Norton and C. E. Stone. Republican leaders, convinced that nonpartisanship would greatly weaken the party, voted against the amendment. Negative votes were recorded by R. C. Dunn, Thomas Frankson, Nolan, Norton, and Rines.

The bill, which also contained numerous amendments to the primary election act of 1912, was adopted by a final vote of 94 to 17 on March 27, 1913. Die-hard opposition came from from the Public Ownership member, a Democrat, and fifteen Republicans, all but one of whom were drys.

Apparently the relative merits and demerits of a nonpartisan legislature never were considered either on the floor of the House or in private discussions while the bill was under consideration. Voting seems to have been motivated purely by questions of political expediency. Eighteen wet Democrats supported the bill, while one opposed it. Most Republican wets favored it, as did a large number of drys, including the Prohibitionist. The efforts of the beverage lobby seem to have been successful.

On March 28, C. H. Warner, a Republican, moved for reconsideration, but the proposal lost 63 to 47. In support of the motion, Nolan claimed that liquor groups had approved the nonpartisan measure and that this alone should be enough to warrant reconsideration.[10] The *Willmar Tribune* of April 2 reported that "the brewery interests, and their representatives, were beside themselves with delight when the House . . . decided to retain this [nonpartisan] feature in the primary election law."

The bill was not yet law, however. Under an act of 1912, the date for the election was set in September. The Senate version of the Haycraft bill proposed to change the time to June, while the House bill suggested October. This discrepancy probably reflected an effort to create a deadlock between the two houses.[11]

A conference committee appointed on March 29 was deliberately "stacked" against nonpartisanship by Lieutenant Governor Burnquist and Speaker Rines.[12] When it did not report promptly, a political writer for the wet Democratic *St. Cloud Daily Times*, in an article published belatedly on April 18, commented: "Though passed by both houses over a week ago the nonpartisan primary bill is still a long ways from being a law. A conference committee composed of members of both houses has it in charge, and . . . they are out to either kill it or make it so obnoxious that neither house will adopt the changes proposed. The objectionable feature is the nonpartisan idea as applied to the election of members of the house and senate and which the house leaders, after giving their sanction, woke up to the fact, or rather they charged it, that unfriendly interests had put one over on them. They are trying to get back now by proposing that the nonpartisan idea be extended to state officers, which would include the governor. This simply means that the bill will never become a law."

Just what the conference committee wanted to do is not certain. According to the *St. Paul Pioneer Press* of April 12, committee members searched unsuccessfully for a precedent in Minnesota legislative history that would allow them to add completely new material to a deadlocked measure. It seems improbable that they believed they could add the state executive officers to the nonpartisan ballot and thus force both houses to reject the bill.

After stalling as long as possible, on April 11 the committee finally reported that its members were unable to agree on the scope of its authority. Specifically, they did not know if they could strike out the provisions concerning the nonpartisan legislature. N. J. Holmberg, one of the House managers, moved that the committee be allowed to consider this question. H. H. Dunn, leader of the wet Republicans, moved that the House committeemen be instructed to confer on only one difference between the House and Senate bills — the date for the primary election. The *Minneapolis Journal* reported on April 12 that G. W. Brown criticized the committee for attempting to say it knew what the House wanted better than did the House itself. The Dunn motion carried, but by a vote of only 64 to 47. This represented eight more negative votes than had been cast against the crucial Brown amendment to override the recommendations of the House elections committee. The changes of heart took place among dry Republicans, who became doubtful as a result of the interest taken in the bill by brewery representatives.[13]

Opposition to nonpartisanship then abruptly collapsed. After a brief meeting of the committee, Senator Haycraft announced that he remained opposed to a nonpartisan legislature, but that he was willing to go along with the majority. When the report of the committee was heard in the House, light attendance forced proponents of the bill to engage in hasty parliamentary maneuvering. The roll call on the adoption of the conference report lacked an absolute majority, with a vote of 48 to 32, and a motion to reconsider had to be made to keep the report alive. On the following Wednesday, April 16, after the dry Republicans had twice tried unsuccessfully to adjourn the House, the bill was repassed, 65 to 48.[14]

The Senate adopted the conference committee's report 36 to 15.[15] Among those who voted in the negative were six senators who had joined in the scheme to inject the legislature into the bill and who had opposed Senate passage earlier. Many confirmed opponents of the bill, including Rockne, found it expedient to support it.

Some senators saw fit to explain their votes. Among them was Senator Edward Rustad of Wheaton, who said that although he opposed the nonpartisan legislative principle, he found the June primary date so desirable that he voted for the bill. Senator George H. Sullivan of Stillwater explained that there were no longer any party lines anyway, since the state convention had been abolished. One might, he felt, just as well vote for a nonpartisan legislature and abolish party lines in name as well as in fact. The bill was signed by the governor without comment on April 19, 1913.

The Minnesota legislature had become nonpartisan without a single word of debate on the merits of the question. The proposal had been introduced without thought or intention that it ever would become law. Wet sponsorship of the bill had been entirely spontaneous and was based upon simple political expediency. The wets hoped that nonpartisanship would help break the strength of the Republican caucus in the legislature and disorganize the forces demanding county option. Subtly, the drys had been influenced to think that they, too, could gain politically by supporting the bill. To add to the confusion, the opposition consisted both of progressive and extremely conservative Republicans. The progressives felt that nonpartisanship on the local level was desirable, but deplored its extension to the legislature. Conservative Republicans thought the plan would destroy party organization.

According to the *Red Wing Daily Republican* of March 31, a nonpartisan legislature "was a suggestion so new and so radical that even the members who voted for it hardly realized what a revolutionary change" they were proposing. In fact, there is no evidence that any legislator expected the new arrangement to cause important problems of organization or to change executive-legislative relationships and responsibility. A few were concerned lest it weaken party strength needed for more important state and national offices. Other provisions seem to have been the determining factors in the final passage.[16]

Contemporary newspaper reports indicate a lack of interest in the new law, as well as of any realization that its application would involve important problems. Many rural papers did not even bother to comment. Country editors who did offer opinions seemed chiefly concerned with the probability that the new law would "hamstring" local party organization. The metropolitan dailies were not enthusiastic about the change. The *Minneapolis Journal* gave the plan tentative approval, although its chief political observer was skeptical and never approved nonpartisanship. The *St. Paul Pioneer Press* opposed the change.

Preoccupied with the prohibition issue, the *Red Wing Daily Republican* of April 26 merely noted casually that "a great change was brought about." On April 24 the *Fergus Falls Daily Journal* stated that the "nonpartisan primary bill is a step farther than any other state has gone and much farther than any member dreamed of going when the session opened."

The *Willmar Tribune* reported that county officials seemed pleased that henceforth they would be elected on a nonpartisan ticket. The paper suggested that the new system would be worth while if only because it would save money by reducing the size of the ballot. After considering the change in the light of the 1912 election, the editor suggested that the nonpartisan feature might well be extended to the office of governor. "Men are elected to office, not parties," read the editorial. "The official state ballot should not recognize any party organization." [17]

The *St. Cloud Daily Times* of March 3, looking toward the passage of the bill, was nostalgic concerning the party system. "Truly the day of political parties is passing away," it said. On March 7 the same newspaper reported that Stearns County officials generally favored the nonpartisan bill on the local level, but felt that it might be detrimental in state and national politics. They proved poor prophets, however, in predicting that the bill would result in shorter official lives, in increased competition for offices, and in the total elimination of party lines in offices elected without party designation. Others thought the plan would work to the advantage of a candidate active in a party, since he would get the support not only of his party but of independents as well.

A hidden danger in the new plan was suggested by the editor of the *Caledonia Journal* when he wrote: "The legislature seems to be determined to so amend the election laws that candidates for the legislature must run on a non-partisan ticket. It is a mistake. Extravagance is rampant now, and when we get a non-partisan Legislature it will be still worse. There will be no minority to watch over the extravagance of the majority." The *Anoka Union* also expressed disapproval. "A nonpartisan ticket finds no favor with the Union," commented the editor. "It believes in party organizations, and particularly the old Republican party. . . . If a non-partisan ticket for county officers does not work out any better than the non-partisan judiciary ticket did last election, it will prove a gigantic failure." [18]

The *St. Peter Free Press* suggested that the new system "means a concentration of political power in a comparatively few people." Opinion was more favorable, however, in Fairmont. "Thank the Lord and the Legislature, hereafter a good and deserving man will not have to wear the brand 'Republican' in order to get a county office or be elected to the Legislature in Minnesota," wrote the editor of the *Sentinel*.[19]

Of all newspapermen, the *Minneapolis Journal's* veteran observer, Charles B. Cheney, proved the wisest. After the Senate added the legislature to the primary election bill, he commented on March 1: "Nonpartisan nominations in local government are sound in principle and work well in practice. But the case is very different with legislative nominations. The Minnesota plan throws the door open to nominations of the liquor and other interests. They find it easy to juggle the contests, once these have degenerated into mere personal struggles."

On March 28 Cheney demonstrated that he had a more truthful crystal ball than did the brewery lobbyists. The final result, he said, "might properly fool the liquor interests. The law would also wipe out the prohibition factor which has divided the temperance forces in many legislative districts. With nothing but the temperance issue involved and the temperance forces united, the demand for county option would very likely be able to make gains in several districts." That is exactly what happened in the election of 1914.

A *Journal* editorial of March 29, however, expressed a different view. It concluded that "the Legislature has dropped the party distinction" because through the adoption of the primary and "other changes," party lines had been all but obliterated and there was no longer a responsible party in the state. The writer expected that there would be some self-seekers, some one-idea men, a scramble for places, and an outcropping of personal platforms. He expressed the opinion that because of weakness in numbers, the Democrats had tended to make secret bargains, "horse-trading" rather than serving as an alert opposition. This the *Journal* writer thought unfortunate, concluding that "A nonpartisan legislature could hardly be worse."

The *St. Paul Pioneer Press* of April 15 expressed orthodox political theory in an editorial which asserted that "The Legislators would do well to consider carefully whether it is desirable to extend the nonpartisan feature to legislative and other state officials. There is no doubt about getting rid of party politics in local affairs. . . . But there is grave doubt if such should be the case in state and national affairs," it continued. "The best check against authority is a vigorous and well organized opposition. One party will keep another up to its duty."

A writer in the official journal of American political science took note of the change in Minnesota politics as follows: "It may be seriously doubted . . . whether the nonpartisan movement is not overreaching itself when it invades the field of political offices as it does for the first time in Minnesota." [20]

The lone enthusiastic comment seems to have come from the muckraking C. J. Buell, an ardent prohibitionist, who wrote: "It is to be hoped, that the time is near when men will be chosen for public positions in state and city, village and county, upon their honesty and fitness instead of how they line up on national issues that have no necessary relation to state and local affairs." [21]

Less than a week after the bill passed, a group of prominent attorneys who were active Republicans publicly announced that the bill creating the nonpartisan legislature was, in their opinion, unconstitutional. They argued that the act violated Article IV, Section 27, of the Minnesota Constitution, since it embraced more than one subject and that subject was not expressed in the title. The new law, in truth, was a fairly extensive revision of the Primary Elections Act of 1912, and it actually amended sections of the *Revised Laws* other than those listed in its title. The attorneys said that the act had not been adopted in a strictly constitutional fashion, and urged someone to test it by filing for office on a partisan basis. No one made such a move, however — probably because both the wets and the drys expected to gain from the law in the 1914 election.

Consequently the legality of the nonpartisan legislature was never tested in the courts. The state supreme court upheld the nonpartisan ballot for judicial nominations and elections, but the court decided that the case did not apply to the part of the law that concerned the legislature.[22] Although the origin of Minnesota's nonpartisan legislature can be traced to an accident resulting from a series of political maneuvers, at mid-century the state is still electing its lawmakers on a nonpartisan ticket under the provisions of the act of 1913.

The Democratic-Farmer-Labor Party Schism of 1948

G. THEODORE MITAU

MINNESOTA'S long tradition of political protest is further illuminated in the following article. Despite the limited perspective afforded by the passage of only seventeen years, it is now clear that the decisions taken by Minnesota's Democratic-Farmer-Labor party in the summer of 1948 had far-reaching effects both for the state and the nation. In view of the election of Hubert H. Humphrey to the vice-presidency in 1964 as the first Minnesotan to hold that office, it seems particularly appropriate to reprint the following piece which touches on an important phase of his early political career. The article by G. Theodore Mitau appeared in the Spring, 1955, issue (volume 34) and won the society's Solon J. Buck Award for that year. Mr. Mitau is James Wallace professor of political science and chairman of that department in Macalester College, St. Paul. He is the author of Politics in Minnesota *(1960) and of* A Selected Bibliography of Minnesota Government, Politics and Public Finance since 1900 *(1960), as well as co-editor of two textbooks on case problems in local government (1963).*

BEHIND THE LIVELY EVENTS of the Democratic-Farmer-Labor party schism of 1948 a long and complex background of political protest can be traced. As one writer has put it, Minnesota "through most of its history has shown symptoms of political schizophrenia. On the one hand, it was the staid dowager, as reliably Republican as its down-East Yankee sisters; on the other, it had skittish moments during which it produced a brood of third parties or helped raise the radical offspring of its neighbors." [1] Especially in periods of economic depression, voices of agrarian and urban protest, often discordant and intense, have risen from the mining pits of the Mesabi Range, from the slaughterhouses and railroad shops of the cities, and from the debt-ridden farms of the Red River Valley to find expression in the platforms and conventions of Minnesota's third and minor parties. Through the Anti-Monopolists and the Greenback party of the 1870s, and the Nonpartisan League and the Farmer-Labor party of the present century, this tradition of protest has continued to exert pressure on state politics.

Thus the fervor for social justice and economic opportunity has long had organizational expression in Minnesota, even though success in national elections has been rare and erratic. Along with other midwestern states, Minnesota witnessed the well-known patterns of protest, genuinely active, rich in condemnation of the railroads, monopolies, and Wall Street, and proud of the righteous blasts from such "tribunes of the people" as Ignatius Donnelly, A. C. Townley, Magnus Johnson, and Floyd B. Olson. The quest for success at the polls, which would translate platform and program into actual public policy, caused leaders of the Populist movement to experiment with various types of political tactics. At times it led them to support a major party contestant, such as John A. Johnson, who ran for governor on the Democratic ticket in 1904, and Charles A. Lindbergh, Sr., candidate for the Republican nomination for governor in the primaries of 1918; at other times it led them to advocate fusion with emerging national parties, as in 1912 and 1924; and in other campaigns, like that of 1892, all fusion attempts were spurned and Donnelly was called upon to head a state Populist ticket as that party's candidate for governor. During the dark, unhappy days of the depression in the 1930s the voices of protest rose to a crescendo. In their commitment to left-wing radicalism, the Farmer-Labor platforms of that period are perhaps unmatched by those of any other American party which has been successful at the polls.[2] Those were, of course, bitter times, and the remedies proposed by the Farmer-Labor administration and party leaders were sharp and dogmatic curatives for deeply felt economic ills, offering many a strange combination of Marxism, agrarian egalitarianism, and Utopianism.

But even in the perilous 1930s, when the party had the popular Governor Olson to argue on its behalf, Farmer-Labor policies seemed to have reached the limits of their acceptability. Olson's legislative program encountered major modification, some features incurring intense hostility and some meeting with outright defeat. This happened, moreover, in sessions like those of 1933 and 1937, when Olson's party had control of the lower house of the legislature. Then in 1938 the electoral fortunes of Farmer-Labor protest reached a new low. Governor Elmer A. Benson was swept out of office by Harold E. Stassen, the relatively unknown county attorney from South St. Paul, after a campaign which stressed charges of administrative incompetence, corruption, and blindness to Communist infiltration. The wave of popular indignation left

Benson with a mere 387,263 votes to the amazing and overwhelming total of 678,839 for the Republican party's nominee.[3]

The Farmer-Labor party lost its one-time broad popular support, according to one scholar, largely because it could not combat the undermining tactics used by internal quarreling factions, and because it failed to provide necessary policy direction through executive and legislative leadership. The same writer concludes his analysis of the "great debacle of 1938" with the observation that "the next six years were to see the final disintegration of the Farmer-Labor party, culminating in its virtual extinction when it was fused with the Democratic party in the Democratic-Farmer-Labor party"; and he describes "the fusion of 1944" as "simply the requiem for a death that had occurred in 1938."[4]

What, in retrospect, can be inferred from these events? Minnesota's eleven electoral votes* never have and probably never will determine the balance of presidential fortunes. Nevertheless, traditions of protest politics make Minnesota a most fascinating laboratory for the study of political dynamics of agrarian and labor discontent. Most populist movements have been motivated by an urge to broaden the base of sociopolitical and economic privilege through such state interventions as a particular grievance seemed to demand. What these movements lacked in the doctrinaire qualities of a European pattern of challenge was counterbalanced by the American tradition of practical and selective state intervention.[5]

Most of this protest, then, was genuine, necessary, creative. Especially relevant in a study of the fortunes of the protest tradition after the Democratic-Farmer-Labor fusion of 1944, however, is the fact that some of the protest lacked these qualities. Largely through union infiltration, the long arm of the Third Internationale seemed at times to reach all the way to the North Star State when efforts to exploit real grievances and to confuse, disrupt, and subvert the democratic processes were made in Minnesota. An early example of a truly dramatic clash within the ranks of the Farmer-Labor movement took place between the doctrinaire and highly disciplined forces of left-wing Marxism and the indigenous and reformist forces of midwest progressivism in 1924. At that time such noted leaders as Samuel Gompers and Robert M. La Follette warned their followers not to attend a convention in St. Paul, predicting political suicide for those who took part in it.[6] The fusion of the Democratic and Farmer-Labor parties in 1944 did

* On the basis of the 1960 census Minnesota's electoral votes were reduced from eleven to ten. *Ed.*

not, and perhaps could not, eliminate this numerically small, but quite vociferous, segment of left-wing Marxist radicals. As a matter of fact, the very presence of some of these radicals within the ranks of the Farmer-Laborites had caused many old-line Democrats and independents to oppose earlier attempts at fusion.

The attitude of the Democratic party — and more particularly its so-called liberal New Deal wing — toward the political far left presented a major ideological problem not only for Minnesotans but for the nation as a whole. The problem was intensified after the Congressional elections of 1946. Two mutually antagonistic groups crystallized into organizations by the spring of 1947. On the left, the Progressive Citizens of America emerged from a fusion of the National Citizens Political Action Committee and the Independent Citizens Committee of the Arts, Sciences and Professions. On the right appeared the Americans for Democratic Action.

With spokesmen like Henry A. Wallace for the left and such well-known New Dealers as Leon Henderson, Chester Bowles, Mrs. Franklin D. Roosevelt, and Franklin D. Roosevelt, Jr., on the right, the issues soon became clearly drawn. The right-wing "non-Communist liberal" Americans for Democratic Action supported the Marshall Plan and President Truman's Greco-Turkish aid program; the Progressive Citizens of America held these to be unwarranted circumventions of the United Nations, conceived in support of European forces of reaction and fascism.[7] Whereas the Americans for Democratic Action approved most of Truman's domestic, security, and defense measures, the Progressive Citizens of America considered them entirely inadequate halfway measures of a party which was doing little better than the Republicans. This clash of ideology and policy, debated at great length throughout the nation and in Congress, was personified locally by Mayor Hubert H. Humphrey of Minneapolis, a national leader of the Americans for Democratic Action, Orville E. Olson, chairman of the Independent Voters of Minnesota, and ex-Governor Elmer Benson, a leading figure in the Progressive Citizens of America.

Wallace himself left the national Democratic party after a now famous declaration on December 29, 1947, in which he denounced Truman and his program. Nevertheless, Benson and his Minnesota friends apparently decided early in 1948 that it would be politically wiser to work through the Democratic-Farmer-Labor party than to revert to the more traditional pattern of third-party politics. Speaking in Chicago at the second annual convention of the Progressive Citizens of America, the former Minnesota governor declared, "if we retain control of the

Democratic-Farmer Labor party at the state convention, Wallace will be the nominee and we will present him at the national Democratic convention. . . . If President Truman runs in Minnesota, he'll have to run as an independent, or however he wants to label it." [8]

Thus plans were made to push Wallace in Minnesota not as a third-party candidate, but as a regular Democratic-Farmer-Labor nominee whose name would go on the party ballot after his faction had captured the state party machinery. When the Democratic-Farmer-Labor state central committee met on February 20, the battle for control of the precincts began to take shape. The Humphrey-led right wing asserted its three-to-one lead over the Benson faction by appointing exclusively from its own ranks the steering committee which was to make arrangements for the precinct caucuses and the county and state conventions. [9]

The hostility which the left wing felt for Mayor Humphrey and his followers is expressed in an editorial in the *Minnesota Leader*, then the organ of the pro-Wallace Democratic-Farmer-Labor Association. "Your association," it reads, "with the unsavory Americans for Democratic Action, created nationally to serve as liberal window dressing for the Wall Streeters and militarists behind Truman and created in Minnesota as a heaven for reactionary elements in the Democratic and Farmer Labor parties, is another indication of the character of your associations." It also accused the Minneapolis mayor of "close and friendly relations" with the Cowles press and General Mills, and of conducting a "reactionary" administration of city affairs; and it told the mayor that "by your associations and your record you have ruined any chance of your being an acceptable progressive candidate in the 1948 elections." [10] In the same paper the state chairwoman of the Democratic-Farmer-Labor Association charged Humphrey with the disruption of the Democratic-Farmer-Labor party in the 1944 and 1946 elections, with disloyalty to the party chairman, with red-baiting, and with giving support to Churchill's foreign policy.

The leaders of the right wing answered in the *Minnesota Outlook*, where they published this indictment of the Wallace-Benson faction: "We are convinced that if the DFL is to win support, it must remove from positions of leadership all those who have represented or who have otherwise aided and abetted the program and tactics of the Communist party which believes — not in progress towards a free world — but in the reaction of totalitarianism and suppression of individual freedom." [11]

A bitterly contested battle of the two factions was to develop in the ranks of the Minnesota Democratic-Farmer-Labor party in the spring of 1948. The party workers who were preparing for caucuses and conventions knew that the survival of their respective factions was at stake. The right wing made a strong offensive move on April 18, when its steering committee, under the leadership of Mayor Humphrey and Orville L. Freeman, who was later to be governor of the state, announced that Wallace's third-party supporters were disqualified from taking part in the regular Democratic-Farmer-Labor sessions. All county chairmen who identified themselves with Wallace were asked to turn their credentials over to the next ranking Democratic-Farmer-Labor leader. In the meantime the state chairman for the Wallace group countered this right-wing declaration by telling two thousand Wallace fans who met in the St. Paul Auditorium that "regardless of 'talk' about keeping them out," they were, in fact, "legally entitled to participate in all DFL caucuses and should do so en masse."

As the factional fight grew in intensity, charges and countercharges raised Democratic-Farmer-Labor tempers to the boiling point. Mayor Humphrey was quoted as saying that the third-party movement was part of a deliberate international pattern to confuse honest liberals and to hobble the functioning of democracy; that it was being used to serve the purposes of the Russian police state; and that, although most Minnesotans in the Wallace movement were non-Communist, Communists and party-line followers in all states were seeking with religious fanaticism to promote a third party as part of Moscow's strategy to split Americans into ineffectual groups fighting among themselves.[12]

Wallace supporters, in the meantime, continued to attack the Marshall Plan, Truman's cold-war strategy, universal military training, and the "reactionary nature" of domestic legislation passed by the Eightieth Congress. Theirs, they claimed, was a fight for peace through supporting Wallace as an independent candidate. Wallace himself was quoted as saying at Albuquerque that the Communists "support me because I say we can have peace with Russia." He further clarified his position by stating: "I will not repudiate any support which comes to me on the basis of interest in peace. The Communists are interested in peace because they want a successful socialist experiment in Russia."[13]

The factional battle reached its first significant parliamentary stage in the precinct caucuses of April 30. Aside from the customary citizenship and residence requirements, all that is needed for participation in such a caucus under Minnesota law is the assurance of a past vote (with the secret ballot precluding any external verification) or the promise of future affiliation with the party which is holding the caucus. When the results of these caucuses were finally tabulated, the right wing claimed a clear numerical majority throughout the state. This claim was loudly protested by leaders of the Wallace-Benson faction. After the county conventions of May 14, the right wing claimed still another victory, pointing out that only 161 of 402 state convention delegates had faced any contest at all, and that out of 76 county delegations, 59 were definitely anti-Wallace, 5 probably pro-Wallace, 4 uncertain, and 8 contested.[14]

On May 23, members of the Wallace-Benson faction, which was still very active, telegraphed Harold H. Barker, state chairman of the Democratic-Farmer-Labor party, demanding that its delegates be allowed to participate in the state convention called for June 12 and 13 at Brainerd. Unless this demand was granted, they said, they would call their own convention in Minneapolis and would repudiate the Brainerd convention as illegal and irregular. While the delegates were assembling at Brainerd, a temporary preconvention committee on credentials submitted a report giving a clear majority to the right wing. It showed that of 402 authorized delegates, 216 had been uncontested. Of the latter, 186 actually were present and ready to vote on the seating of the delegation.[15] The committee arrived at these figures even before contested delegations from Hennepin, Ramsey, St. Louis, and other counties were seated. The Brainerd convention was to serve as a "political court of last appeal" at which the results of the bitter struggle between the right and left wings were finally determined.

One left-wing leader, Orville Olson, protested the convention's opening proceedings and denounced what he felt to be its unlawful and arbitrary conduct of business. A member of the incoming Hennepin County right-wing delegation replied by branding the Wallace "fringe" as "the Communist party in action, a movement of revolutionary character," by asserting that the "Wallace movement is not a third party in the true American sense [and by] inferring that it is serving the interests of Moscow." Whereupon the convention voted "with an almost unanimous roar" to seat the right-wingers from Hennepin County.

The Wallace leaders thereupon held a hasty conference and decided to use the microphone in calling for a rump convention. When they were "greeted by loud laughter and derisive cries," five of the group gathered on the sidewalk in front of the convention hall and solemnly held a meeting, with Francis M. Smith of St. Paul acting as chairman. He appointed a secretary to keep minutes, declared the meeting a rump convention of the Democratic-Farmer-Labor party, and then adjourned it to the American Federation of Labor Temple in Minneapolis, where a gathering of the left-wing faction was already in session.[16]

According to leaders of this group, five hundred delegates from fifty-one counties assembled for the Minneapolis convention. They listened eagerly as Benson termed the "program of Marshall, Forrestal, Dulles, Vandenberg and Co. the most gigantic international swindle of all time . . . intended to suppress common people in every part of the world."[17] The convention then organized itself into the Progressive Democratic-Farmer-Labor League and endorsed James M. Shields of Minneapolis for the United States Senate and Walter Johnson of New York Mills for governor. In addition, five nominees were named for the national House of Representatives, eleven presidential electors pledged to Wallace were agreed upon, and delegates were chosen to attend the convention of the Progressive party in Philadelphia in July. As a final offensive stroke, the Minneapolis convention promptly presented its slate of presidential electors to the Minnesota secretary of state, claiming that since its group represented the true Democratic-Farmer-Labor ruling body, it was entitled to have its name placed on the ballot pursuant to the provisions of the Minnesota election code.[18]

Attorneys for the right-wing Brainerd convention then prepared a petition urging the Minnesota state supreme court to order the secretary of state, as the respondent, to reject the slate of the Minneapolis group as false and fraudulent and to substitute that of the petitioners as the true and legal one of the Democratic-Farmer-Labor party of Minnesota. The secretary of state, speaking through the attorney general, insisted that he had no facilities or authority to investigate or determine the truth or falsity of the conflicting representations, and asked the court to ascertain the facts and determine what course of action he should take with respect to accepting one or the other of the two certificates.[19]

If certain factional and legal complexities which have no direct bearing upon the problem under discussion are overlooked, the case of the Democratic-Farmer-Labor State Central Committee and others v. Mike Holm, secretary of state, raised and answered three fundamental questions: First, are the qualifications of members of a legally called political delegate convention subject to judicial determination and review? Second, is the legality of such a convention's actions affected by improper floor decisions? Third, does such an allegedly illegal action entitle disaffected members to withdraw from a convention, to terminate its legal life by so doing, and to resuscitate in a newly assembled convention such former authority as did exist? [20]

On September 2, 1948, the Minnesota supreme court handed down a unanimous decision in favor of the second slate, the Brainerd right-wing convention thus receiving negative answers to the three main questions raised. In support of its decision the court advanced two considerations: First, with regard to judicial review of the actions of political conventions, "In factional controversies within a political party where there is involved no controlling statute or clear right based on statute law, the courts will not assume jurisdiction, but will leave the matter for determination within the party organization." Second, in the absence of a controlling statute, "a political convention is the judge of the election, qualifications, and returns of its own members." Such a convention is not a select body requiring "the presence of a majority of all persons entitled to participate in order to constitute a quorum for the transaction of business and, if that convention is regularly called, those who actually assemble constitute a 'quorum', and a majority of those voting is competent to transact business. . . . The withdrawal of either a majority or minority from a political convention does not affect the right of those remaining to proceed with the business of the convention, and those withdrawing cannot claim to be the legal party convention." [21]

The Minnesota court accepted the following proposition: "As elections belong to the political branch of the government, the courts will not be astute in seeking to find ground for interference, but will seek rather to maintain the integrity and independence of the several departments of the government by leaving questions as to party policy, the regularity of conventions, the nomination of candidates, and the constitution, powers, and proceedings of committees, to be determined by the tribunals of the party." This clearly reaffirmed the position that the Minnesota supreme court had taken earlier to the effect that "a political party, absent statutory restraints, makes is own reasonable rules for self-government." [22]

The language of the court leaves little doubt that it was the intent of the Minnesota judiciary so to construe applicable statutes that the affairs of party conventions, if correctly convened, are to be placed squarely in the hands of their duly elected delegates. Theirs, and not the judiciary's, is the responsibility for conducting the business of the party fairly and soundly. Legal theory at this point found itself in complete harmony with the well-established democratic principle that political power should always be centered in those whose actions are subject at least theoretically to popular scrutiny and accountability. And this faith in popular sovereignty was destined to be reinforced and mathematically underscored by the results of the primary election of September, 1948, when the right-wing nominees were victorious in all the important contests except that in the Seventh Congressional District. Even more significant were the results of the final election in November, which saw President Truman, then heading the Democratic-Farmer-Labor party ticket, garner 692,966 votes to the mere 27,866 cast in Minnesota for the Progressive party's candidate, Henry A. Wallace.[23] The successful right-wing struggle for control in the precincts, and in county, district, and state conventions provided President Truman with the type of major party instrumentality without which Minnesota's eleven electoral votes might well have gone to the Republican nominee. Not only the president's Minnesota victory, but Mayor Humphrey's election to the Senate and the addition of three Democratic-Farmer-Labor representatives to Congress, were hailed by right-wing leaders as direct results of the 1948 party struggle.

The outcome of the Democratic-Farmer-Labor party schism of 1948 — showing as it does that the will of the majority can be made to prevail over the concerted efforts of even a better disciplined, numerically small, but closely knit party segment — serves to reaffirm faith in the vitality of the major party system. Most assuredly, lack of vigilance there as in other political activities can rob a free people of its treasured political heritage, should they ever grow weary of freedom or supinely take their liberties for granted. The intensity of the 1948 factional struggle within the Democratic-Farmer-Labor party and the resulting schism well illustrate vigilance and a willingness to do battle for the sake of political conscience.

The Minnesota Backgrounds
of Sinclair Lewis' Fiction

JOHN T. FLANAGAN

FROM THE FOREGOING selection of articles, it is evident that the pages of Minnesota History *during its first fifty years have reflected many facets of the development of the North Star State. Politics, art, social life, medicine, sports, commerce, literature, people, and places are all a part of the broad subject covered by the magazine's name. To much of the world, the most famous Minnesotan is Sinclair Lewis (1885–1951) and the most familiar place is his Gopher Prairie. The selection which brings this volume to a close deals with the relationship of the state's best-known novelist to his native region and with the influence Sinclair Lewis' home state had upon his work. The article appeared in March, 1960 (volume 37). It is one of fifteen major contributions made by John T. Flanagan to* Minnesota History *over the years. Beginning with a piece on "Thoreau in Minnesota" published in 1935, Mr. Flanagan has written about many of the eminent literary figures who visited the state, as well as its early literary periodicals and some of its resident authors. He is now professor of English in the University of Illinois at Urbana. Among the books which have come from his pen are:* America Is West: An Anthology of Middlewestern Life and Literature *(1945),* A Long Way to Gopher Prairie: Sinclair Lewis's Apprenticeship *(1947), and* The American Folklore Reader *(1958).*

SINCLAIR LEWIS was once questioned about the autobiographical elements in *Main Street* by a friend whose apartment he was temporarily sharing. The novelist remarked to Charles Breasted that Dr. Will Kennicott, the appealing country physician in his first best seller, was a portrait of his father; and he admitted that Carol, the doctor's wife, was in many respects indistinguishable from himself. Both "Red" Lewis and Carol Kennicott were always groping for something beyond attainment, always dissatisfied, always restless, and although both were frequently scornful of their immediate surroundings they nevertheless lacked any clear vision of what could or should be done. And then Lewis revealingly added this comment about *Main Street:* "I shall never shed the little, indelible 'Sauk-Centricities' that enabled me to write it." [1]

One is tempted to remark that Lewis not only preserved these "Sauk-Centricities" in his later fiction, but that because of them his picture of Gopher Prairie and Minnesota and the entire Middle West became both durable and to a large extent accurate. A satirist is of course prone to exaggeration. Overemphasis and distortion are his stock in trade. But despite this tilting of the balance, his understanding of places and events and people must be reliable, otherwise he risks losing touch with reality completely. Lewis was born in Minnesota, he spent the first seventeen years of his life in the state, and he returned on frequent visits, which sometimes involved extensive stays in Minneapolis, St. Paul, or Duluth. A number of his early short stories and six of his twenty-two novels are localized wholly or in part in Minnesota. Claims in this connection might even be made for *Babbitt* and *Elmer Gantry,* although Lewis places the action for each in the fictional town of Zenith in the equally fictional state of Winnemac. [2] In other words, Minnesota was the birthplace, for a considerable time the residence, and by his own request the burial spot of Sinclair Lewis. [3] It was also in actuality or by imaginative projection the physical habitat of much of his fiction. Lewis' "Sauk-Centricities" were real, and even in any aesthetic evaluation of his work they are important.

In a reminiscent article he contributed to *The O-sa-ge,* the annual of the Sauk Centre Senior High School, Lewis spoke nostalgically of his Sauk Centre days, of the friendliness of the people, and of the indelible memories of boyhood. [4] He still vividly remembered fishing and rafting on Sauk Lake, tramping the fields and woods on October afternoons, sliding down Hoboken Hill which, to the young son of Dr. E. J. Lewis, symbolized the West. Yet twenty-nine years had elapsed since his departure for an Eastern college, and for most of that period he had been out of touch with the town. There were visits, of course, prompted partly by filial devotion.

In the spring of 1916 Lewis took his wife (born Grace Hegger) to Sauk Centre to meet his family. One can infer from Mrs. Lewis' later account of the visit that both she and her husband felt that the experience was somewhat trying. [5] They found the rigid mealtime routine irksome, the bridal dinner party with its formal decorations rather ludicrous, and both relatives and friends impressed by Lewis' money-making ability through writing but hardly sympathetic with his vocation. Mrs. Lewis' portrait of Lewis' stepmother sounds like an adumbration of Carol Kennicott who, in 1916 of course, had not yet been conceived. The doctor's second wife was prominent in civic affairs, had launched an antifly campaign in an effort to improve sanitation in the local stores, and was president of the Gradatim Club, a local organization dedicated to current events. Moreover, she had been a pioneer in establishing rest rooms for farm women when they came to Sauk Centre to shop, an activity which not only anticipates one of Carol Kennicott's great reforms, but recalls a familiar Hamlin Garland short story.[6]

During this first extensive visit to Sauk Centre, Lewis tried hard to re-establish his working habits and engaged an empty room over Rowe's Hardware Store where he could type his three to five thousand words daily.[7] At the moment he was working on *The Job*, an early novel about a career woman which had nothing to do with the Middle West. But it is not hard to imagine that he was storing away material he would eventually use in the novel he first thought of as "The Village Virus" but which appeared in 1920 as *Main Street*. Lewis as always was restless. After a short time in Sauk Centre, he and his wife visited Dr. Claude Lewis in St. Cloud and then began a four-months hegira from Duluth to San Francisco in a newly purchased Ford. Part of this journey, incidentally, was to be reflected in the novel *Free Air*.[8]

In the next dozen years Lewis was frequently in Minnesota and lived for short periods in different places. The year 1917 saw him residing in St. Paul, in a lemon-colored brick house on Summit Avenue, and in Minneapolis. During this Minnesota sojourn, Lewis also visited the Cass Lake lumber camps and slept in a bunkhouse.[9] Two years later he was back in Minneapolis again hard at work on *Main Street;* the novel was continued during a summer spent in Mankato, where he lived in a brick house at 315 Broad Street, and was finished in Washington, where Lewis' stay was financed in part by a loan from his father. In 1926 Charles Breasted met Lewis at a house party on an island in Rainy Lake, where the novelist was somewhat gloomy because of the imminent death of his father and because he felt that Dr. Lewis had always resented *Main Street*. Lewis commented: "He can't comprehend the book, much less grasp that it's the greatest tribute I knew how to pay him." [10]

The decade of the 1940s saw Lewis spending part of his time in Minnesota and on one occasion deciding to make Duluth his permanent residence.* Lewis' Minnesota diary is clear testimony that he felt a very strong pull toward the state, but that his innate restlessness would never permit him to sink deep roots.[11] While feverishly working on a particular project he could adjust himself to almost any locale and could enjoy the immediate environment; the novel completed, he sought other stimulation and the horizon beckoned.

Lewis returned to Minnesota in the spring of 1942. The fall quarter saw him teaching a writing class on the Minneapolis campus of the University of Minnesota. Lewis liked his classroom experiences and the university atmosphere although he was warily conscious of the presence on the faculty of another teacher of writing, Robert Penn Warren. The preceding spring he had rented a house at Lake Minnetonka and in the fall of 1942 he lived in a house at 1500 Mount Curve Avenue, Minneapolis. Lewis relished the society of the city (it was pleasant to see his old friend William J. McNally), but his impression of the downtown area was hardly favorable. He wrote on April 8, 1942: "Minneapolis is so ugly. Parking lots like scabs. Most buildings are narrow, drab, dirty, flimsy, irregular in relationship to one another — a set of bad teeth." [12] The city actually impressed him as an overgrown Gopher Prairie, without either planning or style. On the contrary, Lewis found the Minnesota rural landscape highly attractive and was particularly pleased by the rocky, hilly farms and the wooded banks of the St. Croix Valley near Marine. At this time the novelist was working on *Gideon Planish,* which one writer termed Lewis' "Made in Minneapolis" novel, despite the curious fact that it has few references to Minnesota.[13] The heroine, Peony Planish, however, hails appropriately enough from Faribault.

It was in 1945 that Lewis decided he had had enough of roaming the world and determined finally to settle down in Minnesota; the city he chose for his residence was Duluth. He bought the enormous house of Dr. E. E. Webber at 2601 East Second Street and there installed his personal possessions and his library of some thirty-five hundred volumes. Apparently he also plunged immediately into the composition of *Cass Timberlane.* During his brief Duluth stay he toured the Duluth-Superior Harbor with a party of businessmen, whom he called "good outdoor men," and met such local writers as Margaret Culkin Banning. But the Duluth winter irritated him, and on March 11, 1946, he observed that the ice was too sullen to melt. "Superior Street now seems

* Since this article was written, Mark Schorer's monumental biography, *Sinclair Lewis: An American Life,* was published (New York, 1961). Additional details concerning Lewis' return to Minnesota will be found in Schorer, pages 684–693, 725–745. *J. F.*

meager, ill-constructed and -assorted; a small town — the First National Bank's proud building just a huddle of assorted brick boxes." The novel completed and the long winter over, Lewis' customary nomadism reasserted itself; he sold his house "because it is time to wander again" and left by car for New York on March 21, 1946.[14] This decision spelled the end of any close connection with Minnesota. He returned to the state for short visits and worked in the collections of the Minnesota Historical Society in 1947 doing research for *The God-Seeker*. But there was no further idea of permanence.

Geographically Minnesota is a big state, and even so indefatigable a traveler as Lewis did not see all of it. Indeed certain areas, such as the Red River Valley, the Pipestone region, and even the Arrowhead country seemed never to strike his fancy. On the other hand, he became rapturous about sections which were strongly photogenic, and if he discovered some of them too late to utilize them in his fiction he did not hesitate to recommend them to the public. On one occasion he listed seven areas which he had found scenically memorable.[15] First came the St. Croix Valley, notably the view which the automobile traveler has as he begins to descend the hill on Highway No. 8 leading into Taylors Falls. Second was the Leaf Mountains section of Otter Tail County, with the spectacular view of surrounding waters and woods from the top of Inspiration Peak. Third he cited most of Fillmore and Houston counties, chiefly the region adjacent to Chatfield, Lanesboro, and Preston. Next Lewis was impressed by the Mississippi River bluffs extending from Red Wing to La Crescent, a sight which evoked the familiar comparison to the Hudson Valley. Finally he mentioned two lakes for their special charms, Minnetonka and Minnewaska, and he added the area around New London in Kandiyohi County. When Lewis made this list in 1942 he had not yet seen the North Shore of Lake Superior. His sojourn in Duluth certainly familiarized him at least in part with the littoral of the largest American lake, but he presumably saw no reason to revise his earlier list.

By birth, by occasional residence, and by intermittent travel, then, Sinclair Lewis knew Minnesota. The interesting question is how freely and fully did he convert this knowledge into his fiction. Are specific people and places recognizable, are trends of settlement and economic and industrial development reflected, are specific historical events introduced? Lewis of course was a writer of fiction with the novelist's mandate to disguise and alter his material. Moreover, he wrote only one historical novel, *The God-Seeker,* and was thus little inclined to preserve the facts of history for their own sake. Yet there is ample evidence that his Minnesota heritage played a large part in his literary work.

It would be difficult and probably futile to attempt to establish personal models for many of Lewis' characters. The identity of Dr. E. J. Lewis and Dr. Will Kennicott is probably most complete. There is a good deal of Lewis in Carol Kennicott and probably much also in Carl Ericson, the barnstorming aviator of the early *Trail of the Hawk*. Undoubtedly Lewis knew radicals and liberals like Bone Stillman, Miles Bjornstam, and Seneca Doane;[16] scientists like Max Gottlieb of *Arrowsmith;* sincere editors like Doremus Jessup of *It Can't Happen Here*. It has been contended that certain lineaments of Grace Hegger Lewis appear in Fran Dodsworth. Undoubtedly the Sharon Falconer of *Elmer Gantry* owes something to Aimee Semple McPherson, at that time notorious, and the radio priest and demagogic politician of *It Can't Happen Here* to Father Charles E. Coughlin and Huey Long. But George F. Babbitt is certainly a composite character (even his patronymic was established only after Lewis had rejected such names as Jefferson Fitch, Hornby, and G. T. Pumphrey) in whom many details and aspects were fused. To his great gifts of observation and mimicry, Lewis also added enormous inventive powers and an almost interminable ability to reproduce conversation.[17] Under these circumstances it is unlikely that he would have been content merely to photograph individuals. When he does introduce historical characters like Father Augustin Ravoux, Chaplain Ezekiel G. Gear, William D. Phillips, and Joseph R. Brown in *The God-Seeker,* they are stiff and puppetlike, and are meant to give a sense of milieu which unfortunately proves specious.

With the physical background, the situation is somewhat different. It is true that Minnesota's larger cities — Minneapolis, St. Paul, Duluth — are mentioned occasionally. The smaller towns, however, rarely appear under their own names. Instead Lewis invented place names liberally and used them in several stories — hamlets like Schoenstrom, New Kotka, Curlew, Plato, and the famous village of Gopher Prairie, somewhat larger communities like Vernon and Wakamin and St. Sebastian, the town of Northernapolis, and finally Grand Republic, the scene of both *Cass Timberlane* and *Kingsblood Royal*. Indeed, Sinclair Lewis might well have drawn a map comparable to William Faulkner's chart of Yoknapatawpha County on which he indicated the interconnecting actions of his stories and identified the communities.

In the second chapter of *Free Air* the reader is mired in gumbo with the heroine on "this oceanically moist edge of a cornfield, between

Schoenstrom and Gopher Prairie, Minnesota," some sixty miles north of Minneapolis. Fortunately Milt Daggett, a garage mechanic from Schoenstrom, comes along to extricate both heroine and car. In subsequent chapters Daggett becomes the romantic squire who follows Claire Boltwood from Minnesota to Seattle and is duly rewarded for his fidelity. In the first fifty pages of the novel, however, Lewis refers not only to Schoenstrom and Gopher Prairie, but also to Joralemon and Wakamin, towns which were to become familiar to readers of his later stories. Moreover, he sketches two of these communities in the acid manner of *Main Street.*

Schoenstrom, for example, consisted of a brick general store, a frame hotel, a farm machinery agency, "the Old Home Poolroom and Restaurant, which is of old logs concealed by a frame sheathing," and Daggett's Red Trail Garage, the agency for tires, Teal cars, sewing machines, and binders, as well as the weekly office of the veterinarian. Daggett, incidentally, was the son of a New England-born doctor. Gopher Prairie, on the other hand, as Lewis conceived it in the fourth chapter of *Free Air,* had five thousand people, a commercial club, and an infinitely better band than Joralemon, its neighbor. The lobby of the hotel to which Claire Boltwood and her father went was notable for its poison-green walls, brass cuspidors, and insurance calendars; drummers lounged in the ragged chairs; and of the two baths available to hotel guests one was reserved and the other out of order. Another local color touch in this novel of 1919 was the slangy, talkative waitress who was more interested in learning about her customers than in serving them food. This same dismal hotel was probably referred to by Lewis in an earlier short story, "A Woman by Candlelight," in which the protagonist, a wholesale groceries salesman, proceeded from St. Sebastian via Joralemon to Gopher Prairie in a blizzard. "The rows of two-story brick stores running off into straggling frame houses, which made up Gopher Prairie, were covered with snow like a counter of goods with a linen cover smoothly drawn across them." [18]

Gopher Prairie, of course, receives its fullest exposition in *Main Street,* where it assumes some of the dimensions and color of the actual Sauk Centre but, more importantly, is universalized into the typical small town of the second decade of the twentieth century — shabby, dull, provincial, and strangely complacent. The portrait is too familiar to repeat here. One should remember only that even on the physical level there are two Gopher Prairies, the tawdry, provincial community that was revealed to the disgusted eyes of Carol Kennicott fresh from college and the Twin Cities, and the glittering, inviting city that impressed Bea Sorenson, newly arrived from Scandia Crossing, population sixty-seven.

In 1924, at the request of the editor of *The Nation,* Lewis paid a return visit to Gopher Prairie and "interviewed" Dr. Will Kennicott. He found the Thanatopsis Club still operating and the materialism of the community focused in the general discussion of automobiles and golf. But he emphasized that in the ten-year interval since he had last observed the prairie community vast changes had occurred; the streets had been paved, the lawns seemed prettier and neater, old houses had been rejuvenated, and there was some new construction. When the two men stopped to talk "on the edge of Gopher Prairie — this prairie village lost in immensities of wheat and naïvetés, this place of Swede farmers and Seventh Day Adventists and sleeve-garters," Dr. Kennicott rebuked his creator for his radicalism and his scorn of material success. The physician also announced his intention to support Calvin Coolidge for the presidency in the coming election.[19]

Lewis' town of Joralemon receives passing reference in several stories. In "The Kidnaped Memorial," a Civil War veteran goes from Wakamin to recruit enough ex-soldiers to stage a Memorial Day parade. And it is from Joralemon that Young Man Axelbrod, whose name gives the title to one of Lewis' best short stories, goes to Yale at the age of sixty-four to get an education. Axelbrod learns soon enough that age and youth do not mix well; indeed he is somewhat pathetic as a serious college student. But he conducts himself with dignity, has one or two stimulating experiences, and is content to return to his prairie community without a degree.[20]

Joralemon is also the home of Carl Ericson, a young boy who after leaving high school attends near-by Plato College. Carl is interested in machinery more than in academic subjects, but his devotion to a certain liberal instructor permits Lewis to picture a fresh-water college with corrosive scorn. In due time Carl grows interested in aviation and, nicknamed "Hawk" Ericson, becomes famous as a stunt and exhibition flier in the novel called *The Trail of the Hawk.* The protagonist's subsequent travels take him far from Minnesota, but Lewis devotes the whole of Part 1 — twelve chapters — to the Joralemon-Plato scenes.

In 1935 Lewis to a large extent retold the story of *Main Street* in a magazine tale entitled "Harri." [21] The setting is New Kotka, "a clean town, with birch trees and a few Norway pines and an unusually large water tower, in Otter Tail County, Minnesota, half an hour's drive from Fergus Falls." New Kotka, a dairy center, has seventeen hundred people. Harri, really Mrs. Harriet Braham, arrives with her two children to operate the Old Barne Souvenir and Booke Shoppe; lacking both experience and capital, she nevertheless has unlimited assurance. Indeed, although she resembles Carol Kennicott in her energy, her projects, and her reforming instincts, she is really a sinister opportunist who preys on both her suitors and her benefactors. Her base of operations eventually shifts to the Twin Cities, but not before Lewis has had ample opportunity to sketch the regional landscape and to praise the Leaf Mountains and Inspiration Peak. Of his later tales this is perhaps the richest in its details of the Minnesota locale.

The town of Vernon, the exact location of which is uncertain, is the scene of several Lewis narratives. Most of the action of "The Willow Walk," a curious mystery story in which a bank teller, Jasper Holt, plays a Dr. Jekyll and Mr. Hyde role, takes place there. Holt is so successful in his self-disguise that he is never apprehended as a defaulter; on the other hand, he loses the money he steals and has to resort to day labor to support himself. Palmer McGee, in "The Cat of the Stars," lives in the University Club of Vernon and is an assistant to the president of the M. & D. R. R., which Lewis elsewhere identifies as the Minneapolis and Dakota Railroad. The action of the story, however, has little to do with Vernon.[22] In "Habeas Corpus" the protagonist is Leo Gurazov, a Bulgarian radical who owns a tobacco store in Vernon. The plot concerns his strained efforts to get himself deported so that he can join a homeland revolution, but they result only in landing him at Ellis Island for an indeterminate stay.[23]

A more impressive story is "Things," a satiric account of social climbing and its perils. Lyman Duke is a Vernon real-estate operator who has had extensive interests in the woodland north of Grand Marais and who makes a comfortable fortune. His wife and daughter insist that he lead a social life commensurate to his financial standing. With misgivings, Duke builds an elaborate house in Vernon, fills it with expensive and fragile treasures, including Japanese ceramics, engages an army of servants, and puts himself at the complete mercy of the "things" that he has worked so hard to acquire. When he sees that the artificial life he is forced to lead has begun to warp his personality and bring unhappiness to his daughter, he deliberately sets fire to the house and — a later Silas Lapham by conviction, not by accident — reverts to a simpler existence.[24]

"A Matter of Business" and "The Shadowy Glass" also have Vernon as their locale.[25] In the first tale James Candee, proprietor of the Novelty Stationery Shop, is torn between his normal desire to make money and his ambition to raise the aesthetic tastes of his community. He sells writing paper, cards, bookends, and gifts, but when he finds in the outskirts of Vernon a truly creative craftsman who has a flair for making original dolls, he invests in the Papa Jumas dolls. They are angular and gauche, but authentically different; despite the offer of a large manufacturer to make him sole agent of a conventional line of fluffy, commercial products, Candee continues to back the Papa Jumas line. "The Shadowy Glass" has somewhat more local color, and here Vernon is identified, inconsistently with other references, as being in the state of North Iosota. This is the story of Lelia Corvalan, who, after being reared in a convent, falls in love with Otis Corvalan and sees only too late that he is both deceitful and irresponsible. Life with Otis proves less romantic than she had envisaged it at first. Eventually, when he has been dismissed from several positions, Lelia decides to take up nursing and, abetted by her mother-in-law, she leaves to go into training in Chicago.

Details in several of these stories suggest that Lewis had a kind of fusion of Minneapolis and St. Paul in mind as a model for his fictional Vernon. It is neither the state capital nor a flour-milling center, but it is the hub of a railroad network, it has steel mills and glass industries, and it is the site of a university. Once the terminus of the Red River carts, it was settled about 1840 by emigrants from the East. "Nothing is very old in the Middle-Western city of Vernon," Lewis writes in "Habeas Corpus," but "in Mississippi Street remain the gloomy stone buildings erected by the early fur traders and a mysterious ancientness clings to the dark irregular way." [26] Vernon boasts of an Iosota Club and a Garrick Stock Company, and fashionable people live along its Boulevard of the Lakes. "Vernon society goes to Palm Beach and New York; it is in wholesaling, the professions, or the railroad; it attends either Saint Simeon's P. E. Church or Pilgrim Congregational; and it frowns upon vulgarity, labor unions, and all art except polite portrait painting." [27] To the north of Vernon, incidentally, an iron range richer than what Lewis calls the Mesaba has been discovered.

Finally, there are Northernapolis and Grand Republic. Though details are vague, it is possible that Duluth was Lewis' archetype here. Northernapolis is the scene of "The Ghost Patrol," the rather unconvincing story of an old policeman who refused to stay in retirement but would walk his nocturnal beat, trying doors and watching for pranks, until the authorities finally persuaded him to remain in a county home.[28]

Northernapolis is the locale also of "Hobohemia" and "Joy-Joy," companion stories published in 1917 which deal with the courtship of Elizabeth Robinson by Dennis Brown.[29] Elizabeth, who prefers to be called Ysetta, has artistic ambitions; she wishes to write, to dance, or at least to lead a Bohemian existence. She leaves Northernapolis for the greater opportunities of New York. Dennis Brown, a Northernapolis lumber magnate, follows her and by a succession of remarkable exploits convinces her of his own artistic ability and persuades her to return to Northernapolis as his wife. As the mistress of a luxurious house in the fashionable suburb of Hydrangea Park, Elizabeth is about to sink into suburban opulence when the neighborhood is disrupted by the arrival of Mrs. Henrietta Flint. Mrs. Flint is writing a novel, to be called "Joy-Joy," in which she will preach her doctrine of the need for sunshine, happiness, and gaiety in life and for their symbolic realization in dancing. Elizabeth's original ambitions are dangerously reawakened by Mrs. Flint, but again her husband is more than equal to the emergency and soon brings his wife back to an even keel. Mrs. Flint, it might be remarked, has some of the reform impulses and the aesthetic insistence that were later to characterize Carol Kennicott and Harri.

With the exception of Gopher Prairie, Grand Republic is the most fully pictured of Lewis' fictional communities presumably located in Minnesota. In *Cass Timberlane* it is described as a city of eighty-five thousand people. In *Kingsblood Royal*, the action of which postdates World War II, the population has grown to ninety thousand. Grand Republic is situated eighty miles north of Minneapolis and seventy-odd from Duluth, though the exact direction is not stated. "It is large enough to have a Renoir, a school-system scandal, several millionaires, and a slum." The city lies in Radisson County at the confluence of the Big Eagle and Sorshay rivers; the combined stream then flows west to the Mississippi. Lewis is careful to keep Grand Republic out of proximity to Lake Superior so that there can be no easy confusion with Duluth. But his account of its growth has a familiar ring: "Grand Republic grew rich two generations ago through the uncouth robbery of forests, iron mines, and soil for wheat."[30]

Grand Republic has preferred residential districts, such as Ottawa Heights and Sylvan Park, the latter being somewhat less pretentious than the former.[31] Streets bear the names of Flandrau, Beltrami, Schoolcraft, and there is even a Joseph Renshaw Brown Way. The Radisson County Courthouse, comic in its hideous mélange of architectural styles, might well serve as Lewis' final comment on the ugliness of many of the older public buildings in Minnesota. Built in 1885, "It was of a rich red raspberry brick trimmed with limestone, and it displayed a round tower, an octagonal tower, a minaret, a massive entrance with a portcullis, two lofty flying balconies of iron, colored-glass windows with tablets or stone petals in the niches above them, a green and yellow mosaic roof with scarlet edging, and the breathless ornamental stairway from the street up to the main entrance without which no American public building would be altogether legal." Downtown Grand Republic has other large buildings too, notably the twelve-story Blue Ox National Bank and "the Pantheon of the Duluth & Twin Cities Railroad Station." [32] But across the tracks and along the Sorshay River are decrepit shacks and incipient slums which remind the observer of the frontier village that was to be seen on the same site seventy-five years earlier.

In *Cass Timberlane* the reader is kept constantly aware of the Grand Republic background; buildings and streets continually impinge upon the consciousness, and the social stratification is tied in with the economic development. In *Kingsblood Royal,* on the other hand, the real themes of the novel — race prejudice and the ostracism of Negroes — acquire inflated importance, and interest in the physical scene is supplanted by Lewis' strident exposition of the dangers of bigotry.

Both these novels are tributes to Lewis' social observation, to his amazing ability to accumulate details that are at once amusing, relevant, and suggestive. They also confirm Lewis' interest in the contemporary and the diurnal. Historical fiction in general did not appeal to him (he obviously preferred Dickens to Scott) because it seemed to lack immediacy; he could project through his eye rather than through his imagination. But in the centennial year of Minnesota Territory he published his one historical novel, *The God-Seeker,* the action of which takes place in 1849 in the area around the fictional Bois des Morts, two hundred miles west of Fort Snelling on the Minnesota River. [33]

It takes Lewis fourteen chapters to transport his hero, Massachusetts-born Aaron Gadd, to the West. Aaron is motivated in his decision by missionary zeal, ambition, and a craving for romance. He travels mostly by river steamboat via St. Louis, Dubuque, and Galena; the final stretch of the river he sees from the deck of the "Dr. Franklin," with Russell Blakeley as first officer and clerk. Minutes after his arrival at the muddy St. Paul landing, Aaron meets Father Ravoux, Vital Guerin, and Joe Brown; and Brown in particular is given a full characterization.[34] At Fort Snelling, prior to his departure for his missionary post where he would act as a carpenter, Gadd is introduced to Thomas S. Williamson, to Stephen Riggs, and to the Pond brothers, although none of these figures largely in Gadd's future adventures. Transportation to Traverse des Sioux is later arranged by a trader on Grey Cloud Island, and eventually, by canoe and horseback, Aaron reaches his destination.

Gadd, a shrewd, industrious young Yankee, rises quickly amid his unusual surroundings. In relatively short time he meets Selene Lanark, daughter of the frontier trader and impresario Caesar Lanark, and the two are married, first in a civil ceremony by Joe Brown, later by a Unitarian clergyman using an Episcopalian ritual. When Gadd joins the trading firm of Buckbee, Lanark and Gadd, his subsequent fortunes are assured. Most of the rest of the novel can be quickly forgotten by the discriminating reader. Lewis' gift for caricature is always apparent, and his ridicule of certain evangelists and self-seekers is amusing if superficial. The characters, however, never come alive. He is perhaps least successful in delineating Indians. Certainly his hypocritical Black Wolf, a pureblood Dakota who has attended Oberlin, is the least convincing of all. Black Wolf can discuss existentialism in perfect English; he also participates in the tribal feast of the raw fish and readapts himself to the blanket. As Caesar Lanark says cynically: "The typical Dakota is Isaac Weeps-by-Night, who is merely a little ahead of his fellows in giving up hunting for plowing, building a wretched shack and getting drunk on forty-rod whisky. That's what the children of Black Wolf will do . . . if they get born and survive." [35]

In *Elmer Gantry* Lewis attacked the hypocrisy and excesses of irresponsible evangelism with all the virulence of which he was capable. In *The God-Seeker* he shifted his perspective from the contemporary to the historical, and he also modified his satire. If Aaron Gadd's missionary associates are naïve, ill-informed, and even on occasion unscrupulous, Gadd himself is honest and moral. Lewis' picture of frontier evangelism is unflattering rather than vicious. He could not understand, for example, the consecration to a cause which led Edward Eggleston on the Minnesota frontier to adopt the peripatetic life himself until his health broke down, and then to choose a Methodist circuit rider as the hero for his fiction. Nor could Lewis sympathize with the proselytizing activities of a Bishop Whipple. On the other hand, Lewis also resented the rapacity and cynicism of the Indian traders who exchanged shoddy merchandise and gaudy trinkets for valuable furs. His Caesar Lanark, to whom he ascribes a certain amount of intellectual sophistication, represents the more predatory frontier merchant. But even Lanark is a one-dimensional figure. Indeed most of the characters in Lewis' later novels remind one of a remark of Mark Twain when he was disparaging photography as a source of fictional portraiture. "Observation? Of what real value is it? One learns peoples through the heart, not the eyes or the intellect." [36] Lewis never ventured further from human reality than in his one historical novel.

In a sense, however, Lewis was most faithful to his Minnesota background when he was least deliberately photographic or representational. As a native of a prairie community in Stearns County he was intimately aware not only of the rural area around him but also of the settlers. The German and Scandinavian farmers of the region figure prominently in most of his early stories and provide the often anonymous but always evident background of *Main Street*. Moreover, Lewis practiced his mimicry of speech by rendering the dialect of Teuton and Swede and prided himself on his fidelity of transcription. His protagonists, to be sure, seldom represent these national strains, but his minor figures are frequently of immigrant stock. Lewis was also conscious of other ingredients in the Minnesota melting pot; the Yankees, who came early and quickly controlled lumbering and mercantile activities; the French, more nomadic and less socially important; the Central Europeans, who provided much of the manpower for the iron mining industry. In *Cass Timberlane* Lewis was especially careful to emphasize the fusion of races and tongues in his fictional northern town, though he made less use of them than did Phil Stong in his novel, *The Iron Mountain*. In an essay which Lewis contributed to *The Nation* he labeled Minnesota the Norse State and emphasized the prominence of the Scandinavians in state politics, but he also tried to dispel the notion that Minnesota's population was made up only of emigrants from northern Europe. This was as much of a misconception, he argued, as the belief that Minnesota's topography is uniform or that a commonwealth which contributes dairy products and corn and lumber and iron ore to the nation is a region of one crop — namely, wheat.[37]

History impinges frequently on Lewis' descriptions. The only Minnesota aborigines who appear *in propria persona* are the unconvincing Sioux of *The God-Seeker,* but Lewis was fond of impressing the recent development of Minnesota on his readers by stating that less than a century ago a particular town was a Chippewa-haunted wilderness. Indian legends are alluded to sparingly, the voyageurs are cited, and particular patronymics like Radisson are preserved as place names. The Sioux-Chippewa feuds are referred to occasionally, and Lewis' ear was historically attuned to the creaking axles that characterized the Red River carts.

The varied economic history of Minnesota also is reflected in his fiction, although he wrote neither a novel of industry nor one of labor. No Lewis novel is set in the area of the iron ranges or in the northern forests; when he did tell a story about the wilderness he went across the border into Saskatchewan for a locale, as in *Mantrap*. But lumbering in general has a place in his novels — the streams which floated the logs, the lakes which held the booms, even the banks which pyramided the industry's money. Certainly the Blue Ox National Bank of Grand Republic is Lewis' bow to the Paul Bunyan stories. In the same way the milling industry is alluded to and is said to be one of the mainstays of such a city as Vernon. Agriculture, of course, is the occupation of most of the people who go to market in Gopher Prairie or the adjacent hamlets. Lewis' references to the cornland, the interminable fields in which the tiny communities stand like oases, are usually satiric, but he could grow enthusiastic about the pleasures of field sports and the lure of lake and forest. Not even Mark Twain, recalling idyllic days on his uncle's plantation near Florida, Missouri, was more nostalgic than Lewis writing about fishing and hunting as a boy in Stearns County. Lewis never developed a projected novel about education, but one may presume that if this had materialized it might have dealt with the University of Minnesota, as some of the faculty members of that institution once feared.

After the great decade of the 1920s, during which Lewis' best novels appeared, his work became repetitious, clamorous, imitative. Reviewer after reviewer complained that each new Lewis novel covered familiar ground and used familiar methods. Locale and names might be different, hotelkeeping or the penitentiary system or the dangers of Fascism in the United States might be substituted for small-town provincialism and Zenith real estate, but the technique was unchanged. Lewis' gifts of mimicry and selection of details remained as remarkable as ever, yet the stridency was more pronounced, the humor more labored. Unwilling or unable to change his approach, he wrote in the same way until the end, and his later fiction became attenuated and unconvincing.

It is always interesting to speculate why a writer reaches a point, either midway in his career or later, beyond which there is no development. Some writers say essentially what they have to say in their first book and do nothing but parrot themselves thereafter. Others are delayed in finding their real theme or their happiest medium until several books have come off the presses. Only the rare few progress consistently and reveal increased stature and maturity as one published work follows another.

It seems quite apparent that in Lewis' case his fiction began to decline as soon as he got away from the Minnesota or at least the middle western background. Always a diligent researcher, he filled notebooks with details, names, phrases pertaining to whatever theme he had decided to develop, so that his picture of a location or a career is superficially authentic whatever it may lack in vitality. But "getting up" a subject in this fashion is not quite the same thing as writing from a reservoir overflowing with impressions and experiences. Lewis' youth in Minnesota and his early years as student and companion to his doctor-father were the reservoir out of which flowed six or more novels and many stories. When he tapped this source in his early maturity he produced his best work — *Main Street, Babbitt, Elmer Gantry, Arrowsmith, Dodsworth.* Upon returning to the source toward the end of his career he could still write with some authority, despite the familiarity of his technique. But much of the intervening fiction is stiff and self-conscious, and even the famous mimicry often palls. Lewis never lacked gusto even when not at his best as a storyteller, yet one can tire of excessive exuberance.

In later years Lewis was too restless, too nomadic ever to settle down anywhere. During his creative throes he was not especially conscious of surroundings — chair, table, typewriter, and isolation from society were almost his only necessities. But the book finished and out of the way, he needed change, and his peregrinations were endless and hectic. Nevertheless, he remained conscious of his formative years, and the impressions he gained from them served to solidify his fiction. He once paid sincere tribute to his Sauk Centre boyhood: "It was a good time, a good place, and a good preparation for life." [38] His fiction justifies the tribute.

Footnotes

THE PIPESTONE QUARRY AND THE INDIANS — *Nydahl*

[1] This is a revised version of a paper read on September 23, 1950, before the evening session of the Minnesota Historical Society's twenty-fourth annual tour at Pipestone.

[2] Newton H. Winchell and Warren Upham, *The Geology of Minnesota,* 1:533–536, 544 (Minneapolis, 1884).

[3] R. H. Landon, "The Story of Pipestone," in *Minnesota Archaeologist,* 1:5 (April, 1939); Rose A. Palmer, *The North American Indians,* 31, 32 *(Smithsonian Scientific Series,* vol. 4 — New York, 1938); John W. Davis, "A History of the Pipestone Reservation," 1, 2, an unpublished master's thesis prepared at the University of Colorado in 1934; the Minnesota Historical Society has a copy.

[4] Peter Pond's "Narrative" was first published in the *Connecticut Magazine,* 10:235–259 (April, May, June, 1906); it has been reprinted in several other publications, including Charles M. Gates, ed., *Five Fur Traders of the Northwest* (Minneapolis, 1933). For the present passage, see p. 53.

[5] Davis, "History of the Pipestone Reservation," 7; *The Pipestone Indian Shrine,* 8 (Pipestone, [1933]). The latter, a booklet of forty-four pages compiled by the Pipestone Indian Shrine Association, contains "Indian Legends and Historical Facts regarding the Red Pipestone Quarry, Winnewissa Falls and the 'Twin Maidens.'"

[6] Edward D. Neill, *History of Minnesota,* 514 (Minneapolis, 1882); Winchell and Upham, *Geology of Minnesota,* 1:24; Gates, ed., *Five Fur Traders,* 52.

[7] Another explorer, Count Francesco Arese, moved along the "Red Pipestone River" in the summer of 1837 while hunting buffalo. He failed to mention the quarry but referred to rocks close to the river of a "greyish red" and told that, upon meeting a family of Sioux, "we all shook hands and passed pipes around." See Andrew Evans' translation of Arese, *A Trip to the Prairies and in the Interior of North America,* 95 (New York, 1934).

[8] Prescott's manuscript "Reminiscences," which are addressed to Governor Ramsey, are owned by the Minnesota Historical Society; the extracts here quoted are on pages 133 to 139 of a typewritten copy. No part of the manuscript was printed until Donald D. Parker quoted some passages in an article on Prescott published in installments in the Sioux Falls, South Dakota, *Daily Argus Leader* for October 1, 8, 15, and 22, 1950. Another entry for 1831 is in Lawrence Taliaferro's Journal, also owned by the Minnesota Historical Society. Under date of August 15, Taliaferro, who was the Indian agent at Fort Snelling, recorded: "Ratter and six men start for the Pipes Stone Quarry and are to bring me specimens of the same for several cabinets." William W. Warren noted that the "quarry had been known to, and visited by white traders for nearly a century before Catlin saw it and wrote his book." See his "History of the Ojibway Nation," in *Minnesota Historical Collections,* 5:114 (1885).

[9] The account of Catlin's journey to the Pipestone Quarry as here given is

based upon his *Letters and Notes on the Manners, Customs, and Condition of the North American Indians,* 2:160–176, 201–206 (London, 1842).

[10] Landon, in *Minnesota Archaeologist,* 1:5; Neill, *History of Minnesota,* 514 n.

[11] Davis, "History of the Pipestone Reservation," 11, 12, 112–115; Landon, in *Minnesota Archaeologist,* 1:5; *Pipestone Indian Shrine,* 7.

[12] Winchell and Upham, *Geology of Minnesota,* 1:69; Davis, "History of the Pipestone Reservation," 52; J. N. Nicollet, *Report Intended to Illustrate a Map of the Hydrographical Basin of the Upper Mississippi River,* 14–17 (Washington, 1843).

[13] Winchell and Upham, *Geology of Minnesota,* 1:149, 545, 546; interview with Lyle K. Linch, superintendent of the Pipestone National Monument, 1950.

[14] *Pipestone Indian Shrine,* 12, 13; Winchell and Upham, *Geology of Minnesota,* 1:555–560. The latter volume contains four full-page plates picturing forty examples of the rock inscriptions once to be found at the Pipestone Quarry. Since visitors defaced the petroglyphs, the best of them were removed from their original location. They are now on display at Pipestone National Monument.

[15] Catlin, *North American Indians,* 2:164–166, 168–170; *Pipestone Indian Shrine,* 13–17; Davis, "History of the Pipestone Reservation," 42–46, 53–56; Prescott, "Reminiscences," 138.

[16] *Pipestone Indian Shrine,* 21–24; Davis, "History of the Pipestone Reservation," 63–70. The National Park Service area covered about 285 acres in the 1950s.

[17] Arthur P. Rose, *History of the Counties of Rock and Pipestone,* 261 (Luverne, 1911); Historical Records Survey, Works Progress Administration, *Inventory of the County Archives of Minnesota* for Rock, Lincoln, Murray, and Nobles counties (St. Paul, 1937–42).

[18] Rose, *Counties of Rock and Pipestone,* 262–269.

[19] Rose, *Counties of Rock and Pipestone,* 262, 265; *Pipestone Indian Shrine,* 39, 40; Davis, "History of the Pipestone Reservation," 70–79; James H. Baker, *Lives of the Governors of Minnesota,* 380 (*Minnesota Historical Collections,* vol. 13 — 1908).

[20] Davis, "History of the Pipestone Reservation," 79–97; *Pipestone Indian Shrine,* 24–27.

[21] *Pipestone Indian Shrine,* 7; *Minneapolis Journal,* September 11, 1937; interviews with members of the Pipestone Indian Shrine Association and with residents of Pipestone, 1950.

[22] United States, *Statutes at Large,* 50:805.

[23] Interviews with residents of Pipestone, including Mr. Linch, 1950.

THE STORY OF GRAND PORTAGE — *Buck*

[1] This is a revised version of a paper read at the state historical convention held under the auspices of the Minnesota Historical Society at Duluth on July 28, 1922.

[2] Warren Upham, "Groseilliers and Radisson," in *Minnesota Historical Collections,* 10:506, 513 (part 2 — 1905). Reuben G. Thwaites in *Wisconsin Historical Collections,* 11:96 n. (1888), interprets a sentence in Radisson's narrative as a reference to the Grand Portage. See also Lawrence J. Burpee, *The Search for the Western Sea,* lvi, 212, 307 n. (Toronto, 1908).

[3] William W. Folwell, *A History of Minnesota,* 1:23, 44 (St. Paul, 1921). A statement in a letter of a French officer written in 1722 with reference to the best route from Kaministiquia to the site of a proposed post in the interior is probably a reference to the Pigeon River route. See Pierre Margry, ed., *Découvertes et établissements des Français,* 6:516 (Paris, 1886); Warren Upham,

Minnesota in Three Centuries, 1:276 (New York, 1908); and Burpee, *Search for the Western Sea,* 202.

[4] Margry, *Découvertes,* 6:586, 591.

[5] Sir Alexander Mackenzie in *Voyages from Montreal through the Continent of North America,* viii (Philadelphia, 1802), refers to "the Grande Portage, where the French had a principal establishment, and was the line of their communication with the interior country. It was once destroyed by fire." Benjamin Sulte, "Early Forts in the North-West," in his *Mélanges historiques,* 10:139 (Montreal, 1922), says that "between 1718 and 1720 La Noue erected a fort at Grand Portage," but gives no indication of the evidence on which the statement is based.

[6] Mackenzie, *Voyages,* vi; Louis F. Masson, *Les bourgeois de la compagnie du nord-ouest,* 1:9 (Quebec, 1889); Alexander Henry, *Travels and Adventures in Canada and the Indian Territories,* 195 (New York, 1809); Gordon C. Davidson, *The North West Company,* 33 (University of California, *Publications in History,* vol. 7 — Berkeley, 1918); Folwell, *Minnesota,* 1:53.

[7] Henry, *Travels and Adventures,* part 1; "Thompson Maxwell's Narrative — 1760–1763," in *Wisconsin Historical Collections,* 11:215 (1888).

[8] Mackenzie, *Voyages,* viii; Davidson, *North West Company,* 34; Jonathan Carver Journals. Photostatic copies and typewritten transcripts of the latter are in the Minnesota Historical Society. The originals are in the British Museum, London.

[9] Carver Journals.

[10] Carver Journals; "Abstracts of Indian Trade Licenses, 1768–76," in the Governor-General Papers of the Public Archives of Canada at Ottawa, transcripts of which are in the manuscripts collection of the Minnesota Historical Society; Henry, *Travels and Adventures,* 238, 239.

[11] *Michigan Pioneer and Historical Collections,* 19:337–339 (1892).

[12] *Wisconsin Historical Collections,* 11:142; 19:237, 239, 243 (1910); *Michigan Pioneer and Historical Collections,* 9:356 (1886); 19:345, 372; Davidson, *North West Company,* 28. Davidson states that a detachment was stationed at Grand Portage "in 1777 and succeeding years."

[13] Davidson, *North West Company,* 8–14.

[14] John Macdonell Diary in the Masson Papers in the library of McGill University, Montreal. The Minnesota Historical Society has a copy. A somewhat different version of parts of this document is in Burpee, *Search for the Western Sea,* 306. For other descriptions of the post, see Mackenzie, *Voyages,* xliii; Daniel W. Harmon, *A Journal of Voyages and Travels,* 40 (Andover, 1820); and George Heriot, *Travels through the Canadas,* 203 (London, 1807).

[15] Heriot, *Travels,* 204.

[16] Masson, *Bourgeois,* 2:466, 480; Mackenzie, *Voyages,* xliii–xlv; Harmon, *Voyages and Travels,* 41–43; Heriot, *Travels,* 204; Davidson, *North West Company,* 22, 204, 230; William W. Warren, "History of the Ojibway Nation," in *Minnesota Historical Collections,* 5:379 (1885). See also the "Accounts of the Fur-trade, extracted from the journal of Count Andriani of Milan, who travelled in the interior parts of America in the year 1791," in the Duke de la Rochefoucault Liancourt, *Travels through the United States of North America, the Country of the Iroquois, and Upper Canada, in the Years 1795, 1796, and 1797,* 1:325–334 (London, 1799). The statements are here made that "a fort . . . garrisoned with fifty men" was maintained at Grand Portage and that "in this place there is frequently a concourse of one thousand people and upward."

[17] Alexander Henry, the younger, in Elliott Coues, ed., *New Light on the Early History of the Greater Northwest,* 1:6 (New York, 1897); Mackenzie, *Voyages,* xlii; Henry Y. Hind, *Narrative of the Canadian Red River Exploring Expedition of 1857,* 1:74 (London, 1860); George Bryce, *Mackenzie, Selkirk, Simpson,* 12

(*The Makers of Canada*, vol. 8 — Toronto, 1909); Davidson, *North West Company*, 23, 49 n., 204, 211, 231. For an account of the method of carrying over portages, see John Johnston in Masson, *Bourgeois*, 2:165.

[18] Harmon, *Voyages and Travels*, 43; Henry, in Coues, *New Light*, 1:6; Heriot, *Travels*, 205.

[19] Harmon, *Voyages and Travels*, 40; Coues, *New Light*, 7 n.; John B. Moore, *History and Digest of the International Arbitrations to Which the United States Has Been a Party*, 6: map 57 (Washington, 1898). See note 29 below.

[20] Roderic McKenzie, "Reminiscences," in Masson, *Bourgeois*, 1:46–48; Warren, in *Minnesota Historical Collections*, 5:292; Coues, *New Light*, 220 n.; Davidson, *North West Company*, 48, 105. David Thompson says that a United States collector landed at Grand Portage in 1800 and declared his intention of levying duties. See quotation in Burpee, "Highways of the Fur Trade," in Royal Society of Canada, *Transactions*, series 3, vol. 8, section 2, p. 188 (September, 1914).

[21] Henry, in Coues, *New Light*, 1:218; François V. Malhiot, "A Wisconsin Fur-Trader's Journal, 1804–05," in *Wisconsin Historical Collections*, 19:169; Davidson, *North West Company*, 90.

[22] A map in the British Museum, which is reproduced in Davidson, *North West Company*, 144, indicates that there was a North West Company post at Grand Portage as late as 1818. Hind apparently thought that Fort Charlotte was an important post after the headquarters were moved from Grand Portage. He states that "Fort Charlotte was connected with Point des Meurons [*near Fort William*] by a traveled road in the time of the North-West Company." See his *Narrative*, 1:14, 74. General James H. Baker, on the other hand, in "History of Transportation in Minnesota," in *Minnesota Historical Collections*, 9:9 (1901), says that a road thirty-six miles long was built in the earliest years of the nineteenth century between Grand Portage and Fort William and claims to have seen the remains of some of the bridges. Newton H. Winchell, in the Geological and Natural History Survey of Minnesota, *Final Report*, 4:502 (1899), describes the remains of the dock at Fort Charlotte as they were in 1893. He makes the mistake, however, of assigning the name "Fort Charlotte" to the post at Grand Portage.

[23] Thwaites, in *Wisconsin Historical Collections*, 19:190 n.

[24] *Wisconsin Historical Collections*, 19:378, 430; 22 Congress, 1 session, *Senate Documents*, no. 90, p. 43, 46 (serial 213); Warren, in *Minnesota Historical Collections*, 5:382; Folwell, *Minnesota*, 1:132. The American trader referred to may have been Bela Chapman, who wintered on the north shore of Lake Superior in 1823–24 and visited Grand Portage in the spring. In his journal, which is in the Sibley Papers in the Minnesota Historical Society, he tells of his unsuccessful efforts to prevent Indians from taking their furs to the British, who had given them "credits."

[25] Table in 22 Congress, 1 session, *Senate Documents*, no. 90, p. 50; Gabriel Franchere's "Remarks made on a visit from Lapointe to the Fishing Stations of Grand Portage, Isle Royal and Ance Quiwinan — August 1839"; account of the fur trade around Lake Superior, probably written by Clement H. Beaulieu about 1880. The last two items are manuscripts in the Minnesota Historical Society. Hind found an American trading post at Grand Portage in 1857. See his *Narrative*, 1:75.

[26] Baptismal Records, 1835–1854, St. Joseph Mission Papers, La Pointe, Wisconsin. The Minnesota Historical Society has copies of these; the originals are in the Franciscan Rectory, Bayfield, Wisconsin. P. Chrysostomus Verwyst, *Life and Labors of Rt. Rev. Frederic Baraga*, 384, 386 (Milwaukee, 1900); Joseph G. Norwood, "Geological Report of a Survey of Portions of Wisconsin and Minnesota," in David Dale Owen, *Report of a Geological Survey of Wisconsin*,

Iowa, and Minnesota, 397, 405 (Philadelphia, 1852); letter of Bishop John M. Henni, December 30, 1847, a copy of which is in the Grace Lee Nute Collection of Mission Transcripts of the Minnesota Historical Society; Sister Mary Aquinas Norton, *Catholic Missionary Activities in the Northwest, 1818–1864,* 72 n. (Washington, D.C., 1930). The location of the mission on Pigeon River is indicated on a map, plate N, at the back of Owen, *Geological Survey.*

²⁷ Folwell, *Minnesota,* 1:500–502.

²⁸ United States, *Statutes at Large,* 10:1109; 25:642; Indian Office, *Reports,* 1896, 2:330; 1897, p. 312; 1906, p. 397; 1917, 2:93; Land Office, *Reports,* in Department of the Interior, *Reports,* 1916, 1:163; A. H. Sawyer to Minnesota Historical Society, April 26, 1922.

²⁹ Paul Bliss, "Back Two Centuries over Minnesota's Oldest Highway to Oldest Fort," in *Minneapolis Journal,* July 16, 1922.

³⁰ Ray P. Chase, *Statement to the Nineteen Hundred Twenty-three Legislature,* 65 (St. Paul, 1923).

THE SETTLER AND THE ARMY IN FRONTIER MINNESOTA — *Prucha*

¹ 33 Congress, 1 session, *Senate Executive Documents,* no. 1, p. 6 (serial 691).

² *Weekly Pioneer and Democrat* (St. Paul), June 30, 1858.

³ *Sauk Rapids Frontierman,* June 24, 1858.

⁴ After leading an expedition to the Red River in 1856, Colonel C. F. Smith, commandant of Fort Snelling, reported that the town of Pembina, at the junction of the Pembina and Red rivers, had a thousand inhabitants, and that St. Joseph, farther up the Pembina, had fifteen hundred. Debating in Congress in 1855 in favor of a Red River Valley post, Henry M. Rice declared that four thousand people were living at Pembina and that they were twenty days away from the nearest settlement to the south. See 35 Congress, 2 session, *Senate Executive Documents,* no. 1, p. 427 n. (serial 975); *Congressional Globe,* 33 Congress, 2 session, p. 454.

⁵ *Daily Minnesotian* (St. Paul), August 1, 1854; United States, *Statutes at Large,* 10:608; 34 Congress, 3 session, *Senate Executive Documents,* no. 5, p. 3 (serial 876); 35 Congress, 2 session, *Senate Executive Documents,* no. 1, p. 435–437 (serial 975).

⁶ *Daily Pioneer and Democrat* (St. Paul), April 21, October 15, 1859; 41 Congress, 3 session, *House Executive Documents,* no. 1, part 2, p. 27 (serial 1446).

⁷ Indian Office, *Reports,* 1860, p. 55–58.

⁸ 32 Congress, 2 session, *Senate Executive Documents,* no. 1, p. 71 (serial 659); 35 Congress, 1 session, *Senate Executive Documents,* no. 11, p. 151–153 (serial 920); *Pioneer and Democrat,* August 23, 1857.

⁹ *St. Cloud Democrat,* April 21, 1859; March 29, 1860. Mrs. Swisshelm's journal was established in 1857 as the *St. Cloud Visiter.*

¹⁰ *Minnesota Pioneer* (St. Paul), June 19, 1851; *Minnesotian,* June 2, 1858.

¹¹ *St. Cloud Democrat,* July 12, 1860.

¹² *Henderson Democrat,* July 16, 1857; *Pioneer and Democrat,* July 11, 1858.

¹³ 26 Congress, 1 session, *House Executive Documents,* no. 144, p. 1–4 (serial 365).

¹⁴ William W. Folwell, *A History of Minnesota,* 1:222 (St. Paul, 1921); *Statutes at Large,* 10:36.

¹⁵ Minnesota Territory, *Laws,* 1849, p. 161; *Statutes at Large,* 10:36; *Minnesotian,* August 28, 1852; *St. Anthony Express,* September 3, 1852.

¹⁶ Folwell, *Minnesota,* 1:434, 503–515; Rodney C. Loehr, "Franklin Steele, Frontier Businessman," in *Minnesota History,* 27:309–318 (December, 1946). The details of the sale can be traced in *Fort Snelling Investigation* (35 Congress,

1 session, *House Reports,* no. 351 — serial 965) and *Sale of Fort Snelling Reservation* (40 Congress, 3 session, *House Executive Documents,* no. 9 — serial 1372).

[17] See F. Paul Prucha, "Fort Ripley: The Post and the Military Reservation," in *Minnesota History,* 28:215–224 (September, 1947). A map showing the extent and boundaries of the reservation is reproduced on page 217.

[18] The commandant's order, dated February 13, 1854, is in an unpaged manuscript history of "Fort Ridgely, Minnesota," compiled in the war department and sent to the Minnesota Historical Society in 1880. The narrative shows that before 1866 more than eighty pre-emption and homestead entries had been made within the limits of the reservation.

[19] Photostatic copies of three undated petitions are in a folder of letters relative to abandoned military reserves, 1857–70, among some United States General Land Office Papers in the Minnesota Historical Society.

[20] *St. Paul Pioneer,* October 21, 24, 1869.

[21] 40 Congress, 2 session, *Senate Executive Documents,* no. 44 (serial 1317); 41 Congress, 2 session, *Senate Executive Documents,* no. 6 (serial 1405); 41 Congress, 2 session, *Senate Miscellaneous Documents,* no. 87 (serial 1408); *Statutes at Large,* 16:187, 21:506.

[22] *Statutes at Large,* 16:430, 22:168; 44 Congress, 1 session, *House Miscellaneous Documents,* no. 137 (serial 1702). The part of the reserve in Dakota Territory was made subject to homesteading and pre-emption in 1880. *Statutes at Large,* 21:172.

WILDERNESS MARTHAS — *Nute*

[1] This paper was read at the seventy-eighth annual meeting of the Minnesota Historical Society on January 17, 1927.

[2] The chief sources from which the data in this account have been derived are the manuscript letters and diaries of missionaries. All of these papers may be found, either as originals or as copies, in the manuscripts collection of the Minnesota Historical Society. A large proportion of the letters are copies of the missionaries' correspondence with the American Board of Commissioners for Foreign Missions in Boston, which sent out many of the mission workers. Copies of the diaries of Edmund F. Ely and his wife and of William Thurston Boutwell have been drawn upon to supply data on Mrs. Ely and Mrs. Boutwell. One letter in the papers of Henry H. Sibley, to whom Mrs. Frederic Ayer wrote on May 2, 1835, concerning Mrs. Boutwell's culinary skill, is quoted.

[3] William H. C. Folsom, *Fifty Years in the Northwest,* 276 (St. Paul, 1888).

TWO LETTERS FROM MINNESOTA TERRITORY —
Folwell and McFarlane

[1] This letter was written by Dr. William W. Folwell, president of the Minnesota Historical Society, to be read at the luncheon program of the society's seventy-sixth annual meeting on January 19, 1925, in place of a short speech which he had been asked to make. It is a valuable description of the Minnesota situation in 1849 and is based upon studies and an accurate understanding of early Minnesota history. The letter is so written as to be attributable to Richard Chute, one of the pioneer settlers at St. Anthony Falls. No intimation was given the audience that the letter was not an authentic portrayal of Minnesota conditions in 1849, and apparently most of those who heard it read considered it a genuine pioneer letter. The fact that Dr. Folwell prepared the following footnotes to correct "excusable inaccuracies" in the letter strengthened the impression that here was an original document. Indeed, a newspaper reporter actually described the nonexistent original as "yellowed with the years since 1849." *Ed.*

[2] The Stevens mentioned was without doubt John H. Stevens, who built the first house on the west side at the falls.

[3] The flour mill had been equipped with "bolts" for making flour.

[4] Rebecca Marshall became Mrs. Rebecca Marshall Cathcart. Her "Sheaf of Remembrances," in the *Minnesota Historical Collections,* 15:515–552 (1915), is full of details of life in "the little French and Indian village" of St. Paul, as she calls it.

[5] Dr. Neill did not start the school. Miss Harriet Bishop did that two years before he came.

[6] Joseph Renshaw Brown was his full name.

[7] If Mr. Brown had known the Dakota language as well as Gideon or Samuel Pond he would have spelled the name of the territory *Min-ni-sota.* "Minne" is a mere nickname in English.

[8] The letter ends abruptly without proper signature, apparently because of a lost sheet.

[9] This document is filed in the Curtis H. Pettit Papers in the manuscripts collection of the Minnesota Historical Society. The introductory note was supplied by Grace Lee Nute. *Ed.*

THE "FASHIONABLE TOUR" ON THE UPPER MISSISSIPPI — *Blegen*

[1] This paper was read on June 17, 1939, at the Frontenac session of the seventeenth state historical tour and convention held under the auspices of the Minnesota Historical Society.

[2] Two publications of much interest and value are William J. Petersen, *Steamboating on the Upper Mississippi* (Iowa City, 1937), and Mildred L. Hartsough, *From Canoe to Steel Barge on the Upper Mississippi* (Minneapolis, 1934).

[3] Giacomo C. Beltrami, *A Pilgrimage in Europe and America,* 2:199, 200 (London, 1828).

[4] George Catlin, *Letters and Notes on the Manners, Customs, and Condition of the North American Indians,* 2:590–592 (Philadelphia, 1857).

[5] Joseph Schafer, "High Society in Pioneer Wisconsin," in *Wisconsin Magazine of History,* 20:449 (June, 1937).

[6] Frederick Marryat, *A Diary in America, with Remarks on Its Institutions,* 2:78–124 (London, 1839).

[7] Bertha L. Heilbron, ed., *Making a Motion Picture in 1848: Henry Lewis' Journal of a Canoe Voyage from the Falls of St. Anthony to St. Louis,* 3–11 (St. Paul, 1936).

[8] Heilbron, ed., *Making a Motion Picture in 1848,* 7.

[9] Heilbron, ed., *Making a Motion Picture in 1848,* 35. The scene that provoked this comment was that from Trempealeau Mountain, looking north.

[10] Dorothy Dondore, "Banvard's Panorama and the Flowering of New England," in *New England Quarterly,* 11:821–826 (December, 1938); Theodore C. Blegen, *Norwegian Migration to America, 1825–1860,* 342, 343 n. (Northfield, 1931); Heilbron, ed., *Making a Motion Picture in 1848,* 4.

[11] Hartsough, *From Canoe to Steel Barge,* 163, 164; *Minnesota Chronicle and Register* (St. Paul), August 12, 1850; Petersen, *Steamboating on the Upper Mississippi,* 256, 260, 261.

[12] For an account of this event, see William J. Petersen, "The Rock Island Railroad Excursion of 1854," in *Minnesota History,* 15:405–420 (December, 1934).

[13] The Minnesota Historical Society has typewritten copies of the letters about the excursion printed in the *Boston Evening Transcript* and various other eastern newspapers.

[14] Catherine M. Sedgwick, "The Great Excursion to the Falls of St. Anthony," in *Putnam's Monthly Magazine,* 4:323 (September, 1854).

[15] *New-York Tribune,* June 20, 1854, quoted in Petersen, *Steamboating on the Upper Mississippi,* 279.

[16] *New-York Tribune,* June 20, 1854, quoted in Petersen, *Steamboating on the Upper Mississippi,* 284.

[17] Mark Twain, *Life on the Mississippi,* 370 (Boston, 1883); Petersen, *Steamboating on the Upper Mississippi,* 265; George B. Merrick, "Steamboats and Steamboatmen of the Upper Mississippi," in *Saturday Evening Post* (Burlington, Iowa), November 6, 1915.

[18] Petersen, *Steamboating on the Upper Mississippi,* 353, 357.

[19] Luther W. Peck, "The Upper Mississippi," in *National Magazine,* 9:483 (December, 1856).

[20] H. W. Hamilton, *Rural Sketches of Minnesota, the El Dorado of the Northwest,* 8 (Milan, Ohio, 1850).

[21] Adolf B. Benson, ed., "Fredrika Bremer's Unpublished Letters to the Downings," in *Scandinavian Studies,* 11:192 (May, 1931).

[22] Ida Pfeiffer, *A Lady's Second Journey Round the World,* 431, 432, 433 (New York, 1856); George T. Borrett, *Letters from Canada and the United States,* 135–144 (London, 1865).

[23] Anthony Trollope, *North America,* 1:206–209 (London, 1862).

[24] Charles Lanman, *A Summer in the Wilderness,* 56 (New York, 1847); Mrs. Elizabeth Ellet, *Summer Rambles in the West,* 77, 78, 81 (New York, 1853).

[25] Ellet, *Summer Rambles,* 92.

[26] Ellet, *Summer Rambles,* 89, 126.

[27] Theodore C. Blegen, ed., "Campaigning with Seward in 1860," in *Minnesota History,* 8:167 (June, 1927). The journal of the younger Adams is there published from a typewritten copy in the Minnesota Historical Society.

[28] *Minnesota Pioneer* (St. Paul), July 22, 1852.

KEEPING HOUSE ON THE MINNESOTA FRONTIER — *Swanson*

[1] This paper is a revised version of a chapter from a master's thesis on "Frontier Homes and Home Management" submitted at the University of Minnesota in 1933.

[2] Hans Mattson, *Reminiscences: The Story of an Emigrant,* 54 (St. Paul, 1891); Harriet Bonebright-Closz, *Reminiscences of Newcastle, Iowa,* 39 (Des Moines, 1921); Lucy L. W. Morris, *Old Rail Fence Corners,* 99 (Austin, 1914). See also Edward B. Drew, "Pioneer Days in Minnesota," 122, a manuscript narrative prepared in 1899, in the Drew Papers owned by the Minnesota Historical Society.

[3] *Minnesota Pioneer* (St. Paul), October 11, 1849; July 24, 1851; *Pioneer and Democrat* (St. Paul), January 1, 1857; Seth K. Humphrey, *Following the Prairie Frontier,* 66 (Minneapolis, 1931). The newspapers used in the preparation of this article are in the collections of the Minnesota Historical Society.

[4] The expense book kept by Miss Fuller for her home in St. Paul in 1857 is in the Fuller Papers, in the Minnesota Historical Society. In her balance for 1857 she gives the total cost of lighting for that year as $87.85. Miss Fuller purchased one and a half gallons of sperm oil for $2.75, a ball of candlewick at ten cents, and a bunch of lampwicks at twenty-five cents. The balance, $84.75, was used to purchase 254 pounds of candles. Star candles were less expensive than others, costing thirty or thirty-five cents a pound, while sperm candles were valued at sixty cents.

[5] *Pioneer and Democrat,* November 2, 1860.

[6] J. S. Woodard, "Reminiscences to 1881," 24. The Minnesota Historical Society has a typewritten copy of this manuscript.

[7] *St. Cloud Democrat,* November 25, 1858; *House Journal,* 1865, p. 179.

[8] Jennie Pettijohn Tyler, "Reminiscences," in Thomas Hughes, *Old Traverse des Sioux*, 133 (St. Peter, 1929).

[9] *Pioneer and Democrat*, September 26, 1857; January 30, 1858; August 24, 1859; *Falls Evening News* (St. Anthony), October 2, 1857. Ames's home was the first in St. Anthony to be equipped with gas.

[10] John C. Laird to Matthew J. Laird, November 12, 1850, in *Minnesota History*, 12:163 (June, 1931).

[11] *Pioneer and Democrat*, April 9, 1859.

[12] Lillian E. Stewart, *A Pioneer of Old Superior*, 196 (Boston, 1930). Elizabeth Fuller, according to her account book for 1857, paid from $5.00 to $6.50 per cord for wood except in July, when she purchased five cords at a mill for $4.00 each. On several occasions, she had to pay an additional charge of $1.50 for delivery.

[13] *Minnesota Pioneer*, November 24, 30, 1854; *Pioneer and Democrat*, January 6, 1857; December 21, 1859; December 2, 1860; Minnesota, *Special Laws*, 1866, p. 50.

[14] *Pioneer and Democrat*, January 30, 1858; J. A. Willard, *Blue Earth County: Its Advantages to Settlers*, 7, 18 (Mankato, 1868).

[15] A. J. Russell, *Loring Park Aspects*, 45 (Minneapolis, 1919); *Pioneer and Democrat*, July 6, 1859; September 2, 1860.

[16] *Pioneer and Democrat*, August 21, 1856.

[17] Willard, *Blue Earth County*, 7; *Minnesota Pioneer*, November 27, 1851. The Harrington Diary is in the Minnesota Historical Society.

[18] *Minnesota Pioneer*, August 22, 1850; March 11, 1852; *Minnesota Beacon* (Wasioja), August 15, 1860.

[19] *Minnesota Pioneer*, February 12, 1852; *Pioneer and Democrat*, July 24, 1857.

[20] *Pioneer and Democrat*, July 8, August 13, September 20, 1857; December 30, 1858.

[21] Humphrey, *Prairie Frontier*, 70; J. Wesley Bond, *Minnesota and Its Resources*, 138 (New York, 1853); *Minnesota Pioneer*, August 28, November 27, 1851; *Pioneer and Democrat*, July 17, 1859.

[22] Abby Fuller Abbe to Elizabeth Fuller, December 30, 1860, Fuller Papers.

[23] *Pioneer and Democrat*, February 14, 1860.

[24] *Pioneer and Democrat*, March 28, 1860; *General Laws*, 1866, p. 73.

[25] *St. Cloud Visiter*, June 24, 1858. For a concurrent opinion, see the *Minnesota Pioneer*, June 3, 1852, which asserts that a tallow chandler or a soapmaker settling in St. Paul could make a fortune in three years.

[26] *Minnesota Pioneer*, March 13, 1850; *Pioneer and Democrat*, November 17, 1855.

[27] Morris, *Old Rail Fence Corners*, 19, 77; *Minnesota Pioneer*, January 18, 1855.

[28] Bonebright-Closz, *Reminiscences of Newcastle, Iowa*, 197.

[29] *St. Cloud Democrat*, May 27, 1858; April 12, 1860; T. M. Newson, *Pen Pictures of St. Paul, Minnesota*, 276 (St. Paul, 1886).

[30] Bonebright-Closz, *Reminiscences of Newcastle, Iowa*, 51.

[31] Willard, *Blue Earth County*, 18, 19; *General Laws*, 1867, p. 60; Bonebright-Closz, *Reminiscences of Newcastle, Iowa*, 55; *Minnesota Democrat* (St. Paul), May 20, 1851. For complaints against hogs running at large on the streets of St. Paul, see the *Pioneer and Democrat*, May 6, 1860.

[32] *New Era*, May 31, 1860.

[33] *Pioneer and Democrat*, October 27, 1860. A copy of the Ford company's *Catalogue of Fruit and Ornamental Trees* is in the Minnesota Historical Society.

[34] *St. Cloud Democrat*, May 19, 1859.

[35] Newson, *Pen Pictures of St. Paul*, 308; *Minnesota Pioneer*, August 13, 1855.

³⁶ *Pioneer and Democrat,* June 14, 1857; December 21, 1858; December 18, 1860; January 19, 1861.

³⁷ Hughes, *History of Blue Earth County,* 64; John H. Stevens, *Personal Recollections of Minnesota and Its People,* 84 (Minneapolis, 1890); Bonebright-Closz, *Reminiscences of Newcastle, Iowa,* 42, 46; Morris, *Old Rail Fence Corners,* 13, 97, 130.

³⁸ Bonebright-Closz, *Reminiscences of Newcastle, Iowa,* 45; Drew, "Pioneer Days in Minnesota," 60; Comstock, "Early Reminiscences," 16. A copy of the latter manuscript is in the Minnesota Historical Society.

³⁹ P. P. Quist, "Recollections of an Immigrant of 1865," in *Swedish-American Historical Bulletin,* 4:12 (September, 1931); Mrs. Louis Blum to her parents, November 18, 1853, Cory-Forbes Papers, in the Minnesota Historical Society.

⁴⁰ Russell, *Loring Park Aspects,* 51; Mrs. Blum to her parents, November 18, 1853, Cory-Forbes Papers; *Pioneer and Democrat,* October 25, 1859.

CHRISTMAS AND NEW YEAR'S ON THE FRONTIER — *Heilbron*

¹ Unless otherwise indicated, manuscripts cited in this article are in the collections of the Minnesota Historical Society.

² Grace Lee Nute, *The Voyageur,* 83–85 (New York, 1931); Zebulon M. Pike, *Expeditions to Headwaters of the Mississippi River,* 1:130 (Coues edition — New York, 1895). The Minnesota Historical Society has extracts from McKay's diary, the original of which is in the archives of the Hudson's Bay Company, London. It has been used by permission of the governor and committee of the Hudson's Bay Company.

³ Boutwell Diary, January 1, 1834.

⁴ Lucy M. Lewis to Clarisse W. Burrell, January 1, 1846, Lewis Papers; Sela G. Wright to J. P. Bardwell, December 25, 1845, in *Oberlin Evangelist,* 3:46, 47, 63 (March 17, 1841); *Minnesota Missionary,* vol. 4, no. 6, p. 2 (March, 1881).

⁵ *Minnesota Chronicle and Register* (St. Paul), December 22, 1849; *Minnesota Pioneer* (St. Paul), January 2, 1850; January 2, December 25, 1851.

⁶ *Minnesota Pioneer,* December 25, 1851; *Minneapolis Journal,* December 26, 1920; "A Christmas Dinner," in Orrin F. Smith Papers, Miscellaneous, 1852–1932; Evadene A. Burris, "Frontier Food," in *Minnesota History,* 14:391 (December, 1933); Ramsey Diary, December 28, 1850; Donnelly Diary, December 25, 1873, 1879.

⁷ Mrs. Abbe's letter is in the Fuller Papers.

⁸ Alfred Bergin, "The Westgoths in Minnesota," in *Weekly Valley Herald* (Chaska), July 25, 1935; *Minnesota Missionary,* vol. 1, no. 4, p. 4 (January, 1878); vol. 5, no. 3, p. 5 (December, 1881); vol. 5, no. 4, p. 2 (January, 1882); vol. 8, no. 1, p. 1 (January, 1884).

⁹ Alice Mendenhall George, *The Story of My Childhood,* 35 (Whittier, California, 1923); Britania J. Livingston, "Letters from a Pioneer Woman," in *Fairmont Daily Sentinel,* June 6, 1925; Mitchell Y. Jackson Diary, December 24, 1854; Anna M. Cowan, "Memories of Upper Fort Garry," in *The Beaver,* p. 25–30 (September, 1935).

¹⁰ The traveler was Hugo Nisbeth, whose account of a visit to Minnesota, published at Stockholm in 1874, appears in a translation by Roy W. Swanson under the title "A Swedish Visitor of the Early Seventies," in *Minnesota History,* 8:386–421 (December, 1927). Nisbeth's remarks about the American Christmas appear on page 413. See also *Chronicle and Register,* December 22, 1849; *Minnesota Democrat* (St. Paul), December 24, 1850; *Minnesota Missionary,* vol. 5, no. 4, p. 5 (January, 1882).

¹¹ *The Flower Queen* was published as a pamphlet of eighteen pages at Hastings in 1857. The Minnesota Historical Society has a copy. See also *Red River*

Valley News (Glyndon), December 26, 1879; *Dodge Center Index,* December 30, 1882.

[12] *Chronicle and Register,* December 22, 1849; "A Christmas Dinner," in Smith Papers.

[13] See Walter Stone Pardee's "Autobiography" in the Pardee Papers.

[14] *Minnesota Pioneer,* December 25, 1851; Ramsey Diary, January 1, 1851, 1852; Charles E. Flandrau, "Reminiscences of Minnesota during the Territorial Period," in *Minnesota Historical Collections,* 9:199 (1901).

[15] *Minnesota Pioneer,* January 2, 1850; *St. Paul Pioneer Press,* January 3, 1878; Samuel W. Pond to Ruth Riggs, January 26, 1856, Pond Papers. Neill's address appears in *Minnesota Historical Collections,* 1:17–36 (1872).

[16] *St. Anthony Express,* January 7, 1853. Carriers' greetings of the *Falls Evening News* and the *Minnesota Republican* of St. Anthony and Minneapolis for 1859, the *Saint Paul Daily Press* for 1866 and 1868, and the *St. Paul Pioneer* for 1867 are in the collections of the Minnesota Historical Society.

[17] Nisbeth, in *Minnesota History,* 8:413–416.

HEALTH AND MEDICINE IN ROCHESTER, 1855–1870 — *Shugg*

[1] This is an expanded version of a paper read on June 15, 1939, at the Rochester session of the seventeenth state historical convention held under the auspices of the Minnesota Historical Society.

[2] *Rochester Post,* May 8, 1869.

[3] Newspapers are the chief source for information about the general state of health in the community. There are no official records for the 1850s and 1860s; even the reporting of deaths was a voluntary matter until a law passed in 1870 to provide for the collection of statistics required the registration of births and deaths. See Minnesota, *General Laws,* 1870, p. 44. Until then, the obituary items in the newspapers were the only death records kept, except for census statistics covering the year preceding the enumeration. Scarlet fever, a common scourge in Minnesota at the time, seems not to have visited Rochester during these years. An epidemic in Preston, near by, is described in the reports of the Reverend E. Newton to the American Home Missionary Association, December 31, 1863, and January 14, 1865. The Minnesota Historical Society has microfilm copies of these reports; the originals are in the Chicago Theological Seminary.

[4] *Rochester City Post,* January 9, 16, 1864; *Rochester Republican,* January 13, 1864; *Chatfield Democrat,* January 9, 16, 23, 1864; *Owatonna Plaindealer,* January 7, 21, 1864. More than five years later rival editors were still citing this incident as an example of the ultimate in depravity. *Lanesboro Herald,* August 23, 1870.

[5] *Post,* January 2, 1868; February 6, 27, 1869; January 8, 1870; *Federal Union* (Rochester), February 20, 27, March 6, 13, 1869.

[6] *Republican,* January 28, August 19, November 18, 25, 1863; *City Post,* August 22, October 24, 1863.

[7] "The Climate of Minnesota," in Girart Hewitt, *Minnesota, Its Advantages to Settlers,* 29–31 (St. Paul, 1867). This article is unsigned, but a prefatory statement indicates that it was written by a physician, Dr. Thaddeus Williams of St. Paul.

[8] *Post,* March 24, 1866.

[9] Rochester, *Charter and Ordinances to 1881,* 21, 34, 41, 47–49 (Rochester, 1882); *City Post,* May 21, June 4, 1864; September 23, November 11, 1865; *Post,* March 10, 24, June 2, August 18, 25, 1866. As near as Rushford there were some fifteen cases of cholera in 1866, enough to send many of the inhabitants scurrying from the town until the epidemic should pass. *Post,* September 8, 1866.

[10] The items quoted are reprinted from the *Cincinnati Commercial,* the *New-York Tribune,* and the *Boston Journal,* in the *Rochester Post* of October 28, 1865, June 27, 1868, and August 7, 1869.

[11] *Special Laws,* 1868, p. 99; *Post,* September 10, 1870.

[12] *Saint Paul Daily Press,* August 13, 1870.

[13] *Post,* June 9, 1866.

[14] *Federal Union,* April 18, 1868; February 27, October 2, 31, 1869; *Chicago Republican,* quoted in *Rochester Post,* August 15, 1868.

[15] Supplements to the *Federal Union* and the *Post,* October 17, 1868; *Federal Union,* January 2, 1869; *Post,* December 26, 1868; May 8, 1869.

[16] Minnesota State Medical Society, *Transactions,* 1870, p. 4. This volume includes reports of the sessions held in 1869.

[17] *General Laws,* 1869, p. 52; 1870, p. 106; *Post,* March 27, 1869; State Medical Society, *Transactions,* 1870, p. 13, 14, 18–20; Dr. John M. Armstrong, "History of Medicine in Ramsey County," in *Minnesota Medicine,* 22:257 (April, 1939).

[18] *Rochester Free Press,* October 13, November 18, 1858; *City Post,* February 11, May 26, June 30, July 21, December 22, 1860; *Post,* February 3, 10, 1866.

[19] *Post,* April 4, 25, 1868; January 16, 30, February 13, 27, March 13, 27, April 10, 24, June 5, 19, 1869; *Federal Union,* September 18, 1869.

WHEN AMERICA WAS THE LAND OF CANAAN — *Stephenson*

[1] This paper, read on June 14, 1929, at the Hutchinson session of the eighth state historical convention, is based mainly upon documentary materials discovered in Sweden by the author.

[2] *Nya Wexjö-Bladet* (Växjö), May 22, 1869.

[3] Papers like *Aftonbladet* (Stockholm), *Östgötha Correspondenten* (Linköping, *Norrlands-Posten* (Gävle), and *Jönköpings-Bladet* and writers like Karl J. L. Almqvist and Pehr Thomasson foreshadowed a new day in religion, politics, society, and economics.

[4] *Jönköpings-Bladet,* May 26, 1846.

[5] For a sketch of Cassel and a reprint of his letters, see George M. Stephenson, "Documents Relating to Peter Cassel and the Settlement at New Sweden, Iowa," in the *Swedish-American Historical Bulletin,* 2:1–82 (February, 1929).

[6] "There is peace and prosperity here. I have come in contact with millions of people of all sorts and conditions, but I have never heard of dissension, and we have never been snubbed. There are black and brown people, but all are friendly and agreeable." Letter from Samuel Jönsson, Buffalo, New York, November 22, 1846, in *Östgötha Correspondenten,* May 26, 1847.

[7] This letter, dated February 9, 1846, was published in *Östgötha Correspondenten* on May 16, 1846. It is reprinted, with English translation, in the *Swedish-American Historical Bulletin,* 2:22–28, 55–62 (February, 1929). The abundance of fish and game was mentioned frequently in letters to the old country. See, for example, a letter from A. M. D——m, Taylors Falls, Minnesota, in *Östgötha Correspondenten,* July 27, 30, 1853.

[8] Correspondence from Döderhultsvik to *Kalmar-Posten,* April 23, 1852; *Landskrona Nya Tidning,* cited in *Borås Tidning,* June 13, 1854; *Hwad Nytt?* (Eksjö), February 18, 1869; *Wäktaren,* cited in *Dalpilen* (Falun), July 17, 1869; Aron Edström, "Blad ur svensk-amerikanska banbrytarelifvets historia," in *Svensk-amerikanska kalendern,* 61–64 (Worcester, Massachusetts, 1882).

[9] His first letter was dated at Milwaukee, Wisconsin Territory, October 15, 1841, and published in *Aftonbladet,* January 4, 5, 1842; his second letter was dated at New Upsala, Wisconsin, January 23, 1842, and published in *Aftonbladet,* May 28, 30, 31, June 3, 7, 9, 1842.

[10] Letters dated January 18, 1841, and July 4, 1842, in *Aftonbladet*, April 6, October 6, 13, 1842.

[11] Letter dated February 10, 1843, in *Skara Tidning*, May 18, 1843. Unonius mentions the meeting with Friman in his *Minnen från en sjuttonårig vistelse i nordvestra Amerika*, 1:182 (Upsala, 1861).

[12] Letter dated February 10, 1843, in *Skara Tidning*, May 18, 1843.

[13] Letter from J. C. Melander, Eksjö, June 27, 1843, in *Skara Tidning*, July 13, 1843.

[14] Extracts from several letters in *Skara Tidning*, November 2, 1843.

[15] *Emigrationsutredningen*, 7:131–263 (Stockholm, 1908).

[16] Peter Cassel to relatives and friends, December 13, 1848, in the *Swedish-American Historical Bulletin*, 2:78 (February, 1929).

[17] Letter from Johan Johansson, Burlington, Iowa, November 12, 1849, in *Östgötha Correspondenten*, April 5, 1850. Compare the following statement in a letter from Stephan Stephanson, May 17, 1854: "There is no class distinction here, but all are equals, and not as in Sweden, where the working people are looked down upon and are called 'the rabble,' whereas the lazy gentlemen are called 'better folk.'" This manuscript is in the author's possession.

[18] Steffan Steffanson to relatives and friends, October 9, 1849, in Swedish Historical Society of America, *Yearbooks*, 11:86–100 (St. Paul, 1926).

[19] Unsigned letters from New York in *Norrlands-Posten*, December 29, 1856; and from Chicago, September 9, 1853, in *Nya Wexjö-Bladet*, October 7, 1853.

[20] Unsigned letter, dated January 23, 1852, in *Bibel-Wännen* (Lund), September, 1852.

[21] L. P. Esbjörn to Peter Wieselgren, Andover, Illinois, May 23, 1850, a manuscript in the *Stadsbibliotek* of Gothenburg; Cassel to relatives and friends, December 13, 1848, in the *Swedish-American Historical Bulletin*, 2:81 (February, 1929).

[22] Steffan Steffanson to relatives and friends, October 9, 1849, in Swedish Historical Society of America, *Yearbooks*, 11:97; Peter Cassel to relatives and friends, December 13, 1848, in the *Swedish-American Historical Bulletin*, 2:75.

[23] Letter from Anders Jonsson, Bishop Hill, Illinois, February 9, 1847, in *Hudikswalls-Weckoblad*, July 17, 1847.

[24] Letter from Erik Hedström, Southport, Wisconsin, in *Aftonbladet*, September 20, 1843.

[25] Letter from Jon Andersson in *Norrlands-Posten*, January 12, 1852.

[26] Letter from Åke Olsson, Andover, Illinois, February 20, 1850, in *Norrlands-Posten*, June 3, 1850.

[27] Letter from New York in *Aftonbladet*, reprinted in *Barometern* (Kalmar), June 5, 1852.

[28] Letter from Åke Olsson, Andover, Illinois, February 20, 1850, in *Norrlands-Posten*, June 3, 1850.

[29] Letter from Stephan Stephanson, May 17, 1854.

[30] Letter from L. P. Esbjörn, Andover, Illinois, May 6, 1850, in *Norrlands-Posten*, June 20, 1850.

[31] *Carlshamns Allehanda*, August 3, 1854. Anders Andersson, who for some time after his emigration corresponded with a crown official in Norrland, soon changed his style of address from *ni* to *du*. See his letters edited by Anna Söderblom, "Läsare och Amerikafarare på 1840-talet," in *Julhelg*, 80–93 (Stockholm, 1925).

[32] "Renter" suggests the meaning.

[33] Unsigned letter from Chicago, August 3, 1854, in *Skånska Posten*, reprinted in *Carlshamns Allehanda*, October 4, 1854.

[34] Letter to *Götheborgs Handels- och Sjöfarts-Tidning*, April 22, 23, 1852.

[35] Letter of O. Bäck, Victoria, Illinois, in *Norrlands-Posten*, April 3, 1849.

[36] *Götheborgs Handels- och Sjöfarts-Tidning,* April 22, 23, 1852.

[37] Letter from Åke Olsson, Andover, Illinois, February 20, 1850, in *Norrlands-Posten,* June 3, 1850.

[38] Letter from C. P. Agrelius, New York, April 14, 1849, in *Östgötha Corre-spondenten,* July 4, 1849.

[39] *Chicago-Bladet,* January 13, 1885.

[40] Mary H. Stephenson to her relatives, November 3, 1867, in Swedish Historical Society of America, *Yearbooks,* 7:90 (St. Paul, 1922).

THE LITERATURE OF THE PIONEER WEST — *Commager*

[1] Lewis Mumford, *The Golden Day; A Study in American Experience and Culture* (New York, 1926); Vernon L. Parrington, *Main Currents of American Thought: An Interpretation of American Literature from the Beginnings to 1920* (2 vols. — New York, 1927); Charles A. Beard and Mary R. Beard, *The Rise of American Civilization* (2 vols. — New York, 1927).

[2] Hamlin Garland, *A Son of the Middle Border,* 67 (New York, 1917).

[3] Mumford, *The Golden Day,* 62.

[4] Willa S. Cather, *O Pioneers!* 15 (Boston and New York, 1913).

[5] Garland, *A Son of the Middle Border,* 416.

[6] Mumford, *The Golden Day,* 79.

WENDELIN GRIMM AND ALFALFA — *Edwards and Russell*

[1] This paper was presented at the afternoon session of the eighty-ninth annual meeting of the Minnesota Historical Society in St. Paul on January 10, 1938. In the absence of the authors, it was read by their friend, Rodney C. Loehr.

[2] For additional details on Grimm, see the following accounts by Charles J. Brand: *Grimm Alfalfa and Its Utilization in the Northwest,* 7–9, 17–21 (United States Department of Agriculture, Bureau of Plant Industry, *Bulletins,* no. 209 — Washington, 1911); "The Acclimatization of an Alfalfa Variety in Minnesota," in *Science,* 28:891 (December 18, 1908); and "Ancestral Home of Grimm Alfalfa," in *Fertilizer Review,* 9:8–10, 13 (September–October, 1934). See also Charles F. Collisson, "Memorial Tablet Erected to Grimm Alfalfa Originator," in *Minneapolis Tribune,* June 15, 1924; M. C. Cutting, "Alfalfa from Xerxes to Grimm," in *Country Gentleman,* 89:11, 29 (August 16, 1924); Charles Kenning, "Minnesota Alfalfa," in *Farm, Stock and Home,* 20:112 (March 1, 1904); and J. H. Shepperd, "The Story of an Everlasting Clover," in *Breeder's Gazette,* 83:845 (June 21, 1923). In Germany alfalfa is known as *ewiger Klee,* because of its continuous growth. It is also called *Luzerne,* and *Monatsklee,* or "monthly clover," since it can be cut each month.

[3] Several writers have followed the statement in Brand, *Grimm Alfalfa,* 20, that "in 1899, with the exception of certain counties in New York, Carver was the only county east of the Mississippi and Missouri Rivers that reported as much as 1,000 acres of alfalfa under cultivation." Carver County is west of the Mississippi and only 658 acres of alfalfa were reported within its borders in the agricultural census of 1900.

[4] A. B. Lyman, "Alfalfa Seed," in Minnesota State Agricultural Society, *Annual Report,* 1903, p. 38–44, and "History of Alfalfa," in Minnesota Farmers' Institute, *Annual,* 1922, p. 34. See also the paragraphs entitled "How I Discovered the Grimm Alfalfa" in the sixteen-page sales pamphlet issued by Lyman in at least three versions under the title *Lyman's Grimm Alfalfa* (n. p., n. d.).

[5] Minnesota State Agricultural Society, *Annual Report,* 1903, p. 42.

[6] C. J. Brand and L. R. Waldron, *Cold Resistance of Alfalfa and Some Factors Influencing It,* 50 (United States Department of Agriculture, Bureau of Plant

Industry, *Bulletins*, no. 185 — Washington, 1910); Brand, *Grimm Alfalfa*, 9–11, 13–17; R. A. Oakley and H. L. Westover, *Commercial Varieties of Alfalfa*, 10 (United States Department of Agriculture, *Farmers' Bulletins*, no. 757 — Washington, 1916); P. K. Blinn, "Developing a Hardy Type of Alfalfa," in *Breeder's Gazette*, 63:947 (April 16, 1913).

[7] Brand, *Grimm Alfalfa*, 14.

[8] Brand, *Grimm Alfalfa*, 58; J. M. Westgate, "Another Explanation of the Hardiness of Grimm Alfalfa," in *Science*, 30:184–186 (August 6, 1909).

[9] A. C. Arny, "Alfalfa as a Farm Crop in Minnesota," and C. G. Selvig, "Pastures and Meadows for Northwestern Minnesota," in Minnesota Farmers' Institute, *Annual*, 1912, p. 167–170; 1918, p. 61–66; C. P. Bull, "Alfalfa in Minnesota," and "Nubs of News," in *Breeder's Gazette*, 53:671, 57:618 (March 18, 1908, March 9, 1910); A. D. Wilson, "Why Alfalfa on Every Farm," H. M. Hamlin, "They 'Tried Alfalfa' — and They Failed," and A. D. Wilson, "Getting Started This Year with Alfalfa," in *National Alfalfa Journal*, February, 1919, p. 3, March, 1920, p. 5, April, 1920, p. 5, 9–12; C. R. Hutcheson, "Notes from the Alfalfa Clubs," in *Northwest Farmstead*, 25:465 (August 1, 1924); Minnesota State Board of Immigration, *Central Minnesota*, 45 (St. Paul, 1915); "Failures in Alfalfa Growing," in *Farm, Stock and Home*, 20:377 (September 1, 1904).

[10] [J. Y. Beaty], "Alfalfa Seed with a Real Pedigree," in *National Alfalfa Journal*, March, 1916, p. 5; "Lyman Tells of Saving Alfalfa Seed," in *Northwest Farmstead*, 25:399, 404 (June 15, 1924); advertisement in *Farm, Stock and Home*, 25:207 (March 15, 1909); *Lyman's Grimm Alfalfa*.

[11] R. S. Dunham, "40 Years of Agronomy," in *Red River Aggie*, 12–15 (Crookston, 1936).

[12] W. R. Porter, "N. D. Grimm Alfalfa Association," in *The Farmer*, 36:852 (May 11, 1918).

[13] "Certifying Alfalfa Seed," and "Morris Donates Grimm Warehouse," in *Northwest Farmstead*, 25:359, 506 (May 15, August 15, 1924).

[14] "Northwest Farmstead's Alfalfa Campaign in Minnesota," "Review of Alfalfa Club Activities," and "With Alfalfa Clubs in Minnesota," in *Northwest Farmstead*, 25:294, 352, 403 (April 15, May 15, June 15, 1924); C. R. Hutcheson, "Grimm or Cossack — Why?" in *Farm, Stock and Home*, 41:174 (March 15, 1925).

[15] "Alfalfa on Every Minnesota Farm," in *Farm, Stock and Home*, 41:174 (March 15, 1925).

[16] "Honor to Wendelin Grimm," in *The Farmer*, 42:800, 857, 864 (June 7, 21, 1924); Collisson, in *Tribune*, June 15, 1924; *Northwest Farmstead*, 25:375, 419, 423 (June 1, July 1, 1924).

MONTE CASSINO, METTEN, AND MINNESOTA — *Krey*

[1] This paper was read at the state historical convention held under the auspices of the Minnesota Historical Society at St. Cloud on June 16, 1927.

[2] For information about the Benedictine community the writer is indebted to a volume by Father Alexius Hoffmann entitled *St. John's University, Collegeville, Minnesota: A Sketch of Its History* (Collegeville, 1907); to a manuscript history of the monastery by the same author, which the writer was permitted to read, in the library of the university; and to the kindness of the Abbot Alcuin.

ON THE TRAIL OF THE WOODSMAN — *Larson*

[1] This paper was read on July 15, 1932, at the Moorhead session of the eleventh state historical convention held under the auspices of the Minnesota Historical Society.

[2] "Memoir of Capt. S[tephen] B. Hanks," vol. 2 in the Fred A. Bill Papers. These recollections of an early Minnesota lumberman were written from his dictation by C. B. Paddock in 1907 and 1908. They consist of six notebooks in the manuscripts collection of the Minnesota Historical Society.

[3] William H. C. Folsom, "History of Lumbering in the St. Croix Valley," in *Minnesota Historical Collections,* 9:296 (1901).

[4] George H. Warren, *The Pioneer Woodsman as He Is Related to Lumbering in the Northwest,* 78 (Minneapolis, 1914); interview with Robert Ap Roberts of the office of the surveyor general of logs, St. Paul, June 17, 1932. Much of the material used in the preparation of this paper was gathered through interviews with men who engaged in the logging business in Minnesota, particularly during the pioneer period. Several of the men were more than eighty years of age at the time of these interviews.

[5] *Mississippi Valley Lumberman* (Minneapolis), vol. 21, no. 4, p. 6 (January 22, 1892); interview with J. W. Bayly of Duluth, August 13, 1932. The firm with which this lumberman was connected — Alger, Smith and Company — at one time employed the largest number of loggers of any firm in the Duluth lumber district.

[6] *St. Croix Union* (Stillwater), March 6, 1855; Hanks, "Memoir," vol. 1. Files of the newspapers used in the preparation of this paper are in the Minnesota Historical Society.

[7] *Minneapolis Tribune,* December 13, 1873. There were few white women living near the lumber camps, and the Indian women were invited to the lumberjack's dances. Woodsmen tell that the endurance of the squaws when dancing surpassed even that of the lumberjacks.

[8] In an interview on August 14, 1932, Michael McAlpine of Grand Rapids recalled that "on the drive" he had slept with eleven other men under one blanket.

[9] *St. Anthony Express,* January 31, 1852; *St. Croix Union,* March 6, 1855; Martin Page, "The Camp in the 50's," in *Daily Telegram* (Eau Claire, Wisconsin), February 24, 1916; Hanks, "Memoir," vol. 2. The item from the *Telegram* is a clipping in the William Bartlett Collection in the Minnesota Historical Society.

[10] Wilson P. Shortridge, "Henry Hastings Sibley and the Minnesota Frontier," in *Minnesota History Bulletin,* 3:120 (August, 1919); Edward W. Durant, "Lumbering and Steamboating on the St. Croix River," in *Minnesota Historical Collections,* 10:648 (part 2 — 1905).

[11] *Express,* January 21, 1854.

[12] Daniel Stanchfield, "History of Pioneer Lumbering on the Upper Mississippi," in *Minnesota Historical Collections,* 9:357 (1901).

[13] *Express,* January 31, April 10, 1852.

[14] *Express,* January 31, 1852; January 21, 1853.

[15] Return I. Holcombe, *Compendium of History and Biography of Minneapolis and Hennepin County,* 67 (Chicago, 1914); *Express,* January 21, 1854; interview with O. D. Dahlin of Port Wing, Wisconsin, June 5, 1932.

[16] *Express,* November 12, 1853; *St. Croix Union,* November 3, 1854; April 24, 1855.

[17] Hanks, "Memoir," vol. 2; *Express,* January 21, 1853.

[18] John E. Gilmore of Minneapolis told the writer, in an interview on August 15, 1932, that the peavey was invented by a man of that name at Oldtown, Maine.

[19] In an interview on May 18, 1932, Jesse H. Ames, president of the Wisconsin State Teachers College at River Falls, whose father was an early Maine logger in the Northwest, told the writer that the first loggers in this region did not use crosscut saws. See also William McDonald, "Logging Equipment

and Methods," a clipping in the Bartlett Collection, from the Eau Claire *Daily Telegram,* October 7, 1916.

[20] George W. Hotchkiss, *History of the Lumber and Forest of the Northwest,* 530 (Chicago, 1898).

[21] Stanchfield, in *Minnesota Historical Collections,* 9:321–361.

[22] *St. Cloud Democrat,* November 26, 1863.

[23] J. W. McClung, *Minnesota as It Is in 1870,* 149 (St. Paul, 1870); Warren, *Pioneer Woodsman,* 77. McAlpine, who went to the Grand Rapids region in 1874, asserted that he was one of the first woodsmen in the district. Interview, August 14, 1932.

[24] *Stillwater Messenger,* March 21, 1873; *Tribune,* February 20, 1875; *Daily Telegram,* March 27, 1916; *Duluth Herald,* August 21, 1926.

[25] This call was used on the St. Croix in the 1880s, according to O. D. Dahlin. Interview, June 5, 1932.

[26] *Tribune,* February 20, 1875.

[27] *Mississippi Valley Lumberman,* vol. 27, no. 9, p. 3 (February 28, 1890); Edward G. Cheney, "Development of Lumber Industry in Minnesota," in *Journal of Geography,* 14:194 (February, 1916). Arthur Sjoberg of Mora explained much of the lumberjack's language to the writer.

[28] *Messenger,* March 21, 1873; *Tribune,* April 29, 1876.

[29] Wright T. Orcutt, "The Minnesota Lumberjacks," in *Minnesota History,* 6:11 (March, 1925). J. W. Bayly of Duluth, who was assistant to the vice-president of Alger, Smith and Company and who had dealings with thousands of lumberjacks, told the writer that generosity was very characteristic of them.

[30] *Tribune,* April 29, 1876.

[31] *Tribune,* April 29, 1876; *Mississippi Valley Lumberman,* vol. 19, no. 25, p. 2; vol. 21, no. 5, p. 3 (June 13, 1891; January 29, 1892).

[32] Interview with Willcuts, July 13, 1932. In the winter of 1887 Isaac Staples, who had a crew of three hundred men logging on the Snake and Ann rivers, ordered for their use 18,000 pounds of beef, 104 barrels of pork, 9,000 pounds of sugar, 1,900 pounds of tobacco, 1,500 pounds of currants, and 1,400 pounds of prunes. *Kanabec County Times* (Mora), March 12, 1887.

[33] *Tribune,* December 13, 1873.

[34] In an interview on June 6, 1932, J. C. Daly of Port Wing, Wisconsin, told the writer how these games were played. Even in his amusements the lumberjack did not spare his body.

[35] McAlpine gave the writer a copy of this poem on August 15, 1932.

[36] William T. Cox, *Fearsome Creatures of the Lumberwoods,* 35 (Washington, 1910).

[37] *Anoka Union,* January 5, 1878.

[38] Daly told the writer this story in an interview on June 6, 1932. A similar tale is related by John E. Nelligan, in "The Life of a Lumberman," in the *Wisconsin Magazine of History,* 13:57 (September, 1929). The latter uses the word "gummed" instead of "gunned."

[39] J. W. Clark, "Lumberjack Lingo," in *American Speech,* 7:47 (October, 1931).

[40] *United States Census,* 1900, *Manufactures,* 9:818.

[41] *Duluth Weekly Herald,* May 2, 1900.

[42] William T. Cox, *Timber Resources of Minnesota,* 87 (St. Paul, 1913).

MINNESOTA, MONTANA, AND MANIFEST DESTINY — *White*

[1] *Saint Paul Daily Press,* December 31, 1863; January 16, May 5, 13, 1864; January 16, 31, May 1, August 23, 1866; January 24, May 4, 1867; *State Atlas* (Minneapolis), January 27, 1864; *Winona Daily Republican,* February 1, 1864;

Anoka Star, February 13, 1864; *Mankato Weekly Union,* April 8, 1864; *Shakopee Argus,* April 30, May 14, 1864; *St. Cloud Democrat,* March 10, 1864; January 11, 25, February 1, March 15, August 9, 1866; *Saint Paul Pioneer,* February 12, 20, 1864; January 16, 1866; *Congressional Globe,* 38 Congress, 1 session, p. 37; 39 Congress, 1 session, p. 446, 2 session, p. 471; Minnesota, *General Laws,* 1863, p. 284; 1866, p. 124; 1868, p. 193–195; United States, *Statutes at Large,* 12:333, 642; 13:14, 516.

² See, for example, John Wesley Bond, *Minnesota and Its Resources,* 243–251 (New York, 1853); Minnesota Territory, *House Journal,* 1857, p. 46; *Minnesota Democrat* (St. Paul), December 31, 1850; *Pioneer and Democrat* (St. Paul), July 1, 3, 1858; January 18, 1859; Joseph A. Wheelock, *Minnesota: Its Place Among the States,* 103 (Minnesota Bureau of Statistics, *First Annual Report* — Hartford, Connecticut, 1860). American ideas of manifest destiny to which these Minnesota visions were undoubtedly related are described in Albert K. Weinberg, *Manifest Destiny: A Study of Nationalist Expansion in American History* (Baltimore, 1935). See especially pages 43–71.

³ These ideas are expressed in *Minnesota Democrat* (St. Paul), May 20, December 2, 17, 1851; July 28, 1852; *Daily Minnesota Pioneer* (St. Paul), June 14, 1854; *Pioneer and Democrat,* August 21, 1856; January 14, April 28, 1859.

⁴ Alexander von Humboldt, *Cosmos: A Sketch of a Physical Description of the Universe,* 2:317–335 (New York, 1850), translated by E. C. Otte; Helmut de Terra, *Humboldt: The Life and Times of Alexander von Humboldt,* 355, 374–376 (New York, 1955); Lorin Blodget, *Climatology of the United States and of the Temperate Latitudes of the North American Continent,* 529–534, charts opposite 210, 308 (Philadelphia, 1857). Evidence that Minnesota promoters made use of the isothermal concept may be found in *Minnesota Democrat,* June 22, 1853; *Pioneer and Democrat,* July 3, 14, December 10, 1858; January 28, April 5, May 22, November 13, 1859.

⁵ William W. Folwell, *A History of Minnesota,* 1:358; 2:65 (St. Paul, 1956, 1961); Russell Blakeley, "Opening of the Red River of the North to Commerce and Civilization," in *Minnesota Historical Collections,* 8:46–50 (1898).

⁶ *Daily Minnesota Pioneer,* June 28, 1854. On the cable, see *Pioneer and Democrat,* September 3, 1858. The cable operated only a short time in 1858 and was not finally completed until 1867. On Russia, see *Pioneer and Democrat,* September 16, October 23, December 10, 30, 1858.

⁷ *Pioneer and Democrat,* September 18, 1858.

⁸ *Pioneer and Democrat,* September 16, 1858.

⁹ See *Fort Ridgely and South Pass Wagon Road* (37 Congress, 2 session, *House Executive Documents,* no. 35 — serial 1129); Willoughby M. Babcock, "Gateway to the Northwest: St. Paul and the Nobles Expedition of 1859," in *Minnesota History,* 35:249 (June, 1957).

¹⁰ *Statutes at Large,* 12:333.

¹¹ *Press,* May 2, 30, 1862.

¹² See Theodore C. Blegen, "James Wickes Taylor: A Biographical Sketch," in *Minnesota History Bulletin,* 1:153–195 (November, 1915).

¹³ "Briefly Biographical: Col. Jas. L. Fisk," (photocopy) Fisk Papers, in the Minnesota Historical Society; "Proceedings of the Third Annual Meeting of the Stockholders of the Dakota Land Company," in *South Dakota Historical Collections,* 6:180 (1912); *Weekly Pioneer,* March 30, 1866; James L. Fisk, "Report of Expedition (North Western) to Montana in 1864," 8. A typewritten copy is in the Fisk Papers, Minnesota Historical Society, and the original is in the National Archives.

¹⁴ A draft of instructions for the superintendency of overland emigration dated April 26, 1862, which has been altered in pencil to apply to Fisk and the northern overland trail may be found in File 401W, records of the Adjutant

General's Office, National Archives, Record Group 94. For an account of Mullan's road, see John Mullan, *Report on the Construction of a Military Road from Fort Walla-Walla to Fort Benton* (37 Congress, 3 session, *Senate Executive Documents*, no. 43 — serial 1149).

[15] *Shakopee Argus,* July 12, 1862; *Press,* May 30, 1862; Warren Upham and Rose B. Dunlap, *Minnesota Biographies,* 340 (*Minnesota Historical Collections,* vol. 14 — 1912); Lafayette H. Bunnell, *Winona and Its Environs on the Mississippi in Ancient and Modern Days,* 224 (Winona, 1897).

[16] *Shakopee Argus,* July 12, 1862; *St. Cloud Democrat,* July 10, October 2, November 27, 1862; January 15, 1863.

[17] *Expedition from Fort Abercrombie to Fort Benton,* 4 (37 Congress, 3 session, *House Executive Documents,* no. 80 — serial 1164).

[18] Samuel R. Bond, "Journal Kept on the Fisk Expedition of 1862," 3–24, typewritten copy in the Minnesota Historical Society. The original is in the Ipswich Historical Society, Ipswich, Massachusetts. For origins of the emigrants, see unpublished roster of the expedition in the possession of the author.

[19] *Expedition from Fort Abercrombie to Fort Benton,* 6–27. A more detailed account of the trip is given in Bond, "Journal," 24–129.

[20] Bond, "Journal," 130–132.

[21] *Expedition from Fort Abercrombie to Fort Benton,* 28.

[22] *Press,* March 19, 1863.

[23] James L. Fisk, *Idaho: Her Gold Fields, and the Routes to Them,* 11 (New York, 1863); *Expedition of Captain Fisk to the Rocky Mountains* (38 Congress, 1 session, *House Executive Documents,* no. 45 — serial 1189).

[24] *Weekly Pioneer,* March 30, 1866; *Pioneer,* February 12, April 28, 1864; *Press,* February 16, March 12, 1864.

[25] *Pioneer,* May 22, 1864. See also a circular advertising Fisk's 1866 expedition, preserved in the Donnelly Pamphlets, vol. 4, in the Minnesota Historical Society.

[26] Fisk also issued a map in the same year. Copies of both are in the library of the Minnesota Historical Society. See also Seymour Dunbar, *A History of Travel in America,* 4:1225 (Indianapolis, 1915).

[27] *Pioneer,* February 20, 1864; June 10, 28, 1865; March 21, 25, November 1, 1866; *Press,* March 4, 1864; May 17, 1866; *Weekly Press,* February 15, December 20, 1866; *St. Cloud Democrat,* August 3, 1865; February 22, May 17, July 5, August 30, 1866; *Saint Peter Tribune,* May 30, 1866.

[28] Examples of these bills may be found in 38 Congress, 1 session, *House Journal,* 1863–64, p. 123 (serial 1179); 38 Congress, 1 session, *Senate Journal,* 1863–64, p. 30 (serial 1175); 38 Congress, 2 session, *Senate Journal,* 1864–65, p. 188 (serial 1208); 39 Congress, 1 session, *House Journal,* 1865–66, p. 191 (serial 1243).

[29] *Statutes at Large,* 12:204, 333, 642; 13:14; *Minnesota in the Civil and Indian Wars,* 2:534 (St. Paul, 1892).

[30] On army co-operation with westward migration in the 1860s, see United States War Department, *The War of the Rebellion: A Compilation of the Official Records of the Union and Confederate Armies,* series 1, vol. 34, part 2, p. 258, 622–625; vol. 41, part 4, p. 882; vol. 48, part 2, p. 1150–1153 (Washington, 1891, 1893, 1896).

[31] This estimate is based on rosters in the possession of the author. For references to expeditions not already discussed, see Nicolas Hilger, "General Alfred Sully's Expedition of 1864," in Montana Historical Society, *Contributions,* 2:314–322 (1896); *Press,* October 8, 1864; Charles S. Kingston, "The Northern Overland Route in 1867, Journal of Henry Lueg," in *Pacific Northwest Quarterly,* 41:235–242 (July, 1950). Accounts of all the expeditions are included in the forthcoming book which the author has in progress.

[32] *St. Cloud Democrat,* January 11, August 9, 1866; *Press,* January 24, April 9, 1867; *Statutes at Large,* 13:319; 15:254; James H. Bradley, "Account of the Attempts to Build a Town at the Mouth of the Musselshell River," in Montana Historical Society, *Contributions,* 2:305.

SOCIAL AND ECONOMIC EFFECTS OF THE CIVIL WAR — *Shippee*

[1] This address was read at the annual meeting of the Minnesota Historical Society, St. Paul, January 14, 1918.

[2] Frederick Merk, *Economic History of Wisconsin During the Civil War Decade,* ch. 1 (Madison, 1916).

[3] Carl R. Fish, "The Northern Railroads, April, 1861," in *American Historical Review,* 22:778–793 (July, 1917).

[4] Merk, *Economic History of Wisconsin,* ch. 12.

[5] Merk, *Economic History of Wisconsin,* ch. 14; Minnesota, *Statistics,* 1869, p. 107.

[6] Minnesota, *Statistics,* 1870, p. 116.

[7] Governor's Message, January, 1865, in Minnesota, *Executive Documents,* 1865, p. 19; Merk, *Economic History of Wisconsin,* ch. 6.

[8] Sydney A. Patchin, "The Development of Banking in Minnesota," in *Minnesota History Bulletin,* 2:159–168 (August, 1917).

[9] One of Ignatius Donnelly's correspondents asked his aid in obtaining the payment of a loan of fifty dollars, the interest on which was three per cent a month. Schriver to Donnelly, November 12, 1862, Donnelly Papers, in the Minnesota Historical Society.

[10] Minnesota, *Statistics,* 1869, p. 9; Commissioner of Statistics, *Minnesota: Its Resources and Progress,* 1872, p. 27.

[11] Minnesota, *Statistics,* 1869, p. 127.

[12] Merk, *Economic History of Wisconsin,* 35–37; Minnesota, *Statistics,* 1870, p. 35. John Wass wrote to his Congressman, Donnelly, December 13, 1863, asking for tobacco seed for himself and for the benefit of Minnesota. Donnelly Papers.

[13] Minnesota, *Statistics,* 1869, p. 43; 1870, p. 36.

[14] Merk, *Economic History of Wisconsin,* 61–63.

[15] William W. Folwell, *Minnesota, the North Star State,* 112-120 (Boston, 1908).

[16] George W. Hotchkiss, *History of the Lumber and Forest Industry of the Northwest,* 531 (Chicago, 1898); "Report of the Pine Land Committee" (Senate), March 3, 1874, in Minnesota, *Senate and House Journal,* 1874, p. 541–552; *Testimony Taken by the Committee on Invalid Pensions,* 59 (44 Congress, 1 session, *House Miscellaneous Documents,* no. 193 — serial 1707).

[17] William W. Folwell, "The Five Million Loan," in *Minnesota Historical Collections,* 15:189–214 (1915).

[18] Minnesota, *Statistics,* 1869, p. 105.

[19] In the spring of 1858 the voters of Minnesota adopted an amendment to the constitution providing that the "credit" of the state, to the amount of five million dollars, might be loaned for the purpose of facilitating the construction of railroads. In the following two years $2,275,000 worth of bonds were issued to four companies which had complied with the requirements by grading nearly two hundred and fifty miles of roadbed. The companies, however, failed to fulfill other obligations, and the governor was forced to start foreclosure proceedings which resulted in the transfer of all their privileges and property to the state. The bonds, which had greatly depreciated in value, were in form an obligation of the state, but all attempts to secure payment were of no avail until 1881 when provision was made for the issuing of Minnesota state railroad ad-

justment bonds in exchange for the old ones. The liquidation of these refunding bonds was completed in 1910. Folwell, in *Minnesota Historical Collections*, 15:189–214; Rasmus S. Saby, "Railroad Legislation in Minnesota, 1849 to 1875," in *Minnesota Historical Collections*, 15:30–49 (1915).

[20] Minnesota, *Statistics*, 1870, p. 63.

[21] Commissioner of Statistics, *Minnesota: Its Resources and Progress*, 1870, p. 31.

[22] Secretary of State, *Annual Report*, 1866, p. 113; Hans Mattson, *Reminiscences, the Story of an Immigrant*, 97–100 (St. Paul, 1891).

[23] Charles F. Adams, "A Chapter of Erie," in Charles F. Adams, Jr., and Henry Adams, *Chapters of Erie, and Other Essays*, 4–99 (Boston, 1871); Charles F. Wingate, "An Episode in Municipal Government," in the *North American Review*, 119:359–408; 120:119–174; 121:113–155; 123:362–425 (1874–76).

[24] *Report of the Special Senate Investigating Committee, Appointed to inquire into the Condition of the State Treasury*, 5–7 (St. Paul, 1873); *Proceedings of the Senate of Minnesota, sitting as a High Court of Impeachment for the Trial of William Seeger, Treasurer of State* (Minneapolis, 1873).

[25] The *Saint Paul Daily Press*, in its issue of February 27, 1873, affirmed that this was happening in all the Democratic counties, and admitted that the same thing might have occurred in Republican counties as well.

[26] *Press*, March 6, 8, 1873; *Report of the Special Senate Committee, Appointed to Investigate the Management of the Office of State Auditor, prior to January, 1873*, 55 (1875). In February, 1874, William Murphy wrote that "there is something rotten in the management of county affairs." Murphy to Donnelly, February 4, 1874, Donnelly Papers.

[27] *Press*, February 1, 1873.

[28] In the *Report of the Committee Appointed to Investigate the Management of the Office of State Auditor* the above facts are brought out in the formal report of the committee as well as in the testimony accompanying the report.

[29] Bouck White, *Book of Daniel Drew: A Glimpse of the Fisk-Gould-Tweed Régime from the Inside*, 161 (New York, 1910); George W. Curtis' speech to the New York State Republican Convention, March 22, 1876, in the *New York Tribune*, March 23, 1876; speech of George F. Hoar in the *Congressional Record*, 44 Congress, 1 session, vol. 4, part 7, p. 63; James Ford Rhodes, *History of the United States from the Compromise of 1850*, vol. 7, ch. 1.

RIVALRY FOR A RIVER — *Kane*

[1] 39 Congress, 2 session, *House Executive Documents*, no. 58, p. 29 (serial 1292); Newton H. Winchell, "Recession of the Falls of St. Anthony," in Geological Society of London, *Quarterly Journal*, 34:886–900 (November, 1878). Meeker Island, which no longer exists, was located between the present Franklin Avenue bridge and the Milwaukee Railway bridge.

[2] *Minnesota Register* (St. Paul), August 4, 1849; *Minnesota Pioneer* (St. Paul), August 9, 1849.

[3] *New York Daily Tribune*, May 23, 1850 (transcript in the Minnesota Historical Society).

[4] Captain R. W. Kirkham to John H. Stevens, May 9, 1850, Stevens Papers. Unless otherwise specified, all collections cited in this article are owned by the Minnesota Historical Society.

[5] *The Intelligencer* (Bloomington, Illinois), May 4, 1853 (photostatic copy in the Minnesota Historical Society); *St. Anthony Express*, June 18, 25, July 2, 1852; July 9, 1853; December 23, 1854; July 14, 1855; *Minnesota State News* (Minneapolis), January 6, May 27, 1859; March 24, June 9, 1860; April 20,

1861; *Minneapolis Daily Tribune,* March 30, April 30, 1869; "Agreement," I. F. Woodman and ninety-eight others, December 12, 1856, Stevens Papers.

⁶ *Express,* July 5, 1851.

⁷ *Minnesota Pioneer,* July 1, 1852.

⁸ *Express,* February 14, April 30, August 6, 1852; "Agreement," December 12, 1856; Minnesota Territory, *Laws,* 1855, p. 178; 1856, p. 346; Minnesota, *General Laws,* 1858, p. 367–369; 1861, p. 345–349.

⁹ Minnesota Territory, *Laws,* 1857, p. 230–234.

¹⁰ *Express,* June 16, 1855.

¹¹ Minnesota Territory, *Laws,* 1857, p. 233; Minnesota, *Laws,* 1858, p. 502; 1865, p. 221; Meeker to Ignatius Donnelly, January [n.d.], 1866, Donnelly Papers; 39 Congress, 2 session, *House Executive Documents,* no. 58, p. 45–50 (serial 1292).

¹² 39 Congress, 2 session, *House Executive Documents,* no. 58, p. 45.

¹³ Meeker to Donnelly, January [n.d.], 11, 1866, Donnelly Papers.

¹⁴ Meeker to Donnelly, February 1, 14, March 28, 1866, Donnelly Papers. Elihu B. Washburne, unlike his brothers, spelled his name with a final "e."

¹⁵ Meeker to Donnelly, February 1, 14, March 28, 1866, Donnelly Papers.

¹⁶ Meeker to Donnelly, March 15, 28, April 3, 21, 1866, Donnelly Papers; Donnelly to Curtis H. Pettit, February 15, 1866, Pettit Papers.

¹⁷ Miller to Donnelly, April 6, 1866, Donnelly Papers.

¹⁸ Meeker to Donnelly, April 16, 1866, Donnelly Papers.

¹⁹ Fletcher to Donnelly, February 2, 1866; Meeker to Donnelly, February 7, March 13, 29, April 21, 1866, Donnelly Papers.

²⁰ *Congressional Globe,* 39 Congress, 1 session, p. 579, 2292; United States, *Statutes at Large,* 14:74.

²¹ Meeker to Donnelly, May 2, 1866; Cook to Donnelly, August 15, 1866, Donnelly Papers.

²² Meeker to Donnelly, December 16, 1866, Donnelly Papers; 39 Congress, 2 session, *House Executive Documents,* no. 58, p. 30, 32, 53 (serial 1292).

²³ *Saint Paul Daily Press,* February 19, 1867; Meeker to Donnelly, December 16, 1866, Donnelly Papers. A month earlier, Hennepin County had given Donnelly nearly a two-to-one vote over his Democratic rival for Congress. See *Press,* November 27, 1866.

²⁴ *Statutes at Large,* 15:169.

²⁵ Miller to Donnelly, April 6, 1866; Fletcher to Donnelly, March 28, 1866; Meeker to Donnelly, March 27, April 21, 1866; March 1, 1867, Donnelly Papers; Hennepin County Register of Deeds, Books of Deeds, no. 14, p. 184, among the county archives in the Register of Deeds' Office, Minneapolis.

²⁶ *Minneapolis Chronicle,* cited in *Press,* April 30, 1867.

²⁷ *Press,* April 30, 1867.

²⁸ *Press,* April 23, May 2, 1867.

²⁹ Articles of Incorporation, Book B, 166, in the Secretary of State's Office, Minnesota State Capitol.

³⁰ *Tribune,* February 12, 1869.

³¹ Minnesota, *Special Laws,* 1869, p. 350–352.

³² *Tribune,* August 10, 11, 1870.

³³ *Tribune,* December 31, 1872; *Congressional Globe,* 41 Congress, 3 session, p. 52, 65, 792, 838, 847, 1884, 2004; 42 Congress, 2 session, p. 395, 452; 42 Congress, 3 session, p. 82, 123, 702.

³⁴ *Tribune,* December 29, 1872; January 8, 1873.

³⁵ *Tribune,* December 17, 24, 25, 28, 29, 31, 1872; January 1, 7, 8, 1873.

³⁶ See footnote 35 above and the following items in the Ramsey Papers: Telegram, William D. Washburn and others to Ramsey, April 20, 1872; Eugene

M. Wilson to Ramsey, April 17, 25, 1872; Telegram, Richard Chute and others to Ramsey, April 24, 1872; Edward Murphy to Ramsey, May 1, 1872; Telegram, James A. Lovejoy and others to Ramsey, December 7, 1872; A. B. Barton to Ramsey, [January, 1873].

[37] See footnote 35 above and *St. Cloud Press,* December 12, 1872.

[38] *Tribune,* January 28, 1879.

[39] *Northwest Magazine,* 8:9 (March, 1890); 8:10 (April, 1890); *Weekly Northwestern Miller,* 29:171 (February 14, 1890).

[40] *Weekly Northwestern Miller,* 30:733 (December 19, 1890); Press Clip Book, [n.p.,] Box 148, Henry Villard Papers, Houghton Library, Harvard University.

[41] *Tribune,* March 9, 1890; Edward P. Burch, "The Utilization of Water Power for the Electric Railway System of Minneapolis and St. Paul," in North-West Railway Club, *Official Proceedings,* 5:13–29 (April, 1900).

[42] *Statutes at Large,* 17:562; Chief of Engineers, *Annual Report,* 1906, vol. 1, p. 471; 1917, part 1, p. 1139; 61 Congress, 2 session, *House Documents,* no. 741, p. 2–14 (serial 5732).

[43] Chief of Engineers, *Annual Report,* 1915, part 1, p. 1030; *Tribune,* June 11, 1909.

[44] Northern States Power Company, Scrapbook No. 1, p. 132, in the offices of the company, Minneapolis.

[45] Articles of Incorporation, Book U-3, p. 704, Secretary of State's Office; Northern States Power Company, Scrapbook No. 1, p. 185, 187.

[46] Northern State Power Company, Scrapbook No. 1, p. 219; No. 2, p. 98.

[47] "The Minneapolis Harbor," in *Greater Minneapolis,* 12:15, 30 (May, 1961); Wesley Dibbern, Corps of Engineers, to the author, August 11, 1961.

THE RISE OF ORGANIZED LABOR IN MINNESOTA — *Engberg*

[1] *United States Census,* 1930, *Population,* 1:10, 18, 19. This article is based upon a longer study, covering the period from 1850 to 1890, prepared as a master's thesis at the University of Minnesota in 1939. The Minnesota Historical Society has a copy.

[2] *United States Census,* 1890, *Report on Manufacturing Industries in the United States,* part 1, p. 6.

[3] *United States Census,* 1880, *Report on Manufactures,* 138–140.

[4] *United States Census,* 1890, *Report on the Transportation Business in the United States,* part 1, p. 21; William W. Folwell, *A History of Minnesota,* 3:61, 141 (St. Paul, 1926).

[5] Minnesota, *General Laws,* 1858, p. 154; Minnesota Department of Labor and Industries, *Biennial Report,* 1913–14, p. 23. The department that issued this report was organized in 1887 as the bureau of labor statistics; it has also been called the bureau of labor, the bureau of labor, industries, and commerce, the department of labor and industry, and the industrial commission. Its reports, cited hereafter as Department of Labor, *Biennial Reports,* are not entirely consistent in the information they give about labor organizations. The reason is apparent in the following quotation from the *Biennial Report* for 1905–06, p. 364: "In presenting the report on organized labor in the state as collected and arranged for the year 1906 it has to be stated that the separate reports have been furnished this department by the secretaries or some other official of the respective organizations. The department having no means by which to verify these reports, but having impressed upon reporting members of the various unions the necessity of correct statements, can not accept responsibility for any errors that may be found in these reports."

⁶ Minnesota, *House Journal,* 1858, p. 665; *Daily Minnesotian* (St. Paul), June 15, 1858.

⁷ *Minnesota Daily Pioneer* (St. Paul), October 23, 1854.

⁸ *Minnesotian,* November 1, 1856; *Minnesota Weekly Times* (St. Paul), December 20, 1856.

⁹ *Times,* December 20, 1856; January 3, 1857; *Minnesotian,* December 27, 1856; January 1, 1857; *Daily Pioneer and Democrat* (St. Paul), January 1, 1857; *St. Paul Financial, Real Estate and Railroad Advertiser,* January 3, 1857; George A. Tracy, *History of the Typographical Union,* 17–139 (Indianapolis, 1913).

¹⁰ *Minnesotian,* April 5, 1858.

¹¹ Department of Labor, *Biennial Report,* 1905–06, p. 365, 373; Minnesota State Federation of Labor, *Official Yearbook,* 1915, p. 19; Tracy, *Typographical Union,* 172, 175.

¹² References to Newson's clash with the union appear in the *Minnesotian* for March and April, 1858. For the union notice, see the issue of April 5, 1858.

¹³ Tracy, *Typographical Union,* 187, 195.

¹⁴ Tracy, *Typographical Union,* 187–276; State Federation of Labor, *Yearbook,* 1915, p. 19; Department of Labor, *Biennial Reports,* 1901–02, p. 457; 1911–12, p. 451; 1915–16, p. 178.

¹⁵ *Falls Evening News* (St. Anthony), June 5, 1858; *Minnesotian,* June 8, 1858.

¹⁶ *Minneapolis Daily Tribune,* June 19, 21, 1867; *Faribault Central Republican,* June 25, 1867; State Federation of Labor, *Yearbook,* 1915, p. 20; Arthur J. Larsen, "The Rise of Labor in Minnesota," in *Minnesota Alumni Weekly,* 33:23 (August, 1933).

¹⁷ The Minnesota Historical Society has a copy of the *Constitution.* See also State Federation of Labor, *Yearbook,* 1915, p. 26.

¹⁸ *Tribune,* September 8, 15, 1868; February 17, 1869; Department of Labor, *Biennial Report,* 1907–08, p. 104.

¹⁹ *Lake City Leader,* January 7, 1870; *Tribune,* January 12, 1870.

²⁰ Articles of Incorporation, Book B, 713, in Secretary of State's Office, Minnesota State Capitol.

²¹ Department of Labor, *Biennial Report,* 1887–88, p. 248.

²² *Labor Review* (Minneapolis), September 4, 1914; Department of Labor, *Biennial Reports,* 1905–06, p. 371; 1907–08, p. 101; *Minneapolis City Directory,* 1874, p. 40, 140.

²³ Department of Labor, *Biennial Report,* 1901–02, p. 455; Articles of Incorporation, Book B, 790, in Secretary of State's Office.

²⁴ Department of Labor, *Biennial Reports,* 1899–1900, p. 292–295; 1901–02, p. 498; 1905–06, p. 378; 1907–08, p. 103; 1911–12, p. 430, 452; 1913–14, p. 205, 215, 217, 220, 226; 1915–16, p. 179, 187; State Federation of Labor, *Yearbooks,* 1915, p. 20; 1917, p. 27; Articles of Incorporation, Book C, 225, in Secretary of State's Office.

²⁵ United States Bureau of Labor, *Annual Report,* 1893, p. 138, 139, 321; *St. Paul Directory,* 1873, p. 57; Articles of Incorporation, Book B, 302, in Secretary of State's Office; Albert Shaw, "Co-operation in the Northwest," in Johns Hopkins University, *Studies in Historical and Political Science,* 6:282–287 (Baltimore, 1888); *St. Paul Daily Globe,* February 7, 1873; May 9, June 2, 1878; *Minneapolis City Directory,* 1877–78, p. 26; *United States Census,* 1880, *Report on Trade Societies in the United States,* vol. 20, p. 1.

²⁶ For an account of eastern backgrounds, see Herbert Harris, *American Labor,* ch. 1, 2, especially p. 67 (New Haven, Connecticut, 1938). See also *Tribune,* November 5, 1870; and Donnelly, *Facts for the Granges,* 1, 19. Although this pamphlet is not dated, there is evidence that it was published in 1873.

[27] Selig Perlman, *History of Trade Unionism in the United States*, 81 (New York, 1922).

[28] *United States Census*, 1880, *Report on Trade Societies in the United States*, vol. 20, p. 2, 14–19.

[29] United States Bureau of Labor, *Annual Reports*, 1887, p. 272–289; 1901, p. 554; Hellen Asher, "The Labor Movement in Minnesota, 1850–1890," 1, a term paper in the Minnesota Historical Society.

[30] Department of Labor, *Biennial Reports*, 1907–08, p. 103; 1911–12, p. 430, 453; 1913–14, p. 218; 1915–16, p. 180; *Globe*, January 25, 1883; October 12, 1884; April 19, 1885; Tracy, *Typographical Union*, 359; International Typographical Union, *Report of Proceedings*, 1882, 1884. See also the minutes of the St. Paul Trades and Labor Assembly, vol. 1, p. 48, 49, in the Minnesota Historical Society.

[31] *Globe*, May 5, June 23, 24, 1878; minutes of the St. Paul Trades and Labor Assembly, vol. 1, p. 81; Tracy, *Typographical Union*, 372; International Typographical Union, *Proceedings*, 1884, p. 251.

[32] Articles of Incorporation, Book F, 265, in Secretary of State's Office; Department of Labor, *Biennial Reports*, 1899–1900, p. 294; 1915–16, p. 179; *Globe*, June 14, 1885; State Federation of Labor, *Yearbook*, 1915, p. 22; United States Bureau of Labor, *Annual Report*, 1887, p. 272–281; minutes of the St. Paul Trades and Labor Assembly, vol. 1, p. 46.

[33] Articles of Incorporation, Book F, 107–110; Book M, 75, in Secretary of State's Office; minutes of the St. Paul Trades and Labor Assembly, vol. 1, p. 53, 137; treasurer's record of the United Brotherhood of Carpenters and Joiners of America, Union No. 87, St. Paul, in the Minnesota Historical Society.

[34] The two preceding paragraphs are based upon various sources, including the *Globe, Biennial Reports* of the department of labor, the *Yearbooks* of the state federation of labor, the Articles of Incorporation in the Secretary of State's Office, the minutes of the St. Paul Trades and Labor Assembly, and the papers of the Cigar Makers' International Union of America, No. 98, St. Paul, in the Minnesota Historical Society.

[35] Various items about this union appear in the *Globe* from January to July, 1878. See especially the issues of January 16, 25, 30, February 24, March 13, 19, 26, June 2, 22, and 26.

[36] See volume 1 of the minutes of the St. Paul Trades and Labor Assembly, and the *Globe*, December 31, 1883; December 31, 1884; and June 21, 1885.

[37] *Labor Review*, August 29, 1913; September 4, 1914; *Globe*, July 19, 1885; minutes of the St. Paul Trades and Labor Assembly, vol. 1, p. 72.

[38] *Globe*, June 29, 1878; January 9, 13, 16, 17, 1883; Minnesota Historical Society, *Catalogue of the Library*, 2:105 (St. Paul, 1888).

[39] This summary for the smaller cities of the state is based mainly on the *Biennial Reports* of the state department of labor and the *Annual Report* for 1887 of the federal bureau of labor.

THE PEOPLE OF THE MESABI RANGE — *Sirjamaki*

[1] Lake Superior Iron Ore Association, *Lake Superior Iron Ores*, 252–254 (Cleveland, 1938).

[2] Fremont P. Wirth, *The Discovery and Exploitation of the Minnesota Iron Lands*, 24 (Cedar Rapids, Iowa, 1937); Minnesota, *Fourth Decennial Census*, 126 (St. Paul, 1895); *United States Census*, 1900, *Population*, part 1, p. 226; *United States Census*, 1910, *Abstract, With Supplement for Minnesota*, 560, 626.

[3] The field work upon which this study is based was done in the summer and fall of 1939, and a part of the material was incorporated into an unpublished

doctoral dissertation entitled "Mesabi Communities: A Study of Their Development." It was submitted at Yale University in 1940. Information about the minority groups in the Mesabi Range country was obtained primarily through interviews, inasmuch as relevant printed materials are scant.

⁴ Stewart H. Holbrook, *Iron Brew: A Century of American Ore and Steel,* 51–53, 59 (New York, 1939). Material gathered in interviews supports this analysis of ethnic succession on the Michigan ranges.

⁵ William J. Lauck, "Iron Ore Mines on the Mesabi and Vermilion Ranges," in *Mining and Engineering World,* 35:1269 (December 23, 1911); G. O. Virtue, *The Minnesota Iron Ranges,* 353 (United States Bureau of Labor, *Bulletins,* no. 84 — Washington, 1909).

⁶ The consolidation of mining companies is summarized by the writer in his "Mesabi Communities," 51–63. Excellent material is included in Wirth, *Minnesota Iron Lands,* 186–206; William W. Folwell, *A History of Minnesota,* 4:1–59 (St. Paul, 1930); Henry R. Mussey, *Combination in the Mining Industry: A Study of Concentration in Lake Superior Iron Ore Production* (Columbia University, *Studies in History, Economics and Public Law,* vol. 23, no. 3 — New York, 1905); and Walter Van Brunt, ed., *Duluth and St. Louis County,* 1:285–288, 399–408 (Chicago, 1921). See also James H. Bridge, *The "Carnegie Millions and the Men who made them,"* 257–274 (London, 1903); and Joseph G. Pyle, *The Life of James J. Hill,* 2:210–231 (New York, 1917).

⁷ The distinction between this group and the Swedes from Sweden, on the one hand, and the Finns of Finland, on the other, is important on the Mesabi Range. See Carl J. Silfversten, "Finland Swedes of Northeast Minnesota," a typewritten manuscript in the files of the St. Louis County Historical Society, Duluth.

⁸ Lauck, in *Mining and Engineering World,* 35:1269; Virtue, *Minnesota Iron Ranges,* 353; LeRoy Hodges, "Immigrant Life in the Ore Region of Northern Minnesota," in *Survey,* 28:709 (September 7, 1912).

⁹ Quoted from an article published "forty years ago," in the *Virginia Daily Enterprise,* April 3, 1939.

¹⁰ Virtue, *Minnesota Iron Ranges,* 345.

¹¹ Constantine Panunzio, *Immigration Crossroads,* 45 (New York, 1927); M. B. Cothren, "When Strike-breakers Strike," in *Survey,* 36:535 (August 26, 1916); M. H. Vorse, "Mining Strike in Minnesota," in *Outlook,* 113:1036 (August 30, 1916).

¹² These conclusions are based upon figures published in Minnesota, *Fifth Decennial Census,* 176, 177 (St. Paul, 1905).

¹³ The figures on mixed marriages are discussed by the writer in "Mesabi Communities," 447, 448.

THE ORIGIN OF MINNESOTA'S NONPARTISAN LEGISLATURE —
Adrian

¹ The nonpartisan judicial movement died almost as suddenly as it began. Many states abandoned the plan after a few years. Since it was adopted by Nevada in 1923, no new states have tried it.

² The term "progressive" as used in this article refers merely to the branch of the Republican party that supported the general principles of Theodore Roosevelt, as well as other moderate reform proposals. The progressives were opposed by the conservatives, standpatters, or regulars — all fairly synonymous terms.

³ For the text of the Haycraft bill, see Minnesota Legislature, Thirty-eighth Session, 1913, Senate File 412.

⁴ *Minneapolis Journal,* February 27, 1913.

⁵ For the progress of Senate File 412 through the Senate, see Minnesota,

Senate Journal, 1913, p. 251, 288–290, 337–344, 472–475, 494–500, 513–515, 1055, 1409, 1681.

[6] For summaries of the attitudes of various groups, see the *Red Wing Daily Republican,* March 31, 1913; the *Willmar Tribune,* April 2, 1913; and the metropolitan dailies, especially Charles B. Cheney's report in the *Minneapolis Journal,* March 28, 1913.

[7] Interview with Henry Rines, August, 1949.

[8] For the progress of Senate File 412 through the House, see Minnesota, *House Journal,* 1913, p. 626, 1028, 1166–1170, 1193, 1214.

[9] The Republicans included thirty-four drys and three wets, as indicated by the vote on the county option bill of 1913.

[10] *Minneapolis Journal,* March 28, 1913.

[11] *Fergus Falls Daily Journal,* March 29, 1913; *St. Paul Pioneer Press,* March 28, 1913; *Minneapolis Journal,* March 29, 1913.

[12] Interview with Henry Rines, August, 1949.

[13] *House Journal,* 1913, p. 1621–1623; *Willmar Tribune,* April 16, 1913; *St. Cloud Daily Times,* April 18, 1913; *Red Wing Daily Republican,* March 31, 1913.

[14] *House Journal,* 1913, p. 1745.

[15] *Senate Journal,* 1913, p. 1409.

[16] *Red Wing Daily Republican,* March 31, 1913. The enactment was a surprise not only to the state at large, but to "most of the members responsible for its enactment into law," according to Robert E. Cushman. See his "Non-partisan Nominations and Elections," in the American Academy of Political and Social Science, *Annals,* 106:90 (March, 1923).

[17] *Willmar Tribune,* April 9, 23, 1913.

[18] *Caledonia Journal,* quoted in the *St. Paul Pioneer Press,* April 18, 1913; *Anoka Union,* quoted in the *St. Cloud Daily Times,* February 6, 1913.

[19] *St. Peter Free Press,* quoted in the *St. Cloud Daily Times,* February 7, 1913; *Fairmont Sentinel,* quoted in the *St. Paul Pioneer Press,* April 24, 1913.

[20] Victor J. West, "Legislation of 1913 Affecting Nominations and Elections," in *American Political Science Review,* 7:439 (August, 1914).

[21] C. J. Buell, *The Minnesota Legislature of 1913,* 13 (St. Paul, 1914).

[22] State *ex rel.* Nordin v. Erickson, in 119 *Minnesota Reports,* 152 (St. Paul, 1913).

THE DEMOCRATIC-FARMER-LABOR PARTY SCHISM OF 1948 — *Mitau*

[1] Donald F. Warner, "Prelude to Populism," in *Minnesota History,* 32:129 (September, 1951).

[2] On Governor Johnson's many progressive recommendations to the Minnesota legislature during his administration, see William W. Folwell, *A History of Minnesota,* 3:286–289 (St. Paul, 1926). See also Theodore Saloutos and John D. Hicks, *Agricultural Discontent in the Middle West,* 187 (Madison, 1951); Hicks, *The Populist Revolt,* 258 (Minneapolis, 1931); and George H. Mayer, *The Political Career of Floyd B. Olson,* 171 (Minneapolis, 1951).

[3] Minnesota, *Legislative Manual,* 1953, p. 333.

[4] Arthur Naftalin, "The Farmer Labor Party in Minnesota," 382, an unpublished doctoral thesis submitted at the University of Minnesota in 1945.

[5] Currin V. Shields, "The American Tradition of Empirical Collectivism," in *American Political Science Review,* 44:104–121 (March, 1952).

[6] Mayer, *Floyd B. Olson,* 184–222; Saloutos and Hicks, *Agricultural Discontent,* 358. On left-wing radicalism in Minnesota after 1917, see O. A. Hilton, "The Minnesota Commission of Public Safety in World War I," in Oklahoma

Agricultural and Mechanical College, *Bulletins,* 48:1–44 (Stillwater, Oklahoma, 1951).

[7] William B. Hesseltine, *The Rise and Fall of Third Parties,* 87 (Washington, 1948).

[8] *St. Paul Pioneer Press,* January 17, February 22, 1948.

[9] *Pioneer Press,* January 28, February 8, 20, 1948.

[10] *Minnesota Leader* (St. Paul), February, 1948.

[11] *Minnesota Outlook* (Minneapolis), February 18, 1948.

[12] *Pioneer Press,* April 19, 29, 1948. The latter issue quotes Philip Murray of the CIO as stating that "The Communist party is directly responsible for the organization of a third party in the United States."

[13] *Pioneer Press,* June 4, 1948.

[14] *Pioneer Press,* May 20, 1948; *Minneapolis Star,* May 14, 1948. The attitude toward a third party of national leaders, including Mrs. Roosevelt and J. H. McGrath, Democratic national committee chairman, is expressed in the *Pioneer Press* for April 30. For the law relating to precinct caucuses, see Minnesota, *Statutes,* 1953, ch. 202.14.

[15] *Pioneer Press,* May 23, 1948; "Brief for Petitioners," in 227 *Minnesota Reports,* 52.

[16] 227 *Minnesota* 52, 54; L. D. Parlin, in the *Pioneer Press,* June 13, 1948.

[17] See Carl Henneman, in the *Pioneer Press,* June 13, 14, 1948.

[18] *Minneapolis Star,* June 14, 1948.

[19] 227 *Minnesota* 52.

[20] 227 *Minnesota* 52; 33 *North Western Reporter* 831 (second series, 1948).

[21] 33 *North Western Reporter* 831.

[22] 29 *Corpus Juris Secondum,* Elections, section 88; case of Emil E. Holmes v. Mike Holm, in 217 *Minnesota* 264.

[23] *Legislative Manual,* 1953, p. 165, 335. In the seventh district, James M. Youngdale, who was endorsed by the left wing, won by a vote of 6,452 to 5,958 for the right-wing candidate, Roy F. Burt.

MINNESOTA BACKGROUNDS OF SINCLAIR LEWIS' FICTION —
Flanagan

[1] Charles Breasted, "The 'Sauk-Centricities' of Sinclair Lewis," in *Saturday Review,* August 14, 1954, p. 33.

[2] See *Elmer Gantry,* 81 (New York, 1927).

[3] Lewis died in Rome. His ashes were buried in Greenwood Cemetery, Sauk Centre, January 20, 1951.

[4] "The Long Arm of the Small Town," in *The O-sa-ge,* 1:83 (Sauk Centre, 1931).

[5] Grace Hegger Lewis, *With Love from Gracie: Sinclair Lewis, 1912–1925,* 88–108 (New York, 1955).

[6] "A Day's Pleasure," in *Main-Travelled Roads* (New York, 1903), is supposedly based on a visit to Worthington.

[7] Grace H. Lewis, *With Love from Gracie,* 95.

[8] The copy of *Free Air* (New York, 1919) in the special Lewis collection in the University of Minnesota Library is inscribed by the author as follows: "Written in a bare room behind a photographer's studio in Mankato, Minn. to make it possible to write 'Main Street.'" Mankato, incidentally, figures in *It Can't Happen Here,* 449 (New York, 1935).

[9] Grace H. Lewis, *With Love from Gracie,* 115.

[10] Breasted, in *Saturday Review,* August 14, 1954, p. 33.

[11] Mark Schorer, ed., Sinclair Lewis, "A Minnesota Diary," in *Esquire*, 50:160–162 (October, 1958).

[12] *Esquire*, 50:161.

[13] William J. McNally, in *Minneapolis Tribune*, April 20, 1943.

[14] *Tribune*, January 30, 1945; *Esquire*, 50:162. In January, 1946, Frederick Manfred, his wife, and the young novelist Ann Chidester visited Lewis by invitation at his Duluth home. See Manfred's "Sinclair Lewis: A Portrait," in *American Scholar*, 23:162–184 (Spring, 1954).

[15] " 'Red' Lewis Discovers Minnesota," in *Tribune*, June 2, 1942. A reprint appears in the *Conservation Volunteer*, 4:21 (August, 1942).

[16] Bone Stillman is the eccentric atheist of *The Trail of the Hawk* (New York, 1915); Miles Bjornstam is the village radical and indispensable town handyman of *Main Street* (New York, 1920); and Seneca Doane is the liberal lawyer of *Babbitt* (New York, 1922).

[17] As a young writer, Lewis actually sold some twenty-three plots to Jack London. See Franklin Walker, "Jack London's Use of Sinclair Lewis Plots," in *Huntington Library Quarterly*, 17:59–74 (November, 1953).

[18] *Saturday Evening Post*, July 28, 1917, p. 12.

[19] "Main Street's Been Paved," in *The Nation*, 119:255–260 (September 10, 1924). The article is reprinted in Harry E. Maule and Melville H. Cane, eds., *The Man from Main Street*, 310–327 (New York, 1953).

[20] *Selected Short Stories of Sinclair Lewis*, 281–298, 321–337 (New York, 1935).

[21] *Good Housekeeping*, August, 1935, p. 19, 64–75; September, 1935, p. 44, 166–181.

[22] *Selected Short Stories*, 99–140, 143–158.

[23] *Saturday Evening Post*, January 24, 1920, p. 10, 112, 114, 118, 121.

[24] *Selected Short Stories*, 235–277.

[25] *Harper's Magazine*, 142:419–431 (March, 1921); *Saturday Evening Post*, June 22, 1918, p. 5–7, 81. "A Matter of Business" appears also in a treasury of material from *Harper's*, edited by Horace Knowles and published under the title *Gentlemen, Scholars and Scoundrels*, 460–477 (New York, 1959). It supposedly represents the best contributions to *Harper's* from 1850 to 1959.

[26] *Saturday Evening Post*, January 24, 1920, p. 10.

[27] *Saturday Evening Post*, June 22, 1918, p. 5.

[28] *Selected Short Stories*, 215–231.

[29] *Saturday Evening Post*, April 7, 1917, p. 3–6, 121, 125, 129, 133; October 20, 1917, p. 63, 67, 70, 73, 76.

[30] *Cass Timberlane*, 10 (New York, 1945).

[31] *Kingsblood Royal*, 9 (New York, 1947).

[32] *Cass Timberlane*, 11, 12. See also Lewis' equally scornful picture of the Zenith Athletic Club in *Babbitt*, 54–60.

[33] *The God-Seeker*, 53 (New York, 1949). In an appendix Lewis carefully distinguishes between the historical and the fictional characters. See p. 419–422.

[34] *The God-Seeker*, 113. In his appendix Lewis pays tribute to the ability and virtuosity of Brown. See p. 421.

[35] *The God-Seeker*, 299.

[36] Mark Twain, "What Paul Bourget Thinks of Us," in *Literary Essays*, 148–170 (New York, 1899).

[37] "Minnesota: The Norse State," in *The Nation*, 116:624–627 (May 30, 1923).

[38] *The O-sa-ge*, 1:83.

Index

Index